In The Rear View Mirror

Memories and Metaphysics

Strictly for the Curious

Robert L. Brueck

This book is based only on my memories, some pictures, some scraps of paper here and there, and coin flips when I thought something needed to be recorded but couldn't really determine which might be credible. No names have been intentionally changed. Any resemblance to real people, living or dead, should not be coincidental.

Cover Design by
Jennifer Wauson

Encouragement and assistance have been provided
By
Kevin Wilson, Jennifer Wauson, and Pam Knight

Copyright © 2014 Robert L. Brueck

ISBN-13: 978-1502569042
ISBN-10: 1502569043

Acknowledgement

I am grateful and acknowledge my appreciation to my granddaughter Courtney Brueck Hemperly for encouraging me in this project, to my wife Pat for putting up with me during the course of my dealing with such an open-ended task, to Pam Knight for helpful guidance about publishing it, to Marty Kopra Gretzinger for helpful editing, and importantly, special appreciation to Kevin Wilson and Jennifer Wauson for the encouragement, ongoing dialogue, the cover design, and feedback regarding many details to help guide me thru it. Without their help I would have been out of my mind stumbling in the dark.

Bob Brueck
14 November 2014

Boy: I don't think there is a God.

P: Oh yes there is.

Boy: Then where is he?

P: He is running the projector.

Boy: What projector?

P: The one that is creating Earth.

Boy: But Earth is already here.

P: Yes, but you want to grow up to be a man, don't you?

Boy: Oh yes, I would like to grow up smart, handsome, and rich.

P: That will depend on how you and God decide to run the projector.

Boy: How do I get to help?

P: You will make decisions. God will help show you what they mean.

Boy: How will God show me?

P: He will run the projector.

Boy: What does the projector do?

P: It picks the new picture of Earth every minute, including one of you.

Boy: Is that like a movie?

P: Yes.

Boy: And I am in it?

P: Yes.

Boy: What is the movie about?

P: You.

Contents

Introduction

As should become apparent to anyone who chooses to read this book, I consider myself to be one of the most fortunate persons on Earth.

Along my life journey I received love, kindness, and friendship from many very special people. Many are mentioned as a way for me to express gratitude, though possibly not as often as they deserved. I have also mentioned several who gave me much needed and appreciated guidance to make my life unfold in a way favorable to me and my family. I hope I have succeeded in passing it on and that by calling attention to how people help each other, maybe a young reader will someday find some inspiration to both especially appreciate and offer help along their own path.

There is at least one person I can count on to be happy that I wrote all this. It was originally a project taken on reluctantly at her request. Our oldest granddaughter knows who that is. When I finally acquiesced to write a story about my life, I mean my life story, I did not look forward to the task with glee. However, as I got both my psyche engaged and a little writing under my belt, so to speak, it actually became another fun adventure in this life. But no one told me that it seems to take forever to write about such a small part of forever! This reminds me, I also share my description of the nature of forever late in the book.

The earlier chapters are about what one would expect from a person's memoirs—some detail about where they came from, maybe who they came from, what they did during life, who helped them do it, and maybe a good dose of what they thought about it. I offer all of the above. I describe enough lying, deceit, and irresponsibility to qualify me as an expert, and enough of my teenage love life to convince the experts I was unqualified. In general, I was very sensitive to the likelihood that my granddaughter will have her kids read this early in life, so I refrained from recounting some history entirely. After all, it is not supposed to be a novel. It is only a story! I also met and have mentioned in the book a lot of outstanding people, some having held recognized stature in our world—but the story isn't about my hob-knobbing with greats or having achieved greatness when I haven't. It is simply what I see as life events and some of my thoughts along the way as I look back in the rear view mirror.

I am told that a life story is sort of supposed to say a lot about the world of that time. It strikes me as a little strange that I get such counsel to record something about such a small part of what was going on in the world. (Isn't that what history books are for?) There was a "time" (as we experience "time") about 40,000 years ago when all that had ever been recorded for posterity was written on one cave wall. I would presume that what was recorded was important and worth sharing with the next cave-wall observer.

It is not so obvious to me that what I have recorded along the way will be of such interest, even though aspects of the world around me during my growing up years might have been of a time in the distant past of a reader. It is a matter of well-recorded history that for much of my life there was no TV, no Power Steering or Power Brakes, no Colored Film, no Microwave Ovens, no Interstate Highway System, no Jet Planes, no Computers, no Moon Landings, no Internet, no Smart Phones, and not even ballpoint pens! All that I noticed in my everyday life activity during my youth was pretty much happening within a very few miles around me, with exceptions like the atomic bomb to end WWII and the beginning of the system to draft young men into the military service during the wars in Korea and Vietnam. However, looking back, it is clear that some events or conditions around the world did find special significance in my life, and I presume I am the only one who has recorded that.

There would be little uncertainty about such personal significance these days in the developed world. It seems like there is next to nothing that is not being documented even at very personal levels in some form in the world around me now. It even seems like the clear trend is almost to record now what hasn't even occurred yet. My book does fully explain precognition and clairvoyance, but it seems like a stretch to say that the future is already known. Some mystics say the future has been writ, but my idea of how they do that is sort of far out, so I haven't included that in my book.

Anyway, I have at least recorded some detail about a few things going on in my era related to the evolution of computer software. I was in the middle of that with only a few thousand or million other citizens of the world at the time. In describing my own participation, I have shared for posterity a brief historical blip related to the early days of computing as it existed in the last half of the 20th century. (I can walk through the displays at the Computer Museum and recognize many of the oldest machines.) Maybe my reflections about my role within a small computer software company that survived toe-to-toe in competition with a giant might provide a little visceral feel for that era.

The mid-1950s was a time when it would have been possible for only a very few individuals to be aware of almost everything there was to know about digital computers and computing in that era. I do believe there were such people at that time. There is a lot of their history captured in various archives. On the other hand, however, it is a matter of historical record that there were a few individuals that over-simplified what was there to be known. During the many years between 1943 and 1952, some people thought to be very bright are quoted as having said things like, "It is very possible that ... one machine would suffice to solve all the problems that are demanded of it from the whole country." In 1943 the Chairman of IBM, Thomas Watson, was quoted as having said, "I think there is a world market for maybe five computers." Luckily for me, by the time I first saw in 1955 what an electronic digital computer looked like, those around me knew better, and I was encouraged to pursue learning how they worked and how to use them.

I was fortunate to have had the opportunity to do that. Jumping in early in the age of computers was like riding a big ocean wave that could take one into many fascinating lands. For a few decades, in one way or another, computing in technological and business situations or financing early stage computer and communications technology companies were the focal point of my adult working life. In particular, I especially enjoyed mentoring a few deserving persons engaged in entrepreneurial ventures where I believe my assistance was of benefit to them and those they rewarded by their effort and perseverance. I was fortunate to work side by side with a few people so brilliant that they were never satisfied with their work because they could always see how it could have been better. Over the years I also contributed and gained experience on the Board of Directors of four public companies and many smaller companies, some doing business worldwide. I guess my story shows a little about what one does when doing those things.

This life story covers that ground, and in the process, about what else one would expect—a guy maturing more and learning more and spreading his wings a little after surviving his youth. I think I included enough about my family life to indicate that I know how fortunate I have been. Covering life experiences from birth to about yesterday took me 14 chapters. The last three chapters, however, are a horse of a different color, as we like to say in both Idaho and Texas. They depart from life activity, per se, and get more into the thoughts that came along with that life—in particular, my quest to improve my understanding of the nature of a reality greater than what I saw and see around me every day. Although the subject of my belief in reincarnation is not mentioned until those last three chapters, my life story records a life that may then be reviewed in that context. Thus, I have tried to identify life experiences that in retrospect help give some flesh to the idea of reincarnation.

As the days and years came and went—faster, faster, faster—I had more and more activity to fill my hours than I had hours. It was hard to keep up with family and work responsibilities, let alone have time to cogitate about the nature of reality. But looking back it appears that I did make note during those years that there were an ever increasing number of questions of interest to me with no clear consensus known to me regarding answers. The most significant questions for me were those I encountered that were related to contemporary quantum physics and the growing amount of credible data relating to paranormal phenomena. Over the years I had not found a way to resonate with common religious exhortations relating to the supernormal, but in those areas I did encounter much to think about of a metaphysical nature beyond the normal. Naïve thinking for sure but at least a start down my long agonizing path to put it all together to my own satisfaction.   However, I am reminded that someone whose name I have forgotten said something like metaphysics is only what looks plausibly meaningful, it is not a proof.   That is certainly true with my metaphysical conclusion.

The story of my metaphysical journey might be of interest to some who don't care a whit about my experiences while growing old but might like to twirl around in their heads some more metaphysical thinking to go along with unanswered questions they are already quite aware of.   They might be the seekers of their current lifetime—possibly even another Sagittarian seeker. However, for those who don't care about that metaphysics kind of stuff, I hope they might enjoy the vicarious nature of my growing up experiences to trigger some of their own special memories, and maybe even some new questions relating to their own lives.

If someone were to ask me why this book is so long, (thank you for asking) I would respond that I have a good memory and that I was told not to let it go to waste. If someone were to ask me why they might find this book worth the time to read, I would say, "I don't know."   I know that granddaughter will read it. And at some point she is likely to suggest that her children and grandchildren read it—or they would probably be denied so many picoseconds on their embedded nanochip with which to exchange teenage trivia with their favorite thought-space friends in China. I could speculate about why there might be a few others that will stumble across this book—possibly because there is travelogue content.   The much more interesting question to me would be, how did they find it in the first place? The only one I know for sure who might have a strong desire to find and read it many decades from now is me, but I have not thought of a way to arrange that.

Anyhow, since an introduction is supposed to introduce something, I will introduce myself as the one who laboriously forwent watching a lot of football games, Reality TV, and reading a lot of sex-laden novels so I could write this thing. It has been a very humbling experience.   Because I am looking back at a lot of my life from late in life, it has been a lot easier to see limitations than accomplishments. In a sense, it has taken me 78 years to mature.

To get started reading it, I suggest that one replace the background melodies of Mozart or the beat of whatever is in vogue at the time with the instrumental version of their favorite tales from the Wagner Ring music, turn it up loud awhile to get into the feel of things, then go back to something at least similar to Mozart, find a comfortable chair, and imagine they are about ready to take on a new identity—then go for it!

Bob Brueck
2015

1

The Boy Calf

As the pain grew more intense, even the doctor began to fidget and rock from one foot to the next. Finally, after a particularly loud shriek from Mom, the doctor turned to Dad and suggested that he might help. He immediately nodded and informed Dr. Mack that he had helped deliver many calves, so he knew how to do that. There was another loud shriek but sounding more like anguish than pain. Soon thereafter I became born!

It was Mother who told me that story—after Dad had passed on. She did add that by normal criteria, it was a difficult delivery for all involved. I didn't know it at the time. In any event, that and the fact that it all took place late in the day on 17 December 1935 at St. Alphonsus Hospital in Boise, Idaho, is all I know about it. They recorded my name as Robert Lewis Brueck.

I was Mom and Dad's first child. Brother Harley was born about 16 months later. (Later in life, Mom suffered more than one miscarriage.) Mom and Dad had been married exactly eight months before I was born, and their marriage was the first for each. They had met at the Idaho State Penitentiary the year before when Mom was tending the Warden's children. I think Dad delivered something there, and the rest is history.

A Little Genealogy Shouldn't Hurt Too Much

Mom, Edythe Bernice Pearce Brueck, was the only child of Edna Minnie Davis Pearce, later to become Edna Griffiths, married to a wonderful man, John Henry Griffiths, who became a great influence in my life—but that is getting ahead in the story. Edna married Giles Otis (Dewey) Pearce on 18 November 1914 in Boise. Mom was born in Boise on 31 August 1915. (They lost four children after the birth of Mom.) As the years went by, and as more and more citizens of Boise were born elsewhere, she took great pride in informing others she was a native.

Grandma Edna was born on 1 May 1889 in Minneapolis, Minnesota. She had been married for a short time once before to a Mr. McKeone. She did not have much to say about that marriage. Grandpa Dewey was born on 29 March 1895 in Diller, Nebraska, and was a well-known sportsman in the Boise area at the time of their marriage. There won't be much to say about Dewey or his relatives because Mom was so upset with her father regarding the circumstances that led to his divorce with her mother that she didn't want us kids to traffic with them. She told me later in her life that she regretted that decision. He was never thought of as "Grandpa" by Harley and me. Edna, on the other hand, was not only "Grandma," she was almost "the beloved." That will become evident as I proceed with this venture into life.

In her youth, Mom was very devoted to her father. He owned a sporting goods store, sponsored ball teams, and loved to hunt and fish. Mom was at his side in all that most of the time—and her mom Edna also. The family had a lot of fun, and some might say my mother was somewhat of a spoiled child. All went hunky dory for Mom until her Dad jumped the fence, and her parents divorced when she was still in high school. Then after she graduated and enrolled in a nursing program in Portland, he reneged on his commitment to finance her and she could not complete the program. She met Dad a year later in 1934 and that was a good thing for me.

Dad, Albert Louis Brueck, was the youngest child of Louis Albert and Mary Wilhelmina Saar, who were married in Sioux City, Iowa, on 6 June 1908. Grandpa Brueck was born 21 February 1875 in Aurora, Illinois, and died at age 85 on 19 November 1960 in Niagara Falls, New York. He was one of six children of Peter H. Brück. Grandma Brueck was born in Germany on 12 December 1883 in Doberphal, West Prussia, and died in Boise 1 April 1953. The other children of Dad's family were my Aunt Mary, born 16 March 1910, and Ann, who died in an automobile accident in the Idaho Mountains before I was old enough to remember her. She was with her boss to visit a mining sight, and their vehicle went over the side of the road high up on the Kleinschmidt Grade overlooking Hell's Canyon and the Snake River along the Idaho-Oregon border. I did log time occasionally over the years with her son, Eugene Zeigler. A fourth child of Louis and Mary, Anna, died at childbirth or early in life.

Over the years my Aunt Mary and I developed a very simpatico relationship. I referred to her as my favorite aunt. (She was my only aunt.) One could write what I would consider a fascinating book about that highly intelligent, eccentric woman. In a way, in my youth, she disappointed me on the occasion of every birthday and Christmas by giving me books instead of stuff to fight childhood make-believe wars and sports equipment or other boy toys. Looking back, I know her intent, and she was successful.

Aunt Mary was the perennial student, though the only formal educational degree she ever received was her law degree from the University of Utah in 1946. She was admitted to the Idaho bar in 1948 as the 19th woman ever admitted to the Idaho bar since statehood in 1890. She became the second woman lawyer in Boise. During her life, Aunt Mary devoted most of her lawyering to helping people of limited means, especially the disabled, elderly, the disadvantaged, and others often mistreated by "the system." She even married two disabled men, one of whom was her third husband, Robert T. Poole. She then became a loving mother to Susan Poole Cardwell, Bob's daughter from a prior marriage, and then eventually separated from Poole in 1964. Aunt Mary didn't litigate any memorable lawsuits, but she lived a life of great significance helping others. If I didn't hold her in high regard and with affection, I would not have written even this much about her. She was special. She died in Boise on 24 April 1998 at the age of 88 after suffering Alzheimer's in her later years.

Grandma Brueck, Bob, and Harley

Although there are many memories of pleasant times with Grandma Brueck, I do not remember her as cuddly and nurturing like I do Grandma Edna. She was the one who said, "no work, no eat." She did not respond well when Harley and I had a pillow fight with her nice handmade down pillows, etc. I recall her doing many chores of daily living at their rural home at 2925 Tamarack Drive in Boise. Their home was my first memory of a wood stove and of Grandma often cooking a Sunday dinner for several in the family.

I also recall getting money for picking the bugs off the potato and tomato plants in their large garden. I was unsuccessful in my attempt to get rich when I stole Cousin Gene's penny bank and hid it in a ditch down the road. I don't know where I failed in my great theft, but the next thing I knew Grandma was on my case like a hound dog on raw meat. My chores when there included some care for the goats, calves, and chickens—and in particular, to wring the necks when we "harvested" the chickens. Grandma was a good cook of basic foods, and the bounty of their garden led me to like vegetables at an early age. That is

14

also the place where I tried unsuccessfully to fly by jumping off the roof of the chicken house.

I do remember Grandpa Brueck as someone I always liked to be with. Although I was told that he had a great swear-word vocabulary and could "out swear" anyone in South Dakota, I do not recall him ever swearing in the presence of Harley and me—even when his fishing line was terribly tangled or he banged his finger using a hammer. I recall that his manner of instructing us how to do farming chores was gentle and effective.

When Dad, Harley, and I went on hunting trips in the fall, we often took Grandpa with us. One time when I was hunting with him after he turned 80, when we had to climb a rather steep bluff to get out of the place we were in, I offered to carry his gun to relieve him of the weight. You would have thought I had spit on the flag. I recall at that time hoping I would be able to do as well if I

reached that age. (That was the trip we got snowed in and had to catch a few fish on a bent safety pin and kill and eat a porcupine. Terrible meat but a memory I obviously have not forgotten.)

When I was old enough to drive, I would take Grandpa and his overweight, ailing buddy across the road on fishing trips.

Grandpa Brueck

Most were high pleasure but not when one of them would try to stand up in the little flat-bottomed boat we trailered to the mountain lakes. (I somehow felt responsible for their safety.) I have always felt this picture of him, taken by a newspaper reporter interviewing people on the street, showed his kind and gentle basic nature—at least in old age.

Dad in his youth had to work hard on the family farm in South Dakota. Although there had been a bumper crop in 1914 before his father moved there from Iowa, there were many lean years thereafter, hardly paying for the seed to grow the crops. Aunt Mary reported in later life that Dad was worked very hard by Grandpa in his youth and into his early adult years.

When Dad had been offered a scholarship to attend South Dakota State University in Brookings, he declined it after saying something like, "I never saw a prof who wasn't starving to death." However, he did attend for two years in

1931-32. He returned to the farm, but he had issue after issue with his parents, and Mary said, "I kidnapped him," to get him out of misery.

Somewhere along the trail Aunt Mary had made the acquaintance of a close friend in Emmett, Idaho, and she moved there from South Dakota in 1932. She had started a mimeograph newspaper, and Dad joined her in the endeavor. Dad rode the rails (a "hobo") to Idaho. Their folks gave up farming and also moved to Idaho in 1933 and lived there until Grandma Brueck died 1 April 1953. They had leased the South Dakota land, but at some point during WWII, the lease payments stopped and the land was sold or lost to unpaid taxes.

The written material that has come down in the family indicates that Dad was active in the National Guard and a member of the rifle team. He and Mother made a driving trip to Camp Perry, Ohio, for a national match in September 1939 while Harley and I visited with John and Edna in Twin Falls. Sixteen years later, I was a member of a NROTC rifle team at the University of Colorado (CU). I had shot my first deer at age 12. Firearms training ran in the family in those days.

And of course, my grandparents had parents and so on back into antiquity. I will leave it to the ancestry-focused websites and whatever supersedes them to lead one that direction if so interested—with one exception—the gentleman prominent in this picture.

My father's paternal grandfather was Peter H. Brück. Peter was born 22 September 1835 in Erda, now Germany. We never met, but over the years I learned a lot about him, but we don't have time and space for much of that. Note in passing that my Grandfather Brueck, pictured to the right of Peter in the picture, was one of his six children.

The information we have indicates that Peter grew tired of the obligation to be called up by the then Prussian government to fight wars. He served his hitch, and after an honorable discharge, he apparently didn't like the developing climate for what became the Second War of Schleswig in 1864. We do have a picture of him in a military uniform copied from a charcoal portrait originally created in about 1855-60.

16

Peter, his bride of only a few months, Anna Marie Bertalott, and her father departed Germany from Hamburg on 7 May 1864. They sailed on the Teutonia and arrived in the USA via Castle Garden in lower Manhattan Island, New York, on 1 June. Castle Garden was the world's first immigration depot, which preceded Ellis Island by 40 years. There is quite a bit of information in family genealogical records about Peter, in particular after he became a naturalized citizen of the USA in the state of Illinois on 15 June 1870. He died 14 June 1900.

It appears that I was born into this life in 1935 because of a war in 1864.

Family of Great Grandfather Peter Brück

A Thought or Two Looking Back from Now

Even though some of my progenitors lived in the Boise Valley of Idaho, the sense I take away from writing about them is "rural." And I know there have been some letters preserved for future generations, but letters seem, well, archaic. If anyone reads this on down the family line, I wonder what they will think about my era. It started with letters, and phone calls that cost too much to make except in emergencies. Now we have a worldwide Internet with data rates upwards of 30 Mbps even to hand-held devices, and what are now called "social media," where some people practically inform the world about their every trip to the bathroom! The electronics of the future had better be a lot denser and with currently unforeseen higher speed logic technology, or there won't be enough bandwidth to essentially interconnect everyone and everything of significance in the world—as is certainly the trend.

2

Preschool Years

Before, and for a while after Mom and Dad were married in April 1935, Dad worked bussing tables for $9/week at the restaurant of the Hotel Boise. There he met Ralph and Flossie Searle, who would be lifetime friends and people I knew as neat people in my adult years. Dad had won a state championship in typing and shorthand in South Dakota. So he left bussing to take a job that paid $75/month working as a stenographer for an esteemed architect at what was then Boise-Payette Lumber Company—and later grew to be Boise Cascade, a highly vertically integrated, major company. Five years later, he was paid $150/month and was provided a company car. Harley and I believe that while working there Dad developed both competence and a love for building architecture that served him well in many ways later in life.

It is possible that Mom and Dad lived at 1401 W. State Street in Boise for at least awhile after marriage—at least that is the address on the wedding invitation—Grandma Edna lived where she worked. My birth certificate notes that my parents lived at 1314 Grand Avenue in Boise when I was born, and that is likely where I went when Dorothy Schubert drove us home from the hospital. There is evidence they moved to 2117 Bannock sometime in 1936 for a while but to 1518 Jefferson later in the year. Dad named me, and then called me "Buzzy?" Mom told me that she called me "Bobby Lew," and that if I had been a girl, she would have named me Roberta Lou.

We still lived on Jefferson at the time of Christmas in 1936. While living there, Dad created a small home floor plan to provide Boise Payette an affordable home option to market too many people in the late 30's. Dad used those plans to build the home at 2112 Madison in Boise that we moved to June 1937. I do have memories that go back that far, but the only one I will mention is my fondness for our neighbor across the street, Mrs. Reese. She had a candy jar on the table in front of their couch—thus introducing me to *Reese's Pieces* early in life. I don't recall it, but I am told that on 11 April of that year Mom

18

gave birth to another kid, my brother Harley. We became well acquainted later. John Griffiths and Edna were married in Ogden, Utah, on the 17th while Mom and Harley were enjoying life together without me in the hospital. Harley came home from the hospital with her on the 20th. Busy year!

Mom and Dad and Us Boys

I like this picture of the young family taken in August that year.

Moving on—my baby book records that on the 4th of July in 1938, Harley and I had our first airplane ride, which would have been from the airfield at the current location of Boise State University (BSU). I subsequently have had my bones hauled around in the sky for a few million miles. In those early years, I have vague memories of some of Mom and Dad's closest friends, in particular Larry and Rosalie Brown and Ralph and Flossie Searle. I later met Harley Adamson—yes, Dad's close friend whom Harley was named after.

I can find no record of when and why our family moved away from the home on Madison that Dad built. My baby book records that I had an emergency appendectomy (Dr. Mack) in June 1939 and that Harley lived for a month with John and Edna in Twin Falls. We were still living on Madison then. It also records a tonsillectomy in August 1939. (All I recall about that operation is that I got an ice cream cone after it.) Only a couple months later when Mom and Dad went to the rifle match in Ohio in September 1939, I think we still lived on Madison. After that I have no memory until we lived at 1523 Vermont in Boise, not far from that old airfield, now Boise State University.

Several of us in the family believe we have seen written references or heard inferences from Mom that they lost the home because they couldn't make the mortgage payments. At the Vermont Street home, I recall Dad coming home from hunting with a deer draped across the fender of his car—a practice he later knew to be deplorable—a way to spoil otherwise good venison. That is also the home where he let me sit on his lap and try to steer the car around the block.

During those years, Dad was a staff sergeant in the National Guard, and he later reported to a relative that he had planned on a military career. I do have several pictures of Dad in the Army uniform of those times. This is one of my favorites.

Soon after dawn one morning in early May 1941, I recall accompanying Mom and Dad across the Broadway Street Bridge to the Morrison Knudson Company and witnessing my Dad get on a bus with a tearful Mom waving goodbye. I later learned that he had taken a job to be a truck driver for MK (employee number 2630), which was a PNAB (Pacific Naval Air Bases) contractor working

Dad in National Guard Uniform

to fortify islands in the Pacific. When Dad signed up, the MK records show he gave the name of Ernest Miller of 2112 Madison Street, Boise, as his contact person. There is a record of an Ernest and Ruby Miller in Boise at 703 Union Street in 1940 and that he was a VP in charge of credit at the Idaho First National Bank—further supporting the assumption Mom and Dad lost the Madison home because they could not make payments.

Dad went to work on Wake Island after a few days in Honolulu and a few days on Johnson Island because of a mix-up in MK paperwork. Letters between Mom and Dad during the following months make it clear that there was indeed financial stress, and the job was Dad's effort to significantly increase income. Mom later told me that Grandpa John had counseled against the decision. The letters also indicate that the marriage was undergoing marital stress at the time but that both looked to the future together expecting better days.

I well remember that soon after Dad departed, Mom, Harley, and I went to live in a cabin at Lowman, Idaho—well, sort of at Lowman. Lowman was a wide spot in a dirt mountain road with a Lodge on the banks of the South Fork of the

Payette River. The cabin was separated from the lodge by a large pasture. To go to the lodge for groceries or on upstream to the hot springs to do laundry or take a bath, we had to either cross the pasture or climb a steep hill to the Boise-Lowman road and walk much farther. The big bull in the pasture made crossing it a harrowing journey. I have vivid memories of Mom saying, "Run!" and her with a bull close behind.

The record shows that we were only at the cabin for six weeks. No wonder! The only light after dark was a kerosene lantern. The only way to keep food cool, not cold, was to put it in a hole dug alongside the creek adjacent to the cabin, and then there was the bull. I don't recall the outhouse, but I am quite sure that is where I first encountered much of the world being a place where a guy can easily pee. Harley and I recall a trip to Boise with someone during our stay. Harley recalls that the driver shot a coyote out the window of the car on the way. We wonder if maybe we left the Lowman cabin because our hair grew back in enough that the evidence of ring-worm disappeared. ☺

After a pleasant stay in Caldwell during July with Grandpa and Grandma Griffiths (hereinafter referred to, affectionately on into eternity, as John and Edna), we moved to a rental on Manitou Street, the "Woolsey House," also south of the current location of BSU. A few memories of our sojourn there are also quite vivid. Mr. Smith next door was much more than grumpy. When he found Harley and me playing with matches on the back porch, he was beside himself and reported that to Mom as soon as she got off work and returned home. We could not have lived there more than two or three months and maybe less.

After the Woolsey House, Harley and I lived for a short time with John and Edna at 603 10th Avenue South in Nampa. They had moved to Nampa when John became the city engineer there. While we were with them, Mom moved us to 1216 North 14th in Boise. I recall that this apartment was not far from where the Schubert's were living then. They lived at the kink in the road at the intersection of West Hays and North Harrison Blvd. There was and is a small park at that corner. Just remembering the park makes me recall that there have been a few times in my life when it could have ended, shall we say, "Prematurely." One of those times was when Harley and I went there with bows and arrows. A "not good" thing we did with them occurred that afternoon in that park. One of us would try to shoot arrows straight up in the air—then the other one would try to stand directly under it as it returned toward Earth. It makes me wince just to recall doing that, even though the arrows probably had a rubber tip of some kind. I quickly add that I am glad that doing a stupid thing doesn't necessarily doom one to do more stupid things, or at least not a lot of stupid things, or a regular habit of doing stupid things. Thank goodness. As someone has said, "There is no cure for stupid."

Sometime in August 1941 we traveled to Payette, Idaho, to participate in a short-wave frequency radio link conversation with Dad in Honolulu. I presume a ham radio operator in Payette was in touch with an operator there and arranged the link.

Anyway, I recall three events that occurred at that apartment on North 14th. I recall that the Schubert girls, Pat and Virginia, baby sat Harley and me on occasion. I recall hiding far back under the bed so they could not undress me at bedtime. Strange! I also recall hitting myself on the top of my head with a claw hammer when using the hammer to pound on something, probably one of the black walnuts that grew nearby. Real klutz! And the most relevant memory is the time Mom and one or two other women were packing all sorts of goodies into a big box that was then sent to Dad and Lester Turner, a relative of Grandma Edna and Dorothy Schubert, for Christmas on Wake.

I don't remember hearing whether the box arrived. However, I recall very vividly that one Sunday afternoon I was out in front of the Beberness home in Boise playing with their kids and marveling at acorns that came from a tree. Imagine that. Suddenly Mom came running out to gather us up and try to explain that something far away was happening that was bad. I forget the detail of what she said, but later realized that the adults had just heard the first news of the Japanese attack at Pearl Harbor. Mom's note in a scrapbook reports that she called the Schubert's right away and that they drove us to John and Edna's in Nampa. Ben Schubert and John were the steady pillars in our family life at that time.

In a speech on 8 December 1941, US President Franklin D. Roosevelt declared war on Japan in a speech to a joint session of Congress, describing the day of the Japanese attack on the Pearl Harbor Naval Base as "**a date which will live in infamy.**" Another war was about to have a major effect on my life.

A Thought or Two Looking Back from Now

My youth clearly started in an extended family with meager financial resources but apparently with few concerns about the near-by world around them being something to fear. I don't recall being called a "latch-key" kid, but according to the meaning of the term now, I certainly was. I believe that I have grown up with a basic nature of self-confidence. I wonder if some of that might be from being free so much in my early life to touch the perimeter of my comfort zone on my own. I think it was. I know I later came to believe that self-confidence was a potentially valued male attribute. It was late into life that I realized that so many people lack self-confidence and became a little more sensitive to interaction with them.

➤ 3 ⤬

IBM

The World War II Years

To most people nowadays, IBM is just the short name for International Business Machines Corp. However, to many who worked there a few decades ago, it meant:

I've Been Moved

It is the latter that comes to my mind at the moment, before the war—to eight different houses. As we will see, during the war—to six more houses. Thus, we lived in 14 houses in less than ten years! Until age 13 I had not celebrated Christmas in the same house. Definitely IBM! And as you would not see if you got this far but don't go much further, that was only the start!

Over the years, I read a lot about Pearl Harbor, saw many of the movies (including one I particularly recall, *From Here to Eternity*), and have visited the Pearl Harbor Visitor Center and the memorial at the USS Arizona in Hawaii. I have also read a lot and have seen many movies related to the war in Europe. However, until recently, I didn't know that it was only three days after the US officially declared war on Japan that Germany and Italy declared war on the US. The countries of the world, with only a few declaring neutrality, quickly assembled into the Allies vs. the Axis Powers, the latter anchored by a treaty between Germany, Italy, and Japan. It was indeed a World War II. To me at that age, it was just "the war." It was only on VJ day, 14 August 1945 that I really recall that something very special was occurring to change from "the war" to a whole new perspective. Imagine that, almost ten years old and sort of oblivious. I have since come to believe that should be my middle name— "oblivious." When the days of war subsided, and over time in later life, I learned more and more about both the Battle for Wake Island and what Dad experienced in the Japanese prison camps.

The Battle for Wake Island started when the Japanese launched their battle there on the day after Pearl Harbor. The US Marines had a detachment there with some fighter aircraft, and they successfully with great valor fought off the initial invasion attempt—later known as the first US victory of the war. I later learned that the Marines had help from my Dad and his civilian buddies with their earth-moving equipment to repair the runway, move the placement of anti-aircraft guns each night, and for the creation of battlements in general. That could not be acknowledged for many years because technically that made them "terrorists," and not protected by the Geneva Convention as other civilians are protected. However, many years after the war, and with consistent lobbying by some dedicated relatives of survivors, the US government later made them retroactively Navy veterans. That status provided those still living with some compensation and medical services in their later years.

A few days before the Japanese attack on Wake, Dad had been in the hospital with appendicitis. He later told us that the hospital, with a huge red cross painted on the roof, was the first building targeted by the Japanese fighter/bomber planes. To my knowledge, Dad never said he was in a weakened condition when captured due to his recent hospitalization. He did say that his body fared better than most with the limited and nutritionally poor food they received during captivity.

There are well-written books describing the Battle for Wake and even the movie *Wake Island: The Alamo of the Pacific*, so I won't just repeat what I have read and been told by Dad. The Marines put up a good fight, and as I understand it, have become known as The Defenders—a part of the Corp lore. The Internet is loaded with material describing the defense of Wake and the subsequent events relating to both Marines and civilians.

What I do remember very well is that, about one month after Pearl Harbor, Harley and I moved to Nampa to live with John and Edna for the remainder of the war. Mom was clearly already showing the gutsy stuff I would see for myself in post-war years. She was working. Some letters show that she was communicating with many parties to hold some family interests together. It was hard to stretch what money she could make to pay rent and put food on the table, let alone pay for purchased child care. Mom and Dad's friends were in Boise. Mom knew we were better off to live with John and Edna while she fought the good fight, and I think they were gutsy to take us in. I do have a lot of memories of life with John and Edna during the war years—many—but only the idea of mother, not the actual touch or doing things with a mother—or a dad, either.

25

The rest of this chapter will be my personal memory for those years, with John and Edna as "in loco par entum"—in place of parents.

Some Childhood Memories

If being as oblivious of the war as I was can be excused, it is because those grandparents gave Harley and me as close to a normal or desired childhood experience as was possible in the context of a major war. In my opinion, they did a fantastically good job. Under the banner of "a fantastically good job" of providing child development in a loving, secure environment, all I intend to further record about the war years are memories having very little consequence in my later life.

For some reason, John still did not own a home in Nampa since he had become the City Engineer. They had been living at 603 10th Avenue South since moving to Nampa. Harley and I lived there briefly with them, but soon after we arrived to their care, we moved to "The Dole House," named after the owner I guess. It was located on 12th Avenue just south of 7th Street where an Albertson's supermarket is now located. Before moving in with them in January 1942, we had all gathered there for Christmas.

There are many scrapbook pictures of Harley and me with gifts we were given that year. Before Pearl Harbor, Dad had arranged for a couple buddies in Honolulu, Jim On and Ray Kataharu, to buy and send his list of gifts. In retrospect, it sort of looks like Santa dumped his entire sleigh at our house. Some of those pictures taken at Christmastime are among those I have scanned and added to the rather large amount of genealogically related material I have digitized and have attempted to spread widely within the extended family. We had beds and some play space in the basement, where John was experimenting with making wine. I have since become quite familiar with that delightful odor.

At the time we moved in with John and Edna, Mom lived in Boise (at 415 Idaho Street, Apartment 5, I believe) and worked as a switchboard operator. Back in those days it took such operators at the telephone company to connect one party with another circuit that would be the path to the other party. (There were also "party lines" in rural areas where several families shared a single line, and when one party was using the line, neighbors would sometimes try to listen in without being detected.) For the next couple of years, Mom worked at several jobs and lived at several addresses.

There was a highly informative attempt by Mom and Dad to exchange letters in 1942. In what appears to be early 1942 from the Shanghai camp, Dad was given the opportunity to write home to Mom. He didn't cover a lot of ground but just to say he was alive and not wounded or abused was the important thing. Before she received that letter on 21 April 1942, Mom wrote Dad a letter we know he later received—only because Dad kept and returned with all letters he received from family during his years as a "Guest of the Emperor"—as he later called being a prisoner of war.

On 7 June 1942, Mom wrote Dad a letter making it pretty clear she had received his letter because in her letter she answered his question about Christmas presents. It is also clear that receiving Dad's letter was her first confirmation that he was alive. She starts her letter with, "I am so jubilant at hearing from you." Dad received this 7 June 1942 letter from Mom because it was one he also brought back with him. Sometime between a letter she wrote to someone in South Dakota on 9 March, and her 7 June letter, Mom moved and went to work at St. Luke's Hospital in Boise. From later correspondence, it indicates she was living with her friend Josephine while working at St. Luke's.

At some point in 1942, we moved from the Dole house to another rental at 823 11th Avenue at the corner of 9th Street in Nampa. I know that is where I started my formal education—first grade at Roosevelt School, about six blocks away. Mrs. Keithly was my teacher. It's nice to have a recollection that she was a nurturing teacher that indeed taught us something.

Sometime between the start of school and 22 September, I vividly recall my teacher calling me out of class to tell me to run home as fast as possible, and I think she told me that it was something relating to Dad. I ran home and listened to a short-wave broadcast. In Aunt Mary's letter to Dad dated 22 September 1942, she mentions that a letter with his name as author was read over the Tokyo Broadcasting Station. It seems pretty certain that the broadcast Aunt Mary was referring to is the one I ran home to listen to. Someone had to send info in advance to inform family that there would be a broadcast. I think that was done by the Red Cross. When I was later in the third grade, Harley and I had the similar experience of being told by teachers to run home for the same reason. Predictably in those times, I also had measles and chicken pox during the year with a sign posted each time at the front door to announce to all who might wish to enter that the home was quarantined.

John taught me to play checkers during the year, and we often played a game as he lay on the couch after returning home from work. Our most frequent playmate was Sharon Halverson, who lived in a large home next door or one house removed. A distant relative who joined the Seabee's gave us a blond cocker spaniel named Dawn. Christmas that year was a big deal. Carl Eisenberg, his wife Harriet, and his daughter were there. I recall Carl and John setting up our new model train set and a happy occasion in general. We had a dog, playmates, and caring functional adults who anointed us with what I think were rock-solid values. And again, my memory is "What war?" It was very clear that John and Edna were going all out in devotion to giving us a wonderful youth experience with them.

There are quite a few things about war memories that aren't pegged to a

John Teaching Dawn to Beg

particular time or home. Gasoline was rationed. To drive 15 miles from Nampa to Caldwell was a big deal. I don't recall how much per month, but I recall it was a very limiting amount. John did a little better because he had gas to do his job for the city. To conserve fuel, speed limits were very low. Bananas were only available to babies who needed them for diet purposes. Shoes, sugar, and tires required coupons. The good thing about coupons was that family members could pool the allotment. That is the only way they kept Harley and me in shoes—shoes that were seemingly made with cardboard soles. The pooling of sugar coupons was a big deal because so much of our food was grown in a Victory Garden or purchased locally to be canned for the next winter. The pressure cooker was used more than a frying pan. Occasionally we had air raid drills, where we had to hang blankets over the windows if we used lights at night so as to have a "black out" for the whole town.

Sometime into 1943, John and Edna bought the home at 823 10th Avenue South. It was one block away. That home was across 9th Street from a guy named Jerry Zimmerman, who became a closest friend for a long time. I have many memories of times with Jerry and pictures also, but other than to say I had a buddy, I can't see a reason to go into detail—except that he is the one I liked to go around with jumping fences to steal ripe fruit after dark. There was a time when I thought we knew of every fruit tree in Nampa. We ate the fruit—unlike when we stole fruit from farmers when in high school and donated the fruit and vegetables to the grateful home economics department.

That year, John built in his basement workshop the beautiful bedroom set we still have from wood from the black walnut trees growing on the Griffiths homestead property in Caldwell. That place is where I would live during my high school years.

Another special thing I recall about 1943 was the great gardening experience and that I/we received a set of drums for Christmas. With the guidance of John, we tilled the soil, planted, weeded, watered, harvested and even sold some of the wide varieties of produce from our Victory Garden. I definitely recall that the women of the homes where I went door to door peddling eggplant, celery, carrots, turnips, beets, cabbage, and later, potatoes, were delighted to see me coming with my little wagon filled with the daily offerings. I wish everything I have tried to sell in my life was such a slam-dunk sale.

The drums started Harley and me on a track that led all the way into high school. I seem to recall that Harley remained in band and orchestra all four years of his high school experience. I made it two or three years before getting kicked out. But getting kicked out is what started me on a path to a happy marriage, so maybe I owe something to those drums that I hadn't thought of until just now. Imagine, grandparents so committed to making us happy that they bought us drums even though we would be practicing right under their roof. Nowadays, aspiring musicians rent practice space in old office buildings. One of Mom's letters to Dad said that John had "really developed Bob's mathematical ability." The record shows that a bent toward math won out over any inclination to stick with music in the long haul—but we will at least revisit the drums for a spell in high school.

My only other clear memory of 1943 is that we also got a BB gun. I cringe now at all the little birdies I sent on to birdie heaven. I do recall that once we had a burial ceremony on Jerry Zimmerman's property and buried a robin in the pipe that covered one of the old utility meters of that era. Raise the lid, say the solemn words, drop the bird, put the lid back on, and have the good feeling of a religious rite. Sweet and simple. I cringe. I am told that such deeds make the river Styx into Hades narrower. On the other hand, there is the view that to know white, we must first know black. I later in life came to the view that I would not shoot a bird or animal unless I intended to eat it.

Jerry, a couple other neighborhood friends, and Harley and I spent a lot of time playing in an empty lot at the other end of our block. With inspiration from some kind of war source, movies maybe, we created "forts," and conducted battles of some sort. The forts were quite elaborate. We dug holes a couple feet into the ground, placed sod around the holes, and made some kind of roof. In addition to the entrance, we had openings in the walls for vision and shooting. John made Harley and me a wooden model machine gun that was the envy of all the guys. Great boy fun. My other war-related way to spend time was to build models of American fighting aircraft from balsa wood and tissue paper—before kids started sniffing the glue.

There is a sort of irony that during those days of war between America and Japan another of my close chums in the neighborhood was Japanese. I wish I could recall his name. I think it was Ishihara, and we called him Isshy for short. I know that is close to accurate but would not bet on it. Isshy's family lived kitty-corner across the street from our place. They had been in the US a long time and were not a part of the Japanese citizens living on the Pacific Coast who had been interned to the interior to avoid any collusion with the enemy. There were a lot of internment camps in Idaho, but Isshy's family lived a quite different life. Isshy and I played catch with a baseball often, and once he let me ride his "whizzer" bike—a pretty normal bicycle with a small motor to drive the rear wheel.

And finally for 1943, from letters between Mom and government authorities, I learned that early in the year she was informed that she would receive a check in the amount of $89.38 each month ($1229.10 inflation adjusted to 2014) from the government as compensation for Dad's unfortunate situation to be located between two warring nations. She used part of those funds in May to buy a radio capable of receiving short wave broadcasts. Pat and I still have that old tube radio. I kept it operative for several decades, but I haven't even dusted it off for many years. I presume the vacuum tubes are defuncto and hard to come by these days.

The most memorable event the next year was that Mom enlisted in the Women's Army Corp (the WAC) in June 1944. Of course I didn't understand much about such matters, except that we would be seeing her even less. It was cloaked in serving one's country, and the financial need wasn't mentioned in front of us boys. When she gave up her apartment, the short-wave radio came to our house. I do recall listening to Tokyo Rose propaganda broadcasts but little else, with one exception—Harley and I got to hear our Dad's voice.

A couple months before Mom left, we had listened to Dad's own voice in a shortwave broadcast from his POW camp in Japan. Shortly thereafter, Mom received several recordings of the broadcast made by ham radio operators in America who monitored the sources of such broadcasts, recorded them on a plastic 45 rpm record, and mailed them to the address of kin mentioned during the broadcast. Neat people with a neat way of helping the war effort.

We were gifted our first real bicycles during 1944. Such mobility was a whole new experience. We rode for miles, often well into the country outside of town to fish, swim, or just play in and investigate the drain ditches. One time we were playing in an irrigation ditch only a half-mile from home. At some point, I slid down the bank and my big toe collided with a broken bottle top. We had gone there pulling our wagon, taking turns as to who was pulling and who was riding. We were barefoot, and the pavement on the return home route was hot, hot, hot. Because I had to hold my big toe up in the air as I walked and because my feet were more hardened to endure the hot pavement, I was, for some reason not clear to me now, willing to pull the wagon all the way on the return with Harley worried on my behalf about the bleeding toe but really glad he was in the wagon and didn't have to suffer the burning sensation of feet on hot pavement.

We swam in those ditches for a while that is. One evening John came home early from work, gathered us up and gave us a tour of the filth that runs into those drain ditches—yup, sewer type stuff and agricultural chemicals from farming. I don't recall him saying much, but he pointed a lot. We ceased swimming in canals and drain ditches, but I seem to recall that we still fished in them. Hmmmmm?

The bikes were hard on Dawn. The first day we rode them extensively, Dawn followed us and got bleeding paws for his trouble. We had blood on our hands. We were much more thoughtful in the following days. At some point, we and Dawn worked out a way to distinguish what would be a long ride and what was just roaming around the neighborhood.

31

My life just rolled on. In my mind now, that was about the best that any kid could hope for. Sort of the focus of attention but not spoiled too much. And far off, my parents wore uniforms to work and endured a highly regimented life—without the warm embraces and loving mutual servitude of what they had hoped for in married life. Such was the way it was then. We were all six experiencing a way of working through a difficult time in history for US citizens, and I was mostly oblivious--however, when I now look into the eyes of my parents in these photos there is a lot to see.

Dad During WWII   Mom During WWII

I don't recall much about my second-grade teacher, but I do recall that I liked Mrs. Tipton in third grade, starting that fall in 1944. Some time that year, probably during the summer, we had moved to another house, at about 805 11th Avenue South in Nampa—only about three houses from where we lived when I started first grade. Three grades, three homes.

This third one had a basically empty big room on the second floor with a long work bench against one wall. That is where my chemistry set came into being. I am sure John supervised what I was buying, from where, and for what experiment in what book, so I represented no threat to humans or the house, but sometimes I sure came up with an awful odor. I don't recall any details about what I discovered, but I do remember that the overall experience was positive, even exhilarating at times. The process to take two things to come up with a completely third thing was quite interesting, especially if the third thing smoked, changed color, changed solid/liquid/gaseous state or smelled bad.

The most memorable thing I recall about my education during the third grade is that alliances between individuals can be helpful in many ways. It was about fifty years later I learned from *The Rise and Fall of the Great Powers* by Paul Kennedy that was true for countries also. My lesson in the third grade came from a real downer experience as a consequence of one of those alliance relationships.

Mrs. Tipton motivated us students like John did Harley and me. She offered tangible reward for desired behavior or accomplishment. I wasn't much on the good behavior side (D's in attitude and deportment, year after year), but I excelled on the accomplishment side. She awarded stars for high grades. I accumulated lots of stars, and periodically we could take our little star books to her store of desirable goodies as local currency for purchases. One period I had my eye on one item in her store, worked hard, and knew I had enough stars to buy it and that no one else did. I really, really wanted it.

Well, that's when I ran into this "alliance" phenomena. Before the buying time came to my desk, some mediocre student up the row bought the coveted item. How could that be, you ask. Well, the stars were transferable. I don't know if I ever found out whether the slob bought stars or traded favors for them, but it took him several people working together to get enough stars to rob me. Yes, could have been that a motivation to put me in my place may have been the bedrock of the alliance, but maybe it was just that he coveted the same thing and was a smooth talker with several close friends. I have obviously not remembered a lot of what we were taught as book subjects by Mrs. Tipton, but I do remember the lesson in alliances.

Not surprising, sometime in the summer of 1945, we moved to another house—this one at about 619 12th Avenue South in Nampa. A church now occupies the location. John appears to have bought the house with intent to move it to a vacant lot several blocks away near Roosevelt School—which he later did—and would you believe that was the house where we again lived with John and Edna during the second semester of my sixth grade. The war victory in Europe had been celebrated in May, and the outcome in the Pacific probably looked quite encouraging. Maybe that was a factor in John's decision, but I don't know. It was just another move—and remember, I was sort of oblivious!

I recall few experiences while living there—the minor memory of attending a church not far away—and the several major memories after the victory in the war with Japan was declared in August. From communications now in our records, the family learned via a telegram sent to John that Dad had been liberated from the Niigata 5-B POW camp about 160 miles NW of Tokyo on 10 September. He was one of a few hundred who were moved earlier that year from the 5D camp at Kawasaki because of heavy bombing in that area. (I was glad for that bombing and for the move!)

Mom traveled to the San Francisco area to greet Dad when he returned and then returned to her Army post in Seattle to be discharged on 1 November. Harley recalls greeting Dad at the Nampa train depot, but I don't recall that experience. My first memory is of John and him enjoying Tom and Jerry cocktails during the Thanksgiving Holiday family gathering.

While in the WACs, Mom sent a few pictures, short notes to John and Edna, and an occasional special something for Harley and me, but she never really told her own war story. It did lead to her later employment, but we just didn't learn about the experience of getting the experience. As for the bigger picture, Mom and Dad were able to send and receive some letters during the war years, and copies of those have been scanned and are a part of our genealogical records.

But finally, we became a family again--with John and Grandma Edna a precious part of it.

Family Again--with John and Grandma Edna
34

A Thought or Two Looking Back from Now

Again, I now wonder if all those moves provided the emotional context I have had in my adult life to be able to easily accept changing circumstances in the world around me. Whatever the fact, I have considered that demeanor to be helpful and have seen how the demeanor of fearing change has on occasion negatively affected the lives of others.

Reading what I have written, I am reminded again of the depth of my love for John and Edna, who provided me such a nurturing home life, and how little bonding with a father and mother was a part of my early years. We certainly became a close family in later years, and I found it easy to love my parents, but I wonder if losing the child's way of loving left something missing.

4

A Family Again

It sort of got off to a shaky start, but all the ingredients were in place for four people with great desire to be one family to create our future.

There were a brief few weeks where I don't recall anything after Dad returned. I do indeed recall that very happy Thanksgiving gathering at John and Edna's in Nampa where John and Dad were enjoying those Tom and Jerry drinks, and I recall that they served Harley and me some of the batter. We soon ended up living at 2808 Idaho Street in Boise. That was the then edge of town on the NE side of the Boise River. The river bank in that area was a dimpled landscape of old gravel pits. There were many ponds in the pits, and there were often many ducks in the ponds.

For some reason, Dad bought Harley and me bows and arrows. Here we go again. We did shoot at targets to get the hang of it, but my favorite target was flying ducks. I don't recall ever hitting a duck, but I sure did have a lot of fun. I spent a lot of time trying to recover the arrows. I was happy when hunting ducks.

Meanwhile, things were not really happy around the house. Dad obviously had some adjusting to civilian life to do, and the immediate need to fund a family added additional stress. He had a drafting table and was trying to earn some income as a draftsman, possibly helped by his prewar relationships with people at Boise Payette Lumber Company. Mom was working but experiencing some health issues, including fainting on the job, so was taking prescription drugs to deal with that. I do not know if there is any genetic connection, but I did have fainting spells when growing up that started up about the time I was five or six years old, then infrequently after that. The cause of mine was later diagnosed at about age 65 to be a minor electrical anomaly in my brain, for which I have since taken a daily low dose of a prescription drug.

Now, back to Boise and family life. It was quite apparent that Dad was struggling. Things were occasionally testy between Mom and Dad. There must have been a lot going on that Harley and I were not aware of because we were moved again sometime during the year to Spokane, Washington.

But in the meantime, life went on for us boys. Both of us recall more than the usual number of fights at Lowell School. One of mine was in the middle of State Street, even then a busy street. I was not popular at school for several reasons, not just my basic nature. I transferred in during the middle of the year and rattled the makeup of a couple of cliques. I started getting the highest grades on schoolwork—clearly disturbing some. I did not like the teacher or the fact that I had to cover both the prior semester and current semester of Idaho History, and I didn't think that was too important to start with.

Other memories from that period include the time Harley and I were "fencing" with a couple of trellis lath sticks. I made a lunge thrust and accidently sent the end of my stick through the back of his mouth. He received medical attention, but I felt terrible about what I had unintentionally done. (If it had been intentional, I would have felt quite different, I guess.) Harley and I learned a certain amount, much wrong, about the "birds and bees" from the neighborhood boys. I don't recall the details, but I do recall that I never did get what one might call a good preparation for what was to come.

Speaking of bees or hornet's maybe. One day we were visiting the Schubert's, who by then were living out near Collister a few blocks off State Street. Harley and I were outside roaming around and while walking by the side of the house we saw a box on the ground. Harley was curious, or something, and picked up the box. He was immediately greeted by who knows how many hornets. He started running and hollering toward the front of the house, with hornets on him and behind him, and I out ahead of him headed for a tree to hide behind. Peeking around the tree, I saw Pat Schubert greet him at the steps of the house and immediately strip him of most of his clothes while others joined to swat hornets. It was a wild scene, and of course, peeking out from behind my tree about 30 feet away, I felt very sorry for my younger brother. Hmmm! Well, maybe I did. In any event, in later life he told me he felt very embarrassed to be undressed by that girl.

Dad liked cigars. I don't recall how strong that liking was but enough that I recall him smoking an occasional cigar. One evening when Mom was gone, he was smoking one and offered Harley and me a puff. Being basically risk adverse by nature, I declined. Harley was gung-ho, and after his first puff, asked for

37

another. I don't know how many times he puffed, but when he got up from his sit-down position, his face turned more than pale—it was almost pale green. Then he vomited. Then he...didn't make it to the bathroom. I don't know if that incident is responsible, but I have never had an interest to smoke cigars.

The Sojourn in Spokane, Washington

Our first housing in Spokane was a subsidized low-income barracks unit in Garden Springs Terrace, across Hangman's Bridge on the outskirts of the city. The road over that bridge, which is near the much newer I-90 bridge, is now called West Sunset Boulevard. One could talk to their neighbor through the walls. Mom had to cook over a wood stove. I even recall the wood box along the gravel street 20 feet away from the only door. A truck came by periodically and filled it with wood. Hot water for our quarters came from a pipe through the stove. No fire, no hot water. Dad installed a heater element in the water tank connected to a wall socket—after all, he was studying electrical engineering! That event gave Mom great pleasure.

But the good news was that Dad seemed happy to be going back to college, and that the college was Gonzaga, and Gonzaga was in Spokane. Why Gonzaga you might ask, we being of the Protestant persuasion; my parents liked Bing Crosby music but that could not have been the main reason. Well, not having ever asked either parent, my guess is that it was because two of Dad's closest POW buddies lived in Spokane. Ellsworth Graham came back to his father's furrier business. Wally Fleming created a car dealership, which was doing well. And Mom had found employment in the X-ray department at the Sacred Heart Hospital. All in all, they had a lot of positive stuff going for them, and Harley and I could, as far as they knew, deal with whatever the world put at our doorstep.

We were again latch-key kids. In Spokane, we took over where we had left off with John and Edna—we had a lot of time and space to "do our own thing." We listened to certain radio programs faithfully every day. (Gene Autry, Tom Mix, The Green Hornet, and The Shadow, for instance.) In no particular order, here are some of "our own things" that were more venturesome than being glued to the radio and sending away for pictures of cowboys and magic rings, etc.

We had a hatchet. We strolled what would be a couple city blocks down past the end of our street into the woods. One of us would climb a tree and the other would chop it down—one chop, one gets a ride. We carried a gunny sack and walked along all the major roads to collect bottles of the kind that could be exchanged at the only nearby grocery store for some money. We found a lot of bottles and bought stuff with the money. All I recall buying was Double Bubble bubble gum.

To get to the grocery store, we had to go into a steep ravine and cross the

railroad tracks. While in Spokane a few years ago, Pat and I revisited the two places I had lived there. We found the old Garden Springs site (ground cleared and about ready for condominiums) and sure enough, there were the ravine and the railroad tracks. The thought of ever letting one of our kids near a place like that was unthinkable. However, I had been happy with the situation as a

Garden Springs Railroad Track

kid because I found fossils in the sandstone carved out for the tracks. Fossils were neat things—quite thought and imagination provoking.

Some days, after the sun went down, the neat guy next door would try to arrange a boxing match between Harley and me under the street light across from our unit. One reason we liked the guy was that he was in the ordinance group at the Fairchild Air Force Base southwest of Spokane. He brought us an abundance of little bundles of powder that would make a big time bang when set off on the Fourth of July, year around.

My first recollection of trying smoking was while living at Garden Springs. The area under Hangman's Bridge along the river was basically bushes and tall grass with trails winding around. I think the traffic in the area were hobos and vagrants, whatever. They littered the area with debris. Anyhow, I think we tried some of what we called the tobacco weed. I didn't make a habit of that stuff.

One of the latch-key advantages was that we could ride the bus downtown after school to swim at the YMCA, right next door to the Vaudeville Theatre, where the doorman would usually let us go in for free. Some pretty racy stuff.

In the fall of 1946, I enrolled in the fifth grade at Whittier School—now Whittier Playground with no remaining school—a little less than a mile from our barracks. I had a teacher I liked a lot, Mrs. Belknap. I was good in the classroom, but as I recall it now, sort of a cry-baby on the playground when things didn't seem "fair." She handled the playground stuff also and probably helped me develop a better understanding of what was a form of "fair" that one had to react to, and that some things that didn't seem fair to me seemed quite fair to others, etc. Mr. Henderson, the principal, made it a point to interact a lot with students and provided the "man's" way of dealing with some of those moments.

My best school chum was David Warner. He lived on my path to and from school, so we hooked up a lot outside of school hours. I thought his "girlfriend" was the cutest girl in our class. For some reason, I thought another girl was also cute, and she was the first unrelated girl I ever kissed. She was taller, like girls seemed to be at that age and I had to sort of "jump up" to make contact. I have a picture of that class in a scrapbook and have no trouble picking out Martha, David, and David's girlfriend.

It was in the fifth grade that I developed a love of reading. Of course, it was schoolboy sports and the kid books to provide moral lessons at that time, but by the time I reached high school, the librarian set me up to get books at the public library to permit me to expand my interests. I still recall some of the books I read in high school.

Our family attended a Lutheran Church in town. We were charter members. I received confirmation instruction from Pastor Livingstone. In answer to one of my questions, he is the one who informed me that, if a burglar broke into my house and I had a gun, before shooting I should say, "Friend, I would not harmest thou for anything in this world, but thee standeth where I am about to shoot." I liked going to church because we usually stopped for a hamburger on the way home. They cost ten cents each at that time.

Mom and Dad both liked the out-of-doors. That had been a part of Mom's experience since learning the routine at her father's side in her youth. Mom taught my then flatlander Dad how to fish and camp in the mountains of Idaho after they married, and when in Spokane we went fishing/camping a lot in British Columbia, Canada, as well as in Washington and Northern Idaho. Dad also encouraged our achievement in Cub and Boy Scouts, which were also outdoor-oriented programs at that time in that place. I am grateful for the early fishing and camping experience. I believe there are many life lessons learned during that kind of experience.

Sometime before school started for my sixth grade the fall of 1947, guess what? We moved again. This time across Hangman's Bridge to 2314 2nd Avenue, Apartment B, in the Browne Addition, where Dad managed an apartment house for his friend, Wally Fleming, in exchange for rent. It was real upscale compared to the barracks, and there was a nice park nearby. There was also a small neighborhood grocery store nearby where I developed a fondness for playing the pinball machine with the money I made by collecting and selling old newspaper from the neighborhood. I was just strong enough to pick up and tilt the machine to influence the direction of the ball, and thus the score to win more games without having to pay more nickels.

Our home there was where I first recall Mom and Dad having parties. The Gonzaga gang of older-than-average students liked to get together, and occasionally they would all show up at our place. It was clear to me even then that Mom liked to be a hostess. I remember the drill. We would be called into the living room to say hi to people and then told to go to bed.

Harley and I had a longer walk to school than ever before. Even with our warm coats on, we shivered a lot as we walked across Hangman's Bridge, especially during the snow storms with the wind blowing. (I am not kidding.) I am not sure we even stayed in Spokane for the full winter. At some point, we ended up back with John and Edna in Nampa for the second half of my sixth grade in the spring of 1948. I surmise that it had something to do with Dad's last semester work at Gonzaga University and his job hunting. I recall quite a bit of discussion between him and some of his classmates about the philosophy class focused on the work and thinking of St. Thomas Aquinas. Maybe he needed more time without kid distractions to get by that hurdle. Although I definitely recall Dad's studies being a major demand on his time, I think he clearly left the war years behind and enjoyed himself as husband and father— which had to be a normality much desired by Mom.

Anyhow, there we were in the spring of 1948 with me back to Roosevelt School in Nampa and with some of the classmates I knew in earlier grades there. One gal I didn't recall from earlier years became a close friend. Her name was Margie Gibbons. We used to meet at the rack where we left our bicycles while in classes. I thought she was sort of neat, and I took her picture. I dated Margie during high school and about the time I graduated from high school, I learned that she was Pat's cousin. Small world in those parts!

I had the mumps that semester and learned how to sew from Grandma Edna to pass the time. At some time during the spring, Harley and I dug a ditch across the front of the house to earn money from John. One of the deeds Harley and I wish had never happened is when we stole rope from the construction site for a new church. We both recall that for some reason, either childhood guilt or

41

that John discovered our deed; we returned the rope to the site—again sort of in the dark of the night. If I did believe that feeling guilty was appropriate and constructive for any reason, I would add that experience to the list.

Another learning experience added to the list that spring was when I was caught stealing a candy bar from a dime store in town. The employee who apprehended me marched me right down the street to the police station where a very solemn discussion took place. I was quite scared. Not just because of being caught and the nature of the discussion but also because John's office was right upstairs from police headquarters in City Hall. I thereafter continued to put washers in the gum machines, but I quit stealing in the more direct way. In case it matters, I am nearing the end of any memories of being a thief or even of wanting to steal or lie or cheat.

I started playing baseball as a team sport that spring in 1948. I seem to recall that the "Babe Ruth League" of young 12-13 year-olds was sort of a new program, at least in Nampa. I took to it with gusto. The thrill of the experience was when the St. Louis Browns held a recruiting camp in Nampa. We hung around and watched. As the camp wound down, some players had to leave, and the remaining players let us kids take a position and play (sort of) with them. The star of the camp was Lefty Martin, from Homedale I believe. He later became a star pitcher for the team or some other major league team.

On that day, he was pitching to me when I came to bat. My knees were trembling just to be doing what I was doing. A lot of things were different from our league experience. I think I recall his making some waving motion with his hand to the catcher. The next pitch seemed to be coming right at me. I knew what a curve ball was but had never seen one. I stood in the batter's box as long as I could, then threw myself to the ground half crying and trembling with unrelenting fear. The ball curved right over the plate. I have obviously never forgotten the occasion and how I felt about it.

I did a lot of swimming that spring and summer. Nampa was able to keep the pool open in spite of the epidemic of poliomyelitis (Polio) that was sweeping the country and causing the closure of many municipal pools. Early that summer, Mom took Harley and me and our friend Jerry Zimmerman on a trip to the Oregon Coast. I remember her rowing the boat as we fished offshore someplace. It was a great time with our mother.

Then came the day when Mom and Dad picked Harley and me up in Nampa, and we were on our way to my next home address—this time to a small "prefab" house at 105 George Washington Way in the then small town of Richland, Washington.

My Remembered Days in Richland, Washington

Dad took a job in Richland that really didn't require his Electrical Engineering degree. As best I recall, he was in a procurement department at the Hanford Engineering Works of the U. S. Department of Energy located on the banks of the Columbia River in a secure area north of Richland, Washington. The site was operated by General Electric at that time. Just in case computer technology does not give way solely to psychic communication in the coming years, there may still be a highly informative article describing the history of the Hanford Site at the time you are reading this.

At that time, atomic energy was obviously very popular in Richland and maybe generally within the US. In my opinion, we as a country and world would have been better off in the years since if nuclear reactors had become widespread instead of psychologically feared. Instead, even with fewer people killed in producing nuclear energy than in producing energy by any other means, and with energy the overwhelming need of the underdeveloped world, people in those countries have been left to third-world circumstances because the population of the US has permitted air-brained movie actors, under-educated "scientists," and a couple energy-plant accidents that killed or harmed no one to make them fearful of nuclear energy. Such is life in a democracy.

The entire downtown area of Richland at that time would cover less ground than a modern mall, circa 2014. 1948 was the year of the Vanport Flood of the Columbia River, and I recall driving into town with flooding in the area where the Yakima River entered the Columbia not far from our home.

The flood happened on Memorial Day in 1948. The Columbia River, swirling fifteen feet above normal, had punched a hole in a railroad embankment that served as a dike. The subsequent flood left 18,000 people homeless in the newly developed 648-acre complex near Portland, Oregon, called Vanport, then the largest public housing project in the United States. In Richland, I recall seeing some buildings flooded, including the bowling alley, but very little other high water. Our home was on high ground and certainly safe from the flood waters we could view on the river side of George Washington Way.

During those years in Richland and my seventh and eighth grades, my life became a little busier. I recall way too much to tell all about it here, and I don't know how to distill the mundane from that which might be of some higher quality. So, I will summarize with some memory snapshots of my Richland experience, and then maybe comment on a few after the summary. In no particular order, my summary of life during the seventh grade goes like this:

- We moved to a duplex at 308 Abert Street with more room and off the busy thoroughfare.
- I started my seventh grade in the fall of 1948 at Lewis and Clark School, before the first true "middle school" was established in town.
- I learned something by paying attention to the local grocer. They would hike the price of potatoes by something like ten cents per pound, then announce a "sale" in the store windows something in the nature of potatoes now on sale, now eight cents less per pound. I've seen that tactic employed over and over again in my life.
- Harley broke his wrist one day during his sixth grade recess, and I recall seeing him at the water fountain enroute to medical attention. I learned that one should not drink water if one is to soon have an anesthetic. He barfed all over the medical staff when they were working on setting his wrist in a splint. (Pat says it is more complicated than that but that I am in the ballpark.)
- Our scout troop was fantastic. Two good leaders, one named Leo.
- For reasons I do not want to go into, the scouts were going on a big campout that I wanted to go on. My folks said no. I stealthily prepared and went out a window before daybreak and was off with the troop. Yes, my folks figured it out, but all the time I was gone I knew there would be hell to pay upon my return. There was—it was a very intense few minutes with parents, especially Dad.
- The trip was not without memorable incident. A storm hit the camp. During the storm, the tent pole in my tent broke, and the ragged end of the top part came down like a spear a few inches from my head. One of the several times in my life when I was lucky to survive through an unanticipated life-threatening experience.
- I had an early morning paper route to earn money. Generally, that meant out and back before daylight. I recall that it was 24 below zero the morning I got frostbite.
- During the season, I made more money per week when I sold Christmas cards door to door. I took orders for later delivery. The cards were very good and sold well. I learned if I could "get my

foot in the door," I could show them and make a sale. That was my first selling experience.

- A major portion of the Lewis and Clark School burned down one day. For the rest of the year, we were bussed to another school, far across town. We sang songs all the way there and back.
- The most embarrassing time of my youth was when I was invited to a boy and girl party at a girl's house. Walking from the car where I had been left off to the door, I stepped in some dog poop. I didn't know it, so after I was greeted at the door by the girl's mother I proceeded to track poop all across the rug for several steps. Bless her, the mother worked hard to make my embarrassment as little as possible. I think I was 13 at the time.

Sometime during the summer in 1949, Dad arranged for Harley and me to spend time at a logging camp in Northern Idaho where he had handled the purchase of a lot of telephone poles for the Hanford site. At that time, telephone poles were made from cedar trees. The taller the pole that could be made from a tree, the higher the price. Where we were on the North Fork of the Clearwater River, the cedars were tall and the poles valuable. Hanford wanted tall poles, so there we were.

I think Dad thought he was paying the logger for us to have a couple of weeks "at camp." I think the logger thought he had slave labor. Harley bought into the idea, but I seemed to smell a rat and offered resistance now and then so I could hunt squirrels to make a Daniel Boone belt of tails. I made the belt before it began to smell real bad from the rotting core of the tails. There was another example where I later regretted shooting animals just because I had a gun and thought they were fair game. Aaaargh!

Logging work is not kids' play. It is dangerous stuff. Trees were cut on the mountains, and the logs or poles were pulled out by teams of horses to the road where they were then trucked to the river and stacked and "stamped" to await the spring flood waters for the log drive downstream to the mill. The "stamp" was essentially a brand on the end of a heavy sledge hammer pounded into the butts of the logs and poles to identify who owned them. A log might be 16 feet long. A pole might be up to 100 feet long when it washed away at the start of the drive, and hopefully, not busted up enroute before the owner could reap the high price.

Some of the loggers were essentially criminals. When pursued by Montana law enforcement, they drove to the end of a road where the Idaho side had not been built and jumped off into the woods. They then bush-whacked down to the river, put together some kind of a raft, and floated down to the first logging camp where they could sign on. Mom would have had a fit if she had known where Dad was sending us.

Three more stories about my logging experience. I could write a book about those few weeks. One day the logger said he had to go to the nearest town, Orofino, for supplies. He took his "niece" with him. She was the camp cook, and when they were unable to get back because of the muddy roads, I became the cook for the small group of loggers. They all complained about my boy-scout kind of cooking—but ate.

The head guy kept a whiskey still going all the time to make high alcohol booze from raisin mash. Some, if not all, of the loggers liked booze too much. One of my jobs was to hide the jugs in the woods. I always had loggers trying to follow me.

One day the head guy took Harley and me, the two he trusted, to an old broken-down cabin off the beaten track. He firmly believed that the original owner had buried something valuable, maybe money, around the cabin. So we dug around all day hoping to find buried treasure. Still makes me smile.

Somehow that summer, I was able to be a steady member of a local Little League Baseball team. I loved it. I still have the little copper medallion they gave all of us, regardless of how well our team did in competition. Ah, that word, "competition." I learned to be a competitor!

Also, I learned how to drive. Dad had bought a new car, a 1950 four-door Ford. He took me into the sage brush paths of a nearby desert, put me behind the wheel, went over some basics, and then said, "Drive." I drove right into the sagebrush. Some wise person has said that whenever you get a new vehicle, one should shortly thereafter scratch or dent it—to get it over with—so as not be upset when the next time it happens. So, I helped Dad out on that one.

A very sad note during the year was that my Grandfather John—bless him throughout Eternity—died in Caldwell in his sleep one night from a blood clot that moved to his brain. We conjecture that the clot came into being at the time he was injured when someone broadsided his car at an intersection on Black Cat Road off toward Boise. We made the long drive from Richland to Caldwell. That was my first "viewing" of the deceased in my life. I recall being very tearful throughout the entire memorial service.

I have often wished that John would have lived longer so I could have known him as a young adult. There were so many of my experiences he would have related to, and I know he would have added greatly to the wealth of wisdom he passed on to me over the earlier years. To this day, I think of him often. His initials were JHG. Occasionally I see those initials someplace, and each time I feel like I should stop to pay respects. One time I rented skis, rode the lift up the hill, got them on my boots, and was ready to start down the slope when I looked down at the top of the skis. Their prior owner had carved the initials, JHG.

When I occasionally think back with gratitude about those special people who were exceptionally strong influences in my life, John is always at the head of the list.

So much for that summer. Sometime during the summer, we moved to another home in Richland—an upscale for Richland—a "ranch style" government-designed and built home on Olympia Street. (All houses in Richland at that time were government-owned houses.) That fall brought on the eighth grade. That was the start of raging hormones for some guys but not for me. I was a little slow on the up-take. I do not recall a single thing about my social life that year.

What I do recall are two of the best teachers a young guy could ask for. Mr. Hanson was one. He taught algebra far beyond the usual eighth grade requirements. The metal-working shop teacher was the other. I will never forget the lesson about electricity he demonstrated in shop class by holding on to both poles of a spot welder in action. Electricity takes the shortest path! That insight didn't get me through electrical engineering in college, but it gave me a comfort-zone feeling on other occasions during my life.

I was still active in Boy Scouts—this time from a troop sponsored by a local Mormon Church. When the elk hunting season got under way in the mountains toward Yakima, there was a big snow storm. With a little help from my scout master, Dad was able to borrow the use of some snow shoes from the local scout district. He shot his elk that year while on snow shoes.

Other than the good teachers, I don't recall much more that school year—except for the leaky roof of the school. I believe the record will show that, thanks to Senator Bourke Hickenlooper from Iowa, Carmichael Jr. High became national news because of that leaky roof as evidence of some malfeasance within government contracting.

By the time the school year was over, I knew we would be "moving on." For reasons still unknown to me, Dad left his job and informed us we were moving back to Idaho. I didn't know where in Idaho but assumed it would be where we had some sort of roots.

A Thought or Two Looking Back from Now

It appears that my love of reading either started back farther than I can recall now or indeed about the time I was in fifth grade. In any event, it started sometime, and grew, and grew. I wonder why I read so much. I will never know for sure! Was I trying to get away from something or attracted by something?

It was a good feeling to recall my two special teachers in middle school, especially Mr. Hanson who mentored my innate ability in math. I think I was fortunate to have started off under his tutelage. Later in life, I taught mathematics while at the Universities of Colorado and Texas. I think there was evidence that I did as much for some students there, even though others struggled. I regret that I didn't seem to help the struggling ones much. That may have been the first time I began to see a problem when expecting equal results when only offering equal opportunity.

I note that a lot of the activity I recall from the Richland days is what I now think of as being beneficial in some way, not just childhood play. In particular, I think the paper route responsibility and the connection between what *helps* to get Christmas card orders and *getting* the orders was enlightening. Nowadays, I would probably be violating some child labor regulation. Not a good thing!

Reading again about John dying, moves me to a very sober feeling. It makes me realize how some people, like John, were so important in my life to guide and inspire me. Just now I recall how it was John who guided me away from dreading to have to go "work" to mow the lawn toward an attitude of just "to mow the lawn"—where "work" was not the operative word or at least not a word with an emotionally bad connotation. Other life lessons from John's influence on me are streaming through my head at this moment.

⊱ 5 ⊰

Those Forgiving Years

I think of my high school age years as "forgiving" because those were developmental years, and kids our age did things that could have brought on serious problems at other times or in other places. But we lived in a small town, we went to a relatively small high school (120 in my class, about 600 in the school), and those times were the 1950s. A lot has been written about the 1950s in America. The baby boom was picking up speed. The post WWII economy was robust with work for everyone willing to really work. The war in Korea was over early in the decade, and in our little part of the world, I wasn't the only one oblivious to any major problem in the wider world that maybe should have been a concern of ours. We did not have to choose to avoid or succumb to a drug culture. We were just busy "expressing ourselves"—with good days, and not so good days. Same for dates! (Just ask the girls.)

Our moving to Idaho had two moving parts. Dad, with some help from Harley and me, built a big trailer on the chassis of an old Cadillac (1912?) that had been his family pride and joy back in South Dakota. I have no idea how it made its way to Idaho. In early mid-June, Dad and friends loaded our household belongings onto that trailer, and he and Mom towed it to Idaho. Harley and I had earlier gone by a separate way.

Our separate way was to ride in an open truck with about 10-15 other Boy Scouts to the Sawtooth Wilderness Area (SWA) of Idaho. Our leader and truck driver was a neat scoutmaster. He was a mailman in Richland and member of the sponsoring Mormon Church. He was outdoors oriented and also had a great knack for guiding and motivating boys our age, just like the two scoutmasters I mentioned earlier when we lived in a different part of town.

The goal of the trip was to hike a certain loop of trails in the SWA for a week. The part I recall was from Yellowbelly Lake, about ten miles to Toxaway Lake, then over the mountain to Twin Lakes, then down via Alice Lake to Petit

Lake, and on into base camp at Yellowbelly where the truck was to be left. That was known as the Toxaway Loop, which became a favorite backpacking trip for our family in later years, starting from Petit to loop the other way around.

By later standards, my surplus Army rucksack was a terrible backpack, but with it loaded for the week, we all hit the trail after a night at a base camp on Yellowbelly Lake. Earlier that morning, we woke to see a moose feeding a ways out in the lake.

Most of us hikers were slower than the leader who was really hot to trot and more physically able to do it. The rest of us were whining and grumbling a lot as we trudged along the trail upstream. A memory I will never forget was our leader coming back down the trail toward us with the news that Toxaway was still frozen over.

This was one of my earlier experiences with switching from a Plan A to a Plan B. The new plan was to drive up to the headwaters of the Salmon River, then on over Galena Summit into the Wood River watershed to camp, fish, and hike there. We camped a few miles north of Ketchum, Idaho, a.k.a. the Sun Valley Resort area. Fishing was good, and we enjoyed several days there.

After a few days, we piled back in the truck and traveled to a large city park in Boise (Julia Davis?) to camp, drop Harley and me off, and where the rest would take off to return to Richland. We arrived at the park to find a large group of Boy Scouts already camping there. They were all decked out in washed and starched fancy uniforms, and we had been wearing most of our stuff for a week and probably smelled like it. We sort of made fun of them but visited enough to learn that their being there was a dry run for how they were going to set up camp in Valley Forge, Pennsylvania, as part of the big National Boy Scout Jamboree in 1950.

Mom and Dad picked us up at the park, and we proceeded to our next home, the old Griffiths' homestead ten acres in Caldwell. Our family home, including Grandma Edna, was the rather ancient original house, as added on a few times over the years, with the street side on the right in the picture facing 2110 South 10th Avenue. I grew to love that home, and my high school years we lived there.

Griffiths Homestead

Looking at the picture brings a flood of memories, starting with the slanted doors to the basement that I see as two little rectangles in the picture at the base of the structure. Down the steps was the coal-fired furnace that created "clinkers" as a by-product of burning the coal that was fed by an auger from the coal bin to the fire—somehow controlled by the thermostat in the house. Of course, Harley and I removed the clinkers.

The peaked thing sticking up from the roof on the right was called a cupola. My bedroom beneath it included windows looking out over the yard, past the rows of flowers and the crab apple trees and the irrigation ditch, and then to the corner intersection of 10th and Ash beyond. I was able to paint the walls and ceiling of my room. The colors I chose were navy blue, chartreuse, and deep maroon. I forget which were for walls and which for the ceiling—or maybe the bedspread. I really liked the result.

The upper-floor bedroom in the right-front corner of the picture was Grandma Edna's room—right across the hall where I could go to tell her all about my experiences that I wanted to disclose but didn't want my parents to know about—like the escapades stealing watermelons during dark nights—or some occasional fights. I don't recall telling her about heart-warming things. Hmmm?

There was a barn out in back, outside the picture to the left. The picture was taken from one corner of the probably about eight acres of pasture. With Dad's encouragement and help, Harley and I had some pigs and a milk cow. We sort of took turns milking the cow and slopping the pigs. We separated the cream from the milk and sold the cream to the creamery and the milk to our parents. Milking the cow gave me well-developed muscles in my forearm that have been on occasion very helpful and that have remained (in a "relative" sense) to this day.

The Jersey milk cow was my first experience with the difference between income and capital gains. I had income when I was younger from the paper route and Christmas cards, and now from the milk and cream. At some point we bred the cow, which was done by artificial insemination, and in due time had a female calf. We later sold the original milk cow for what I learned later was "a capital gain" and milked the offspring for income. That experience was undoubtedly the inspiration for my "rent a cow" business idea (not implemented) later in life.

One other memory particularly tied to the property itself, was my fondness for apple butter jam. When they were ripe, I would do all possible to cause crabapples to drop from the trees above the irrigation ditch, and then I would run down to a plank across the ditch, and grab the crabapples as they floated by. Afterwards, I would pick up those that missed the ditch, and present them all to Grandma Edna—bless her throughout Eternity. She would then do the magic to create the apple butter jam. You just can't get it from a store in a jar or can like Grandma made.

Anyhow, Dad started his Brueck Construction business that summer with his plan to develop the acreage and build houses. The ownership of the homestead property had been deeded to Dad in a transaction between Edna and my parents, the details about which I know some but not enough to represent it accurately in full. The good news for me was that she would live with us. Mom quickly found employment working as the X-ray technician for the private practice of two highly respected doctors in Caldwell.

That was the summer I worked in the fields—work available to all comers on the certain street corner at the break of dawn and with payday and a ride back to town about noon. I liked to do piece work, not work by the hour. Piece work including being paid to hoe beets by the row, but I couldn't make much money doing that because the migrant workers from Mexico worked so much faster that the pay-rate was tied to their productivity that was far beyond mine. I picked crops where the pay was also dependent upon how much one picked and sometimes on the quality of the work product. The migrant workers lived in a government-provided housing camp outside of Caldwell, where I later played drums in a dance band and made good money.

52

Events of high school sort of blur together for me. So for a while here, let

me just mention enough to possibly suggest how my life was changing each year. After a summary like that, I will list in no particular order nor related to a particular year, some memories that may have contributed to my development during my teenage years.

High School Freshman

Fall came, and I entered Caldwell High School as a ninth-grade freshman. I weighed about 104 lbs. I did not play football that year. I did play on the baseball team as a member who "occasionally" got to play in a real game. I was really fond of the baseball coach, who later became the assistant football coach, Wes Johnson. He was a strong influence on me in many ways throughout high school. My contribution to the teams came after my freshman year.

I did play in the school band that year and, especially for me, the pep band. I do not recall having played drums since receiving our first trap set in 1942, but there I was, first-chair drummer, much to the chagrin of Janis Hull, my friend then through high school and, later in life, when Pat and I reconnected with her and her husband. She earned her PhD at Cal Berkeley and went on to be an outstanding public-school administrator. I met many fine musicians and new friends in band. Our band master, Jack Snodgrass, was outstanding. He turned our band into the number one performing band in the Northwest High School Band Competition held in Missoula, Montana, that year.

My main other memory from my freshman year in high school was of my algebra teacher, whose name shall go unmentioned out of kindness on my part. Compared with Mr. Hanson in my Richland eighth-grade math class, she was bush league—at best. It would hurt too much to give some examples. She became upset with me sometime through the ordeal, I mean semester, and we sort of discussed why each was disappointed about something!

The summer that followed my freshman year, I worked for Dad in construction. That was great experience as well as better pay than working the fields. I continued to milk the cow, but we slaughtered and ate the pig. As a family, we did a lot of camping and attended church quite regularly. I think I started American Legion summer baseball that year. I enjoyed it a lot, including the travel to other cities. Summer baseball gave a certain bunch of us a lot of

53

good playing time together, which was to help create a winning high school team the next three years.

High School Sophomore

In many respects, high school years have a lot in common—classes, lot of the same friends year to year, mostly same teachers on the faculty, and certainly in my case, the same building and its quirks. For me, the areas where change took place my sophomore year were in my becoming more social and better at sports. For the first time in years, there was no change in my home address.

In sports, I started on the junior varsity football team and along with others was moved up to varsity to get more experience. Wes Johnson was the assistant coach. He gave me quite a bit of playing time and helped me improve my game a lot. In baseball, I still had too many upper classmen ahead of me. I warmed the bench but learned a lot from Wes. In band I played in both the pep band and the dance band.

Playing in the dance band was a big deal for me that year. I had the least talent of the bunch, but as long as I did my basic stuff on the drums, I kept the ball rolling and added a little fluff once in a while. The other musicians were top flight—really top flight—with capability far above average for their age. To our credit, many students who enjoyed the after-game school dances during the football and basketball seasons liked our band better than those who were available professionally in the area. We were also hired to play for adult dances around the Boise and Payette Valleys. We made good money for those days. The musicians' union did not like us and occasionally made waves in our otherwise low-key "business."

Once we played for an adult ballroom-dancing group. Now that was different—I loved it. Another memorable "quite different" gig during the summer months was playing for the migrant workers' camp weekend dances. They loved our band. They put a guard on our cars. They provided escorts between the cars and the dance hall. They almost threatened the Caldwell government functionary who was responsible for booking their recreation if he didn't treat us well. Each night we played, just before our pay-time was up at midnight, we would play three numbers in a row—Green Eyes, Amapola (Pretty Little Poppy), and La Cucaracha—then pass the hat. They were quite pleased to part with some of their hard-earned money that therefore wouldn't be sent home to family in Mexico. Just before 1 a.m., we would repeat—and usually stop playing by 3 a.m.   That is where we made the money—at quitting time—several quitting times.

Aunt Mary's then-husband had played with a major nationally recognized band in his past. A couple times our dance band rehearsed with him present to make suggestions and provide perspective. One time he and I did the play-to-the-crowd then pass-the-hat routine when we played an organ and drums gig for an Air Force group from Mt. Home Airbase. I had a hard time believing that anyone would want to hear an organ and drum combo. I felt a little embarrassed when we got there. It was a party that started at noon with us playing back a little from first base as they played beer baseball. The day ended with a dance at a grange hall out in the boondocks somewhere nearby. I had to drive all the way back to the Boise Valley in the middle of night after that one. He and I were the only sober people from noon on.

I screwed up all that good stuff when I got kicked out of band early the next year. The reason had something to do with a personality clash, but I have forgotten what I called the new bandleader who replaced our beloved Mr. Snodgrass. However, there was a major side benefit to that event, which will be described in due time. I learned a lot while being in the bands and orchestra. I can still "feel" every instrument when I hear them these days.

Socially, I started dating and dealing with awakening hormones.   Very awkward year for me! In reading back through my yearbook, it seems like I didn't date the girls who I thought were pretty neat and did date the girl that made others wonder why.

Again during the following summer, I worked for Dad and played American Legion baseball—basically same team and all of us getting better with experience. Nothing like having to bat against some really fast-ball pitchers to get over being a little scared while trying to stand in and hit something. I learned some special moves to make me much faster than anyone else running the bases and a way to advance a base by getting into a "run-down" where I could manipulate the outcome. Didn't always work but did often enough to have me looking for opportunities.

That was the summer when I could legally drive at night, so my social life did improve somewhat. If I didn't get permission to use my parents' car but had some passionate reason to want to spend some time with someone late in the day, I would go to bed—but not. And as soon as the coast was clear, I would leave the house via the window in Harley's bedroom that was not high above the roof on that side of the house and away from Mom and Dad's bedroom. I would have left the "hoopy," as we called the old '36 Ford coup, on the building job site on the other side of the ten acres. The starter was a button under the dashboard, so the car required no key. Later reentry was by the same route.

High School Junior

Far and above the best thing that happened to me my junior year was to get kicked out of band. I was sent to the school office to see the principal. The student office volunteer/aid at the time was a girl in the class ahead of me named Pat Benedict. She asked why I had come to the office. I said, "To see Tom." Tom Turner was our principal but still "Tom" to most of us. She asked why I wanted to see him. I said something to inform her that I had been kicked out of band and was told to do so. Anyhow, as she tells it, she had some inkling to want to learn more about me. (I will not dwell here on the fact that I had dated her cousin, who lived in a nearby town Nampa, and that I had once gone to Pat's home looking for the cousin.) So while waiting for Tom, we chatted a bit. She says now that chat did raise a little consciousness—wondering about what made this guy tick—and according to her story, it wasn't all bad and even looked somewhat special.

I had very high grades in high school. If I hadn't somehow offended a (very lousy) teacher and the band guy, I think I would have been elected into Honor Society as a junior. Pat was in Honor Society and later informed me that she thought one or both of them might have "black balled" me, an expression I did not hear again until its application in college fraternities. Yes, it is quite possible, or even probable, that denying me Honor Society was a heads-up to moderate my thoughts when others would be upset to hear them. An object lesson! I really think that experience led to my slow but growing process of maturing. I should add that over the years many lessons in what was unacceptable behavior had been made clear in my home life, and bad behavior was strongly discouraged. However, to use a phrase I learned from one of the people who later influenced my life the most, "I did not, and do not, suffer fools gladly." I just needed to learn how to tolerate those I deemed so afflicted—or to learn they were not fools at all, and sometimes I was. Aaaargh!

However, Grandma Edna used to say that "In every cloud there is a silver lining." In this situation, that was Pat. At the time I was passed over for Honor Society, she heard others say I should have had grades high enough to be qualified for Honor Society. She now admits that while working in the office sometime later, she went to the files and looked at my grades and some other

56

information in the records. Apparently what she found did not turn her off. Even though she was a senior and I was a junior, we did bump into each other a few times by being in a group engaging another group that year, but we didn't get much better acquainted in the process. That was yet to come.

Strictly based on reason, those situations could have been the experience I might have had with anyone working in the office at that time. But fast forward to the end of the year, when yearbooks come out and are passed around to friends to write something for posterity, although we did not know we were then writing for posterity—sort of like all those posting to a social networking site called Facebook in this era. Pat says she doesn't know to whom she had given her book—but that person then passed it to me. Thus, the book and pen ended up in my hands. What I wrote in her book was a mystery to her, her mother and even to us in the years since. I wrote, "Watch out for that neat guy who is going to catch you and keep you forever." She thought it was sort of strange, but the thought of putting up with me for now about 58 years and birthing our three kids didn't occur to her then. Looking back, I think that must have been my first confirmed paranormal experience.

By comparison, my experience with a growing number of friends that year is overshadowed in retrospect by my catching Pat's eye—and I guess, the evidence says, her catching mine. In a more active social sense, the girl I spent the most time with that year and the next was Janet Hanson. Janet had had what I would call a steaming romance with my friend John Platt, and I don't recall exactly how or why we started spending time with each other. I don't think it could have been classified a typical high school romance of hugs and kisses—although over time we enjoyed our fair share. It was more like she was one of the many who tried to teach me to dance, I liked her mother more than the mothers of other girls I dated, and she was not averse to going pheasant hunting with me instead of to a dance. She was a terrific retriever of the soon to be dinner birds. I love pheasant to this day and would still be hunting them if there was the hunting-accessible land we had then.

During our dating in both junior and senior years, Janet and I bonded in a very special way that is hard to describe, and I still sort of think of her as special, even somewhat like a sister I never had. There were other reasons Janet and I hit it off and spent a lot of time together, but later in our senior year, we discovered a few conflicting worldviews regarding a future together. Janet sort of left me for a new path in her life late that year. Pat and I remain friends with Janet.

John, Ron Haile, and Buz Hoff were the friendships originating that year that I recall the most vividly—I say "vividly" because I had unforgettable experiences with each. They were not close mutual friends of each other, but I would say I was a close friend of each.

Buz lived kitty-corner to our home on South 10th and Ash. Both the summers and during the year, Buz and I logged time as baseball teammates. He played second base, and I played at either third base or shortstop. Ernie Keys was our first baseman and was tall enough and talented enough to catch the sometime off-the-mark double-play efforts of Buz and me. Buz did then, and throughout the rest of his life, have a great sense of humor. In addition to being a loving husband and father of three, he became an acclaimed neurosurgeon, a head of that department at the University of Michigan, and a major contributor to the betterment of mankind via his research relating to the treatment of strokes.

Ron Haile's father was the sheriff in those days. One time in the fall, Ron, Buz, my brother Harley, and I were out stealing watermelons late one dark night. We were in Buz's father's pickup that had "Hoff Building Supply" written in big letters on the side. Harley had an injured ankle, so we left him in the pickup, crossed a plank bridge over a drain ditch, and crept stealthfully along the ditch bank toward the field of melons. Suddenly, the farmer rose up from behind a clump of sage bush and fired his shotgun into the thick dust about ten feet in front of me.

In a loud voice the farmer pronounced that he was taking us in to see the sheriff. That would have presented a very awkward situation! However, the shotgun "happened to fall" into the ditch, and we all ran like our lives depended on it with the farmer in pursuit. Harley had taken off down the road in the pickup as soon as he heard the shot, and Ron was off like a bolt of lightning. He had the experience of many similar situations. Buz was a little traumatized, being the innocent of the three of us, and I had to prompt him anonymously into his best base-running speed. We out ran the farmer and managed to regroup with Harley and our ride back to town quite some distance down the ditch.

I will never understand why I liked Ron so well. He constantly seemed to get me into problem situations—all too often also called fights. On Mother's Day, he sort of challenged me in the presence of others to have a fight with a guy that had come home from the Navy to become the boyfriend, and later husband, of the girl I had spent time with in my sophomore year. I didn't care one way or another about the guy but didn't want to appear a chicken in the local guy culture. Ron arranged the time and place, and with fear and trepidation, I was sort of dragged there. I got lucky, and all the blood on my clothes when I returned home to mother had belonged to the other guy.

Speaking of blood, one time when Ron and I decided on short notice to hike into the headwaters of a certain creek above Lowman, we left late in the day. I drove Dad's International ¾ ton pickup, not that the size matters. It was dark as I started down the grade into Lowman. A deer bolted out of the woods right on to the road in my headlights. I hit the brakes with gusto. Ron had been snoozing, slumped over toward the door on his side. My holler and the pickup sliding on the dirt road startled him upright. As that occurred, the hunting knife attached to his belt came out of the scabbard and sliced into his buttock. He screamed, and I stopped to see what the matter was.

He was having a problem removing his pants and trying to discover what was going on with his butt. Soon the blood was quite visible—seemed like it was all over the place. As luck would have it, somewhere in our gear I had a surplus WWII belt attachable first-aid kit. In it was a bandage for a gunshot wound. We managed to find it, and with effort, to find a way to bind up the big cut. We went our way, camped that night, and Ron walked in several miles the next morning to where we wanted to fish, and after a good day fishing, he walked out, bandage still in place. To my knowledge, no one ever said he lacked guts.

Ron was a good halfback on our football team when he could stay in the game long enough to do some good. One of the times he was kicked out for unnecessary roughness or unacceptable language, he wanted to put on a jersey with a different number and go back into the game. Coach would have none of that. One might truthfully say that I even have too many memories of Ron. We did not stay in close touch after graduation from high school, and after a life of bouncing off walls and possibly taste-testing too much beer, Ron died a friend to many, but young. I didn't know his dad well but admired what I had seen. When I was getting ready to head off to college, he turned to me and said something like, "Bob, I know you will never do anything illegal, but if you ever do and get caught, never admit it." I took that to mean that there was more to the criminal justice system than I understood.

My most complicated relationship with a guy friend was with John Platt. We hunted together often, worked jobs together, and even ended up having dated the same girl. John was the only person I knew well in high school who "had a nontrivial flair" about him. I knew his parents well enough to believe that his father had some grandiose plan for John's life akin to molding him into a true

Renaissance man. John was the first person our age I heard speak French—both words—Bonjour, monsieur! His basement bedroom had what I took to be up-town art instead of old WWII posters. He wore a scarf around his neck. You get the idea.

John seemed to work overtime to try to act-out a role as directed by his father. Most of the time, I was impressed with things he knew—that I did not—and I'll admit to a little fascination with that flair. In the end, however, I came to believe he worshipped an unworthy god. He was the model when I learned one of the implications of being an agnostic-inclined person—who I viewed as one without his own values who took values from the situation he was involved in so as to be able to function well in that situation to pursue a personal end. I did not like the way he influenced people I liked, and finally, he showed some low class when he tried to move in on Pat during the summer after my first year at college while I was on my midshipman cruise in the North Atlantic. Pat didn't like it either. John had transferred to the Shattuck Military Academy for his senior year in high school. I later wondered—was there something other than his dad's vision that prompted that?

Later in life, I learned that John was killed when the plane he was on went down during a training mission. That must have hit his father especially hard—to put it mildly—and I feel sad when I think about it. There still remains a certain fond memory of my days and experiences with John. Now that I think I understand how reincarnation works, I wonder what plan John had in mind for that incarnation.

Other than those and many other friends, I don't recall much about my junior year. That which I do includes:

- Mainly sports. I had a good year in football. I played both offense and defense. I think it was the year we beat Nampa in a somewhat bloody football game on their turf. In the last few minutes or seconds, I was so tired that I sort of laid down in front of a guy for a down-field block. I picked the wrong guy. He was a dirty SOB, who tromped down on my head and just missed my eye. Mom had to haul me back to Caldwell and get her surgeon boss out of bed to come stich me up. She got the right guy—a perfectionist. The scar hardly shows. The SOB became a champion Navy fleet boxer—but died early from a cause of his own doing.
- All I recall about baseball is that we had a good year winning and a lot of camaraderie on the team. I do recall learning my first

60

Spanish swear words on the baseball field. Buz got a hit and made it to second safely with a good slide. The player covering second was Latino and said something nasty to Buz in Spanish. Buz had taken Spanish and knew enough to reply in kind—something like, "besa mi culo," which translated loosely is "kiss my ass." Buz was buzzing about it and was quick to share the incident with the rest of us. Fire up the troops by identifying a bad guy enemy.

- For some reason that totally escapes me now, I tried out for the All School Play that year—the roll of Snazzy in the play, *Life of the Party*. The only thing I recall about the play was that I got to kiss a girl, in this case, a friend of Pat's. After much practice, we put a lot into the kiss, and it drew loud and sustained applause. That was the only thespian performance of mine since Vacation Bible School when I was around eight years old. To add to the experience, Janet Hanson and I created the tall back set for the play. We chose a wallpaper pattern and then applied it to the set panels as if we were pros.

- I was selected that year for what was called "Boys State." That was a several-day experience of guys from around the state at the Idaho Capitol to learn how laws were made—or something. There was another fight, but I will not go into the detail except to record that the guy (son of the richest man in Idaho) was looked upon as a ne'er-do-well by most who knew him then, and he never outgrew it. I am not sure who came out better on that one.

I worked for Dad the summer following my junior year. I did a lot of painting on homes being built on Crescent Drive at the far end of the ten acres. I also recall painting my Brueck grandparent's home on Tamarack Drive in Boise. That was during the 1953 Democratic Party Convention that summer. I heard hour after hour of it on a radio.

High School Senior

Sports are again my strongest senior year memories, but this year there was more competition from other activities also. During the year, I had a very light class load, especially the second semester, but enough credits to stay eligible for baseball in the spring. Grandma Edna loaned me her old Nash car much more this year, so my social life picked up. I would say that I was the plutonic friend of many other girls while still first and foremost fond of Janet, and we spent a lot of good times together during the year.

I continued escapades with Ron and Buz, and also enjoyed very genuine friendships with several other guys. I still enjoy seeing many former classmates as grownups when we have reunions or parties these days. I have also renewed special friendships with a few former teammates with whom Pat and I golf and travel with occasionally. Upon returning to live several months of the year back in Idaho after about 35 years living elsewhere, I discovered that my old friends were still my friends. Great feeling.

Pat had moved on to nurses training, and our romance still had not yet become the most important relationship of my experience in this lifetime.

We had a new head coach in football that year, Eddie Troxell. He had been an assistant coach under Bud Wilkinson at Oklahoma during that dynasty and brought the Oklahoma split-T formation to our program. Compared to those we played against, our team was smaller but faster—and the split-T fit our situation perfectly. We were very successful, including a big win over Boise after more than a decade of losing. I had an especially good game that day, but I will spare history the details. I went on to be chosen an all-conference end and had a very good day during the All Star Game the following summer.

I think I learned a lot from Coach Troxell. One thing I recall him telling us has stayed with me ever since. He said, "Just remember, the other team puts their pants on one leg at a time also." He was just as committed to teaching us how to grow in character as he was about winning games. His goal was that each of us could stand in front of a mirror after each game and simply, honestly, say to ourselves that we had played our best—win or lose.

During the football season, I received a hard kick to the head during a practice. Our helmets were not high tech in those days, so I suffered a concussion of some unknown degree. For months, maybe years (I forget), I would occasionally start to see star-like sparkles visually, followed soon thereafter by a headache. The only reason for mentioning this is that in later years I occasionally would have a seizure of some sort. For many years, the fainting or passing out episode was just a mystery. However, on one occasion I banged my head hard again when I passed out and was certifiably coo-coo when taken to the emergency room.

Eventually in my late fifties, I had a neurological exam after years of panic-type episodes during my sleep, and finally, some more typical seizures during daytime. The EEG data shows an electrical anomaly in a part of the brain. It cannot be known for sure if that condition is directly related to the hit(s) in the head, but that is my presumption, so I do not expect our genetic descendants to experience seizures just because I have done so. I hope I am right.

Our baseball season was also exceptionally successful. We ended up in the title game at the end of season district tournament against Boise. Earlier in the series, we played and defeated Payette, where Harmon Killebrew played before becoming a many-year major league all-star player. I have a lot of stories involving Harmon, but alas, other matters wait, in particular—that title game. We might have won it if I hadn't made the most egregious error of my high school playing days. Late in the game, I got a hit, stole second in my special run-down process, and then stole third. I was in scoring position with two outs and an outstanding freshman player up to bat. To cut to the chase, I missed a squeeze-play signal from our coach Wes Johnson and was left standing flat-footed, so to speak, while our batter laid down a perfect bunt. I think that would have been the winning run in the title game. Even if not, the way I feel about it remains the same—bummer! (End note: in our sixties, our pitcher, Ed Hopper, and I invited Wes to Ed's resort property in Oregon for a delightful evening of reminiscing and catching up on lives after high school. Wes remembered that game quite clearly! It was clear that he was with us that evening to be honored. His wife was proud. He claimed that we were the best baseball team he had ever coached. I believed he meant it truthfully.)

One of the most fortunate experiences I had in high school was to get hired by Chuck Banks who was half owner of the Nafziger Banks men's clothing stores in Nampa and Caldwell. Although hired to be a floor sales person, I later also became the bookkeeper and janitor. (As janitor, it was not unusual for me to go vacuum, mop, and wax the floors late at night after a date.) The sales experience turned out to be invaluable in helping me find part-time work after Pat and I were married. Chuck became my "Dutch Uncle" when things got dicey between Dad and me. Chuck's wife, Betty, also worked at the store and both became life-long friends whom we miss. While working there during high school and some summer work while in college, I was able to buy clothes and shoes at cost, and some of the nicer things were gifts from Chuck and Betty. I still have and can wear my old favorite sport coat of college days and the white dinner jacket I wore to formal dances, on special dates, and when Pat and I were married.

Beyond those strong memories, there are lesser ones, including:

- Sometime during the year, Harley and I sold the cow and went out of our quite successful dairy business—at least successful if labor expense is not included.
- The teacher who influenced me the most, other than a coach, was Ted Gruver. I took chemistry from him my junior year and physics my senior year. I clearly believe he opened the door to my strong and enduring interest in physics. I think my appreciation for him as a teacher far exceeds what I am capable of explaining and what others might understand. In later years, Pat and I endowed a scholarship for graduating seniors at the Caldwell High School in his name, to be awarded via a process I specified, to a student headed for college with intent to major in science or a medical profession.
- During my senior year, I took the standard battery of intelligence, aptitude, and psycho tests administered by the school counselor. I don't know much about the results, other than when I asked him some questions he just said you can pursue whatever you want to do. I'm not sure if that meant something about me or if he just didn't know much about what he was there for.
- I applied for a competitive scholarship provided by the US Navy to fund college. I was selected based on the tests and my high school record. All that remained was to pass the physical. I rode a bus to Salt Lake City, and with the help of Mom and Dad's old friends, the Searle's, I showed up at the appointed time and place for the physical. The first thing they did was check my blood pressure. The nice doc told me to go in the other room and relax before he would try again. They were somewhat concerned about a heart-murmur condition I experienced in my very early youth which apparently led to a somewhat enlarged heart, but they passed me and I did receive the scholarship.
- I chose to attend the University of Colorado (CU) over Stanford because I liked the mountains, and I didn't think I would fit in with the upscale culture of Stanford. I am glad I did what I did. Without the scholarship it is highly unlikely that I could have received both the educational and developmental experience I did at CU. I have no way of guessing how things would have turned out if I would have had to earn my way through college at a less expensive school—most likely a school with fewer outstanding professors to influence me. As it was, I worked summers and most of the time while at school as a hasher in a fraternity or a sorority house to augment the scholarship.

- All through high school our family continued to attend the Lutheran Church in Nampa where we were charter members and where Elmore Carlson was Pastor. I think Pastor Carlson was very perceptive and gave me a lot to think about during those years. He also was a driving force for building a church camp at Alturas Lake in the Sawtooth Mountains. With direction from Pastor Carlson, Harley and I and very few others our age helped do the first work ever done on the property. It has been greatly expanded and continues to function to this day. We help it financially.
- At some time during the year, some members of the local Mason's organization decided to form a DeMolay chapter for us young guys in Caldwell. They put together a list of guys spanning their desired age range, enlisted those willing to become founding members, and we were off and running. I was elected Master Councilor and served in the short time until graduation. I don't recall accomplishing much, but it was a very positive experience in several respects. It was my first experience with serious ritual.

The summer after my senior year, a friend and baseball team member, Bob Farish, and I worked in a fruit orchard on Sunny Slope—a very major fruit growing region to this day—now including vineyards. We were up and driving out to work shortly after sun-up week days, and work ended mid-day. While working we were usually not far from each other and engaged in a lot of discussion. Bob's parents found pleasure in the two of us being close friends. Bob became the dentist he intended to become after he left high school behind. We have kept in touch and visited occasionally during the intervening years. Recently I was informed by his sister that he has been put in hospice care.

Late in the summer, a friend of Dad's ended up with no work for a sizable truck, and between the two and eventually the three of us, he gave me a bargain truck-rental rate so I could go in the peach-peddling business to make some more money before heading off to college. My first load went something like this.

With Harley to help drive and possibly to share in any profits, I loaded up a truck load of peaches purchased at the "peddler's rate" from the orchard where I had worked earlier in the summer. The owner believed I could sell them to a store he named in some city in Southeast Idaho. We headed out. At a rest stop somewhere along the road before we got there, we met a peddler coming back with an empty truck. He described what appeared to be a more lucrative place to sell our load, Elko, Nevada.

So, we turned south and headed for Elko. When we arrived, we found the store the other guy had described and went to see the produce manager. He wasn't there. A worker there said he was across the street at a casino. (Nevada laws allowed gambling establishments and still do.) We located him there playing a slot and tried to talk business. He wasn't really into our conversation—until he hit a jackpot. He then pulled up his apron to catch the coins as they came gushing out of the machine. Then with the apron held secure with both hands, he turned to me and said, "Now we can do business."

Well, the business wasn't nearly as good as the rest-stop guy had said it would be. We were left with a truck still more than half full. Downer! I drove away and soon heard a police siren behind me. The officer informed me that I needed a peddler's license to sell in Elko. I asked for directions to the building where licenses could be obtained and drove off in that direction. As soon as I could see in the rear-view mirror that the officer was no longer following, I headed out of town!

I really didn't know what to do next. Poor planning! I began to worry. The peaches began to ripen right before my eyes. Harley had a cigar and began to smoke it, not appearing to me to be near as concerned as I was. I seem to recall trying one other town with no luck. We headed back north without really knowing what to do next. I felt somewhat sick—maybe even scared. At another road stop, some guy driving an empty truck came over and asked how things were going. Not well. He then said he knew of a store in Southeast Idaho where he thought he could sell the peaches. We made a deal, good for him and a bail-out for me, and transferred the ever more ripening peaches to his truck. Whew!

It took a while for my gut and emotional state to get out of crisis mode. However, I still did not look forward to the report I would have to provide to Dad and the orchard owner. Both chastised me for abandoning the original plan. I have looked back on several times in life when it seems to me now that I was sort of "bailed out" when up against a wall and not feeling that I knew what to do next. Some might call getting bailed out just "providence," or "blind luck," but I am now of the opinion that there can be more in play than luck in those situations. I don't recall praying, but now I believe that every thought is prayer, and that some kind of intensity or strong emotion associated with the thoughts may have something to do with whether they have actual physical effects.

However, Dad turned things positive—bless him! After discussion with Bud Kaufman, the orchard owner, we decided that Western Oregon should be a good market because their crop had failed that year or was at least meager. Dad agreed to underwrite (a.k.a. guarantee that I wouldn't suffer a loss) my loading up again to head west, this time without Harley as a sidekick. I still remember driving into Prineville, Oregon, and to a grocery store there. The manager was overjoyed to see the high quality fruit, bought the entire load, and said he would buy all I could haul back to him before I ran out of time or peaches to haul.

Both Dad and I made money—I from the peach business and Dad because he found a source of hardware in Portland (he paid for the additional driving of the truck from there) that he could buy and sell to a hardware dealer in Boise where Dad bought hardware for his construction business. From then till I left for college, I would haul peaches west, the hardware east after the seller loaded the truck overnight, then again peaches west after the orchard loaded my truck overnight, etc. There was a lot of significance in "relationships matter" in that trucking business experience.

I don't recall the detail of what I had to do in Oregon to evade the highway patrol so as to avoid buying a peddler's license for selling in Oregon. I do recall hauling heavy loads up hills in a truck with a four speed transmission and a four-speed "Brownie auxiliary transmission"—most of 16 gear shifts to go from high to lower when heading up a steep grade, and in those days, there were steep grades on two-lane national highways. Four-wheelers were typically very unhappy when stuck behind a slow truck, and still are today. Guilt about avoiding buying a license is just another on my "guilty as stated" list as I have been thinking back over my growing-up experiences.

Before moving on to my college experiences, I am adding another high school era experience that has remained with me all my adult life. While working on the church camp at Lake Alturas one summer, Pastor Carlson and I went out in a rowboat one evening to fish. During our conversation, I said something unseemly like, "Yes, I have misbehaved in all those ways in my life so far, but I haven't suffered in serious ways for my sins." He gave me a serious look and in return said something like, "Maybe, but have you ever given thought to the fact that you may have kids someday?" He knew I would think more about the nature of morality than about having kids. I admired that man for many reasons but that one stands out in my memory.

A Thought or Two Looking Back from Now

I think there is a reason these are called the formative years. In earlier years we look around to gain some views about how the world works. But with puberty and in a few immediately following years, we push a lot into high gear. We form a lot of beliefs and attitudes we take into later years—good or bad. I am glad, even very glad, that I didn't make a really bad choice in my high school years that would have shunted me off to a different future life of less opportunity. Even though I think I remained a rather immature person in some respects on into early adulthood, I think I did improve a little in that respect during these years. However, I think it was probably my developing sense of responsibility that kept me out of a lot of trouble.

If I were to focus on the most important part of high school experience that helped me in later life, it would be athletics. Football and baseball each presented different but still very personal challenges. There were metrics of performance that could not be fast-talked away. There was the locker room, the calisthenics (which I led and which helped develop a voice that I could later project when I have wanted to!), and the crowd cheers and jeers that were so emotionally charged. We had to learn how to lose as well as how to win. Looking back, I was again mentored by two fine coaches. It was a coach that provided a standard for self-appraisal I have never forgotten—"when the game is over, look in a mirror and ask yourself, did I do my best?" It wasn't did we win; it was if we exhibited a commitment to our best effort.

I can't pass over two other men who, in different ways, mentored me as much as the coaches—Ted Gruver, my physics teacher, and Chuck Banks, my employer and "Dutch Uncle." My life would probably have been a lesser experience had it not been for those two.

I was fortunate to live in forgiving times and with parents who offered a stable and supportive home life. Looking back, I think I was very fortunate indeed.

6

Life Picks Up Momentum

Leaving behind my trucking business, family, high school friends, and most of what had been my focus in recent years, my attention, planning, and activity turned toward college.   Up until then, one could say that I had just been going "with the flow." Now I had to think in terms of new terrain and a new course.

Looking back, it seems to me that there are two ways to recall college: (1) to recount memories and activities before marriage to Pat, and (2) experiences directly related to being both in college and married. I will start with the primary areas of focus before marriage.

From My Old Familiar Digs to Totally New Digs

First, just getting to and situated in Boulder, Colorado, was a big deal. It didn't have a banner label, but it was a whole new dimension of personal responsibility. I was going to be "on my own." Even if I wanted to stay close to home while far from home and close to my family and friend relationships, the cost of a long-distance call was high enough to be outside my budget unless very damn important. There was little that was very damn important, and there was little room in the cash flow.

Our family owned a 1950 Ford sedan. There were few flights to Denver, and they were expensive. I had enough belongings to take to school that flying wouldn't have been a practical solution even if there were flights and money to pay for a ticket. The Ford was the way, and the problem that presented was how to get it back to Idaho if it got me to Colorado? Mom and I made the trip together shortly after Labor Day.

We stayed somewhere along the more than 800 miles of two-lane road and arrived in Boulder just before lunch. We drove to the University area and looked for a place to eat. We saw a sign that said "The Sunken Garden." I guess the word "garden" gave us confidence, so we found a place to park and went there.

It was a beer and hamburger joint that I later learned was really called "The Sink."

With the help of both Mom and the wheels, I looked for some solution to housing. We both found pleasure in exploring the beautiful campus and even Boulder itself. For some reason now forgotten, I had decided against the freshman dorms. I ended up renting a room in the basement of a faculty member's home about a half mile up the hill from the campus. After unloading my few belongings, Mom departed to drive back to Caldwell by herself.

The room had a bathroom in an adjacent space and a 1½ by 3 foot window that looked out about even with the lawn. I had two electrical outlets, one for a study lamp and one for a baby bottle warmer that I frequently used to warm canned goods, primarily soup. The typical weekday became a walk to the campus before 8 a.m., go to classes and the library until classes were over for the day, then back to my dungeon room unless there was some special event to defer returning to the dungeon until later.

The immediate mundane events after arriving in Boulder were registering for classes, buying books, and checking in with the NROTC unit before classes were to begin. The first special events were related to "rush week"—the merry mix-up between existing fraternity and sorority members, and the newbie's on campus like me who had an interest in looking into the Greek organizations. It was a pretty intense experience compared to anything previously in my life. I met a lot a people and had a lot of new kinds of interactions with them. I met a few other rushees, one of whom became a close friend while at CU.

I received bids from several fraternities, including Sigma Chi where two guys from Boise were members. I was inclined toward that fraternity but somewhat undecided about the cost and fraternity experience itself. I chose not to become a pledge at that time. Only one other fraternity was of interest to me. Often during my first semester, I would be invited to each for dinner and further mutual inspection. I finally decided to pledge Sigma Chi. More later on that special experience in my life.

Some Commentary about My Scholarly Life

My plan was to get a degree (to be) offered within the College of Engineering. It was called Applied Math, and in addition to the math it required a strong minor in physics. Even though it was not formally offered when I enrolled at CU, I was told by an engineering math professor I met at Trinity

70

Lutheran Church the week before I started school that it had been approved by the higher-ups and would be. That professor, Paul Hultquist, was to be one of the two most influential men in my life while in Boulder.

I carried 19 credit hours in six classes during my first semester—not a glorious one grade-wise (3.2 on a 4-point scale), but it got me started on what college study was like. I had excelled in math in high school but soon found I was struggling with the basic freshman algebra class. My professor was Dr. Britton—later to become my second best faculty relationship throughout college. I went to see him to discuss my difficulty in learning the material and hopefully to get his advice. I did get advice. He said, "Work harder."

I got my lowest college grades the first semester of my sophomore year (2.9 average with a D in a power lab in the Electrical Engineering Dept.). That was not uncommon and was called "the sophomore slump." That was my only D, and I only had three C's in college. That D did get my attention, and I changed my study and play life habits. I seem to recall that I was spending more time than I should have with the fraternity and Luther Club. They were pretty much the extent of my social life. That is to say, dating was not.

By the time I graduated with the BS degree, I was strongly—as in "chained"—in love with mathematical physics. That knowledge "turned me on" in ways hard to explain. I could not get enough. The more I learned, the more I wanted to learn. The pyramid of my math-physics knowledge got bigger and bigger. It even seemed "powerful" in some strange way. My perspective was opened up to include a much greater "nature of the physical world." The farther along I got in undergraduate courses the more I loved each, got mostly A's, and was cited for superior scholarship within the College of Engineering.

During college, I was elected to three honorary scholarly fraternities—one for general scholarship, one in Physics, and the one most meaningful to me, Tau Beta Pi (the Phi Beta Kappa of engineering school). I was awarded the Maurice Davies Memorial Award by the regional professional association of people educated and employed in occupations utilizing statistics, and I developed a strong interest in probability theory, which has served me well in work and in thought processes in years since.

Along the way, I was granted a teaching assistantship and a National Science Foundation (NSF) stipend to attend a Numerical Analysis Summer Institute at UCLA one summer. (That was after marriage and two kids, so it was quite an eventful summer.) While in graduate school I received a Research

Associate NSF grant the summer of 1961 to support independent research. More on that summer later.

After a somewhat slow start, I didn't burn up college (3.44 out of 4.0 grade point) but what I learned—I really learned. In addition to my engineering college classes, along the way I took additional courses (to make a 21-hour load one semester) in the Business School (Accounting) and other courses across campus: Educational Psychology, Shakespeare's Plays, Masterpieces of Literature, and Social and Intellectual History of the United States. The accounting courses helped my grade-point average, the others didn't.

In general during college, I was challenged academically—and I loved it!

Naval Reserve Officers Training Corp (NROTC)

As earlier mentioned, this scholarship was very important to me. It provided payment for my tuition, my books, and $50 (equivalent to about $428 in 2012) per month cash to augment what I could earn from working along with classes and during summers. In exchange, I signed a contract to attend Naval Reserve classes while in college, take cruises during three summers, to be commissioned Ensign when I graduated, and to serve for 2-4 years. I have forgotten the exact term. At the time I accepted the scholarship, I did not know if after college I wanted a career in the military, to go to seminary and into the ministry, or to become a teacher. As it turned out, it was none of the above.

I really enjoyed NROTC. The classroom coursework included naval history, specifically including a thorough coverage of WWII, and a lot about weapons and waging of war—as war was thought of at that time. Part of every course and special unit activities were in a low-key way devoted to teaching us how to be an officer and a gentleman. (Midshipmen are the lowest officer rank in the Navy.) We had reading assignments and wrote papers on the subject of leadership. I was a member of the drum and bugle corps, and we played and marched in the various parades that were a part of University celebration weekends. I was a member of the unit rifle team that competed with the NROTC teams at other conference universities.

Often those rifle matches competing with NROTC teams from other universities were scheduled on days that were on the "away" schedule there for CU athletic teams. Two of the officers of our unit were pilots. To get to the away matches, they would check out a plane at Buckley Field in Denver to fly us there, and we would be in uniform in the officer's seating area at the games. I in particular liked Cmdr. Zimmer. He had a long career flying multi-engine submarine-hunting aircraft. He was my model of an officer and a gentleman.

One time we were flying a twin-engine plane back from a match and lost one engine. He was at the controls when it happened. He feathered that engine and did what he had to do to get us flying along on one engine. He then turned to Cmdr. Krebsbach, who had been the air officer on a carrier, and said something like, "You take it now. You're the single engine jock around here!" It was an interesting landing at Buckley, but we don't need to go into that.

Another time, we had a match where we were to land at a SAC base in South Dakota. They had a long and wide runway for the large bombers. As we approached the field, Cmdr. Zimmer asked the Marine sergeant, our rifle team instructor, if he wanted to land the aircraft. He did, and we bounced and bounced and bounced down the runway enough to draw comment and questions from the control tower. I presume one could get in deep water for letting him pilot the plane, but it didn't happen.

The most engaging part of my NROTC experience was the summer cruises. My first summer cruise was in 1955 between my freshman and sophomore years. I was assigned to the midshipman division of the USS Damato DD-871. The outline of the cruise was to depart from Norfolk, Virginia, cruise to Oslo, Norway, with a stop in the Canary Islands for mail and provisions, then to Stockholm, then to Guantanamo Bay in Cuba for anti-submarine exercises, then back to Norfolk for the ship to go into dry dock for some maintenance and refitting of armaments. I recall interesting events and situations all along the way, even from Caldwell to Norfolk.

While home for the summer and working for Dad and occasionally for Chuck Banks, I received travel orders for the cruise. Although the time between the end of school and the time to leave for cruise was short, Pat and I had several dates and the relationship that started when I got kicked out of band had matured slowly but surely. The point where that relationship had accelerated was during the Christmas holidays the prior school year. That story is worth a few lines before I get back on the train to Norfolk.

During the Christmas holidays, John Platt and I were catching up over a few beers on our first-semester college experiences. Late in the evening, we left the bar and for some reason decided to drop by a party we had not been invited to. (Bad behavior, but for an important "life" reason, I guess it was supposed to happen.) Pat was there, and as the party was breaking up, some guy she didn't care for was moving in to offer her a ride home. She accepted my offer, possibly as the lesser of evils. (An offer I made even though it was John's car.) Pat encouraged one of her friends to join us, so with Pat and me in the back seat, off we went into the night.

But "off" didn't mean straight to anyone's home—first we went out to a nearby lake where we could park and visit. Pat was wearing a very heavy coat. I managed a few kisses but contact was dominated by the coat. Maybe that is why we talked more and kissed less. The talking seemed to stir up some raging hormones, possibly even more than the kissing. We clearly hit it off. The first intimate conversation of our lives uncovered a lot in each other that we liked. I was smitten! Those additional times together early the next summer before I had to leave on cruise built on a growing fondness for each other. As I departed for cruise, I was on one hand excited about what lay ahead, but on the other hand, I ached a little to be leaving Pat.

Traveling on orders meant that we had to travel in uniform—dress blues in this case. On the train to Norfolk, we switched train stations in Chicago. I carried a full duffle bag from station to cab to other station in about 99 degree temperature and 99 humidity while in dress blues. Sweaty mess. On the train, I met an army guy returning from Korea for the funeral of someone in the family. He seemed neurotically committed to explain his military life to me. Then he met a woman. They go off together in Philadelphia well short of his and her intended destinations.

Midshipmen stayed in a hotel before boarding the ship the next day. The bottle of booze the Army guy had given me was a big hit with other midshipmen there for the same reason that night. I was not a heavy drinker and just sort of cruised along getting acquainted with the others. (That was well before I discovered wine.)

The next morning some of us got in uniform and traveled together in a cab to the dock. We got out of the cab and just stood there on the dock near the gangplank to a ship tied up at the dock. The ship was ours. I finally took the lead, walked across the gangplank onto the Damato, saluted the stern, and then saluted the Officer of the Day standing amidships at the other end of the gangplank. Before I could say a word, he reamed me out big time in a loud voice with how dumb I was to not know that in port the flag was flown amidships rather than on the stern. That was another time in my life when I took initiative without being as smart as I thought I was. Somehow all of us got to our bunks with our stuff and tried to get our heads into what was happening.

USS Damato DD871

As we departed the port, there were heavy ground swells and some who were inclined toward sea sickness had not had enough opportunity to obtain their sea legs. At one time, I saw a junior officer and an enlisted man standing side by side at the rail barfing over the side. Eventually the enlisted guy took some crackers out of his pocket and would eat one, then barf. After a few cycles of that, he kept some crackers down—and offered the remaining crackers to the officer—his comrade when rank didn't matter. At some time we joined up with the other ships in the task force—the battleship (I think it was the Mississippi), a heavy cruiser, and a bunch of destroyers, including one of the newer, much larger and faster DL class. There was no other person from the University of Colorado reserve unit as a midshipman on the Damato.

Enroute, a plane went down somewhere in the Atlantic. My bunk was in the forward compartment next to the hull. I woke up with a rapid pounding of ship against slapping water as we moved at flank speed. Eventually it came to an end, and I never did know what terminated the episode—but it did get my adrenalin going.

Anyhow, before I record some of what I remember as interesting, or even exciting, experiences that happened while on this training cruise—a few words about the training.

I really haven't given thought to this before, but it seems to me that the scope of the cruise instruction/experience basically covered three things: about ships, a little about being underway in a task group, about some weapons uniquely available on ships, and sort of in between the lines, a little about the Navy. In summary form, we learned about what must be perfected to be able to fight from the water in a war. It is a matter of record that the same physical resources, administrative capability, logistics systems, communications, and command capability to bring those resources to bear near any ocean in the world have also enabled the US Navy to administer to the needs of millions of people around the world by providing humanitarian aid in times of disasters.

A lot about ships had been studied during classes our freshman year. Now it was time for the "hands on" of it all. During the cruise, midshipmen were rotated among all major functions taking place on a ship. We performed the same tasks usually performed by enlisted sailors—we were part of the ships complement. The fact that we were to be viewed as officers led to some interesting situations, but no time for that.

First, we were given stations we were to man during any and every call to General Quarters—GQ in the lingo. GQ basically describes how to man the ship to function in a combat or other readiness situation. My duty station during GQ was as crew inside the forward 5" 38 mount, in the lingo. That is the forward turret with two guns in the picture of the Damato above. (I think the numbers represent the diameter of the projectiles that could be fired by the gun.) A battleship had 16" guns. During live-fire exercises, we bombarded the shore or fired at targets towed on the water by distant ships with all four of those largest guns on board. The exercises also included firing our ack-ack guns at targets towed at a safe distance by airplanes. Most destroyers of our class had six of the five" guns, but the Damato was outfitted with a new anti-submarine weapon called "Hedgehogs" that was (for its time) a high-tech depth charge that had some smarts for exploding where it would do the most good. The Hedgehog mount replaced one of the forward five" gun mounts.

My task in the gun mount was to transfer the casing with the powder from the elevator that brought it up from below into the tray (breach) of the gun. Another midshipman transferred the projectile in a similar manner, then the breach loaded the gun, and then we braced and just waited for the firing of the gun. The actual firing of the gun was controlled by an officer in the Combat Information Center (CIC). When fired, there was a loud sound within the turret, the breach retracted with great force to eject the empty casing onto the floor of the turret where it would bounce around, hot enough to burn anyone on contact, until it found the hole in the mount to fall to the deck below. Then as rapidly as possible, we would reload and prepare to fire again. A ship's complement Chief Petty Officer commanded the mount.

The boiler room was manned by very few personnel. The function was generally all fuel-related duties—in port and refueling at sea and underway. Constant maintenance was required. I was on duty in the boiler room when we were purposefully stressing the ship with depth charges launched to explode at distances closer and closer to the ship while enroute from Guantanamo Bay back to Norfolk at the end of the cruise. The temperature in the boiler room could reach into the 130 range, and did during stress tests, when pipe joints and other stuff I can't recall were giving way. Boiling hot water and steam seemed to pop out everywhere. It was quite tense in there at the time.

One compartment was devoted to the details of the operation of the turbines. I don't recall much about duty there except for an interesting-to-me incident that occurred on duty there one day. A red-headed seaman third class didn't like midshipmen. He probably thought we were weanies and wanted to prove it when he approached me on a narrow walkway with his fists clenched. I was maneuvering to reach a big pipe wrench on the shelf beside me when I felt a presence behind me and watched the complexion of the aggressor's face change from aggressor to docile. I seem to recall that "the presence" said something to indicate that no one should give these midshipmen a bad time. The presence was that of the "chief colored person" in the ships enlisted complement. I learned that ships officers worked through him to deal with issues involving all colored crew members. He was a big guy, with a very congenial nature. We sort of became friends for the rest of the cruise.

The two most interesting duty stations were on the bridge and in CIC. Both were intensely engaged in communications functions much of the time. Communications from the bridge included signaling flags and Morse code transmitted by a searchlight-type unit in addition to radio and the ship's intercom system. Both centers engaged in radio contact with other ships in the task force, in particular the group command ship, which was either the cruiser or the battleship—I've forgotten which.

Duty on the bridge was more intense than in CIC and was somewhat exposed to weather conditions. After being on duty on the bridge one time in foul weather and heavy seas, I later wrote to Pat: "We were the most versatile weapons platform in the military—in heavy seas we would often be like a dive bomber. On occasion with big waves coming over the bow, we were like a submarine, and in calmer waters we actually performed like the surface ship we were." I recall one time in foul weather we were heeled over so far I wondered how far we could heel before we couldn't right ourselves.

77

Duty in CIC was my favorite. I became pretty chummy with the ship's officers usually on watch there. They tried to teach us as much as we could handle. Most of the communications were with the task-force command, but sometimes they were just spreading "scuttlebutt"—news of some kind. There were both radio and teletype forms of communication—the teletype was for those occasions when for some reason a printed record was necessary. CIC was sort of like a comfortable small ship cockpit below deck.

My favorite watch in the CIC was the mid-watch, 12-4 a.m. (When underway, we served watches on an 8-off, 4-on schedule—meaning off eight hours then on four hours then repeat, day after day.) Sometime early in the cruise, I had made friends with the ship's baker. During mid-watch, I was permitted to go to the bakery, the source of that wonderful smell of baking bread, so I could bring back goodies from my friend for the CIC personnel. I recall that on some occasions I was even able to bring back jam. I do not want to suggest that activity in CIC was casual—it wasn't. There were radars to be watched continually for obstructions or to keep track of other ships and radios for different frequency bands that sent information necessary for maneuvers. During live-fire exercises, I did not have a watch in CIC, but during the cruise we received instruction about the battle-command functions performed there.

Of course, larger ships had many kinds of activity to perform additional types of functions. The displacement of the Damato was about the same as just one 16" turret on a battleship. The DDE class destroyers were even smaller. Our mess, bakery, and laundry functions were like closets. Those were major functions on the larger ships as one might find in a large city. In port we could tie up at docks. Often the larger ships would have to anchor out and lower small motor craft to move people and supplies between ship and shore. I was told that the atmosphere on larger ships was much more formal than our often very informal interpersonal relationships on the Damato.

There were a lot of remembered moments on cruise that I could describe in great detail, but I will only summarize a few in no particular order.

- Going into Oslo, the lead ship took on a Norwegian Pilot, and one after another the task force cruised up the long Fjord at dawn with girls on the balconies of homes along the water waving towels at us. I had duty on the bridge and therefore binoculars to take in the "attractive" sights.

- Before going on liberty at a port, we always had a ship's division officer brief midshipmen about wayward women, venereal diseases, and the shipboard availability of contraceptives. We were told in Stockholm that the young women wanted to go to the US and would even get pregnant to get there. (I have no way of knowing if that was true.) Dress Blues were the uniform of the day when in port. For us, that was a wool uniform at a time in a particular summer when that part of the world was experiencing a major heat wave.

- Also, before going to port, we had to "holly stone" the deck to make it as shiny clean as a table top. The Chief in charge of the forward gun mount, where I had duty at GQ, would have us scrub it down and practically douse it in perfume while he practiced his guitar. All that in preparation for the day that the populace was invited to come aboard and tour this warship.

- We went swimming while on Liberty one afternoon in Oslo. There was a 10-meter high diving platform, and we began egging each other to go up and dive or jump off. It became my turn and up I went. When I got to the edge looking down at the water, every cell in my body went into panic mode. It was not the fear of death experienced years later on the mountain snow bank, but to some degree, fear is fear! I think a few episodes of experiencing fear in early life helps perspective later in life. The fact that I jumped is another very good example in my life of what peer-pressure can do.

- I will never forget sailing in to tie-up at the docks in Stockholm. There are bluffs above the water that at that time were lined with what appeared to be housing structures. It occurred to me that those structures could be centuries old. Years later, I was in Stockholm a few times on business and found much more that was old by the standards I grew up with.

- Equipped with pad and pencil, I went to the beach in Stockholm one afternoon when I had a Liberty Pass with the intention to write a letter to Pat. I got there and looked for a structure to be used by people to change into swimwear. There was none. I looked around and noticed that all new arrivals were just changing out there under God and the blue sky. I did the same and tried not to show how intent I was while "noticing" young women doing the same. Some had a big dress so they could change part of their body without disclosing it, but the upper body always seemed to be displayed without care of who might be watching. In fact, some went all afternoon without covering their upper body. So I lay on the sand

79

with my pad and pencil trying hard to just concentrate on writing a love letter to Pat.

- I met a gal named Cristina at the party (reception?) for midshipmen at the US Ambassador's fine home. Mrs. Lodge had gone out of the way to cover my buddy's and my embarrassment when we arrived well before we were supposed to. Cristina and I later enjoyed time together on several occasions during the days we were in port. The last night before leaving Stockholm, liberty for all ship's personnel was cut short because of a Communist demonstration planned for then. However, I was confident that Cristina and I could stay out as long as we desired. I had noticed that my favorite officer on board would be on mid-watch duty. Somehow I had learned that he was a coin collector seeking a five-Kroner piece, and I had found one a couple days before. With a five-Kroner piece in hand to offer, I knew reporting late without undesirable consequences would be a lead pipe cinch. Wrong.

- Shortly after midnight Christina dropped me off at the dock, and we said our goodbyes. My uniform was as it should be, while the drunks arriving in the care of the Shore Patrol were quite disheveled, if not worse. Our ship was the farthest from the dock. (There is a reason for that but I will not go into it.) As I reported aboard and requested permission to cross each of the three ships between the dock and ours, the Officers of the Day on watch would look at me with that look that said, "Boy, is this kid going to catch Navy hell." I was quite at ease and confident that would not be the case.

- I crossed those, boarded the Damato, and saluted the officer on duty. I quickly and fearfully realized that there had been a duty switch, and that before me was the one I respected the least, not the most. I quickly reported aboard and disappeared down the hatch before he could get his wits about him. It was quite some time later when a seaman showed up at my bunk to inform me I was on report and would have to appear at a Captain's Mast—not a good thing.

- However, without going into the detail, good things about me were offered forth by both the midshipman and ship's division officers, and I was given a very light sentence—one less than some got for nasty swearing. I again avoided highly undesired consequences when I thought I was smarter than circumstances proved me to be.

- While cruising in the Strait of Skagerrak in very foul weather, I was so tired that I took a short nap in the flag-bag while on duty on the bridge, again without consequences. That night I noticed some of the ship's complement sleeping on deck—which was also a no-no, but they were not being harassed by the OOD. I later found out that was because the skipper had once run a ship aground and, in general, was viewed in a very dim light. They were quite smart enough to know that if the ship might run aground, better not to be below in a bunk. The Damato was at the bottom of the totem pole in the task force because of our Captain's poor record.

- While underway we replenished at sea. That was a somewhat exciting and ticklish process. The ship to be supplied would come along the supply ship, ropes would be thrown, and eventually a cable would be pulled between the two ships as they bobbed up and down while underway. Once the cable was secured, supplies would be sent across in a large basket hanging from the cable as the ships continued on course, and personnel would unload them and stow the supplies below. I learned that the ship's crew who performed that duty were masters at "two for the ship and one for the locker in my quarters." Some of the stories they told were hilarious, but all I will further say is that it was in many ways and situations nice to be on good terms with the enlisted personnel. When we were not receiving supplies, the Damato was assigned the duty of following the ships involved in the resupply so as to recover any man falling overboard during the process. That was the mission assigned the lowest ship on the totem pole. I did get many pictures of the resupply process. In fact, I got pictures during many cruise experiences.

- Once when I was on duty as the forward lookout, stationed as far forward on the bow as one can get, I failed to report a floating empty ice cream container that had obviously come from some ship belonging to someone or nation. The officer on the bridge chewed me out big-time for not reporting it, pointing out that it could have been a floating mine. He wanted to make it a consciousness-raising occasion, and he succeeded.

- While in Guantanamo Bay, we conducted anti-submarine exercises every day and were given a liberty pass every evening with some curfew that allowed a long evening ashore. I played on the ship's baseball team and very much enjoyed the camaraderie the game and after game at the bar provided. ("Rum and Coke" was ten cents a drink.) I got well acquainted with the Damato officer I most admired. When I observed a fight after one game, he was appointed to handle the defense in the subsequent proceeding.

81

Before cruise ended he deposed me to acquire detailed and accurate information about what I saw. I know it was favorable for the enlisted guy he was defending.

After my 1955 summer cruise, I returned home to Caldwell long enough to enjoy more dates with Pat and to join some of the Boise CU bunch to drive back to Boulder.

My NROTC experience during the summer after my sophomore year consisted of about six-weeks training at the Naval Air Station (NAS) in Corpus Christi, Texas, followed by about six-weeks training with the Marines in Little Creek, Virginia. Before leaving Caldwell for the summer, I bought a diamond ring on a time-payment plan. After I parked the car at the Miramar dance hall in Boise where we were to meet Gene and Mary Kromer for the evening, I gave Pat the paper sack that contained the ring and proposed to her—marriage that is. As they say, the rest is history!

I don't recall how I returned to Boulder, but I do recall the drive from there to Corpus Christi. It was my first exposure to Texas—a place that seemed to me to be so hot as to be uninhabitable. Of course, there was a civilization there, and many years later we went to live and raise our family in Texas. However, arriving at Corpus Christi was a real shock—seemingly unbearably hot and humid. Our barracks were not air conditioned then as they would be now. It was so hot and humid that to get to sleep at night I had to soak a towel, get in my bunk, cover my body with the very wet towel, and hope that I would fall asleep before it dried out and afforded no further cooling from the evaporation of the water.

The NAS part of the summer was more or less a pleasant one. We received lectures day after day about flying and about Naval Aviation in general. We were given rides in jet training planes—my first, and never to be forgotten. When the pilot found out that I would not get sick, he really showed off with many fancy maneuvers. He then made a practice bombing run on some island used for that purpose off the coast, after which he let me fly it for a similar run. Of course, he was in the front seat ready to prevent disaster and may have helped, but I recall it as a very successful run. That was a big-time thrill for me. As he later approached the runway to land, I was sort of overwhelmed by the speed at which everything had to happen in order to descend, line up, and land the plane. My life had never knowingly experienced so many complex considerations being taken into account while so much was happening all at once. I now think it was an experience that helped me get used to the need to think ahead in terms of a lot having to happen in a short period of time—and the perspective, preparation, and possibly training—usually required if one wanted some positive result.

The training with the Marines at Little Creek was quite different. Again, a lot of lectures to learn new things—this time primarily warfare relating to attacking beach emplacements. Every day we were up early, made our bunks and stowed loose gear, then lined up outside our barracks for inspection. On several days we had to put on special gear, grab our unloadable rifles, board a small boat to take us to a landing craft in the bay, then make an assault upon the beach, crawling under barbed wire—the whole nine yards except for live fire. Then, singing raunchy songs as we marched, we returned to the starting point to do it again, and again, and again. We learned that the Marines and Navy were experimenting with high-speed hover craft that were considered necessary for dispersion of landing-craft forces in a theatre with atomic weapons. Years later, the hover-craft concept had been perfected to the point that Pat and I were passengers on a large one to cross the English Channel.

I was given permission to end my summer cruise early so as to attend a workshop in Gettysburg, Pennsylvania, of student leaders from Luther Clubs at campuses all across the country. I rode a bus there, and when the workshop ended, I bummed a ride with one of the other attendees to Chicago, then train back to Caldwell. Pat (by then my fiancée of about two months) and I managed to see each other several times, but soon thereafter, I again departed for school, this time with Don Kromer. More later about "Uncle" Don, the younger of the Kromer brothers from Boise whom I first met during fraternity rush week my freshman year. I quickly grew to like and respect Don. We have been life-long friends.

Sigma Chi Fraternity

During my college years, being a Sigma Chi fraternity member was high on my list of positive experiences. The reasons are hard for me to explain. The moral teaching of the objectives, standards, and values that all pledges had to learn before initiation were meaningful to me then and still are. There were obligations that I took seriously. Living in the fraternity house was a new kind of experience. All in all, it was just a really worthwhile experience. It was the kind of experience that I think would be neat for any guy if they wanted it to be.

Soon after pledging to join the fraternity, I become acquainted with many new friends and spent a lot of time there on my way to my living quarters up the road a piece. I even spent a lot of time at the chapter house on Euclid after moving from my dungeon room to live the spring 1955 semester with Al Kosmata and another guy in a funky one room plus bath second-floor apartment above a run-down house on West Pearl. My bunk was in a small screened-in porch attached to the combined kitchen/dining/living room. Even though the price was right, and we budgeted $1 per day per person for food, it seemed that I always had some end of the month left after the end of the money. ($1/day then, adjusted for inflation, is the same as $8.63/day, thus about $260/month, in 2012.) Al and I had played together on the football team at Caldwell High School. He was the valedictorian in his class, graduating two years ahead of me. He transferred to Colorado after two years at Northwestern and was in the Engineering Physics degree program--more relating to Al later.

The Sigma Chi chapter had a social chairman and always an active social program—often joining with a sorority for a special function. Except for chapter parties, I didn't date much my freshman year. I did enjoy a dance date with Marilyn Kelly from Boise, when we first got acquainted and were both rather short on dating relationships after arriving in Boulder, but otherwise, not much dating. Marilyn later deservedly became one of the most outstanding girls at the University.

The fraternity was part of the reason for my sophomore slump. I lived in the chapter house, ate meals there, horsed around there, listened to stories there, counseled freshmen there, attended weekly meetings of the chapter and other meetings when on various committees there, and oh yes, studied a little there. I earned my board by hashing there, three meals each day. In short, I did not exercise enough self-discipline managing my time that semester. But I learned.

And there was also a personal benefit being in the fraternity. I became friends with many, and close friends with a few. I learned a little about male bonding, which remains somewhat of a mysterious process to me. The close friendships continue to this day, especially with brothers Don Kromer, Bob Sheets, J. Dennis Hynes, and C. C. Robinson. Years later in the 1980s, we had a several day "Bay Bash" mini-reunion in San Francisco with several brothers attending. Subsequently, Bob, Dennis, Curt and I were again together—sadly— to celebrate the life of Don, who passed from this chapter to the Chapter Eternal on April 3, 2015.

Don went on to fly jets in the US Air Force, including duty in Vietnam. After retirement from the service, he devoted his working years to helping young boys and girls who need that help the most. Until Don retired a few years ago, he ran the Boys and Girls Club of America in Arlington, Texas—each year with a multi-million budgeted program. One of the branch program facilities is named after Don. I served on his Board when he earlier directed the program in Austin, Texas. Don has been close enough to our family to be considered "Uncle Don." He was indeed like family.

Bob went on to serve a hitch in the Marines and to become the director of a program to bring performing arts to the smaller towns in Colorado. That program was highly successful. He brought an appreciation of the arts to hundreds of young people. Many of them valued his contribution to their lives to the extent that they as adults like to visit with Bob in Denver when they can. Later in life, Bob has devoted years preparing to write the definitive story of the Salem Witch Trials. All who know him well await with high anticipation the publication of that book—but have doubts that it will ever happen. During the mass hysteria of that time, a distant relative of Bob's was one of those hung. Bob also has been close to our family over the years and is affectionately known to us as "Uncle Bob."

Dennis was a member of Phi Beta Kappa at CU and the Editor-in-Chief of the Law Review while in Law School. He worked in a prestigious New York law firm before returning to CU to teach in the Law School. He retired in 2001 as a full professor and is on the Emeritus Faculty in retirement. He is the author of over five books on law, including the book *Agency, Partnerships, and the LLC* which continues to be the required reading for law school courses covering that subject matter. Dennis has been and still is always available to be the helpful father of three adult children.

C. C. (Curt) Robinson graduated from medical school and served his residency while on active duty in the US Air Force. While stationed in the US, when he could get Air Force transportation, Curt flew to bases in Asia on his own time to provide otherwise unavailable medical attention to the local citizenry. He and his family, Sheila and their two children, moved to Albuquerque, New Mexico, where he created an ENT practice, with Sheila as one of his nurses. He became the "go to" doctor for ENT surgery in Albuquerque and was an early and highly successful adopter of improvements in that kind of surgery as they were created in many parts of the world. We enjoyed skiing with Curt and Sheila and have visited with them in Albuquerque and Denver over the years.

While writing these memories, I pulled an old CU year book from our library and looked at the active chapter picture in 1956. I was quickly recalling friendships enjoyed over the years with many brothers pictured there.

85

The annual Homecoming Celebration and football game was a great party time at CU, a.k.a. a "party school" in most publications describing US institutions of higher learning. For those weekends, fraternities and sororities constructed quite elaborate outside decorations at chapter houses in competition for worldly recognition. We also held parties on that weekend. In the fall of 1955 that Sigma Chi "Homecoming Ball" was very special for me. Pat, Mother, and Don Kromer's mother drove all the way to Boulder to visit at that time. While there at the Ball, there was an interruption in the action for all to witness my "pinning" Pat—that is, giving her my fraternity pin to indicate that we were officially in love and would not be dating others, etc. (Recall, we did not become engaged until a year later.) Don's and my mother experienced the chapter and their dates singing to Pat, "The Sweetheart of Sigma Chi." That remains a special memory for both of us. Pat recalls that at the time I told her something like, "My pin shall never belong to another girl." And it didn't.

As I participated more in fraternity activity, I had a chance to learn how we were all individually unique, with talents and warts, and yet could share an appreciation of the objectives, values, and standards set forth in our vows and rituals that have been handed down since 1855 from the Sigma Chi founding fathers. As an alumnus, I occasionally have provided personal and financial assistance to my own chapter and two others. Over the years, I have observed many good and a few totally failed chapters. The failed chapters hurt because they represent poor leadership, hypocrisy in lip service to the values and rituals, and disgraceful behavior that reflected poorly on Sigma Chi—and even on fraternities in general. I was fortunate to be a member of a chapter that was about as good as they get.

Other College Years Memories

During college, there were many more pleasant and/or developmental experiences that come to mind, though less of a big deal than those I have mentioned. In particular, I think of:

- One of most long-term beneficial experiences was the training in the second semester sophomore year to become a student counselor at what was to be called "Freshman Camp." It was a new University program planned to be a week-long experience each fall where entering freshmen could attend to get up the curve a good bit before embarking on the college experience. I am told that the program continues to this day, probably with a different name. For me, the training experience gave me the opportunity to get acquainted with many outstanding upper classmen. Most importantly, I learned a lot about group dynamics. That helped me to be effective to lead people in many group endeavors later in life.

- While students all through college, Don Kromer and I were volunteer assistant Boy Scout leaders for Scoutmaster Glen Powers. For years, Glen had the longest list of boys trying to get in the troop he led. There were many good reasons. The troop was clearly the most active and well-led troop in town! Excellence matters! Don and I attended troop meetings, helped and participated with them to develop and perform projects, and camped with them. In addition, we went deer hunting with Glen and another assistant scoutmaster. Glen and his wife Dorothy were at times extremely helpful to Pat and me as newlyweds and young parents. More on Glen and Dorothy later.

- After receiving my BS degree (I have never liked that abbreviation), I became a full-time instructor in the Applied Math department. There were seven of us with four of us having offices together in what we called "the bullpen." I guess we might have been congenial to start with, but in any event, we also bonded and have kept in touch and even skied together and visited many times over the years. They are friends high on my list from those days.

- I mentioned Paul Hultquist earlier and that he was a member of the church Pat and I attended. Paul and Prof. Britton were by far the most capable teachers I ever encountered since Ted Gruver back in high school. Both taught the most difficult math and math-physics classes. Paul was more applied in both his interests and the specific courses he regularly taught. I learned a fantastically great amount of advanced mathematical physics from Paul. In addition to a relationship with Paul in the classroom, we worked together within the church. He was also the faculty advisor for the Luther Club where I was the leader for a couple of years. Late in my undergraduate years and continuing into graduate school, Paul provided consulting work (badly needed finances) for me at Ball Brothers Research Corp, where he was the senior consultant on two very high-profile projects. The experience on those projects was very valuable professionally. Paul and I worked together with one of the very early digital computers for computational support. We solved several fundamental problems encountered in design and engineering of the first US Orbiting Solar Observatory. It was successfully put into orbit in 1962. It seems like most of the work I

87

did with Paul helped me bring forth my genetic capability to engage in synthesis as well as analysis, which was to be a very helpful later in life. It is hard for me to say which was more important, the professional experience or the income—both were tangibly valuable. The experience clearly helped me get a nice job offer from Texas Instruments (TI) for a professional challenging first nonteaching job of my career. More later on the TI experience.

- When I joined the faculty, I qualified to get seats in a special section at CU home football games. The seats were annually renewable. Even a lowly instructor was provided seating on a first-come first-choice basis when new seats became available, the same as could full professors. When I went to the athletic department office to get seats, a full professor's seats had just become available after he retired. I got them. Pat and I had seats on the 50-yard line for two years when CU had ranked teams. (They later fired the coach after recruiting violations surfaced, and CU was penalized by the NCAA.)

- This might appear contrived by some, but a very real "ah ha moment" for me occurred one dark, cold morning during the winter of my freshman year. As I walked down the sidewalk into the engineering building, say about 7:45 a.m. for my first class, there was a workman with a shovel digging along the edge of the sidewalk. The ground was frozen. He was elderly. His wages and benefits for that type of work could not have been much. In any event, it looked like a situation I would not like to experience that late in my life. There is no doubt in my mind but that thought somehow increased my interest in being educated and otherwise equipped to do better. I think that experience helped me transition from being sort of oblivious and just "going with the flow" to a new psychological state.

- Once during those years, our minister at church, John Rupley, asked me to preach at the Sunday morning worship service in his absence. I believe that I had been developing communication skills over the years working as a salesman and leading small organizations, but this was experience of an entirely different kind. I think I did better many years later when I had a similar experience as the preacher one Sunday at our church in Austin, Texas.

The description of my college years' experience could go on and on. It has been enjoyable to summarize some of my experiences of a social or scholarly nature. What are hard to recall, let alone describe with words, are the experiences that influenced my growing sense of morality. Almost all I can say is that there were many—some from "feel good" moments and others from "feel bad" moments. Those were the days when I grappled with (deep for me) thoughts about discrimination, belief in God, the nature of personal responsibility, what constitutes truth, the exercise of leadership...and of course, the boundaries of good and evil. Participation in the Luther Club on campus provided a lot of direct focus on topics like that. The fraternity living, special retreats, and the general socializing environment frequently touched on those topics more than most people might imagine. And there were forums and lectures by national figures that periodically brought to the fore relevant topics. Across campus they taught courses focusing on those topics, but in the College of Engineering, we were sort of left to learn from the world around us.

The most specific glimmer of enlightenment for me was the opportunity to see a lot of lying and deceit in general. It might have been a small sample to generalize from, but it seemed to me that the people engaged in that behavior encountered one directly related problem issue after another. I think that in a subtle way that observation helped make me sensitive to situations involving virtue, where there were not so many problem issues, and where there was a lot of good stuff to dwell on. Ipso Facto, as we say in math, it seemed like something might be proven there. (In case one might wonder, I have not had a physical fight since high school.) There is no doubt but that is when I more consciously set myself on a path toward truthfulness while attempting to see the right thing to do in life situations.

All those big questions, and the things the visiting experts and faculty talked about on special occasions, led me to think in terms a little broader than when would be my next classroom test. In later life, I devoted a lot of time and thought to those "broader" topics and learned that they more or less fall within the meaning of the word "metaphysics." [Metaphysics = attempts to clarify the fundamental notions by which people understand the world, e.g., existence, objects and their properties, space and time, cause and effect, and possibility. A central branch of metaphysics is ontology, the investigation into the basic categories of being and how they relate to each other.]

But before I could spell "metaphysics," I learned a lot by just observing what was going on all around me. That is when I finally put what I had observed in college into words I believe to be true—if we are not hesitant to lie, we will encounter a lot to lie about, and have to live with the consequences; if we recognize goodness in people when we encounter it, we will encounter more of it, etc. In my terminology now, and more generally, I started to recognize that our beliefs have a relationship with the reality we experience.

Beginning to think a lot about those kinds of issues then has clearly helped guide me in later years. Even with some wavering of certainty along the path, I am sort of proud that more than casual focus on virtues has at least been a strong guiding light. It does seem to me that I arrived in that headspace by observing the negative rather than with a discerning eye observing the positive. Later in life I ran across a quote from some wise person that one cannot know white without knowing black. I found philosophical, spiritual, and metaphysical significance in that message.

I have occasionally looked back on life to contemplate the branch-point circumstances that resulted in my life proceeding in one way significantly different from another. A few circumstances were clearly the ones most important in determining futures most directly related to why I am so pleased to have ended up where I am today. At the top of the branch-point list are the circumstances that placed me in the nurturing care of John and Grandma Edna. The second was an automobile accident.

A Thought or Two Looking Back from Now

I view those early college years as sort of a watershed when my love of learning really set in. My good high school grades were sort of the result of "if you are going to do it at all, do it well." My college grades were not shabby, but for the most part, they were a result of my really wanting to learn—a growing love of learning, per se.

It is clear to me that it was in those years I started to think about some bigger questions about life than had ever occurred to me before—questions that have been worth dwelling on in later years.

In the category of what was totally unplanned and unexpected but a highly valuable experience, I would say it was the training in group dynamics during our preparation for being counselors in what we called "Freshman Camp."

And finally looking back, the most formative experience was in the NROTC. Sure, it was the serious studying of war and what was important within the military and the developmental experience of my two summer cruises, but it was much more in ways I find difficult to express. Some of the unit officers viewed my violation of my contract as a result of my immaturity. Looking back, I think dealing with the consequences helped me to mature in ways no other college experience could. I was fortunate to have had two instructors, Zimmer and Lewis—who were models of what it meant to be "an officer and a gentleman"—a standard I think I have had in the back of my mind in gauging the professionalism or lack thereof in associations with people from all walks of life in later years.

⇒ 7 ⇐

The Big Step

If marriage isn't a big step, I wouldn't know one if it hit me in the head. There was certainly more involved than purely rational thought processes, but on the other hand, rational considerations were not entirely absent either. I don't necessarily believe that all who decide to get married view marriage to be a life-long commitment and responsibility. I did and I do.

In December 1956 during the Christmas rush, I again planned to work for Chuck Banks as a floor salesman. Through Don Kromer's father, a lending officer at a Boise bank, I arranged to drive back to Boise a "repo" car the bank had repossessed in Denver. I drove all night. In the early morning of the 17th, my 21st birthday, I had an automobile accident on ice in Southeastern Idaho.

With the early technology power steering, which I was not familiar with, when turning, it kept turning until you corrected. Under normal driving conditions that was fine. However, when sliding on ice, once the turning started one never knew which way the wheels would be pointed when sliding off the ice onto something where the tires could react to the direction they were pointed. Even though I thought I was driving slow enough to be safe, I did start to slide. I then started swerving on and off the ice until the car rolled.

The driver-side door flew open, and I flew out on the second roll. I was thrown clear of the car, hit the ground, and started to turn to my side to get up. Then I caught a faint glimpse of the car rolling back on me just before it hit and crushed my hip. It was a serious accident. I could have died feeling warm with no pain lying face down in a foot of snow on frozen ground with the car on top of me. I believe it was first-aid training from Boy Scouts that made me realize that I was in shock. I personally experienced that innate will to live that lies unconsciously below the surface within most, if not all, humans not already emotionally committed or at least ready to die.

I clawed and wiggled my way out from under the car. I managed to reach up and grab the edge of the car and pull myself up without using my legs. I sort of tested my legs and realized that my lower body wiggled from side to side with no bracing at the hips. To keep the weight off my legs, I put my weight on my arms crossed along the edge and slumped forward with my legs sort of dangling. I waited, slumped over the edge of the car for what seemed like an eternity, before I saw a vehicle slowly approaching on the road. I feebly tried to wave my forearm to get their attention. I felt a moment of terror as it looked like they were going to pass on by and not see my car off the road in the ditch. Then I saw them slow and stop. I passed out and fell over backward.

I awoke looking up into the faces of two men in farming attire looking down on me. One of them said, "Do you think he's hurt?" I instructed them on how to use their coats to make a makeshift stretcher and roll me on to it. They carefully slid me into the back seat of their car on my belly with my legs folded at the knee so as to be able to shut the door. They drove me to the hospital in Montpelier, Idaho.

Although they are still clear to me, I see no reason to describe in any detail the events that occurred between then and my arrival a day later at the emergency room dock at the hospital in Caldwell after a flight in a small chartered plane. Mom, Pat's brother Dean, the team doctor from my high school sports, and the staff of the medical facility in Montpelier, Idaho, all helped along the way.

Pat (my fiancée, remember) had graduated as a registered nurse from three years of nurses' training the prior spring and was working as a surgical nurse at the Caldwell hospital. I do recall seeing Pat standing on the dock when I arrived in the ambulance from the airport on Tuesday the 18th. For the rest of the week, I was in somewhat of a coma—in and out of awareness. I "came to" and stayed that way the following Sunday morning. During the week some friends visited me, but I only have faint recollections of their presence. A couple of doctors gave good counsel and care until I went home from the hospital sometime after Christmas. A "special" nurse looked in on my status each day and may even have kissed me once or twice.

As the injuries started the healing process, I became anxious to get back to try to salvage a semester's school work. Course finals were over, but sometime in late January, I flew commercially (with special seating) to Denver with a "private" nurse to assist me along the way.

It is sort of interesting that a few months earlier a doctor described the Children's Hospital in Denver with high praise to Pat. At that time, she considered moving to Denver and contacted that hospital to inquire about employment. They desired to hire her, but she would have to get registered in Colorado, and she was not yet 21, which was a requirement. She subsequently went to Colorado anyway—as that "private" nurse!

Bob Sheets met us at the airport and transported me to the fraternity house in Boulder. The brothers cleared stuff from an old library room and moved me to a small living space on the first floor. I remained there on crutches, occasionally being pushed in a wheelchair by Bob through snow and ice to salvage some classwork. Eventually, I was able to get out and about on my own to pick up my relationship with University classes and professors. (I only managed to complete 19 credit hours from the two semesters that school year—about half a load.) Bob and other fraternity brothers helped Pat hunt for an apartment until she found one and got settled a bit. She turned 21 soon after we arrived in Boulder and found employment as a nurse at a sanitarium there. She soon thereafter became a surgical nurse at Boulder Community Hospital—a considerably more satisfying job for her.

Now the plot thickens. I healed nicely from my broken bones. Rather than discharge me for not being able to attend classes nor to prepare for or be obligated for summer cruise, the NROTC unit had put me on leave. Instead of summer cruise, I attended summer school to catch up on at least seven lost credit hours, still leaving about ten hours short for the year. I applied for and did receive a tuition scholarship for summer school, but the Sigma Chi house was rented to female summer students so I needed to find another place to live. Pat and I considered marriage. It didn't seem to me to be an unthinkable idea; I rationalized, even though it would be in violation of my NROTC contract. I had met several married NROTC Regular Program scholarship recipient midshipmen from other schools the two prior summers. We decided to get married and set June 1st as the date. There followed something like a four-act play with high drama and many characters.

Early Marriage - Act I

The great day arrived, and on Saturday 1 June 1957, we were married at Trinity Lutheran Church, Boulder, Colorado, with the Reverend John B. Rupley Jr presiding. (The announcement of the wedding was withheld at my request by the Boulder Daily Camera newspaper to prevent disclosure to the NROTC.) We had many in our families there, including Pat's mother, Pat's brothers Dean and Glen (Butch), Glen's wife Betty and daughter Sharon, my parents, my grandfather Louis Albert, my brother Harley, and cousin Pat Schubert Zippin. Sharon was flower girl, Dean sang a solo, and the Sigma Chi Quartet sang The

Lord's Prayer. Harley was best man and Bob Sheets was groomsman. Judy Elliot was the maid of honor and Ellen Keyser the bridesmaid. Don Kromer and Curt Robinson were candle lighters—with Don in charge of placing a little kick in the punch bowl. (Thar's a story there, of Don crawling on hands and knees trying to reach the punchbowl.)

Our Wedding

Pat and I both looked young—and still looked young even after David was born. We often heard, "Look at those teenagers with a baby. Poor things."

We stopped at a liquor store for a bottle of bubbly as we left town with a bunch of stuff dragging from the underside of that old 1950 Ford that Dad and Harley had driven to Boulder to leave with us. (We later returned to her father the Studebaker he had earlier provided to Pat.) With the bubbly to toast our new life together, we proceeded to a cabin up Boulder Canyon in Nederland that belonged to Bob Sheet's uncle, Charlie Sheets. It was very late and cold upon our arrival. Trying to start a fire in the wood stove proved more than I could handle by then, so we just slurped some bubbly and were off to what must have been the coldest bed sheets in the universe. We can't recall whether that was a one- or two-night stand, but we do recall that Pat had to return to work and I to complete my class finals, so we headed back down the mountain not long after we went up. We lived for several weeks in the apartment Pat had lived in before our marriage.

Early in the summer, we moved our few belongings to a neat little house at 2901½ Baseline Road, originally built to be the carriage house on a small farm at what was then the edge of Boulder. I worked at Thornton's shoe store downtown, Pat at the hospital, and I completed work on the seven hours of classes that I had been unable to complete in the spring semester. Many summer weeks passed, until—until …

Early Marriage - Act II

Sometime soon after we settled in our new home, my longtime friend from Caldwell High School football and a couple years at CU, Alan Kosmata, had some leave from the Marine Corp and dropped by the NROTC unit in Boulder to visit with the Colonel who directed the Marine option of the unit. At some time during their afternoon visiting, they decided to leave the unit wardroom to have a beer. Al said, "Let's go to Brueck's," and they did. It was no surprise to the Colonel when Pat came home after her 7-3 shift and walked into the living room of our humble dwelling where they were drinking and visiting. The Colonel said, "Good afternoon Mrs. Brueck." He had seen enough pictures and other evidence to know that I didn't live alone! (Let me hasten to add, that Al and I have remained friends lo these many years, but I will never understand why the class valedictorian was so incredibly unthinking in heading to our place for a beer with the Colonel. On the other hand, I thank him!)

There followed some suspense on our part, waiting to hear what the Colonel would do. In due time, we learned. He had reported our marriage to Capt. Wideman who was the senior officer in charge of the NROTC program at CU. The Captain took action, probably starting with calling me to his office to kick me out of the program. Looking back, he did us a favor. But at the time, it was a real downer. I had been becoming increasingly interested in the Navy as a career. I did not feel good about violating a contract. And I really didn't know what the consequences would be. It is clear to me now, based on experience since then that aspects of my nature were not really compatible with a military career, but that is 20-20 hindsight. My life took a new direction for probably good reasons, but those reasons were unknown to me at the time. One's purpose in life remains a somewhat philosophical consideration but looking back, and with later-in-life insights, does give one perspective if we take the time to think about such things.

I don't recall when the ax fell, but one day I was informed with a letter from the Navy that I had received an honorable discharge from the US Navy, but for disciplinary reasons. I was given the opportunity, and used it, to write a letter to some very high-ranking officer in the Navy to say whatever I had to say for myself.

I said something like: I thought permission to marry would give the NROTC Unit officers and their wives an opportunity to bring a young officer and his wife up to speed on the nature of being a Navy officer's wife, instead of the usual "marry on graduation day, husband officer leaves for his assigned duty, often to sea, and new wife is often left sort of adrift." And I made reference to the negative effects of the "double standard" that existed where marriage by those with NROTC Regular Program scholarships was inconsequential in some university units but not in others, like at CU. And with that letter, my NROTC experience was history.

I later inquired and received the official military service records in my Navy file. They included a copy of that letter and an assessment as below showing why I failed to pass muster for forgiveness or a waiver. One of the forms was filled out to declare "above average" regarding various criteria, and intelligent, but it also had a blank for "Statement of evaluation of student's character, ability, aptitude and desirability as a naval officer." It was dated 12 July 1957, and the entry reads as follows:

Brueck has rationalized his breach of contract to where it is the Navy's fault in requiring this obligation of him. He is headstrong and once convinced in course of action, little can deter him. He has the makings of a fine officer when he matures. This breach of a moral obligation is not typical of his character.

They were probably right and looking back—whoever wrote it was correct for sure as to the rationalization and lack of maturity. It is not clear to me that the officer who filled that out thought I would be kicked out. The assessment was understandably not intended to speculate about my being in love.

Early Marriage - Act III

The next shoe fell when I was called into the office of someone in administration at the University one Friday afternoon and told that I was kicked out of school by the University Disciplinary Committee at the request of the commanding officer of the NROTC unit, Capt. Wideman.

As best I recall, one of the first calls I made was to Glen Powers to tell him what happened. Glen, bless him, was a cool head and a serious thinker, in part from years of work at the Rocky Flats Atomic Energy Facility where they dealt with highly dangerous materials. In summary, Glen told me to get to work to identify and arrange meetings to visit with all members of the Disciplinary Committee to tell them my story and answer their questions.

97

I learned later that the following Wednesday when my "case" came up for approval on the agenda of the Executive Committee at the University, Dean King of the Law School rose to say that he understood there were extenuating factors that should be discussed with this case. After discussion, my case was referred back to the Disciplinary Committee for further review. I should mention that our scout troop had included the sons of the Deans of the Music school, the School of Business, and of that articulate Dean of the Law School.

Glen called me as soon as he was informed about what had occurred and asked me what I had to say about my visits with members of the Disciplinary Committee. I told him that all but one seemed to be more supportive of my case than inclined to make a federal case of it but that the representative from the School of Architecture had not been satisfied with any other action than to kick me out. I then learned a management tactic I have never forgotten. The meeting to reconsider my case was set at a time when that member from the School of Architecture had a conflict and could not be present.

Unbeknown to me, Bob Sheet's father had been in touch with, and probably influencing, persons in the administration to support my re-admittance to the University. Newt was well acquainted with Harry Carlson, Dean of Students, and with Joe Keen in the Office of Admissions and Records. (Joe Keen had signed the letter awarding me the scholarship support for the prior summer school.)

Early Marriage - Finale

I was soon thereafter informed that I was readmitted to the University but would lose all credits (18 credit hours of straight A) from NROTC courses and the scholarship that had been continued after the summer. Not good but better than the alternatives. That left only the Army draft board as a potential major obstacle beyond my control on the path to a college degree. It didn't take too long for me to learn that the draft board in Caldwell had found reason to give me a student deferment. As a matter of full disclosure, I should mention that I later found out that the lady who was head of that draft board was sort of the best friend of Grandma Edna—but I did not know that at the time.

So, I was still enrolled with a full class load at CU, without financial support from the NROTC program or from the University scholarship that had paid for my tuition, and—we had earlier become certain that Pat was pregnant! But on the other hand, we had a lot working in our favor. Glen and Dorothy Powers, Newt and Shirley Sheets, and a few other adult friends were there to provide friendship and helpful contacts. I had a part-time job at Thornton's with a boss I

98

respected, Pat was employed at the hospital, and we had an understanding landlord. However, not long thereafter, Pat passed out during a surgery at the hospital, and her employment was terminated soon thereafter because she was considered a risk to pass out again, possibly during a surgery.

That was a tough semester. Pat found some income working for a doctor in his office, in the kitchen at the Sigma Chi house, and some other odd jobs nursing. We both stayed with Glen and Dorothy Powers boys a few times while they traveled—overpaid each time. Pat's folks visited us over Thanksgiving, and my recollections of the Christmas holidays were the paper decorations we made for our little Christmas tree and the times we spent with the Sheets family in Denver. I received all B grades, except for one A, but chalked up a few more necessary hours for a degree. We had that turbulent semester behind us—and David on the way.

A Thought or Two Looking Back from Now

I view the violating of my NROTC contract to have been a serious moral failure. Oblivious was no longer an okay operational posture. I felt bad then and do now. But having said that, if viewed from the perspective that there are life changing influences that arise from a greater reality beyond our physical world—those events were clearly in hindsight meant to be.

It is also clear to me now that my experiences earlier in life equipped me to be a "survivor" when encountering the challenges and stress that I did following my auto accident and getting kicked out of the NROTC. I am grateful to all those who in some way cared about me enough as a child, student, teammate, friend, or member of a group to provide the experiences that resulted in qualities that helped me navigate the complications of the post-NROTC experience. In particular, Pat and I are grateful that Glen Powers was there when we were in the midst of our crisis situation.

I do wonder if the depth and scope of my extensive reading earlier in life might also have helped me figure things out and respond in a useful way when necessary. Looking back, seeing how much help we received from many people makes me hope that I have been helpful to others in similar ways along my path. In some important respects, it clearly took both Pat and me together to deal with what I put on our plate—but we were survivors.

8

Career Development

The following four years were much less stressful and contributed greatly to my future. I became a father twice with a greatly enlarged idea of being a husband, I gained additional communication skills while teaching interesting courses, I completed two degrees and was fortunate to have had advanced courses in the design and operation of computer systems, I applied my math-physics learning to make nontrivial contributions to an early US satellite project, we bought a home and then upgraded to a better one, and I was recruited to a good job and new opportunities when my MS degree was completed and I was able to consider leaving teaching at CU and Boulder.

My father had provided the funds for tuition for the spring semester of 1958. I continued working part time at Thornton's Shoe Store while taking classes. Pat's brother Dean had received financial support from their dad when he was in medical school. At Pat's father's request, Dean repaid that loan by providing monthly funds to us, which we would then later pay back to her parents. We received that support all semester, and it was not then necessary for Pat to find employment.

David Alan was born at Boulder Community Hospital early on Easter morning of 6 April 1958—both he and mother fine after delivery. It goes without saying, but I will say it, that life has never been the same thereafter.

The night before, the friendly owner of a gas service station let me use the mechanic's bay and tools so a fraternity brother with more car savvy than I could help replace the brake linings on our 1950 Ford. It took longer than we expected, and late in the evening he offered to take me home and we would finish the job in the morning. For some reason, I chose to stick with it and was able to get home with car sometime before midnight. I arrived home to find Pat in labor. We sat around until midnight, thinking that the cost would be one day less if we waited until "the next day." After Dave was born I hurried off to church to proclaim the good news.

We received a lot of advice and assistance from Glen and Dorothy Powers, the Sheets family, and friends at church. The Sheets loaned us a bassinet that had been in their family for generations. Dave never lost an ounce after birth. He gained weight steadily thereafter. I recall holding him early in his life, filled with the vision of a small bundle being cradled in the arms of a loving father. It was a little different. He would fuss, I would reposition him to my chest—and he would try to crawl right up and over. So much for the infant infant.

School, work, and home life went well that semester. Soon after finals, we moved our few belongings to storage made available by the owner of the property and headed out to Idaho with Dave in a cardboard box behind the front seats. We lived with my parents, and I worked most of the summer for Dad in home construction. During the summer, we made two trips to California, one with Pat's mother and grandmother and one with my folks. On one of the trips, I interviewed for employment at Livermore Labs. The financial challenge of continuing college was weighing heavily in our future, and by then I could get what I thought might be a reasonable civil service job. I looked into how I might complete my degree work at a couple of universities in the Bay Area. I learned enough to decide I would rather deal with what I had to work with back in Boulder.

When we returned to Boulder, we were fortunate to be qualified to rent University housing—in our case that meant one-half of a standard-size government-issue Quonset Hut. We had a small front section facing Arapahoe Road with kitchen on one side and leisure space on the other, then a small bathroom and two small bedrooms. Our rent included utilities and was $43/month. (About $344 today in 2012 after adjustment for intervening inflation.) We were very fortunate—again.

I don't recall much about life during the two semesters of the 1958-59 school year. I recall that whenever I could I tutored students for $3 an hour and we would then run to the grocery store to buy food, adding up the cost as we placed things in the basket. I quit smoking for some length of time to help make ends meet. During the Christmas holidays that year, Don Kromer came through on his way back to Idaho on leave from his pilot training in Oklahoma. We invited Glen and Dorothy Powers over while he was there, and we drank and visited until we heard the morning paper hit the front door.

I have a transcript showing that for the fall semester 1958 I received all A's in course work except for two courses I took "across campus," Educational Psychology and Social & Intellectual History of the United States. I still recall a lot about those two—maybe not what the authors of the books had in mind. Luckily I got BS, especially even after being tested on the nonsense taught in ed psych, e.g., "the purpose of education is to socialize the child." During those early marriage years, I also read several books describing various "Religions of the World," which gave me that background to have in mind ever since. That was my first awareness of the "Far East" religions.

Sometime in 1958, the College of Engineering purchased an early model digital computer, a Bendix G-15. The going cost for that computer at that time was about $60,000, equivalent to about $480,000 in 2012. Compared to 2012, the Bendix G-15 computer had less memory, computational speed, and useful features than the lowest cost cell phone or maybe even some child's toys in this era. I took my first course in computing in the fall of 1958 and was able to use the machine a lot on my own time, thanks to Professor Hultquist who was in charge of that departmental activity.

In January 1959, Dave had his first train trip—to Harley and Maxene Hammond's wedding. I was the best man, and Pat was the matron of honor. Driving that time of year to Idaho was treacherous, and time was short, so we made the trip by train. On our return, Bob Sheets met us at the Denver train station to take us back to Boulder. While in the restaurant there for lunch before our drive, Dave stood up in the booth and made a noise heard all over the place when he pooped in his pants. Now part of the family legends. That spring he helped me study classical mechanics.

Study Time

During the 1959 spring semester, I was informed that I could have a job as an instructor in the Applied Math Department in the fall if I wanted it. I did because my plan was to push on for a master's degree. Teaching paid $385 per month for ten months (equivalent to about $3,000/month in 2012).

Late in the spring semester, we bought a house. It was $10,000 for a nice three bedroom, 1½-bath house with 1,000 square feet on a nice corner lot. I used one bedroom for an office. Pat's parents loaned us the $1,000 down payment, and a fraternity brother arranged the mortgage loan at the bank where he worked. The house was not ready to move in, so a realtor friend from church found us a home we could rent for a month after graduation and take good care of it while they were trying to sell it. They found a buyer while we were there, so it was win-win. Our neighbors had girls in the family. That is where I first heard the Beatles—through their and our open windows!

I did graduate with my BS in Applied Math and minor in Physics at the end of the spring semester. Mom and Dad came for the occasion and brought Grandma Edna. All that happened as it should. Pat remembers that we moved into our new home at 3000 E. Euclid Street in July. I rode a bus to Denver and back each work day to work at a summer job with Shell Oil. I learned a lot, and the income enabled us to buy the beanie-weanies and tuna fish casseroles we ate and to handle our monthly home payments with enough left over to repay Pat's folks for the loan to buy the house.

Our social life picked up during the summer. But the big news late that summer was that we were expecting another child. Pat had more bad days with morning sickness that time but soldiered on, otherwise in good health. We had time and money to drive to Idaho around Labor Day. Harley's wife Maxene was also pregnant when we were together in Idaho—both wives experiencing unpleasant morning sickness at the same time. Their daughter, Wisti, was born the next spring a couple of weeks before Dana.

I don't recall my full teaching load that fall, but I do recall teaching at least one class in calculus. That continued to be my favorite subject to teach. I took graduate courses in numerical analysis from Professor Hultquist both semesters that year. What I learned in those courses helped me many times during my employment in later years and helped me get a National Science Foundation stipend to attend a summer institute at UCLA during the next (1960) summer. The institute was created to teach academics more about computers. I learned a lot about the internal workings of all major parts of the early computers by working with the UCLA experimental computer, the Standard Western Automatic Computer (SWAC), and with lectures from and personal time with the designer of the National Bureau of Standards computer with a 64 bit-size word.

Dana was born 2 April 1960 at Boulder Community Hospital shortly after my hernia operation there in late March. Pat's mother and dad had come to Boulder to help look after Dave and help in general over a week before. An event during that period is now also family legend. One day when Ethel was vacuuming under the couch, the end piece of the vacuum came off and was caught under the couch out of easy reach. Two year old Dave, who had been watching closely

103

over Ethel's shoulder, was heard to say, "Oh Shit." It is presumed that he did not learn that around the house from his father.

The trip to UCLA in the summer after Dana's birth was through Caldwell and on to California. The summer was full of new experiences—more than should be

recounted here. With difficulty, we found an apartment in a remodeled old home in West Los Angeles; close enough to UCLA that I could walk to classes. (We discovered that landlords would rather rent to people with pets than to people with kids!) Dave had become quite sociable, and quickly became well known in the neighborhood. It was a summer of many fine memories.

Pat Reading to Kids in Los Angeles

I found time away from classes and studies to visit several industrial firms with computer technology and products. In addition to wanting to learn more related to computers, I wanted to see what they had to say about the curriculum for science and computer-related classes they thought would most help their new hires to be successful. In a nutshell, they said they would like the graduates to have done more "problem solving"—with greater challenges within the nature of the problem. I went back to teaching classes the following semester and gave the students some real doozies. (I had to deal with some doozies myself with seven hours of graduate math courses that fall semester.)

We passed through Caldwell again on our way back to Boulder. That was the last time I saw my wonderful Grandma Edna before she suffered a debilitating stroke sometime that fall. I only saw her twice again, once the next Easter break in 1961 when she was being cared for at my parent's home, and later that year at Christmas time when she was in a nursing home. I vividly recall there were tears in her eyes when she obviously wanted to speak her thoughts but could not. That is my strongest remaining vision of her. By coincidence, Pat's grandmother was in the same care center, and they both died on the same day in January 1963.

In the spring semester in 1961, I started research work on my thesis project to mathematically characterize the boundary layer between two dissimilar fluids in laminar flow. Before the end of the semester, I applied for and received a National Science Foundation (NSF) grant to support my research during the summer. Before I learned that I was to receive the grant, I had received and accepted an offer from IBM to work in a research lab in New York. We had even sold the beloved 1950 Ford with about 180,000 miles on it and purchased a used 1956 Mercury so as to have a more dependable car while that far from home—so to speak. Receiving the NSF grant late in the semester created two awkward, situations: (1) we had planned to be gone and had committed to rent our home to a professor and his family coming to the University for a summer program, and (2) the commitment to IBM.

The people dealing with summer hires at IBM were very understanding, no hurdle there. However, we were not going to attempt to renege on the house rental, so we were looking for a place for the summer. We ended up renting a cabin on the edge of the St. Vrain River in the Peaceful Valley area, about 35 miles (one-hour drive) from Boulder. We drove into Boulder about once a week for me to consult with my thesis advisor, for Pat to do laundry at a laundromat, and often to visit with some friends.

So the summer started with our relocation to that cabin with no washing machine and children ages a little over one and three. Soon after setting up residence, we did get an old spin-dry washer that we could wheel in off the porch to connect to the faucet water and drain in the kitchen. We had electricity and Pat's pre-marriage Webcor Inc. phonograph player and a few records but otherwise quite a primitive situation. My favorite record that summer was Beethoven's most challenging composition for a violin. When I couldn't figure out how to make progress on my work and needed a break, I would try to catch a big trout in a pool in the river below the cabin. Late in the summer, I was finally successful.

At some point, the owners of the cabin wanted to use it for a couple weeks, and in accord with the deal we had made, we vacated. We loaded some clothes, camping gear, and other stuff I don't recall into our new used car and headed off for a 3-week tour of the Northwest, camping along the way. It was great; I could write a book just about that adventure.

However, just summarizing, we camped in Colorado, then near Pinedale Wyoming, then at a campground just short of Jackson Hole (with bears brushing the tent during the night), then Jenny Lake, then Yellowstone Park for a couple of days, then an out-of-the-way campground on the east side of Glacier National Park, then the heavy rain forced us to a cheap cabin at Many Glaciers, then a visit with family in Caldwell, then on to a stop at the Bonneville Dam fish ladder, then on to Eugene, Oregon. Pat, Mom, and the kids returned to Idaho with a stopover in Portland, while Dad and I drove a pick-up pulling a trailer loaded with Harley and Maxene's possessions to their new home in Concord, California, after which Dad and I returned with trailer to Caldwell. After Dad and I returned, Pat, the kids, and I returned to Boulder. I think that is a summary kind of summary!

We returned to the cabin. Soon thereafter, when we could return to our home in Boulder, I started another 7-hour class load in the math department and life went on much as before. Except—the renters had abused the lawn and the interior, so it took a lot of effort to really get back to "before." For some reason we cannot recall, with help again from Pat's folks for a down-payment, we purchased a house at 730 South 43rd Street before Christmas and rented our Euclid home. The new house had an unfinished basement where the kids could play, which was a blessing that bitter winter in Boulder and throughout the West.

We flew back to Idaho for the Christmas Holidays, where I had my last visit with Grandma Edna, then back to Boulder and into a very busy last semester at CU. We became tired of our poverty, and I was becoming concerned that if we stayed longer in Boulder we would never leave and we would miss out on a greater expanse of life. So, I planned to quit teaching there and interviewed for a job after graduation. I finished my thesis and the other requirements for an MS degree, and much to my mother's disgust, chose to depart Boulder before the long march to be handed a diploma.

Starting in late 1960 and all through 1961 into early 1962, I had engaged in consulting work for Ball Brothers Research (later, Ball Aerospace)—who had the government contract to manage a major satellite design and build project. Strange enough, the company was owned by the company that made Mason Jars for home canning a household word.

As mentioned earlier, I was sort of a sidekick to Paul Hultquist. We did a great deal of analysis to support the design and orbiting of OSO-1, the first of several Orbital Solar Observatory (OSO) satellites put into orbit to study the sun and galaxy. As of this writing, the history of the OSO program remains described on the Internet. Among other things, we did the analysis of heat-transfer issues when orbiting through the shadow of the sun, determination of the physical characteristics of a system unit to maintain spin stability, and some implications for the orbit originating from the effect of the oblateness of the Earth. Many a night I mothered the G-15 all night as it ground through program code performing mathematical calculations that could be done now in a blink of an eye—on a laptop!

The satellite was successfully placed into orbit on 7 March 1962, and as best I recall, all experiments on board worked as designed. The key principals on the project from Ball Brothers and NASA first thought the orbit failed—until they realized they had the telemetry tape flipped over in the punched-tape reader. YES, program code and data input and output in those days was via punched tape or punched cards!

During the spring, we shared a "good bye" with many friends of our Boulder days. We sold the house on 43rd, moved back to the Euclid house for a short time, and then sold it also. At the end of the semester, we enjoyed a few days at the McGraw Ranch near Estes Park where, during the prior few years, I had interesting experiences hunting, as well as horseback riding with Pat. We sort of felt like family to Frank McGraw, his wife, and the girls. I graded the final exams for the classes I was teaching, we drove through Boulder to drop off the grades at the University, and we were then on our way to Texas. I had accepted a job with Texas Instruments (TI) in the Apparatus Division Research Department at a little over twice my CU teaching salary. TI took care of the move of our household belongings, and we had what was left in the car as we four drove south.

A Thought or Two Looking Back from Now

It has been neat to recall the ways in which what I had learned in classroom study led to the early days of professional employment—my teaching, the summer at Shell Oil, helping Paul to solve problems never encountered before in history at Ball Brothers Research, and some statistical analysis consulting to pick up income when opportunities arose.

We did receive financial support from family, which we repaid, but it is nice to see in the record that we lived early marriage life with many pleasures and sources of satisfaction within our financial means. We did not carry a financial debt burden on into our future.

➤ 9 ➤

The Corporate World

I recall my summer work at Shell Oil in Denver and, more significantly, earning a good bit of money via my consulting work for Ball Research while in Boulder. Paul would meet with the team there, learn their problems, and decide what we could work on to help things along. Those "internships" (sort of) were as close as I had experienced of the corporate world until then. Things were about to change.

After a long drive, during which we experienced Texas temperatures in early June, we attended the wedding of "Uncle" Don in Sherman before driving on to North Dallas to look for a new home. (Don's marriage did not last and did not restart when his former wife approached him later to remarry.) We were fortunate to soon find a nice house to buy in Richardson at 1603 Provincetown Lane. At some point we moved in, acquired some furniture, and I went to work. Richardson was a pretty small community at that time. It grew rapidly over the years with the growth of Texas Instruments (TI) and other employers in the area.

The furniture was bought on time, of course, and while we were at it, I purchased a new piano for Pat as a symbol of the luxury my new salary would provide. Here in 2014, we still own and she still plays that piano, fifty years later. (Don't take that to mean that we couldn't have bought her a better one by now if she wanted it.) Late that year we bought our first ever brand-new car, a 1963 Citroen ID 19, the lesser costing four-door Citroen model. I loved that car and Citroens in general. Dad bought one, the plusher DS model, and he eventually became a good Citroen mechanic. We later bought a Citroen station wagon.

Pat and New Citroen

108

I really liked my first real "corporate" job—working for a corporation, even a sort of big one for its time. I was extremely fortunate in many ways—ways not defined and promised to me before I signed on—ways I could not have foreseen, and even in ways I couldn't even have known enough to wish for. Smoke that in your metaphysical pipe for a while.

I met some very well-educated and experienced people working there. By far the most impressive was Pat Haggerty, the then President of the company. Once, after a research project of mine turned out well and saved the company a failure on the contract, he showed up in my office to recognize the achievement. Wow, what an occasion. Of course, I didn't know what he looked like at the time, so I was wondering who was this older guy entering my cubicle. I subsequently attended meetings of the technical personnel where he would discuss goals and the why and when they were important to TI. He impressed me every time, and his guidance of the company resulted in great success.

While working for TI, I successfully completed the most challenging project I had encountered up till then in the application of math-physics theory, in this case relating to macro photon-phonon interaction phenomena. I had three layers of technical staff bosses at the time. My former direct boss, whose name I will not provide out of sympathy to his being so stuck in inertness, didn't even understand the problem, let alone what might be a solution. His boss, my next boss layer, Doug Ziemer, may not have understood the detail, but he believed that I knew and accurately represented that it was a solution. His boss had a PhD in physics from MIT (again name withheld out of kindness).

Doug marched me into that guy's office one day and announced that the problem had been solved. I was to present the detail. I did, but apparently not well enough for him to understand the solution, let alone how it was derived. Doug and I left his office very depressed. But soon, Doug came to me and told me he had friends down in the bowels of TI who could build an instrument to test the theory. They did, the solution was confirmed, and I moved Doug up a notch in my view of him as a manager. I learned a lot from him throughout my tenure at TI.

Doug was the one I first informed that I had decided to leave TI only a year and a half after going there. However, he knew why almost before I told him. Shortly before, I had written a poem to express what I thought of the recent change in senior management at TI. All I recall now is that it mentioned Chicken Little. I had also been put on a project with managers who would not accept the fact that the approximations they were making to "solve" some non-liner

109

differential equations in the design of some avionics equipment could likely result in a crash and the death of the pilots. I decided I did not want to work for what I called at the time, "mathmagicians." Doug understood but enlightened me concerning the corporate world. He said that sometimes one just has to put up with something like that and eventually "outlive the boss". By that he meant, suffer a while but move on and things will be better with a new boss someday (when one is working for a basically well-run company). I appreciated his counsel but moved on in a different way.

Although I had learned the basic components of financial statements from high school and college accounting courses, before TI I had no idea of what the operations and decisions behind those statements looked like in a sizable corporation. I learned a lot other than technology while working at TI, including how something of societal and commercial value can be created starting with basic scientific theory. In particular, I brushed up against a lot of marketing activity. Eventually I grew to view the most important focus within a business as marketing, marketing, and marketing.

By the time I left TI, the seeds had been planted to think about how my mathematical knowledge and computer capability might accomplish more if employed more directly to the business of business. In addition to my technical work, I had gained a lot more communication skills in people interactions quite different from teaching. I also had traveled and presented technical papers to groups of knowledgeable people, some who had a vested interest to try to diminish the significance of the work I was presenting. Good experience!

While working for TI, we had planted quite a few good roots in the surrounding community. We made friends with our next-door neighbors—real Texans who talked funny—but we learned that was how one could tell they were real Texans. (Now, it seems like almost everyone in Texas is from somewhere else and talk so you can tell they are not native Texans!) We also made friends at work.

In particular, we became very close friends with the Whitely family—Dick, Ruthanne, and their four children. I worked in the same area with Dick at TI and later did consulting work for the company he and another ex-TI'er, Jimmy Jones, started after leaving TI. That relationship led to a very important event in my life not many years later. And years after that, I hired Dick and Jimmy to work for the company I helped found. Our friendship with the Whitley's lasted for many years, with annual visits and occasional travel together until Dick died. We continue to keep in touch with Ruthanne and to visit occasionally. We are also friends to this day with two other families we met through work at TI. I also provided consulting help to a company another friend founded after leaving TI. All were strong bonds of friendship, several including family friendships that often involved Dave and Dana just as much as Pat and me.

We especially met many new friends through membership in a church in the area. I played on a fast-pitch softball team, Pat sang in a very good choir, I taught another high school age Sunday School Class, and we partied often as a group. One of those parties was where I first learned that I could experience a weird sense of pleasure by pretending to be someone different than who I was. Maybe not always with a contrived name, that came later, but with a contrived educational background and occupation. My favorite was the party where I identified myself as a washing-machine salesman to a bunch of Collins Corp electrical engineers. I asked them to explain how color television worked. I greatly admired their ability to communicate to this guy asking questions but who seemed not to understand up from down about electronics.

When we moved to Richardson, Dave was a little over four and Dana a little over two. They quickly made friends with neighbor kids, and the kids of friends we met through work, church, and those in the families of guys I played with on the softball team. The first Christmas time we were there, Don Kromer and Bob Sheets came down from Sherman, Texas, to spend some time with us. That was the beginning of a family tradition that lasted for decades, to decorate the Christmas tree on my birthday, December 17th. During the winter of 1962-63, we had about nine inches of snow. I helped many drivers rescue their cars after they tried to drive in it. The kids were unhappy that we had given the sled away when we left Boulder, and I found it inconvenient that we had also given away the snow shovel. At Christmas time in 1963, our parents drove to Texas together to join us for a few days. Dave had chicken pox in late November and Dana in early December. The pictures taken at Christmas still showed the "holes" where she had had pox.

Our life in Richardson continued after I left TI. Before I left, I became one of several who were early employees of a new organization. In 1962, Erik Jonsson, co-founder of Texas Instruments and then Mayor of Dallas, announced the formation of the Southwest Center for Advanced Studies (SCAS) to be administered by the Graduate Research Center of the Southwest (GRCSW) and housed on a new campus in Richardson. The land and funds for the buildings were raised from private donations. The idea was to interface with universities to provide graduate education and research opportunities that would encourage the accumulation of intellectual and scientific talent in the Texas area.

The creation of GRCSW by Dallas "city fathers" was a bold effort to attract and compete for scientific talent with growing areas of technology in Massachusetts Route 128 near Boston, the Research Triangle in the Raleigh–Durham–Chapel Hill area, Silicon Valley in California, and the North Star research endeavor in the Minneapolis St. Paul area. I was an early hire within the Laboratory of Computer Sciences at the center, headed by Carl F. Kossack, PhD. GRCSW later became The University of Texas at Dallas.

At SCAS I had two responsibilities—as director of a project to survey technology within the USA related to the storage of large amounts of data in the future, and to perform mathematical support for the science projects and scientists in other laboratories at SCAS. The support of scientists was the most interesting and enjoyable for me. I was able to dig deep in my math-physics and numerical-analysis knowledge and provide enough computer support work to deliver a major help to their research efforts. And I liked the several people I worked with.

The survey project was a horse of a different color. I had to learn a lot about the current state of the technology, in particular as related to the then very limited devices for random-access storage of digital data on computers. It soon became clear to me that the technology then available to find data on the devices would certainly not scale up to large amounts of data.

With the sponsorship of SCAS and travel budget of the laboratory, I was able to visit several research laboratories around the US where research staff were quite aware of the issue and were birthing new ways to grow up a technology to handle the future—and make money for their employers. I also spent time studying the views of those in organizations that would be, or at least wanted to be, creating large amounts of data to be stored on a computer system. And, of course, they would rather be able to retrieve data from the data pool in a more reasonable amount of time than days or weeks. The project report was over an inch thick, and I have no idea if it was ever read by many people.

The head of the lab, Dr. Kossack, came out of academia. Helping young people learn and excel was in his blood. He looked at me as one to nurture. At some point, I believe it was in the spring of 1964, he decided to devote some of his budget to helping me get a PhD. (The degree was his idea of achievement.) He offered to pay me half-time at my then salary level as a consultant to the lab if I would pursue a PhD in mathematics at The University of Texas at Austin (UT), with no obligation to return to SCAS, although that door would be open.

After Pat and I gave serious consideration to the idea, we gave it a go. I visited UT a few times, decided to concentrate on numerical analysis, established a relationship with a professor interested in sponsoring and monitoring my degree plan, returned to Dallas to take the GRE exam, applied, and was accepted at UT. Sometime during the summer, we sold our Richardson house and moved to a rental in Austin. The math department had offered me a teaching assistantship, so we weren't staring poverty in the face. (That rental is another story but no time for it here.) We were physically on the move again, and I was jumping into a new pool again.

As mentioned above, while working for SCAS I did consulting work for Dick Whitely and Jimmy Jones who had left TI to form their own company that engaged in electronic countermeasures technology. The largest investor in their company was a Mr. Alfred King, who lived in Austin.

Soon after we got settled in Austin in our un-insulated rental in the summer heat, and after becoming members of First English Lutheran Church, and after I was well into a semester of taking classes and teaching one, I decided to meet this investor, Mr. King.

I got his phone number from Dick Whitely and called him up. I introduced myself as the smallest investor in Dick and Jimmy's company and that I would enjoy meeting the largest investor if he had interest. He had probably heard my name because of my consulting work and maybe even wanted to get my take on how the company was doing, but for whatever reason, he invited me to join him at lunch. I later learned that the Headliner's Club in the historic Driskill Hotel where we had lunch was a very special organization in Austin. I also learned later that Alfred was a member of the then prestigious Town and Gown Club that held its meetings there. A couple years after our first meeting, Alfred sponsored me for membership in Town and Gown. I became the youngest member and remained the youngest member for at least a couple of decades.

I had told Pat I would be gone for lunch. When I had not returned by late in the afternoon, she became concerned. She had no way to contact me. When I finally showed up, I had to explain. About all I could say at that point was that we "hit it off." We found a lot of mutual interest to talk about.

Later I realized that I could sum it up this way—deep down, I had an interest to take what I had learned about computing and analysis into a business environment where I thought I could see untapped potential. Deep down, Alfred had been observing the growing significance about what computers were going to do to change the basics of many functions within business. We had found plenty to keep lunching and talking about.

About the same time, I was realizing that to pursue what I wanted to in a degree plan, I had to take some math courses where I had neither interest nor, seemingly, enough smarts—group theory and topology. I liked the professor in group theory and later hired his daughter, but I just couldn't get interested in the subject in the depth that was required. Before the semester was finished, Alfred and I had agreed to start a small consulting company, and I had dropped or abandoned the group theory course. I soon thereafter walked away from the degree program, ended my association with SCAS (after expressing heart-felt appreciation to Dr. Kossack), completed teaching my class in differential equations, and "moved on."

We named the consulting firm Management Services Associates (MSA). A longtime friend of Alfred's, Bob Mallas, had experience in performing consulting work in management and administration and had some good client contacts. I was to pursue my desire to do operations research (a.k.a. management science) work for businesses. I had no client base, and I knew little about how to develop one. It turned out that Mallas was an investor or owner of a few small businesses. Alfred convinced him that I could improve their operations and profits with some analysis and computerized reporting. I did. It was fun. It was a great demonstration for Alfred.

Bob and I were not close friends, but we did spend time together. He had written a book related to the exercise of power by management, which I read. The topic wasn't on my list at the time, but I recall learning something from it. However, if someone asked me now what did I learn, I could only think of one thing to tell them. It was the same thing I learned from Glen Powers that I mentioned earlier—schedule meetings when your adversary has a conflicting obligation and cannot attend.

Our first MSA employee represented that he had worked a lot for Ford and other big companies, knew many executives, and could generate business for us. He traveled a lot but generated no business. We later discovered he was a text-book example of a psychopath. He lied about almost anything but didn't really know he was lying. That was an expensive lesson, but I did learn one important thing from him. I learned to have all mail opened by, and only by, a trusted employee. At times when he scheduled to remain "working" at our offices in Austin, he had been coming in before anyone else and removing letters that he expected would have blown his cover—so to speak.

But other than Bob Mallas's businesses, I was not having much success finding clients. However, as we know, there is often in life unforeseen good fortune. I had become well acquainted at church with John Bickley, a professor and then head of the Finance Department in the UT College of Business. John sort of looked at things much like Alfred. He thought the insurance companies he advised should be getting into applications of technology like I represented as my capability.

John felt so strongly about it that he bought me a ticket to accompany him to St. Paul, Minnesota, to visit with the senior executives of the St. Paul Property and Casualty Insurance Company. John just told them they needed me, and it was sort of up to me and them to determine how. They were to pay MSA for my work. They agreed. Wow, wish it would have been that easy to get more clients!

St. Paul became a client for something like ten years and later an important customer. They used some of the operations-research work I did for them until a few years ago—for about 40 years—during which the company had grown to have revenue exceeding $5 Billion. The friendship between me and John Bickley grew over the years until his death in 2008. He was a remarkable man in many ways and is honored in the International Insurance Society, Insurance Hall of Fame. With introductions from John, I later did Operations Research (OR) analysis, computer modeling, and simulation work for several big-name insurance companies. In addition to the revenue, a good side benefit that I received from working with corporate clients was to gain a little more perspective about basic corporate business operations that served me well in later years.

One of my exceptionally interesting OR projects was to build a model of the road and plant-building layout and simulate road-traffic congestion for the then major TI semiconductor site north of Dallas. It was very successful in the eyes of the customer. Based on information provided by the simulation of traffic under different assumptions about shift times and flow control, TI changed work-group shift times, reduced traffic congestion, and increased employee satisfaction along with it. I thought it was a fun project and enjoyed the pleasure that comes from a happy client.

115

While all this business stuff was going on, Pat was doing the heavy lifting of running a household (a job she has never been able to get rid of) and being a terrific mother to Dave and Dana. As soon as we were able after I quit at UT and did not need to be within walking distance of the University, we found a good deal and purchased a house in March 1965 in a highly desirable location at 4608 Crestway Drive in what was then northwest Austin. With major gyrations with our one car to provide him transportation, Dave finished first grade where he had started back in our old neighborhood.

Our new home was on a hill overlooking a lot of Austin, including the UT Tower. From our home on 1 August 1966, Pat could see the white puffs of smoke as Charles Whitman killed 14 and wounded 32 others from a location on that tower. I was at work downtown. A few hours later, I learned that an employee, Jim Tillinghast, had been pinned down within rifle range behind a rock wall during the shooting. Jim was one of the earliest employees. He became a long-term employee, partner in ownership of a sailboat, a dear friend to this day, and we occasionally vacationed together where we could scuba dive.

We made friends with many in our new neighborhood, and the kids had plenty of other kids to spend time with after school. After Dana finished kindergarten, both of them were going to the same elementary school and could walk together from our home. For several years, other than neighbors, our closest friends were from MSA or church. I played on the church (this time, slow-pitch) softball team several years (over ten) and the family continued to be my most loyal fans. Both the MSA group and a small contingent from church liked to party at our home—as did I. I discovered that I enjoyed the wine best when I could crawl to my bed on my hands and knees—rhetorically speaking.

My parents came for a visit our first Christmas in our new home, and together we also traveled to Mexico during the holidays. We enjoyed a couple days at the Ramada Inn in Monterrey and touring the city for a couple of days. Alfred and I were investors in the Inn, and we knew the manager well. The seven of us (counting Rob, our "bun in the oven" as they say now) were in the then small village of Saltillo southwest of Monterrey on New Year's Eve. There occurred a fascinating experience we will never forget.

In summary, we rescued a couple of German girls from an old guy moving in on them in the hotel bar where I had hired street musicians to come entertain us. Minutes before midnight we crashed a big party of locals with a message on a scrap of paper from the hotel clerk saying, "See Armando Flores, he is my friend, he will welcome you." We arrived at about one minute 'til midnight and opened the closest door, which happened to be a "side door." The party came to a screeching halt, including the vocalist singing something with a lot of "amour's" in it.

The scrap and message were produced and viewed by the matronly woman obviously in charge, with about 200 soon-to-be friends watching. She nodded her head in approval, and they then proceeded to treat us like royalty for several hours of customary music and more courses of food than we could remember by the time we departed about 3 a.m. You will have to use your imagination to grasp the experience: add racing through the village at high speed minutes before midnight in a small Volkswagen with the German female at the wheel pretending to be a Formula 1 driver. Mom and Dad had retired within the hotel before the excitement—Dave and Dana with them.

Later in 1967, Alfred and I were on a business trip together in New York City. One evening while we were enjoying a Mai Tai before dinner at Trader Vic's, Martin Luther King and others were seated in the booth next to us. I didn't even know who he was. Alfred clued me in, but the main reason I recall the occasion is that during our conversation Alfred brought up some reference to paranormal events. That led to his mention of Edgar Cayce and Cayce's ability to retrieve information while in a trance state about the present and past lives of people he didn't know from something he called the Akashic Record. That kind of thing was all new to me.

When I indicated curiosity, Alfred suggested that I might want to read a book by Gina Cerminara titled *Many Mansions*. The book described how she investigated Cayce as a skeptic but came to consider what was happening as credible. I read the book. It was the first time I recall really understanding that "paranormal" was a word to describe experiences that lie outside the range of normal experience or scientific explanation. It also introduced the idea of reincarnation to me, which for many decades was a topic that intrigued me—but also confused me. I view the evening as a major passage in my life.

I had offered to be paid a minimal salary at MSA when business was touch and go, so discretionary funds in our household were minimal. Part of the "have fun but do not spend money" plan was to play cards almost one weekend night weekly with our minister and his wife, Merle and Ginna Franke. At first, they taught us to play Whist, but soon I moved them into learning Bridge. Long after Pat and I dropped Bridge as a priority entertainment, they continued—becoming quite good and enjoying the pleasure of teaching others. The last time we

117

played with them, a couple of years ago, it was clear that they could play much better than we.

The weekend evenings with the Franke's went on even after Rob was born in May 1966. He was about six years younger than Dana and eight years younger than Dave. To this day, Rob can describe early life sibling abuse in great detail. We vacationed each year in Idaho with family, sometimes Pat and the kids staying longer than me. When Pat's father died in 1968 and she returned there to be with her family, Dave got left with me for a few days before the two of us traveled to Idaho. That was the year our pet purebred Border Collie dog, Sam Houston, was poisoned while we were holding down the fort together in Austin. We were quite sure he was poisoned by a neighbor down the street whose purebred dog of some other breed bore pups fathered by ours. Rob and Sam Houston had spent a lot of time at home together and had bonded, so I was glad Rob was not there when Dave and I were holding a quivering dying dog with those eyes beseeching help we could not give.

In early 1965, it had become clear that the two Bobs of MSA were focusing on business where one had nothing to do with the other—we just shared the same roof and some interesting conversations together. Working under the same roof became more difficult when some language in one of Bob Mallas's consulting reports was widely picked up in the media and created questioning from some of my clients. I approached Alfred, told him I wished to distance my identity from the work of Bob, and left it to him to decide what to do. Alfred decided to continue along the trail that had brought us together. We wished Bob good hunting and went on to pursue my work ideas. MSA morphed into Management Research International (to get a research name through the Texas Secretary of State office), and later into MRI Systems Corporation.

We enjoyed being a profitable small consulting firm for roughly four years, then decided to attempt to become a product company instead of a consulting business. We bit off more than we could really chew, but my lack of experience actually helped get into the Data Base Management Systems (DBMS) business of MRI. If I had been wiser and experienced enough to assess the risk-reward prospects of what I was doing, we would never have embarked on that adventure. MRI became a major challenge for the next ten years of my life.

Before embarking upon that venture, a little perspective might be of interest for anyone reading this life story some years from now. As mentioned earlier, my own experience with digital computers started in 1956 with the "humble" machines of that era. The growth of the computer industry, and of the growing

118

significance within our society and many individual lives, was a major technological evolution of the latter half of the 20th century. If nothing else had registered on the generalized psyche of the world to indicate the rapid acceleration of the rate of change in our worldly environment, this was it.

The rapid introduction of digital computing machines into the societies of the developed world was a change of unprecedented proportions. Businesses and governments were challenged to drastically change their way of life. Employment opportunities became highly skewed toward opportunity within the industry itself or within those challenged by the need to incorporate computers into their business organizations—or die—as a business. Business leaders who failed to recognize the need for their organization to incorporate computing were eventually replaced. It only took a few decades for computers and computing to grow exponentially within industrialized societies. In most respects, the USA led the way, primarily because of our free-enterprise economy of then healthy capitalism.

One measure of the growth in supporting more and more societal activity with digital computer capability was the growing amount of data that could be or should be processed by the computers to accomplish some desired end result. The need for devices to store data grew rapidly, and so did the industry innovation to fulfill the need. As the size of the piles of computerized data grew, the way to find and look at any particular piece of data became a major challenge in data processing. That was the problem foreseen at the time of my work for SCAS in Dallas. I knew the dimensions of the issue pretty well.

The industry had grown from a beginning with punched-card processing machines to machines with capability to store small amounts of data being processed within the machine itself and then on to the capability to store data on devices external but attached to the processing machines. The evolution then ran right smack into a problem that had to be overcome, or the juggernaut would stall out and disappoint those who had invested so much blood, sweat, and tears to incorporate computers into their organizational way of life. Programming computers using basic machine language became more complicated as the parts of the system grew and had to work well together. Growth was bogging down.

All along that growth path it was "software" that provided the instructions wherein a computer user could get the computer machine hardware itself to accomplish a desired result. There was first the tedious writing of instructions in the form that a machine could interpret—then the development of a more user-

119

friendly level of programming language that would permit more complex control of the machines. The advanced programming language interpreted easier to use commands into the kind of machine language needed for executing on the computer hardware. That evolution was followed by higher-level languages that could take an even more powerful expression of what was to be done and compile from it a large number of smaller chunks of computer code as building blocks for computer hardware to execute. A few words of code could then permit the machine to accomplish as much computing as would have taken thousands or millions of words of code to accomplish a few years before.

A major gestalt had come into being—the whole was greatly more than the sum of its parts. Small aggregates of computer instructions could be given names and used by more than one larger program—especially those aggregate routines used to bring data into the computer or to store and retrieve data files on an attached storage device or to print out the results of processing. Highly complex processing involving highly complex logical determinations could be created and debugged much more efficiently using these high-level collections of software routines.

The next major improvement in the power and sophistication of programs to do big jobs occurred when methods of rudimentary file management were extended to permit machine processing of many files instead of a single file at a time. A new kind of software was becoming necessary to support larger amounts of data being utilized in increasing degrees of logical complexity.

This was the beginning of the age of generalized database management. MRI was one of the few companies that developed, sold, and supported a major database management software product. We were only one of a small handful of companies that led the entire world of computing into vastly improved computing capabilities when there was a combination of large amounts of data and many complex processes to be performed—all potentially using the data in different ways. That was the computing frontier of that time, and we were on the front lines. The year was 1970, but we called our product SYSTEM 2000.

MRI was a small company, but as one of my football coaches had said years before—"If the competition was too big to push aside, one had better learn ways to move around them instead"—and there could be no greater mismatch in size than MRI and the giant of the industry, IBM. Our work was cut out for us.

A Thought or Two Looking Back from Now

It is clear to me that the next important branch point in my life after our marriage was meeting Alfred and Ellen King. Alfred was much, much more than a business associate in my life. For one, through our friendship, he exposed Pat and me to many forms of culture that were new to us and to social situations involving groups within a level of society we could never have enjoyed on our own. These experiences brought world knowledge and many friendships and pleasure into many years of our lives.

Also, it is impossible for me to imagine how different my life would have been if not for that short conversation during dinner with Alfred in a restaurant in New York City where I first recall hearing the word "paranormal." I had read about mystical experiences of religious persons of varying persuasions in history but had not read anything about the paranormal in general, except the occasional mention of ghosts and healing miracles. Sure, my spiritual journey had started in my early family experience in church—but I didn't think much about it anymore. Life experience wasn't explicitly advancing that journey. Then, that short conversation opened up what would become a new perspective about what life was like, including life before and after death.

As will be noted often later in my story, Alfred and I (and his wife Ellen) became very close friends—a friendship that continued until his death in 2006 and with Ellen until her death in 2013. I guess it should be noted sometime in this story that Alfred was a descendent of the riverboat captain, Richard King, who sailed up the Rio Grande River in the mid-1800s, became very wealthy as a result of his entrepreneurial nature, and who had amassed about 600,000 acres of land by the time of his death in 1885 that was known for many subsequent generations as the King Ranch.

Because of his wealth and my relative poverty, I requested and Alfred accepted, that our private relationship be such that I always paid my own way and was not to expect or receive personal financial benefit from his wealth. (We always even split the cost of lunch together.) To me, his wealth of character, intelligence, and integrity became far more noteworthy than his net worth. Looking back, I view it a rare life experience for anyone of my age and life situation at that time to have such a long-term and close relationship with someone like Alfred.

Alfred Ashbrook King

➤ **10** ◄

The MRI Story

The formal history of MRI Systems Corporation was recorded for, and published in, the November 2009 journal of the *IEEE Annals of the History of Computing* that focused on the large computer Data Base Management Systems (DBMS) that brought that technology to marketplace. Here is the editor's preface to that article.

> System 2000 was developed in 1970 and then successfully marketed by a small firm of DBMS technology entrepreneurs in Austin, Texas. Before the company was acquired by Intel Corporation in 1979, System 2000 was installed at more than 300 customer sites and used by more than 400 other organizations via Remote Computing Service firms. It remains in use today.

I do not intend to tell that "SYSTEM 2000" DBMS story again here. It is available as a historical document of the IEEE. I intend to write here about some of the *more* personal significance of this entrepreneurial experience in my life—in particular as to how it affected our family, about some of the new things I had to think about and learn, and to mention a few of the many people I came to know as a result of work-related experiences. As it happened, this timeframe was also the trailhead of my metaphysical journey, and I think that important enough to also warrant sharing what I mean by that.

The thought a reader should keep in mind is that, from the time in 1969 when we started our transformation into a software product company, MRI was for the most part OJT (on-the-job training) for me and also for most of us who worked together many years. It seemed like everything we learned month by month pointed toward even more that remained to be learned. For several reasons, we would not have survived had not it been for Alfred King, from whom I learned so much about the business of business—and of life.

Alfred invested in our venture and continued to do so long after most others would have lost faith and bailed out. Over the years of working almost day by day with him to accomplish what we started, he came to be the most important mentor of my life and certainly one of my closest friends. But before getting into some MRI business-related stories, I would like to spotlight the family story during these years.

Dave and Dana were young when we moved to Austin, and I have mentioned some of our family experience with them earlier. Rob essentially grew up with MRI but, of course, was only 13 by the time MRI was history for me. What he might remember most, and in fact, what Pat and all three kids probably remember most, is my "frequent" travel. In fact, it is also what I recall at the top of the list as effecting family life. The word "frequent" is intended to convey "a regular occurrence," which is how I recall it. I think the family will remember that although I might have been away a lot and that much of the time when home I worked six days a week, Sundays were strictly for family. There were a lot of other days with rich family experience, but Sunday was the one that could be counted on with near certainty.

In the summer of 1969, MRI held a series of week-long Seminars in Vail, Colorado, for senior corporate executives to learn about computers and some of the implications for planning within their firms. During the weeks, I sort of bounced in and out. Each time, I met and got well-enough acquainted with the attendees that several later became MRI customers. During one week, I had the whole family at a beautiful rental home at the base of the ski slopes.

During that week, an important customer flew into Denver for an important meeting with Alfred and me. It turned out to be 20 July, the day of the first manned landing on the moon. We were meeting in a motel conference room. We broke off our discussions to crowd around the computer during the TV broadcast of what was happening with Apollo 11 as it landed. I heard the first words spoken by a man on the moon. It was one of those once-in-a lifetime kind of experience—mankind beyond Earth into the new frontier. It also reduced a little of the anxiety associated with our national ability to keep up with the Russians during the Cold War of the time. While we were in Denver, Pat and the kids huddled around a small TV with a fuzzy picture viewing the same event. It was a historic occasion for all of us.

Over the Thanksgiving break in 1969, we moved into our new house on three acres in an area northwest of Austin called Pecan Park. We had the house built to our floor plan for $32,000. Country living was a real change and mostly for the good. Certainly, we were much happier with the school experience for the kids. However, being so far from town was a negative until the town and MRI grew out toward us.

I drove the ten miles between home and our office on Hancock Drive in town each day—and often a drive to the airport about 15 miles away. Pecan Park was located near the intersection of Texas FM 620 and US 183. One corner of that intersection is now one of the largest shopping centers in Austin, but it was mostly surrounded by a thousand acres of pastures then. The closest grocery store was about as far as the office. The road between our Pecan Park home and the Hancock Drive office and stores of any kind was a paved divided highway with a 70-mph speed limit. We both drove it often.

The situation was much improved when in 1971 MRI was able to build our own facility on property we owned three miles away from our home. Fortunately, and by accident, my corner office was built on a county line. My door and part of my conference table were in Williamson County, but my desk was in Travis County. That situation helped a few years later when I was subpoenaed to appear for jury duty in a high-profile murder trial at a stressful time at MRI when I didn't think I had time to serve. The subpoena was from Williamson County. I instructed the receptionist to inform the person delivering the summons that I was located in Travis County. He departed, and I never heard further from the court. I did serve on a Grand Jury in Williamson County years later.

And guess who "held the fort" while I traveled—either in town or much farther? Pat essentially was the parent in charge—mother, household manager, driver, and chief cook and bottle washer—as the saying goes. She did get some property maintenance help from the kids. She handled all that was important at home while three kids were growing older. It seemed like there was something important quite often.

I wasn't there when there was a broken jaw or a meeting with a teacher or a birthday party after school and so many other times. But I was there Sundays for church and after church and many other times when there was a special reason. For instance, one such very special reason was when I was there to go with David when he had to appear in Justice of the Peace Court because of the traffic citation for trying to outrun a police officer. And I do recall being on the sideline or in the stands often as the kids worked through kid sports, including Dana's gymnastics competitions and Dave's varsity basketball.

Fortunately, I was in town when our three-legged pet dog Happy was partially run over by the school bus. Happy was clearly on the verge of death. I was immediately called home from the office only three miles away. I took one look at Happy and went for my heavy hatchet thinking that I might relieve his

125

suffering by finishing what the bus had started with one hit to his battered head from the blunt end of the hatchet. However, as I raised the hatchet, I for the second time, looked into a pet dog's beseeching eyes. That was enough to convince me that we should take him to the vet, so I loaded him into the car. I had to depart pronto to catch a plane, so Pat and Rob drove Happy to the vet.

Pat probably broke speed laws all the way. The vet assessed the damage, fixed his broken jaw, and kept him at the clinic a day or two. He then called and said something like, "He might die if we leave him here. If you take him home and show him some loving attention within the family environment, he may live." We did, he did.

Even though I am not able to remember all those special reasons and special times now, there were many more, and at the time they were very significant for me. I cared a lot, but I would guess there were days Pat might have thought I cared more about work. My side of the story is that, in spite of the days and weeks I traveled and days I left early and came back late, we did manage to do a lot of things as a family at times other than just Sundays.

Pat's family and my parents still lived in Idaho. We always made at least one trip a year to see them, other family, and Idaho friends. From the time Rob was six, we also started our annual back-packing trek to the Sawtooth Wilderness Area while there—which was much more wilderness than it is now. We seldom encountered any other people on the trails.

Rob's first backpack had only his "blankie". After his older siblings cut his blankie into small pieces to end the "blankie" days of his youth, we put as much weight on him as we could, just like the rest of us. Dave had attended a wilderness survival training camp in Idaho for a week when he was about 13, so backpacking was old hat to him. He could even "live off the land" for a long time if he had to. His later backpacking at the Boy Scout Philmont camp was more of a breeze by comparison.

We were usually on the trail three days and two nights. Pat and I then noticed that the kids come out a lot faster than climbing up in altitude on the way in. However, we always stopped on the way out and discussed whether we

Our 1973 Backpacking Trailhead

126

wanted to backpack together again next year. The answer was always "Yes." Our usual trail was what was called "the Toxaway Loop," up from base camp at Petit Lake, to Alice Lake, then Twin Lakes, and then up over Snowyside mountain to Toxaway, and on down to Yellowbelly before crossing the ridge back to base camp.

When the kids were older, we also climbed longer and higher, past Hell Roaring Lake and on to Imogene, a very special place for me. Of all the places we have hiked to in years since, Imogene Lake is where I would like to fly away on magic wings to be there again. At any moment's notice, I can imagine being there, viewing almost any direction from my little orange tent. I even "feel" being there. All those lakes were good fishing at the time.

It was on the Toxaway Loop where a couple years later I slipped while hiking across the snow bank on Mt. Snowyside and started to slide toward the edge of the high cliff—with my father looking up and observing from Twin Lake below. I experienced a terrifying sinking feeling of fear and closeness to death, but then I stopped sliding. When trying to recover, I slipped again. This time as I was sliding toward the cliff, I truly thought that was it, my life was over—I had a second chance, but I screwed up. Oh shit! But I instinctively flattened out and stopped sliding again, helped by a rock sticking up a couple inches above the snow. This time I carefully jammed the butt of my fishing pole into the snow bank below my boot. When I quit trembling, I carefully worked my way back up and off the snow bank.

During high school spring break in 1975, David and some buddies went on a "ski trip" to Colorado. Dave had never skied, but there had to be a first time. His first time was in deep powder on Wolf Creek Pass. He claimed that the deep snow was perfect because he fell so much, and it was so soft. My view is that he might not have fallen so much if not for the deep powder. Anyway in 1976, when Pat turned 40, we were with our close friends Larry and Fran Collmann in Vail, Colorado. Pat and the Collmann's took ski lessons for a day or two, and maybe I should have. Pat then became a skier. For many years thereafter, we skied as a family in Colorado and many other places at least sometime each year.

We had met the Collmanns when they moved to Austin in the early 1970s and joined our church. They had grown up in the same small town in Iowa, married while young, and then lived in Illinois and California as a result of Larry's employment with the then AT&T in the telephone industry. Larry was employed in Austin by a company that eventually was acquired by 3M and then started his own company to serve the industry that by then he knew so well. His firm became very successful, and a major part of it was sold to a larger company with his boys each running a distinct part of the remaining business. They also had three children about the same age as ours. Our two families have been very close friends all the years since we first met.

In 1978, the Collmann's and we bought a condo overlooking the lake in Dillon, Colorado. Although we had it in the rental pool, we used it for at least

Our 1992 Last Trip to Dillon Condo
Front row left to right: Courtney, Kristin, and Autumn
Rest of us: Dave and sons Ross and Nick--Andy, Dana, and son Kyle
And last but not least, Pat, me, and Rob

two weeks a year. It became home base for subsequent skiing trips and many summer weeks until it was sold in 1990—with a condition that we continue to be able to use it a few times thereafter. The last "big fling" there for our family was over the Christmas holiday in 1992.

In April 1971, I spent a week helicopter skiing in the Bugaboo's in British Columbia with Brian Lea, an executive at one of our customers in New York City, Weedon and Co. The trip was the result of Brian telling me that I needed to take a vacation some time—as if I didn't take vacations? Brian became a lifelong friend of Pat's and mine. I would love to write about travels with Brian, but that would be another book. He was the "free spirit" of all my guy friends. With Brian I learned not to be totally "intent" 100 percent of the time. I miss him. Every time a butterfly flutters by close to me I wonder if it might be sent by Brian.

Several times during the 1970s, Pat and I worked in quite a bit of other travel together. In early March 1972, we made a trip with four other couples to the island of Cozumel off the coast of the Yucatan Peninsula, staying at a funky little hotel in the center of San Miguel de Cozumel, now greatly upgraded and called the Hotel Plaza Cozumel. At that time, Cozumel was pretty much undiscovered as a tourist destination except for scuba divers who wanted to dive the Palencar Reef. Dan Appleton was one of those. He gave me my first scuba lesson in a bar the night before my first dive. He followed me down the anchor cable eyeball to eyeball before deciding I had gotten the lesson.

We had great dives on the reef and great times exploring the island in search of "the lost lagoon" I had read about in an old library manuscript when preparing for the trip. The lagoon was reported to be a source of water for pirates. They would bring their ships into the coast, anchor, go ashore, climb over a large berm, and fill containers with fresh water out of the lagoon. We decided we would like to find it and snorkel in it, if possible, but at least swim.

We searched one whole day for the lagoon to no avail. We explored the northern part of the ocean side of the island and south from San Miguel but couldn't even find anyone who thought there was one—until during a conversation with a bartender that night who said he had heard about it and that the grubby-looking guy at the end of the bar knew about it and might take us there. With the help of the bartender to translate, the guy nodded his head that there was such a lagoon and that he could take us there for some amount of money that I can't recall.

Early the next day, we grabbed dive gear and proceeded in our two Volkswagen Jeep-like "things" south from San Miguel to a spot where our guide motioned to drive off the road and into the local version of a jungle. We drove along what appeared to be an old railroad track until the jungle overgrowth barred our further progress.

At that point, our guide motioned for us to follow him, and with his machete he headed into the jungle cutting a tunnel-like clearing with us following behind. Unfortunately, our guide was short, and his tunnel had a low ceiling. Anyhow, he led, we bent over and followed. After what seemed like a long time, he pointed, indicating that the lagoon was nearby in that direction. I climbed a tree enough to indeed see a body of water not far away. We proceeded to the lagoon. After some exploring, we decided not to try a dive or to go for a swim. It had taken a long time to get there, and we were sort of tired. We took our pictures, including one of me looking afar from my perch in the tree, and our memories—and reversed our path back to the bar. We paid and praised the guide for his knowledge and assistance.

In case one might wonder about the frequent mention of a bar, the so-called potable water in the area was known to be rich in "Montezuma's Revenge," so we drank beer to extend our bottled water—so to speak. I recall beer for breakfast. Seemed to go well with the egg, potato, and bacon tacos!

Some year after the Cozumel trip, we chartered a 70-foot sailboat with a name something like "The Thamila" to sail and dive in the Grenadines in the Caribbean. We were joined by two couples, my aforementioned scuba instructor and MRI customer friend, Dan Appleton and his then wife Nancy, and Jim Tillinghast and his then wife Kathy. Our boat owner and skipper, Serge, was a former officer in the French military who served in the branch where they were trained and prepared to function on land, on sea, and by parachuting in behind the lines. He had one very competent crew member to handle the galley and to assist with the sails. That "Second in Command" guy could create and serve gourmet dining out of a galley only as big as a twin bed. Again, that week could be the subject of a small book. The skipper had wry humor, great vigilance, a sense of theatre, and unquestioned competence. On one occasion, he performed a sailing maneuver that made those on nearby boats come to the bow, enthusiastically clap their hands, and wave. They knew of him. He was the legend.

Following those two trips, Pat and I chartered boats several years in the Virgin Islands. We chartered with Phil and Nancy Richards three times. Our last trip was in 1980 when we took Dave and Dana with us for a week. After scuba-diving book instruction during the late night flights

David

from Austin to San Juan, Puerto Rico, (and serious testing of what they learned), we gave Dave and Dana their water checkout the first day of the cruise. Dana decided to pass on anything further. Dave learned well enough to make his first dive with Phil and me on the wreck of the Rhone, about 120 feet below, his Mom and Dana waiting anxiously above. Later, he looked like a pro on a more challenging, though less depth, dive off Little Dog. The reef at Bitter End was so crowded we passed on a dive there and only had one more good dive before the week was history. I was sort of addicted to taking pictures of boats on each trip, so we have over a hundred picture slides of different sailboats underway and many at the anchorages where they anchored nights.

In 1969, we, Jim Tillinghast, and a soon-to-be MRI board member, Al Dale, went together to buy a 20-foot Cal 20 sailboat, which we named "The Trinity." Our spinnaker sail was beautiful. It was white and blue with the shades of blue graduated from dark at the top to less so at bottom with three large interlocking black rings to form the spiritual Trinity symbol. We three guys raced it, often together as crew, and sometimes with help from Dave. Two years in a row, we competed in the Governor's Cup Regatta around the 4th of July and won both times. I still recall some of the most thrilling moments (our brilliance and sailing skill, of course) in each race.

Our family belonged to the Austin Yacht Club. The facility at the club was quite nice for picnics, sometimes with friends as guests, sailing as a family, and after race occasions. The club had a nice pool that Pat and kids enjoyed often in the summer when I was racing weekends. Dave liked to sail, and when in college, we let him take the boat out with friends. On several occasions, Pat and I sailed late into the night with adult friends, sometimes with one playing a guitar and others singing. There are many stories to go with those occasions also—many stories!

The most memorable story started with a late-day picnic while Jim and I were recruiting a guy to join MRI. Right after it got dark, we heard some guys holler and the faint sounds of rocks scratching their hull as they ran their motor boat aground not far down the peninsula from us. The boat was owned by a club member we knew, and it was his son who was soon in deep trouble. However, that little crash was nothing like the big crash in that direction we heard an hour later. We heard the crash, and Jim Tillinghast and I were the first to reach the scene about 100 yards away. It was by then pitch black. We had flashlights. We shined them around. The first thing that I recall seeing was a whiskey bottle floating in the water near the shore.

There was a boat still in the water near the rocky shoreline. There were two bodies up the embankment on the shore and one at shore line. To make a gruesome story short, with Pat's triage help, we determined the woman on the bank was dead, her skull like a bumpy marshmallow. The guy nearby and the

131

one along the shore were moaning but unable to communicate. Jim had jumped in the lake and soon came up with the dead body of another woman.

The noise of the crash and the shouting of our group at the scene aroused a doctor and his wife who were staying the night in one of the club's little cabins. He came down about the time we knew the situation. He assessed the injuries and knowing how far we were from any kind of medical facility, he had us load the two injured males into the back of his station wagon, and he took off for town. We left the scene before authorities arrived, but as soon as I got home, I went to the office and dictated a complete recollection of the experience. That record was later used in litigation.

Several months later, I was doing some consulting work for a state agency. In the course of conversation with the project director for the agency, we somehow put two and two together. She knew one of the men and knew of the accident. He had survived. She later told me that all four were airline employees from Houston. The guys were out on the lake with women married to someone else, and all were drunk. When she later told him about meeting me, he sent back the message of a very grateful person.

One Sunday morning late November 1970, Rob became quite ill with obvious high fever and an aching hip. Our pediatrician was not available, but through our doctor neighbor, another doctor agreed to go to his office to look at Rob. Practically one feel of Rob's hip and a look at the data was enough for that doctor to say something like, "we need to get him over to Breckenridge immediately." We did, and they soon packed Rob in ice and extracted the bodily fluids they needed to send to the lab to be cultured and identified. He had a major infection in his hip. After

Rob in 1974, Age 8

several tough days, in particular for Pat, Rob was diagnosed with osteomyelitis from a somewhat rare bacterial infection in his hip bone. He was able to come home on Dec 3rd after 11 days in the hospital, but it took time for him to heal and again get around on his own. That was a very scary time for me.

Of course, Pat was just as concerned, but she seemed to me to be able to view the situation through professional eyes and conversations with the doctors and not feel as panicked as I was.

When we built our home in Pecan Park, we fenced a pasture and were able to buy Dana a horse—a long-held wish of hers since starting to ride and work with horses at the Double Creek Farm day camp near Round Rock. (Just one of the many places of kid activity where Pat provided the transportation.) I received horse-buying advice from Alfred King, and we started looking at the "horse for sale" ads in the paper. We finally bought a small horse named Cricket. Our neighbor, Frank Toussaint, had adjacent pasture and a horse named Dun Boy. We did not put a fence between the pastures, and Frank built an enclosed shelter, and we stowed the minimal gear and feed for Cricket in a shed attached to our garage. We purchased a large horse tank for the water.

Dana was then only 100 feet away from a horse to feed, groom, and ride. When we made trips, Frank looked after Cricket. The experience with Cricket ended with great sadness. She developed an intestinal blockage related to the fact that undisclosed to us, she had floundered (colic) before we bought her. The vet said that about all we could do was to keep her walking and see if her internals straightened out. We had been walking her for well over 24 hours when it became my turn late one night. At some point during our walk, Cricket stopped, looked at me with beseeching eyes, and fell over—dead. That was a sober life experience for us all.

Dana started gymnastics in her eighth grade and competed regularly as a member of the high school team. Except for an upper-back injury from a "bad landing" off the high bar and a badly sprained finger playing football, Dana managed to avoid more serious injury (until a bicycle accident in her mid-fifties). Dana worked one summer as a wait person/assistant manager in a Pizza Parlor. The summer before going off to college in 1978, Dana worked during the summer as a gymnastics counselor and van driver at the Double Creek Farm.

Dana in 1969, Age 9

Dave had a good year playing high school junior varsity basketball his sophomore year, a broken ankle that interfered with his junior year, and a lot of playing time his senior year. During high school, he worked a summer and part-time during the school year at the most popular Bar-B-Q restaurant in the area. He then worked one summer on a framing crew, followed by a summer selling books door to door in Kentucky (didn't meet expectations), before returning to be rehired onto the framing crew again. Dave had learned how to swing a hammer and use power tools working for my dad a couple summers in Idaho earlier in his high school years.

While Dave was still in high school, say the 1975-76 school year, Jim Tillinghast from MRI and I taught basics of computer programming one night a week for six weeks to Dave and three other kids. We made them pay for it with the proviso that they get their money back if they attended all sessions and passed our (easy) test at the end. Dave then later worked one summer at MRI/Intel working with the programmers there, a job he interviewed for without my help. Of course, he has gone on to a career in corporate Information Technology (IT) with Intel and Motorola. Two of the others we introduced to computers also followed computing system careers. All four were very sharp students.

At Rob's age during these years, 3-13, he was mostly interested in playing with friends, watching TV, and starting into Little League sports experience. He played baseball for several years, but after the Town and Country kid sports program started soccer, that became his favorite. He has enjoyed soccer (along with 2-person volleyball and some basketball) on into adulthood.

During the Carter presidential-term depression in 1974, we had an opportunity to buy a two-bedroom single-bath 1700-square-foot condo at Horseshoe Bend, about an hour's drive from our home. The condo was not "fancy" but was on a hill, had a beautiful view of LBJ lake, and attractive grounds that included a swimming pool and a tennis court. We also could use the main resort tennis courts, and Pat and I started playing tennis often and for the next 20 years. The kids made more use of the swimming pool. We enjoyed many weekend trips to the condo, sometimes with friends. One time Pat's brother, Dean the doctor, flew his plane in to the Horseshoe Bay airport (FBO) less than a half-mile away.

Of course, the above represents a small part of ten years, but years are only a measure of ... years. There was much more our family will remember. Pat and I remember the experiences in New York City while we stayed in the company apartment overlooking Lincoln Center, the two times we trod the grounds at the Breakers Hotel in West Palm Beach, played tennis on the courts there and at The Broadmoor in Colorado Springs, a memorable meeting at the Homestead in Virginia, and dining on the bay in San Francisco—as well as the dining tables at meetings of industry organizations in many other nice places.

We recall the beginning and many fine subsequent affairs of the local International Wine and Food Society and our friend and local wine guru, Bob Lowe—where Pat and I started on the journey of enjoying wine. (Bob Lowe was my idea of the Renaissance man—broadly educated, creative, with flair, asking the deep questions, and was a special spiritual brother. I miss him.) In general during my travels, including business trips to Europe, my business activity provided me a lot of educational exposure to sights and personalities. I remember serving awhile on the Board of the local Boys Clubs of America when Don Kromer was the Exec in Austin. The kids probably recall the house parents while Pat and I traveled.

Dave and Dana remember when they accompanied me at different times on business trips to New York City in the mid-1970s. Dave probably remembers Bette Midler and the Broadway show *Grease*, while Dana remembers the Ballet and Symphony in Lincoln Center across from our company apartment at One Lincoln Center. Each of them remembers New York City as an environment quite different from Round Rock and Austin Texas! Those are trips I still recall vividly with pleasure, and I would guess that they do also. Rob's trip to New York City was years later in 1984, and both Pat and I had the pleasure of showing him more art than he ever wished to see but also a baseball game at the Yankee Stadium in the Bronx, a Broadway show, the Barnum and Bailey Brothers Circus in Madison Square Garden, and a boat trip around Manhattan. Dave and Dana probably also recall when they got their first driver's license and when they headed off to college. They will also probably remember their first kiss from a date and all that goes with being teenagers. For sure, Rob remembers when Dana left for college, and he was then the local recipient of more immediate parental love and attention.

In addition to the above, I recall the 1970s as when I began my quest to understand what I naively called the physics of reality—where reality had to include the credible evidence of parapsychological (psi) phenomena I had been learning about since the late 1960s. I viewed parapsychology as the scientific and scholarly study of certain unusual events associated with human experience. (The scope of parapsychology does not include, or even refer to, subjects like astrology, UFOs, witchcraft, paganism, pseudoscience, etc., no matter that they are generally viewed as not normal.) I thought then, and still do, that understanding bonafide parapsychology has implications for what is generally considered a spiritual nature of mankind, but there is no hidden agenda when engaged in sound research, so evidence of the paranormal proved nothing then.

For a long time I just cruised along on my prior education in physics and focused new thinking on the depth and scope of the paranormal—**Telepathy** (the transmission of information from one person to another without using any of our known sensory channels or physical interaction), **Precognition** (perception involving the acquisition or effect of future information that cannot be deduced from presently available and normally acquired sense-based information), **Presentiment** (a form of precognition creating an emotional response before the stimuli is perceived), **Psychokinesis** (the ability to influence the movement of matter or energy through mental processes— sometimes referred to as "mind over matter"), **Clairvoyance** (seeing objects or actions removed in space or time from natural viewing—nowadays most often referred to as "**Remote Viewing**"), and variations thereof, etc. I devoted a lot of time to reading that would help me to weed out the wheat from the chaff.

Such phenomena were then inexplicable by science—but I became convinced from reading and personal experience that they were probably real. The question for me was: What would bring physics and the paranormal closer together? And I really didn't have enough time or recall enough physics to do other than "wonder about it."

During those years, I did sign up for a study related to some sort of "psi". I still have a piece of paper somewhere that says I scored 75% on a certain test compared to a chance threshold at 50%. I recall it was a test where the administrator gave me a word, and I was to report the first word that came to mind. I called it intuition. About the same time, I recall reading study results that reported that in similar tests, administered to senior executives and those with less responsibility, the executives scored higher on intuition. For many years, I wondered a lot about where intuition came from, until I found an answer acceptable to me later in life.

I joined a couple parapsychological organizations and often spent hours late into the night reading related journals and books. One of the groups I associated with met every few weeks for the leader to talk about various kinds of paranormal phenomena. Meetings included a group experience attempting to "go to alpha" and actually experience an "impression" related to the exercise of that evening. The "alpha state" is a simple kind of meditative state designed to produce brain waves (neural oscillations) in the frequency range of 8–12 Hz which result from synchronous and coherent electrical activity in a certain bunch of neurons in a part of the brain. To get there, one must relax and quit thinking and then impressions can just "pop up." People are easily trained to "go to alpha." That state is also achieved early in any meditation technique.

Pat and Fran and Larry Collmann participated in the group also with Pat and Larry less than enthusiastic about it. Fran and I usually worked together for the two-person exercises. More often than not, I seemed to "pick up on" whatever was the object of the exercise. It was borderline disturbing to me at the time. I recall staying awake late into the night wondering what the heck was going on. After an experiment where I was able to describe a very unusual feature of a target person in another state, I realized that we could not in this simple kind of exercise differentiate one form of psi from another. For instance, I am convinced that I was experiencing a very elementary form of psi called Telepathy.

I think I was just picking up the information from the person in the group who had suggested that exercise and who, of course, knew the target. I do not think I was experiencing what later became to be called Remote Viewing. I learned later that what we tried to do in the exercises was being demonstrated in laboratories with research protocols providing highly controlled conditions so that one form of psi could be studied independent of confusion with another. (Of course, later in life I came to believe that all such phenomena are really just different aspects of the same fundamental characteristic of reality.)

As a member of the American Society for Psychical Research, I received their journal called *Proceedings of the A.S.P.R.* In Volume 31, February 1974, Ian Stevenson, M.D., published an article titled "Xenoglossy: A Review and Report of a Case." I learned that Xenoglossy was a technical term referring to a particular kind of evidence for the existence of something most often called reincarnation. (Stevenson did not claim the evidence confirmed something that specific.) The detail and results he reported seemed credible to me, so there was something else that I wondered a lot about—much more than I had after reading about Edgar Cayce.

I read many other books and papers devoted to forms of paranormal evidence. In particular and most significantly, I read the many books channeled by Jane Roberts with material from a nonphysical personality named Seth. (I have included background information related to Seth and channeling in general in Chapter 16.) It was content from Seth related to phenomena, generally considered the domain of physics, that stirred me to start thinking about all that had been added to mainstream physics since my college days. In particular, it was the 1977 two-volume Seth book, *The Unknown Reality*, that really sped up my neurons. It was later on into the 1980s that the physics research work of Bell and Aspect significantly expanded the foundations of physics to bring physics closer to the paranormal, but my quest had started in that direction during the 1970s.

By the end of the 1970s, I was well down a trail in my metaphysics journey that intersected nicely with quantum physics in future years. I began to have new thoughts about reincarnation and about troublesome issues trying to relate the time and space commitment within physics to possibly more encompassing views of reality. I learned the meaning of the word "ontology."

But while the family and I were growing up together in the 1970s, I was also slowly growing up a bit in business experience. One can read a lot between the lines of the IEEE history article about MRI, but I will add here a couple of things I would like to mention that also belong between those lines.

First, the way I now view the importance regarding the "culture" of an organization. I think culture is one of the most important matters that management should pay attention to and is responsible for—whether within a small or large organization. As Peter Drucker famously said, "the culture eats strategy for breakfast."

Good men will argue that point, but that is my firm stand. I think those of us who worked at MRI collectively evolved a culture working with many of my own views, but I know I learned from the views of others. We did not just take something out of a book—although I read a book or two about organization theory. Obviously, the nature of a culture and how it got that way and stays that way is too complex for this record, but I can't help but share my belief that we got the "culture thing" right at MRI.

First and foremost, I tried hard to make clear that I expected those with management or supervisory responsibilities to work for those that reported to them, rather than the other way around. I think it helped that managers were required to conduct performance reviews annually with subordinates. Both had to sign off on the content of the review that would go in the files and to note the detail if there was any form of difference in any aspect of the review.

At MRI it was also the responsibility of those in management positions to see that those that reported to them knew well what they were supposed to do as part of the bigger effort, were capable or trained enough to do it, and had the resources required to support their effort. I eventually learned that when plans were due, they were to speak to results, not activity! We learned that from our friend and guru, John Narciso, then a dean at Trinity University. One of John's

138

messages was that "what do we want to happen" was a really good frame of reference for communicating—at home as well as at work. We called that "being operational" and that talking in terms of activity is a poor substitute. And I think most of us understood that we were dependent on each other—top to bottom of the salary structure!

I believe I knew each of the first couple hundred employees well and sometimes even their families. I made a point to spend time out of my office "walking the halls" to visit with employees with the understanding that any kind of question from them was acceptable. I made it clear in many ways, some quite overt some rather subtle, what I wanted to see as the "culture" that gave us common cause. All of us at MRI worked hard by any reasonable standard. There were usually a number of cars in the parking lot late into the night and on Saturdays; however, long hours were an employee's choice, not a requirement. Sure, those who worked long hours usually accomplished more, learned more, and were able to take on additional responsibility with commensurate compensation more often than those who could not or chose not. Women were encouraged to work toward management responsibility and knew that they could do that while still picking the kids up after school if they worked hard 40 hours per week. Everyone knew how I felt about one aspect of culture by just reading the sign above my desk:

> Do Something
> LEAD, FOLLOW, or
> Get out of the way!

I learned that once there became a critical mass of a "fair" culture, with a little monitoring and tweaking now and then, employees would generally desire and do things to keep it that way. New hires were selected with that in mind. Anyone, new or old, who strayed from the unwritten behavioral rules were likely to hear about it from another employee they worked with.

I think it was also well understood within the culture that "rules come into being as the consequence of abuse of privilege." Because many, if not all, of the technical personnel had an intrinsic disdain for rules, they could be counted on to lead by example. After Intel acquired MRI, they introduced many "big company rules." In particular, they required employees to sign in by some unreasonable hour each workday—8 a.m. It didn't take long to see noticeably fewer cars in the parking lot evenings and Saturdays. However, I think it continued to be true that the most notable exception was my car!

Speaking of "new hires" (I just did), back in the MSA days I was introduced to a lady in New York City who was verifiably accurate at hand-writing analysis. Her name was Sara, and I affectionately called her "Madam Sara." Alfred and I had her analyze our handwriting and that of my secretary to see if we thought that Sara was accurate. There were a few laughs, but on balance, we were amazed and impressed. We tried a few others experimentally, and I shortly thereafter required applicants to write a short essay while waiting to see someone for an interview. Of course, an applicant wasn't able to type in our lobby area, so it was handwritten. We quickly sent it off to Sara, and along with other important factors, the results became one part of what was considered during a hiring decision. I later came to believe Madam Sara was psychic and maybe the analytic part of analysis was secondary.

I learned along the way at MRI that as the size of the organization grew the policy manual must grow with it. However, my view was that a policy manual supports a culture—it is not one. And I could go on. Some of the things I have mentioned are probably reasons we all really liked to work together, but undoubtedly there was much more. Whatever it was, when we had a well-attended reunion ten years after the company was acquired by Intel, it was a love-in. All evening one heard over and over again the expressions of how much we had liked working together at MRI.

In my opinion, given our inexperience and the difficulty of what we were attempting to accomplish, MRI would not have survived and been as successful as we were if the MRI culture had not been so well established and accepted.

One of the most sobering experiences for me during my MRI tenure was an aborted merger plan. I am convinced that it is a good thing it was aborted, but I was deeply discouraged by many aspects along the way. In my opinion, a key person financing the other company in the process turned out to be a thin reed. He was blustering instead of thoughtful, his judgment was poor, and many of his assumptions about how things could be brought to fruition were in his favor and were clearly indicative of his poor ability to judge the facts independent of his personal bias. We entered into merger discussions believing he would be adding great experience to the prospects of the merged entity. We learned otherwise and eventually believed his desire to micro-manage would be a path backward.

There may have been a little justice of a kind in the situation when, after we refused to agree to late-in-the-deal demands, the people in the other organization that he chose to champion ended up ineffective in part as a result of his influence. It is my belief that, if their financial backer had not killed the plan, they would have achieved their potential with the expertise and operating experience MRI would have brought to the merger. Not only did the intended merger partner fail as a company, the people the financial guy chose to support, failed to protect the ownership of work product his investment paid for. His senior management permitted others to essentially steal from the company potentially valuable work product that he thought he was to acquire. It was one of the two times I recall when someone mistook our lack of experience as lack of intelligence.

The second experience of that kind was when a person more experienced in many ways in our kind of business thought he could take over management of the company. It was actually humorous. He approached MRI, praised what we were accomplishing, and described how his greater experience could help. We put his talent and experience to work and received benefit. Based on his helpful performance, we made him an officer and gave him additional responsibility and compensation. Being a small company and as an officer, he came in personal contact with Alfred King and represented himself well in those instances. Because of his broader experience, we added him to the board of directors.

Soon thereafter, he approached Alfred with the suggestion that he replace me as president—a plan we think he had from the git-go. That is when it really turned humorous. He failed to realize that there were also other qualities important to Alfred than just experience and business acumen. There were personal qualities Alfred believed to be more important. Alfred and I discussed the turn of events, and soon the three of us were walking together across a street while on business together in Washington, DC. Alfred turned to him and said something like, "The jig's up, and we have no further need for your services."

At some time during those years of dealing with men in the business environment, I came to hold the view I continue to hold today. It seems to me like there are some evolutionary traits of males that might be more counter-productive than helpful in business and life more generally in this era. In particular, and to exaggerate, over the years I have grown to believe that being a brute is no longer a drum to march by. It seems to me that in this era, to pick one word, "negotiation" should be the style of living rather than behavioral strategies to try to always get one's way in order to "look good" in the manner of "the brute." It seems to me that successful teamwork is best supported by a style of low-key negotiation of ideas to pick leadership when leadership is important. Battering the timid may work in some organizational environments, but who expects basically insecure fearful people to get a job done?

It bothered me every time I encountered an up-and-coming business guy who manifested the belief that the way to rise was to push the other guy down. To them, winning in the halls of business seemed so important that it did not matter how it was achieved. That seemed to me to have been particularly prevalent during the time when things were good—good economy, growth opportunities—and a shortage of people to manage within the growing organizations. But then in the 1970s, the stuff hit the fan to make business more challenging.

It seemed to me that was when more fundamental qualifications for success came to the fore. Mutual support, cooperation, and back to the basics of effectiveness became winning qualifications—and not tactical maneuvering. Other things equal, I thought I saw evidence that the brutes were the first to go when a reduction in force became necessary throughout many businesses in the United States during the early to mid-1970s. There was still work to be done, but those with qualities to work together seemed to become more valued.

Of course, there are many memories from the MRI years that are more "in passing" than a topic for the above kind of attention. Before going on to the buyout of MRI by Intel, here are some memories that come to mind.

Thanks to a very talented person, Barbara Wiggins, who managed advertising and public relations in the mid-1970s, we began to get good industry press coverage. Often that coverage was just as beneficial in pumping up the psyche within MRI as it was to influence the marketplace. A good example was when PR

MRI's 10,000th Student

was generated by making a big deal recognizing the person we believed to be the 10,000[th] person trained to be able to use our SYSTEM 2000 products. We managed to get this picture into quite a bit of the media communicating to our marketplace.

One year, the US Dept. of Commerce organized a conference in Washington to provide US companies to describe what they had for sale or to offer to a partner and for those from Japan to describe what was of interest to them. Through church, I had met Scott Baird who had taught English in Japan for several years. He was a neat guy and of limited financial means. I paid him to join me at that conference. I presented MRI in the first morning and indicated that we had interest in knowing more about our business potential in Japan and whom to partner with. I explained why we thought there was opportunity and that we could provide the technology to exploit it. While in the men's room at a break in the sessions later that morning, Scott told me the Japanese delegation was more interested in business intelligence than in establishing business deals. After some discussion, he made his case. We went home.

A few years later, after we and our software products were better known, we sent someone to Japan to meet with a few organizations we thought we might want to partner with. (One was headed by a very competent and successful woman known within the computer industry there as "The Dragon Lady.") Shortly thereafter, a group from the Japanese government and a few business firms came to visit us with interest to indeed, do business. I again asked Scott to join in the sessions.

We quickly noticed that the older men did not understand English and depended on the younger men to translate for them. (Of course, we did not speak Japanese—except for Scott—and we chose not to disclose that he could.) At a break, I took Scott aside and asked how we were doing. He said that our informal style and presentations by several executives confused them in the following sense. They could not tell who was the senior person—me! When we reconvened, we rearranged our chairs and after a few "leadership" remarks from me, we heard murmurs of "ah so," "ah so."

MRI became the first software company to join the Computer and Communications Industry Association (CCIA). I chose to join it rather than the ADAPSO organization of software companies. The CCIA membership companies were required to be represented by their CEOs. Of course, I represented a very small company, which was also the only software company. The other companies were typically much more established in the marketplace, much larger, and represented by CEOs with much more experience. The meetings included many relevant presentations and a lot of opportunity for attendees to get acquainted and discuss common interests. I learned a lot from others, and I think they may have learned a little something from me and our senior technology guy, Gene Lowenthal, who gave presentations a couple of times.

At the time, software/firmware was finally being recognized as a critical technological capability for hardware companies to remain competitive in the marketplace. The hardware executives not only knew little about software, but deep down they were aware of that and were up-tight about how to handle it. Relying on their existing business model, software appeared to them as an expense that did not earn revenue and profit like hardware. It seemed to me that they were more comfortable talking to me and Gene about the situation and how to deal with it than with their own employees.

It was my participation in the CCIA which led to my being an expert witness in the government antitrust case against IBM because our Board of Directors believed it was a "corporate duty." I wish we hadn't agreed to that, but once involved, the government wouldn't let me withdraw. Testimony before Judge Edelstein in the 2nd District of New York was quite an experience. Our MRI attorney (board member and dear friend, Howell Finch) and I got along better with the Judge than did the legal counsel for IBM. The discovery phase had been quite a challenge for us at MRI, but we had a little fun forcing IBM attorneys to copy a bunch of nonsense—like reams and reams of hexadecimal printouts of unimportant machine-language code. We also maneuvered the discovery process to require IBM to forever inform us of the change in employment title and duties of anyone who had ever looked at any of the MRI discovery material, some highly proprietary and confidential, that they had received from us. We received such notices for years thereafter.

I met Mike Faherty as a result of my participation in the CCIA. Mike had a career in accounting and finance and was the chief financial officer at Datapoint Corporation, a successful company, which at that time made programmable data entry and communications workstation products. I first met Mike at a meeting called to discuss proposed financial accounting principles that would apply to software companies. He was the one I thought had contributed the most to the morning meeting, so when it was time for lunch, I picked him out to sit with. I subsequently got acquainted enough with Mike to ask him to do a review of our management processes at MRI and report directly to the Board of Directors. We all thought his review was well conducted and helpful. As will be set forth in due time, Mike and I in later years became partners in a significant business venture.

144

He and his wife Pat have been close friends and traveling companions of ours for over 35 years.

In 1978, President Carter requested that the CCIA provide some experts to meet with his staff in the White House to listen to a presentation about some processing of information they thought might be subject to computerization and then offer advice. I was part of that group, and it was another time I was impressed by Mike Faherty. In the discussion, "Mike the CFO" contributed like a sales executive, and Datapoint workstations were eventually acquired by the White House. As our group left the White House, we and everyone else in the area were witness to President Carter saying goodbye to Menachem Begin—surrounded by the discreetly armed athletic young Secret Service agents and helicopters hovering above. Impressive show in my view, and I tried to sort of "inhale" the moment—the closest I ever expect to be to the Commander in Chief.

After the first MRI shareholder meeting following the initial outside money invested in our company, the technical staff revolted. They viewed the situation as one where they do all the work and create all of value, but financial gain would go to those investors who did neither. After that, I tried year after year to make sure all employees had an adequate understanding of the many factors that influence the growth and success of a company—and the connection to the financial statement!

I learned a lesson in doing business internationally with a transaction in Spain. We had success in a major sale there. We were desperately in need of funds to meet payroll (a common occurrence), so I requested the check be expedited. I was soon informed that the payment in pesetas (not euros then) could not be sent out of the country without the approval of the Finance Minister. For reasons I have forgotten, we were told that there would be some considerable amount of red tape to make that happen. We scraped by with payroll some other way, and I continued to work the problem of getting paid from Spain. We were experiencing a problem where we could not determine what the problem was! About that same time, one of our large customers was embarking on a major project in Spain and would be paying for work there in pesetas. I quickly sold them pesetas in Spain for dollars in the US. The lesson was, before doing the work or expecting to get paid for the sale, check to see if the funds can be taken from the country!

One can say that travel to foreign countries is a desired side benefit of being in business there—and I would agree. Although the trips usually involved very little time for being a tourist (less than four hours passing through Paris for a business meeting my first time there), I did travel for business reasons in several countries, including Spain, France, England, Sweden, Canada, and Mexico. We did business in Australia, but I didn't travel there. I did let a valued employee, who was an avid scuba diver take care of business there on one occasion so he could stopover on the return flight to dive in Tahiti.

I learned that sometimes there are conditions beyond one's control that prevent payment by a customer. One time when we again desperately needed to receive payment for a sale we had made to Univac, I was told the paperwork was complete and the check would be sent the following day. That night some anti-war activists burned down the building where accounting had the paperwork, and we had to start a lot of paperwork again—from scratch!

There were many other unusual situations over the years, but I won't burden this story by recounting but a few: the details of helping a bright young son of a business acquaintance avoid the draft in Holland by coming to work for us in the United States; the story of cooperation on a couple of occasions with our government CIA beyond normal debriefing after foreign travel; why and how I met in his chambers with Justice of the US Supreme Court Warren; what management should do and not do when an employee is selling illicit drugs on premises to other employees; and what can happen when phone service after working hours is made available to employees for free long-distance calls (then called a WATS Line), etc.

Many of the people who made noteworthy contributions to the survival and success of MRI are mentioned in the IEEE historical account. They were primarily the officers who managed the basic business units of the company. The editors did not permit the additional content to express appreciation relating to the MRI troops in the hallowed halls of buildings 1, 2, and 3 in Austin and on the front lines elsewhere nor express appreciation to those from customer organizations who were helpful beyond what might be expected. There were many, and several have been close friends of mine in the years since. I recall with gratitude many we worked with on the other side of the business table, but my experience with co-workers at MRI is the most cherished of memories from those years.

What was not appropriate to recount in the IEEE history article is how I felt personally about my work experience between the Intel acquisition of MRI and when I resigned from Intel. Here it is.

From the time the acquisition was finalized at the end of August 1978, I steadily encountered one disappointment after another. The single source from which all else followed was the decision by Intel senior management that I would report to Bill McCalmont. Bill had been hired by Intel senior management (who I otherwise greatly admired) to head up a new systems business for the company. Intel had grown as a semiconductor-parts company but wished to evolve upward in product integration. I did not understand why they thought he was qualified then, and I still don't. They fired him not long after I left Intel. He later tried to get hired by Storage Technology Corporation (STC) while I was on the Board of Directors—a fact that I guess was unknown to him. I gave the STC CEO a briefing, and McCalmont was not considered further.

But back at MRI/Intel, I consider myself collateral damage related to Intel's well-intended decision to have me report to him. Yes, there had been some very positive experiences for me since the acquisition but not enough to outweigh the dis-ease that I had picked up from McCalmont. Prior to the formal closing of the acquisition and before he showed up on the scene, I had participated in the process Intel used to develop five-year plans. Our MRI subsidiary-management team worked hard to prepare our plan without much involvement from Intel. When our turn came, we presented it. The SYSTEM 2000 DBMS product business was presented with considerable growth potential beyond the then $10-$12 million ($36-$44 mil in 2014) annual revenue.

Also presented, and the part of greatest interest to Intel management, was the plan for development of the product that had brought MRI and Intel together in the first place—a specialized database-management computer. When that plan was presented, it was interesting to me to observe qualitative differences in the questions and discussion that followed. When MRI was acquired, there were several in Intel senior management who knew essentially nothing about the Austin operation, other than what was included in the news release.

Intel executives were generally very bright and had a lot of business experience—but it was not experience that gave them much of a handle on the depth and breadth of a "systems" business, let alone "mainframe software." They were used to rapid product obsolescence and development cycles of six months—with little and simple software. The planning, development, and deployment of a major system product took years, and with maintenance process totally funded by customer revenue, the resulting product often remained productively in use for many years. System product lifetimes of about five years were common. SYSTEM 2000 even continues in use today, about forty years after the first modules went to market.

147

Even with some difficulties communicating, I think we helped senior Intel management develop headspace for the work that lay ahead as they all nodded their heads as to why they needed to learn what we had to offer. We were acquired to help them get into a higher level of integration of computing functions—a systems product-line strategy to accompany their core business. I felt good about trying to help Intel in that way, and I gained business experience by participating in their planning process.

I also learned a lot by being invited to participate in the senior management enrichment programs at Intel. It seemed like I was often in the same small break-out group with the Intel Chairman of the Board, Bob Noyce. Although I had met him and visited on several occasions previously, I got to know him up close and personal—to engage in thought and expression while discussing significant questions—and I grew to respect and like him even more. One month before my misery came to a head, Noyce had flown his plane into Austin accompanied by Art Rock (an icon of investing in Silicon Valley and an Intel board member) to visit with Alfred and me. We had a delightful evening of conversation at the Headliners Club overlooking the Texas State Capitol building.

However, the brighter part of the picture was receding into the past as the darker side came to dominate in the form of Bill McCalmont. I guess I can simplify the problem a little and just summarize it by saying that Bill wanted me to be responsible for something his micro-management would not let me be responsible for. My view of the relevant management guideline was then, and still is, summarized by a principle of Responsibility, Authority, and Accountability (RAA). His modus operandi did not include the authority. And in particular, I had no authority to select and hire the people to be added to execute the new product-marketing plans. I have no idea as to whether Bill was just trying to get rid of me or was just incompetent. If I had to guess, I would guess the latter. He would come to Austin for meetings and spend the evening before our working session holed up in his hotel room reading books about great men of history rather than spend time getting better acquainted with the MRI team and noodling some issues together.

Week after week I felt more and more as if I were hitting my head against a brick wall. I finally came to a thought I hadn't considered once in all the tough times as MRI struggled to stay alive and succeed—I could quit!

That thought came to me one weekend as I was sitting alone in a lawn chair out back pondering my situation. It was like a lightning bolt. I reacted as if it was. Then, as I gradually settled down, it occurred to me that I should examine the thought rather than shunt it aside. By Monday, I had decided to request senior Intel management to accept my resignation.

My demeanor dramatically changed. It felt like a ball and chain had been removed. I am sure I was much more excited about what unknowns lay ahead for me and our family than was Christopher Columbus. I could take my deeply embedded caring about the future of MRI with me—my caring didn't have to go away just because I did. (However, I well knew that I would have to stay strictly away from the operation and people for quite some time so as not to be thought of in any way as interfering with the conduct of business in Austin.)

Although I had been given options on a large number of Intel shares as part of the terms of the acquisition, I had decided that I was (surprisingly) quite willing to give up considerable monetary gain rather than endure another six months trying to improve my situation. My resignation request was accepted after I talked by phone with Gordon Moore, the then CEO of Intel, who was another person I greatly admired. On the Friday following my request, Friday the 13th of July 1979, and after briefing key people in the organization, I sent out a memo to announce my resignation. I did not trash McCalmont, but I did say that our relationship was like a square peg in a round hole.

Other than to report that my resignation was received in total disbelief at first, there are only three touching moments I would like to mention. A few hours after the release of the memo, my secretary came to me with a very unusual expression on her face and said someone wanted to see me. She obviously had decided that needed to happen. I invited him in. She closed the door. Ben just sat there, not saying a word, until finally saying, "My father died on Friday the 13th." Many years later, Ben sent me a copy of *The Man Behind the Microchip: Robert Noyce and the Invention of Silicon Valley* (the biography of Bob Noyce) with a very nice note inscribed on the first page.

The other two especially touching moments were a personal note from Bob Noyce and a memo to all MRI employees from Gene Lowenthal, one of the earliest technical gurus to join MRI, and a dear friend. Gene was our R&D vice president and although his PhD was in computing, his written composition was better than any English major in the company. Gene reflected in a very insightful way on our years together growing MRI and included some words quite favorable to me. Noyce wrote something that indicated that we understood each other well.

So back to metaphysics for a moment. I believed then, and I do now, that our beliefs create our reality. Early on, that was just an opinion derived from reading the Seth books and watching and reading about human behavior. Over the years, I also learned why that view is supported by some notions from quantum physics and credible evidence from research relating to the so-called paranormal phenomena. Accepting that our beliefs create our own reality raises the question, "What beliefs may I have held deep down in my psyche to bring the MRI chapter of my life to an end?" There were obviously many and certainly more than I am aware of. However, more than any other, I believed that Alfred should be repaid so his $2 mil loan to the company was no longer at risk. I believed that I had a great personal responsibility to make that happen. I strongly believed that what he had done just had to turn out well. Once there appeared to be a distinct possibility that could indeed happen via the acquisition interest of Intel, the die was cast.

I also believed then, and still do, that life experiences provide the feedback we can think about to really learn a lot of important things about ourselves and the world. In particular, life experiences are what help us evolve the values that define the morality and perspective that we carry into our thoughts and behavior every new day. In that light, I wonder if I subconsciously believed that I needed opportunity to encounter new forms of responsibility and to experience new cannon fodder for personal development. Or as Pat says—she sees that in me every year; maybe I just had a delayed "spring fever" that year. Maybe I just believed more than I realized that I wanted to offer more time to Pat and the kids. Maybe all of these and more. A great deal of effort is required to unearth the core of our personal beliefs that determine our behavior and resulting experience. The passage of time, as we think of "time," makes it even more difficult.

Many who knew me in the 1970s at MRI and know me now probably believe MRI was the major defining experience of my life. I know otherwise. MRI was a great developmental experience for me—that also created meaningful developmental experience for many others. However, in retrospect, for me it was more accurately just a highly creative part of a much larger picture. I love the memories. I love the many people who came into my life then. And I feel quite a bit of satisfaction that, by overcoming my weaknesses and lack of business knowledge, I helped to accomplish something noteworthy that was highly challenging and highly enough successful. However, it was time to move on.

A Thought or Two Looking Back from Now

The MRI years of my life provided an abundance of valuable business experience rarely available to people my age at the time. Looking back, however, I wonder if it left me a little too "cocky"—believing more favorably about my executive qualities than was warranted. There were a couple experiences in the immediately subsequent years that clearly indicated I was still a little immature in my self-assessment. I thought I had more business savvy than some of my subsequent behavior indicated. However, I do think I worked through most of that over the next decade.

The IEEE history article and what I have recorded in this chapter seem pretty self-explanatory as reflecting my thoughts about MRI. The special, and quite unrelated from MRI experience, was the introduction to the Seth material during those same years. The awakening that led to my later thinking and beliefs about a greater reality had grown some roots from the thought-provoking experience of reading those books. In looking back, it is clear that I found something in those books that helped me to be open to new thoughts and generally more inquiring as I pursued my quest.

My last memory looking back during these years is the sheer terror I experienced when sliding down a snowbank headed for what my brain sensed as certain death. I now believe there was a reason it didn't happen.

➤ **11** ⤫

On to the Unknown

As has been noted, the switch from a day-by-day focus on MRI and family changed quickly to being unemployed and family. I had no going-forward plan. Nary a thought about what I would do when I grew up! Two things came to mind right away: try to put the family at ease with the situation and to build a nice office and swimming pool addition to our home. But it was August, so the first, first thing was for us to load up Rob and head for Idaho for some R&R before he had to be back for school. Dave and Dana were both in college, employed for the summer, and could be trusted to take care of themselves without turning our home into the local party house.

As it turned out, the decade of the 1980s, my age 45-55 years, was for us the epitome of work hard, play hard. It was the most worldly "experience rich" period of my life. In addition to providing Pat and me more time to "play" and travel, I experienced much less of a burden or responsibility. I didn't say "no" responsibility, just less, and of a qualitative different form. During the decade, I performed serious work helping others to run small companies, evaluating business plans for at least four hundred companies seeking venture capital, providing a variety of consulting services for several different companies, and by serving on corporate boards, two of which were public companies.

Before I try to summarize the decade as such, I want to share two more aspects of my being unemployed. First, we had some Intel stock we could sell or borrow against to put food on the table and cover other living expenses. Secondly, I still had this void to fill—what am I going to do? I decided on the 3x5-card plan. I would just follow my nose for a while and record all the thoughts regarding the nature of future work on a card in my pocket, and when I quit adding to the list of possibilities, I would go back and seriously consider each. It took well over a year but the plan worked.

We traveled some, I did some consulting, and I invested in a couple of start-up ventures. While wandering around doing those things, my 3x5 list grew. The ones I recall on the list included going to law school, going into full-time teaching or the ministry, join the CIA, find a niche in venture-capital investing, or even (perish the thought) to seek an executive position in a large company. In the process of examining the ideas one by one, I at least discovered what I considered important to me no matter what I decided. There were three things. I wanted to be compensated. I did not want my compensation to be based on a time clock of hours or months worked; I wanted it based on the results I generated. And finally, and most importantly, I wanted

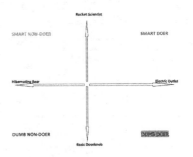

RATE YOURSELF

Performance Review Aid

to be able to pick with whom I worked—whether boss, colleague, partner, or work-team members. And certainly, I did not want to spend time with the lower right quadrant (dumb doer) of the performance review aid (pictured above) I liked to discuss when interviewing those wishing to join MRI. As it turned out, I ended up satisfying all three criteria until the day I retired at age 71 from working obligations to others.

Before summarizing some of that "rich experience" during the decade, I will describe in more detail one of the most unique of those experiences—venture-capital investing. In the 1990s, I found great satisfaction mentoring the management teams of young companies. A lot of what I learned in this early 1980s venture-investment partnership with Mike Faherty served me well as a mentor and board member in those later years.

Sometime during the first year of unemployment, I visited with Mike. Our conversations uncovered several things we each felt important, and neither of us were tied to other commitments at the time. We ended up discussing the fact that the Southwest was growing as a technology center with many start-up ventures but little venture capital at that time. (It has a lot now.) We each knew people in a few "blue-chip" venture-capital partnerships investing in other parts of the country. We talked to them about partnering with us where they would provide the funds as limited partners, and we would do the hard part by making initial investments in raw start-ups. We would attempt to get the entrepreneurs far enough along to have a good business plan and many of the start-up risks behind them and then sort of hand them off to our limited partners to provide further investment and nurturing.

We bounced the concept and our role in it off those we would most desire to partner with. Our four favorites bought in to the idea. We formed Business Development Associates (the two of us) and a partnership where we would be the General Partners and our four limited partners would fund the venture. We called that partnership Business Development Partners (BDP). (How novel.) Although there was much more to the relationship, we would invest, assist those we invested in, and monitor the early stage growth of our portfolio companies. Hopefully, at some point when our partners made investments to continue growth in those meriting further investment, we would distribute the ownership—most to our limited partners but with Mike and me to get a percentage as a return on our effort.

Our limited partners were all in the top ten of venture-capital firms in the country: Rothschild, Brentwood, Hambrecht and Quist, and Norwest. We worked together quite well, but Mike and I eventually found a flaw in our idea. The way typical venture-capital firms work, one partner "champions" each new addition to their portfolio. When it became time for us to "hand off" the most successful of our own portfolio, we found a shortage of willing champions. Our partner's lead investor partners, the potential "champions," desired to invest in and nurture companies they were already working with rather than devote time and effort enough to be confident that Mike and I had done our job well enough for them to pick up where we left off. We invested the first round of money provided by our limited partners, and a little more in some special investments, but did not continue the original concept further other than to follow through with helping our own portfolio investments. Overall, our return on our effort with those funds was quite respectable for both our limited partners and us, but we closed BDP down, and I refocused to other endeavors going on at the time. I am quite sure that no other portfolio company start-up we invested in became more famous and successful than Orbital Sciences—whose space business has by now even taken their rockets to the International Space Station.

We let BDP slide into history as the need to devote time to portfolio companies came to an end. However, we passed the venture-investing passion on to our noble assistant, Jack Biddle. Mike and I knew his father well and liked him as a class guy. He asked us to consider Jack when he graduated from U of Virginia, and we knew he wouldn't do that unless his son was sort of a chip off the old block that we liked so well, and he thought it would be good for both Jack and us.

I interviewed Jack and liked a lot of what I saw—his strong desire in particular—but we had a discussion about the significance of "attitudes" and how here out West things were a little different than the East Coast where he was raised in his formative years. With that topic as something for him to think about, Mike and I agreed to offer him a low-paying job to replace my secretary; he accepted, worked hard, and did so with no arrogance. He says he learned a lot screening all our deals and the deep discussions, in particular when our view was different than his.

After BDP, Jack did a couple more stints working with successful people on the front lines with early-stage companies. He later fulfilled his heart's desire, and with a partner, raised money from limited partners and started his own venture-capital firm. It has been successful and has raised four more rounds of limited partner funding with a greater amount of money to work with at each round. Mike and I have enjoyed seeing his success and have invested in his funds.

While engaged in BDP, in addition to serving on boards of our portfolio companies, in 1981 I went on the board of a public company, Management Assistance Inc. (MAI), based in New York City. The compensation was reasonable but the major benefits were the company insurance and the experience. Later in the decade, I joined the board of Storage Technology Corporation (STK) as one of the new board to bring the company out of a billion-dollar company bankruptcy. I was a member of the audit committee at MAI and of the strategic planning committee at STK.

In addition to the personal investments in start-ups before BDP, I continued to invest in other early-stage businesses, most of which didn't pay out well—except two that did. I also invested in some property with, Dad, Lynn Albers (a former employee at MRI and longtime friend), and with Larry Collmann. All of those proved to be good investments. And sort of half successful, the investment we had made in the Dillon Condo with the Collmanns was unrewarding financially but very rewarding in terms of our enjoyment of it. We also devoted a lot of attention in the eighties to our investments in four duplexes in Austin. It was about 30 years and with many ups and downs, but those duplex investments eventually paid off well in 2007.

Subjectively, the best land investment of all was the mountain parcel in the God's Acres Subdivision that became the home of our Valley County, Idaho, cabin. In 1981, with funding from Pat and me, Dad and my brother Harley

155

constructed the cabin that has provided pleasure for our extended families beyond words to describe—continuing on to this day in 2014. More on the cabin as we go along. The cabin was a dream fulfilled for Mom. Most of her life she had wished for a place to enjoy in the mountains and escape the summertime heat. Now she had it—and the retirement lives of her, Dad, and many of their friends were enriched by its availability. I wrote a Blessing for the cabin, and on 3 July 1982 with many of the family present, I read my blessing, which is copied here:

A BLESSING OF THIS PLACE
3 JULY 1982

Dear family and friends,

In these next few minutes, let us speak, hear, and think some of the thoughts we would like to be a part of this place forever. We ask that our Creator hear our praise and thanksgiving and empower us to bless this property and those who will abide herein. May they, as we do now, give thanks to our loving Creator for the beauty that is present throughout creation, and for the inspiration we receive in places like this. We pray that our stewardship may be found worthy as we enjoy shelter and fellowship in this place. May it long exist as a symbol and reminder, to all who are welcomed here, of the many ways our lives are enriched by the abundance our Creator has entrusted to us.

In each sunrise, we pray we will be reminded to seek growth in love and understanding in the new day.

In each sunset, we pray we will be reminded to be grateful for the experience of another day and for rest and shelter in the night to come.

In each sound and sight of this place, we pray we will be reminded of our individual uniqueness in this universe, of the harmony in its nature, and of the blessings available to us if we seek to protect and preserve it for all to enjoy and share.

In each storm that passes by, we pray that within this shelter we will be reminded of the power and vastness of our Creator and of how the storm helps us to know the calm and how, in the silence of the calm, we may receive insight to guide and enrich our daily lives.

In each mouthful of fish, fowl, or game we harvest from the water, air, and land here about, we pray we will be reminded to give thanks for our daily sustenance; however it might be delivered unto us.

In each rainbow seen from this place, we pray we will be reminded of our oneness with the Creator, that we are also an expression of, a part of, the All That Is, and that when so reminded, we will see less separation and greater oneness in relationships with other people and, therefore, be in closer harmony with the world around us.

In each season of the year, we pray we will be reminded that there is purpose in all change that is a part of our worldly experience, and that in change, we find growth and renewal opportunities provided with purpose by our Creator.

We give thanks that we have been instruments within creation to build upon this place. Bless this structure—the result of our labor and our desires—that it and we who enjoy the pleasure of its use, shall be protected from adversity in this place.

rlb

In 1984, we sold our property in Pecan Park and purchased a home built by a dear friend, Tim Atkinson, on Pin Oak Street in Round Rock. We loved that Pin Oak Street home. We tailored it to our wishes before moving in, and in 1988 built a large office next to the pool, resulting in buildings on three sides of the pool. Of course, I added audio speakers to be able to pump my quadraphonic music to the area where we, our family, and our guests spent so much time. I would sometimes interrupt my work in the office to go float in the pool, listen to the music, and think about the work a while if necessary.

During the decade, David, Dana, and Rob all graduated from college. After Rob went off to college at Arizona State in 1984, Pat and I became free to travel more, and travel we did. In the fall of 1984, we made a three-week trip to several areas in England, France, Italy, Innsbruck in Austria , and Germany with our friends Larry and Fran Collmann, who were mentioned earlier as co-owners with us of the condo in Dillon, Colorado. This trip was a big deal for me. After quite some time where I had tried unsuccessfully to quit smoking, I finally succeeded. I had quit before the trip, not smoked during our trip, and the real test came at the end of the trip. I stayed in London on business relating to one of our BDP portfolio companies after Pat and the Collmanns departed. Even though I was there alone for a few days between them leaving and my business, I managed to divert myself over and over again from the desire to have just one more. 1984 was a very important year for me! I may still be alive because I quit smoking!

In 1988, we made a six-week trip to Europe, traveling again for three weeks with Larry and Fran in Germany, France, and (mostly in) Spain, then followed by another three weeks on our own to see more of Spain, new areas of France, new areas of Italy, Vienna and Salzburg in Austria, and back to Germany. The office addition to our Pin Oak home was constructed while we traveled and was finished soon after our return.

At other times in the decade, we traveled to Mexico, another yacht charter to the Virgin Islands, a trip with my parents for three weeks to British Columbia, Canada, and a week trip with friends to two of the Hawaiian Islands—our only trip there. All of our foreign trips were filled with great memories, most of which we associate with a "follow our nose" tactic—translated to mean, that many of the most memorable places or activities were unplanned. We encountered people and places that guided us to those special experiences for us to take home.

In addition to foreign travel, Pat and I were on the road much of the decade and almost every month after we bought a customized Ford Van in 1985. In

1986, we made another six-week trip, this time west from Texas to California, then with many stops for business or pleasure in between, all across the US to the East Coast, after a swing through Eastern Canada and a visit to Niagara Falls enroute. Larry and Fran flew into New York City after we exited Canada where we

Groton Lake, Vermont

met them, stayed with friends in Connecticut, and traveled up to our home for the next week in Roxbury, Vermont. Brian Lea owned the house in Roxbury and was exceedingly gracious to let us use it. He loved the area and so much wanted us to see it during the height of the "leaf peeping" season that he practically forced us to use it. I took many pictures on the trip. This one of Groton Lake is representative of those I got in New England.

We loved Brian. As I mentioned earlier, he was the most outstanding free spirit of my life. He was born and then orphaned in England during WWII. He somehow got to Germany after the war, worked in a US Military mess hall, and liked what he saw in the nature of "Americans." He lied his way into Canada, then again to get a visa to come to the US. He somehow got drivers' licenses in three states when the law said it was legal to have only one. He never married, but there was always a woman in his life. Many women loved Brian, but he was too much a free spirit to offer a long-term commitment to any.

Early in our acquaintance, Brian was both MRI's most important customer at the time and a man clearly resonating to offer friendship. In his role as customer, he "required" me to accompany him skiing, sailing, and to the New York City restaurants he considered special. In one of those trips to Europe mentioned above, the Collmann's and we even rendezvoused with Brian for a delightful visit in London. After MRI, Brian welcomed me to stay at his apartment when in New York City anytime I was there on business. Later in life, he visited Pat and me in Idaho, Texas, and at a couple of ski areas.

Pat and I returned to Brian's farmhouse in Roxbury again in 1989, this time with Brian. He had a couple months earlier learned that he had prostate cancer. In what I treated with humor at the time, but not now, Brian called me one day and said something like, "Bob, I have been told I have cancer. I need to talk to someone. You are the only one I know who hints of spirituality. Can you come see me?" I viewed that as more of a statement about Brian's friends, many of whom I had met by then. I told Brian we had a trip planned to travel to New York City in a few weeks; we could visit then. Brian said, "No, I just want to talk with you, not with Pat." I sort of told him in a loving way that it was both of us or nothing.

Our flight to New York City experienced some delay, and we arrived late. Brian had invited us as guests of honor at a party on the roof of his high rise on Broadway in upper Manhattan. Then we were all to attend a concert at the Cathedral of St. John the Divine that was very special, as guests of the featured performer, violinist Eugene Fodor, Jr. The concert was to honor Theodor "Teddy" Kollek, the Mayor of Jerusalem. Pat and I checked in at the New York City club for University of Virginia alumni arranged for us by former protégé Jack Biddle. We quickly changed clothes, got a cab to Brian's, rushed through wine and snacks with quick "glad to meetcha's" at Brian's, and went roaring up Manhattan in several cars, none of which could find a place to park by the time we reached St. John's.

Brian told Pat and me to get an usher to help us find the reserved seats and dropped us off at the door. The place was huge. An usher took us to our seats—up the long isle through the whole church right up near the front on the left. The concert was about to begin. Brian joined us at some point, but by then I was totally engrossed in the talent. The Jewish community of America had arranged what seemed to be all of the Jewish talent they could identify to perform that night, except for Buddy Hackett. It was soloists, vocal and instrumental. It was entire orchestras and choral groups. It was poets, Hollywood stars, and cantors. And it was Eugene Fodor pushing the limits of a violin. By then, I had vinyl recordings of Joshua Heifetz, Yehudi Menuhim, and Itzhak Perlman, but this guy blew me away that night! For me, being treated to the talent level that evening classified as a once-in-a-lifetime experience. I wish I could have heard a Jewish master on the famous E. M. Skinner organ at St. John's, but the organ was hardly heard all evening. Anyway, beggars shouldn't be choosy, so I left in a glow of pleasure that remains to this day. It was indeed an evening to remember, and I just had to share it here.

The next day, Brian, Pat, and I journeyed to Brian's farmhouse in Roxbury, Vermont. We stayed several days, took many walks, drank a good bit of wine, and talked about some important things in one's life. By the time we departed, Brian was so fond of Pat that I had to take a back seat on our return to Manhattan. Soon thereafter, Brian started his search for a meaningful spiritual outlook. He investigated many established and fringe manifestations of religious philosophy and belief. He also studied what people had to say about various

diets and kinds of diet food. When I visited him, I often had to "try it." Brian lived an active, and as always, somewhat tumultuous life many years until the cancer took him down late in 1999. When it did, as appropriate, he died in the arms of a woman while in Australia at a clinic that had advertised a miracle cure.

My Last Picture of Brian Lea - May 1999

There were many other trips. Although most of our trips that involved several weeks away were to Idaho, we made one or two trips to our Dillon condo every year and some to the West Coast to visit friends and load up on wine. After Rob moved to Sacramento, we more frequently worked in a visit there on trips West. During the 1980s, we skied at 18 ski resorts in Colorado, Utah, Idaho, and California—many times with kids and spouses or friends along for the trip. The Idaho trips were primarily focused on family. Pat's mother and my parents both lived in the Boise Valley of Idaho where we grew up. On two of those trips, we also attended family reunions of Pat's large extended family.

In March 1981, the year after he graduated from college, David and Autumn Maxwell married, and in May 1983, Dana and Andy MacLaren married. Both families grew with children in the following years. A lot of our travel has been devoted to trying to keep in touch with and enjoy times with them.

Dave and Autumn met while in college at Texas State University in San Marcos, Texas, where Dave had been a University cheer leader for two years. The story is that the first time she laid her eyes on Dave, she told her roommate, "He's mine!" They were married in Corpus Christi, Texas, where Autumn's parents lived. Her father, Don Maxwell, had served in the US Navy for many years. Autumn was born in Naples, Italy, while her father was stationed there. He had retired from the Navy and worked with a Navy contractor in Corpus a year before Autumn went to college. Dave and Autumn have three (now adult) children, Courtney (born 1982), Nick (1984), and Ross (1988). Dave has been employed in information-technology positions within three large corporations since his graduation from college. During the early years of raising their family, Autumn worked part time for several years, then became a full-time stay-at-home mom.

Courtney went to college a few years but then dropped out to become an airline cabin attendant (what we used to call a "stewardess"). She then married Ryan Hemperly while he was stationed in San Antonio, Texas, in the United States Air Force (USAF). Our first great grandchild, Ryleigh, was born there on 27 March 2007. USAF then assigned Ryan to duty in the Las Vegas, Nevada, area, and their son Cory was born there in 2011. Be it recorded, Courtney did finish college in 2012 after working many months from her home taking college classes on the Internet. Ryan completed his master's degree this year, also after long hours of classwork via the Internet.

Courtney is the first member of our extended family to dig seriously into our genealogical roots and life experiences. She is known within the family as "that girl," Mom's nickname for her after Courtney spent many weeks in Idaho visiting with Mom to discuss her life and all she knew of genealogical significance. It was Courtney's prodding that moved me to engage in this life-story project.

Ross completed college at Northern Arizona University (NAU) in 2011 with a degree in Hospitality (food and hotel management) and has been employed in different kinds of firms since to earn his spurs. Nick attended NAU one year, but then decided he would rather pursue work more closely related to his interests. He focused on welding and has been very successful. Nick has a "significant other," and is engaged, but no wedding date has been announced yet.

Dana and Andy also met while both were in college at Texas State University in San Marcos, both majoring in business accounting and both became employed in Austin after graduation. They were married at First English Lutheran Church (FELC), our family church in Austin. Dana became a CPA, and after earning her spurs working as an accountant for a few years, began her own practice working from her home. Early on, she obtained a client with several restaurants in the Austin area. Over the years, her work for that client has grown significantly, and as many other clients as she can handle, now makes a nice practice. Andy worked a few years for Travis County but then left accounting to become a successful CFA (Chartered Financial Analyst). Both have had successful practices over the years since. They have two (now adult) children, Kristin (born 1986) and Kyle (1990).

After a fairy-tale quality romance, Kristin married Neil King in a fairy-tale quality wedding on New Year's Eve 2010 in Austin, also at FELC. They had met in 2009 in the Santa Monica area of Los Angeles where Neil was completing his research work/dissertation for his PhD in biochemistry from UCLA. Kristin had graduated from Texas Christian University in 2008 majoring in Radio/TV/Film, had worked as an intern in Los Angeles the year before, and while working as a film-industry intern again in Los Angeles during the year after graduation, she was offered a full-time position. The new studio, Illumination Entertainment, was producing their first computer-animated comedy film, *Despicable Me*, which was released to acclaim during 2010.

Neil finished his PhD in 2011 and accepted a post-doc position at the University of Washington in Seattle where they currently live. Kristen and Neil had their first child on 15 April 2013, Ellie (Eleanor June), our third great grandchild. Dana was able to file or defer tax returns for her clients in Texas and fly to Seattle late that same day. Kristin is employed by Amazon Corporation and will be returning to work in early September with Ellie in child care close to where she works. Neil's research has gone well, exceptionally well. He is well on his way in his personal plan for how to help mankind.

Kyle graduated with his MBA from Texas Christian University in May 2013 and joined the practice of KPMG in Fort Worth, Texas, late that year. He had successfully passed all of the four CPA exams. Kyle started college with almost a year of advanced-placement credits and had very challenging and rewarding intern experiences during two summers, plus a semester of work that led to being hired by KPMG.

162

Late in the decade, our Idaho trips (at least mine) grew longer and longer. In the early part of the decade, I would take two brief cases of business plans from those seeking funding from BDP. (Only about two in 100 were funded.) Those were shorter trips, in part because there was not yet telephone service at the cabin. Later there was telephone service, but I had less reason to use it. By then BDP had ended, and it was just personal investments, consulting, and work related to companies where I was on the board. That left a lot of time, and most generally when there was a season that meant time to go hunting.

I hunted elk, deer, pheasants, ducks, and geese in those years. Although the elk-hunting trips were the least productive for the dinner table, they provided some of the most memorable moments. The many pictures are reminders. Dad had looked forward to his fall elk-hunting trips ever since he returned after WWII. I had been on several of those trips, and I took him on the last three elk-hunting trips of his life. One of those was a 1987 expensive guided hunt in an Idaho wilderness area, where I also invited Harley and a friend from Texas to join us. In 1988, Dave joined Harley, Dad, and me on a hunt in Dad's old stomping grounds on the Nez Pierce Trail. His last hunt was more touching for me—it was just Dad and me alone in 1989 to tramp through the woods along the Artillery Dome Road, maintain our camp near Landmark, and talk a lot. Dad was 78, and I was 55.

As Pat complains, most of the best meat when I shot a deer returned to Texas to become a special feed when I hosted the next BS Group meeting at our home on Pin Oak. The BSG, as we referred to it, was a group devoted to Beautiful Sayings (don't you believe it) that met in the evening of the second Tuesday each month. During the decade, Pat and/or I became active in several groups, but it was the BSG that was certainly the most unique for me. It began in 1986 with a meeting of eight guys to decide if we ever wanted to meet again. I returned home after the meeting and told Pat I was the only one who had not experienced the often tragic death of a wife or child. It met on the second Tuesday of each month with one member in charge of picking the venue and the major topic for discussion. The invitations sent to the others for each meeting were a challenge to outdo any other in terms of creativity and enlightenment. We continued to meet regularly for 16 years until 2002, after two of the original members had died, two more were coming close, and I grew disenchanted with two of the remaining three others.

The gatherings were often hosted by several of us at our homes where the ground rule was that we would have no help in picking the menu and preparing the meal. Each member was expected to bring a bottle of wine and contribute a small amount toward the cost of the food.

Fred was an ex-US Navy nuclear technician who sort of turned counter culture in the 1960s and as a journalist for the Austin biker community in years since. Bob had a master's degree in chemical engineering but developed an interest in culinary arts so strong that he became a successful restaurateur, first in Houston, Texas, and later in Austin. He loved to write on many subjects, including a many-year wine column for the Austin newspaper, and even a novel I thought well done where some paranormal subtleties were woven within the plot. I have a sign on my wall that he created. It says:

I am fussy about wines
Exacting and proper
With a leaning toward those
Not hard to unstopper!

We continue a close friendship with Bob's widow Joan. Don is a clinical psychologist.

Here is a picture of the entire group, sans the Brueck, taken at our Pin Oak home in the late 1980s. Left to right in the picture they are: Fred Meredith, Bob Lowe, Don Reynolds, Pruett Watkins, Dick Hodgkins, Newt Millen, and Crutch Crutchfield.

BSG Meeting at RLB'S Pin Oak Home

Pruett, a family-practice physician who conducted his many-decade practice without protection of liability insurance, was another favorite of mine. After his first wife died, Pruett became interested in his own metaphysical quest. While participating in a small group of like-minded people, he met and married Janice, who was about 20 years younger than he. Their deep love of each other continued to the final hour of his life, where he died at home with Janice holding his hand and a friend playing a harp. Pruett was soft spoken, but when he spoke, I listened.

Dick was the personality and a past beyond description. He was a former Air Force pilot, who on a whim flew under the Golden Gate Bridge one day, and was given a choice to spend the rest of his life in the brig (so to speak) or start flying for "the company." He became a pilot for the CIA in Korea, and when shot down and captured, he strangled his tormentor in a prison and escaped to rejoin the CIA working with the Israeli Mossad to bring back former Nazis from behind the Iron Curtain—and it goes on and on.

After departing the CIA, Dick went into the early mini-computer software business and over the course of several years saw great financial highs and lows. In his later years, Crutch and I helped him celebrate his last year of life on a picnic each year for several years! This picture of Dick was from the last such picnic.

Last Picture of Dick Hodgkins

Crutch grew up in Corpus Christi, Texas, attended Stanford University for his undergraduate work in Electrical Engineering, married Danna his senior year, then into the Air Force, then on to the University of Texas for his MBA. He and Danna chose to make their home in Austin. Crutch's father was successful in the Texas oil business and over a period of time Crutch became active in several areas of money management and investing. We met when he became interested in venture capital and real estate investing. I have benefited via investing with Crutch over the years. He has been a major contributor to the Conspirare choral group in Austin since its formative years, while also providing counsel relating to strategic thinking and planning. We are close friends.

Newt's career included three quite different kinds of work. I forgot the first, but it was followed by a long stint in the US Navy where, for most of the tour, he was one of a small group responsible for sifting through intelligence to pick the targets if the US were to launch a strike during the Cold War years against the Soviet Union. After retiring, Newt attended law school and practiced law for many years in Austin before beginning a long health decline to his death. I have already mentioned Crutch, so I will only add that after Bob Lowe started a group in Austin known as "The Original Zinners" to meet monthly to drink and discuss Zinfandel wine, after Bob's death, Crutch took over and has kept the group active for many years, continuing to the present.

Bob, Pruett, Dick, Don and Newt are now deceased. I was in Austin and bedside often with Pruett and Newt in their final days but in Idaho and only often on the phone with Bob and Dick. I miss the friendship of all four.

In 1989, Bob Lowe (remember, that special spiritual brother of mine!) put together a nine-day trip to the northern California wine country in Napa and Sonoma. Six of us made the trip—another trip of a lifetime for me. In 1995, four BS'ers made a week-long trip to Idaho where we all stayed at the cabin. Pat consented to invite us to one dinner in McCall one evening, but otherwise we were on our own. In addition to good food and much wine, each afternoon we toured our part of Idaho as far as the Hemingway grave in the Sun Valley area. However, the mornings and evenings were the main focus. At those times, we gathered to take on the most challenging issues of life and death. I would consider two of the others to be true scholars and all five of us able to hold our own in the discussions.

In the 1980s, Pat and I enjoyed event after event with the International Wine and Food Society. We joined when the Austin chapter was started by Bob Lowe in 1980. Each event was planned by the person voted to plan the food and the person to pick the wines to match the menu (often me). In practice, the food and wine guy usually worked together on each venue and menu. That required interviewing and sampling the talents of chefs and the diligent tasting of wines before selecting the ones that matched the food and our budget. The cost of the evenings was always a bargain. Some events, especially around Christmas, were black tie with special guests we hired to entertain us. There were also picnics and field trips to locations with a cultural offering. It was good for the many years it lasted and— with a lot of help from Bob Lowe—was clearly the entry point of my appreciation of wine.

In addition to the approximately dozen corporate boards I was on during the 1980s, I volunteered to be on the boards one time or another with many nonprofit groups. The ten-year stints each as Treasurer of the Child Development Center at our church and on the Advisory Council of the College of Natural Sciences at The University of Texas at Austin required the most time and provided the most pleasure. I was also on the national board of the Lutheran Foundation of the Lutheran Church in America, the local group of the Boys Clubs of American where Don Kromer was the Exec, and Discovery Hall—the local group pursuing similar but less extensive objectives as The Exploratorium in San Francisco—to make science interesting to young people via a hands-on museum of science. For one month during the 1980s, I was on a Grand Jury in Williamson County. That was another especially unique and enlightening experience of the decade.

Most of what I have reported on involved physical activity—the action of going somewhere, being with someone, or doing something. I also wish to share that the 1980s were a time when I could start my climb back into some grasp of quantum physics. It was tough going—just ask Pat about my moaning and groaning about having lost the base of the pyramid of higher math built upon more basic math. Without the advanced math, one just can't do advanced physics, and I had completely lost the details of it—I recognized the symbols and names but couldn't "do it." However, with month-by-month effort some of that came back, and the physics became something I could remember longer than when I had my last shower. My business schedule began to allow me time for that.

It was clear to me that being able to read scholarly work in quantum physics was the only way I was going to find personal satisfaction in deciding how to reconcile the evidence of parapsychology with the then-current equations and models of physics that have evolved over the centuries. The older foundation that had evolved was important, but the quantum level of equations and models to describe how all change in our physical world takes place at the microscopic level of detail were not described within physics until the early 20th century. At that time, the sequence of Planck, Einstein, Bohr, Pauli, Heisenberg, Born, Schrödinger, and Dirac gave birth to modern physics. (I consider Planck, Heisenberg, and Dirac of greatest interest.) Although it was not until the first years of the next century when I did think I had a handle on the quantum issues, I had to start someplace. As things have turned out, the effort was most worthwhile.

In 1989, we made three trips of duration more than one month with most of the time spent in Idaho. The last of those was from September 9th to November 1st. As we drove our van across the 2,000 miles back to Austin in November, Pat took a deep breath and said something like, "There is something wrong with this picture." Here we were, leaving our nice Texas home much of the year—not being able to enjoy the pool much of the summer—and when we were gone having the expense of someone take care of the property. We had aging parents and extended family in Idaho. We owned a nice cabin in the mountains there. And I could just as easily fly out of Boise as out of Austin to do consulting work and attend board meetings. She raised the question: "Should we essentially relocate to the mountains of Idaho for at least half of the year and down-size in Austin?" There we go again—another one of those unthinkable thoughts became thinkable!

We did think a lot about it. We decided that we could continue to enjoy much of what we liked about Austin and our Austin family and friendships and still spend half the year in Idaho. The rest of the matter was easy—we would rather have a primary residence in Idaho and a smaller residence in Texas than the other way around. (We have remained all these years officially as residents of Texas and eventually expect to live there later in our retirement years.) During 1990, we did much of what we had been doing for several years—my consulting and boards, skiing, other travels, including spending time with the kids at their places during the year, and planning for our move to Idaho in 1991.

Pat and I spent a lot of time in Idaho in September and October in 1990, a lot of that time looking for a house to buy. We had thought of building next to the cabin, but neighbors there made a big deal about the regrets they had being so far from a town that we decided to look in the McCall area. Then the decision was whether to be in town or out in the country with mountain and valley views. We decided on in town and eventually found what we thought to be a good buy—if we did some serious remodeling and replacing of carpet and window coverings. Dad came up and checked out the quality of the construction before we closed the deal. We bought the house, returned to Texas, and the remodel took place during the winter in our absence.

On January 16th, the first day of Desert Storm in Iraq, Dad had a major stroke during the night. We were headed out on the 19th for the condo in Dillon enroute to Idaho. After talking to Mom, we decided to continue with that schedule. The first time I recall talking to Dad after his stroke was while we were in Dillon. His speech was very much impaired. After another conversation with Mom, we decided to finish our week in Dillon, then head on to Idaho. We

returned to Austin on February 13th. The rest of the spring we were busy planning our move, saying goodbye to friends, drinking down some wine with the BSers when I last hosted the gathering at Pin Oak, and selling furniture and assorted other items, like patio furniture and cat houses. We finally did what we had to do-- prepared Pin Oak to be rented,

Trucking to Idaho

loaded all our household possessions in a truck, and were on the way on June 7th—with Pat driving the van with air conditioning and 16 cases of the best red wine and my driving a Ryder truck with no air conditioning.

A Thought or Two Looking Back from Now

I recall these years, correctly or not, as the generally least stressful periods of preretirement years. Of course, there were some stressful situations, but they were few and far between. Days and weeks would roll by unburdened with more responsibility than to pay attention to what we were doing. It was certainly a lot of "work-hard play-hard," but the work was for the most part invigorating more than stressful.

There may be a couple of special reasons! First, we thought we were finally on solid financial ground—sort of. We had more money for discretionary purposes than ever before in life. For most of the decade of the 1980s, I earned more than we spent on family needs. We were essentially free from debt. And we had resources to buy our Pin Oak home and add much to make it much more than just a home. We could pay for the Idaho cabin that meant so much to my folks in their later life.

Secondly, I was my own boss and a boss without business obligations to others that were stressful near as much as they were exciting and responsive to my effort. Mike was a super partner. The public company corporate boards required time and effort but provided contact with people bringing to the board a variety of life experience and responsibility that I found personally enriching. I learned about board "perks" but have never felt comforable with them.

We could easily schedule our plans around those obligations. Life was good! We were happy without even thinking about it that way.

➤ 12 ◄

The Same—But Different

Pat Quickly Learned to Operate a Wood Splitter

Life in Valley County, Idaho. Really straight forward. You can heat with electricity or with wood. You can buy electricity or wood, or you can make ready your trailer, chain saw, chain oil, and file to keep your chain saw teeth sharp, and then go drive to the forest with a "wooding" permit—or permits—depending on how many cords of wood you expect to need to get through the next winter. Oh yes, you must seek your wood in the time between when the snow has melted and the ground has dried and some future summer date when the forests might be closed because of the forest fire danger. We chose to fetch it!

Step 1. You find a dead but not too-dead tree—but not white fir—cut it down (yell "TIMBER"), cut it into rounds (see in picture above), carry all rounds to the trailer, learn the special technique for getting heavy ones up into the trailer and up on top of the ones already in the trailer, load the trailer, drive back to town, reverse the loading process, stack the rounds, and then prepare for

Step 2. (Note, the bigger the tree, the greater both the amount of wood and the difficulty of handling large rounds from near the base of the tree! Life is full of "trade-offs." Ever notice that?) A typical tree was about 100-feet high before introducing it to a chain saw. This wooding process is very environmentally positive, in part by opening up the forest to sunlight, and also by the thinning out of fuel to reduce the fire hazard from lightning strikes. It is not unusual for summer thunder storms to include 2-3 thousand lightning strikes as they move through.

Step 2. Decide where you want your woodpile. That is, where did you build the shed or shelter to store your wood once it is split into pieces of a size that will fit in your stove? You want the shelter to be strong enough to hold up under the heavy winter snow load. (All the neighbors snicker and even laugh behind your back if your shed crumbles under the snow load.) You want the shelter to be as close to a doorway as possible, after taking all considerations into account. Remember, distance means more snow to shovel to keep the path to the pile open and the extent of the exposure to the elements on those winter trips to the woodshed. Also, have a plan that will make it possible to get the wood from the trailer to the splitter to the shelter.

Oh yes, the wood splitter. There are some hearty souls who split their rounds by hand with a heavy maul and wedge. That either makes them live longer or shorter lives—one can make a good argument either way. However, when they can afford an engine-powered wood splitter, most people will use it. The splitter is the blue thingy in the picture above. A good one should be strong enough to cut big, wet, heavy rounds and of a quality that won't break down half way through one season's usage. That is serious money so try to join with friends to own one. Of course, the splitter needs gasoline and oil for the engine and hydraulic fluid, plus some maintenance after each use to keep it in good condition. And a splitter sitting around without operators is like an upside-down rowboat on saw horses—just something to mess up the view. That brings us to:

Step 3. A single experienced and strong person "can" operate a splitter to split rounds into firewood—I know because I saw one once—just once. However, splitting wood with a power splitter usually takes two people, one to lift the rounds and position them on the tray lined up for the desired cut, and a second person to push the lever control to make the hydraulic system drive the steel wedge into the round. That usually, but not always, causes the round to split and some piece(s) of wood for next winter's fire to fall on the ground alongside the splitter. It helps for the two operators to be highly coordinated in their work—fewer doctor bills and divorces.

171

So with two healthy people (one with strength well matched to the size and weight of the rounds) working together as described, it is possible to cut more wood than you might imagine in a single day. As you can surmise from the picture above, when cutting enough firewood to make this whole exercise make any sense at all, there are intermediate tasks, such as picking up split pieces, and at some point, carrying them to the shelter and stacking the pieces so they will not avalanche and injure whomever has the chore of fetching wood when needed. The stack of cut wood along the garage door in the above picture was temporary, until I took time off handling rounds to fill a wheelbarrow with the wood and haul it to the woodshed out back of our new home before going back to handling the uncut rounds to continue the process. So, HAPPY NEW HOME, June 1991.

"Wooding" was not the only thing we had to learn about our new home and McCall. We learned that since there was no occupant during the prior winter the water pipes had been drained. Thus, all the faucet washers in the home were then dried out and defuncto. It took several trips back and forth to the local hardware store to return the inside water system to normal functioning.

We learned that there had been somewhat of a "revolt" at the local church we wished to attend. Those left were somewhat desperate for new members, especially younger members like us—we being only 56. We learned that there was a local summertime business called "Ice Cream Alley"—sort of a hole in the wall selling big scoops of really good ice cream for a modest price by large-town standards. We learned what huckleberries were, that they went real well with ice cream, that they grew wild in the area, and that the locals were reluctant to let anyone else know the location of their favorite huckleberry patch.

We learned that our walk to the local post office (there was no home mail delivery) each day was sort of nice—only a mile walk and an opportunity to eat the ice-cream part of the food pyramid sitting on a log at the edge of Payette Lake. It is a beautiful lake, named after Francois Payette, a French-Canadian fur trapper who worked for the North West Company. He was one of the first people of European descent to settle in the Payette River area. We learned that the typical summertime afternoon temperature might be 75-80 degrees, instead of the much higher summer temps we had left behind in Austin.

We learned that I could generally count on 2½ hours to drive to the Boise airport during the summertime. We learned that between visits to my parents in

172

Boise and Pat's family in the Nampa/Caldwell area, we were making about one trip to the Boise Valley each week.

We learned that although it was only 30 miles from McCall to our cabin on West Mountain, it would generally take 50 minutes—which we later qualified by saying, providing there is no ice and snow. We learned that guests could really enjoy our environs—we had many dear friends from out-of-state spend a spell during the summer. We enjoyed showing them around, and especially when we could include them when attending one of our several musical events.

The main two summertime events in McCall were the Folk Music Festival, the third weekend in July, and the Summer Music Festival held on the edge of the lake the first weekend in August. A very special treat were the Sunday "Jazz at the Winery" events at the St. Chappelle winery on Sunny Slope near Caldwell. That is where we listened to and visited with Gene Harris, one of our all-time favorite pianists. He later was the featured entertainer on one of the nights of the Summer Music Festival every year. We enjoyed learning and experiencing many new things that first summer in McCall.

The time with my father after our move to McCall is hard to describe. On one hand, he had recovered from his stroke enough to be mobile and interact with other people with pretty good speech. However, he had little eyesight in one eye and enough mental slowness that it was too risky for him to drive. He sold his boat, and with great mental angst, he sold his beloved pickup. Harley and I took him on a several-day trip that included revisiting many of his favorite mountain locations/surroundings. He enjoyed specific experiences during the trip more than the trip experience more generally. He seemed sort of relieved to return to his familiar home surroundings upon our return.

Looking back, we think that is about when he started losing interest in his life experience. He didn't follow the physical therapy that was prescribed or work hard on improving his ability to verbally express a mental desire to speak. Then finally, his eyesight deteriorated to the point he could not read his favorite news magazines nor watch TV. He also essentially refused to follow the diet prescribed for his diabetes.

I found the people at the State Library to be very helpful in providing equipment and content from their Books for the Blind program. He could even get recordings of those weekly news magazines—but for reasons we didn't understand, he just didn't have interest enough to take advantage of what was readily available. We thought Mom was doing a terrific job of caring for Dad and

173

maintaining their relationship as best possible. To do that, she was gone frequently, and Dad would get anxious and somewhat cranky, and the longer Mom was gone the more so. In 1993, he decided he would like to move to the Veteran's Home there in Boise.

Dad as I Like to Remember

After the civilians who had been on Wake Island were granted Navy Veteran status, he was proud of the fact and decided he would like to live where there were more people always around and staff to look after their needs. The move went well, and Mom, Harley and I, and other members of the family visited Dad often.

However, as time went by, Dad seemed to become angry more frequently, even over very small matters and behaviors of others in his living area. He either found it physically impossible to speak his thoughts or he psychologically just tuned out. He eventually became solitary, possibly as a result of medications he was required to take. Dad passed away on 2 January 1996. He was buried at Cloverdale Memorial Park in Boise with military honors.

When Pat's brother, Dean, died in 1989, her mom Ethel never did recover from her sorrow. After a period where someone was retained to provide the assistance she needed to continue to live alone, she moved to assisted living in 1990. When in Idaho on our frequent trips to the Boise Valley, we would visit my mom, Dad at the Veteran's home, then often Pat's mom at her independent-living apartment, and the rest of Pat's family in Caldwell. In early 1992, Ethel's health declined, and she passed away on 25 May 1992. Pat had made several trips to visit her earlier, but when she died, we were in Texas. The memorial service was delayed a few days, so we could drive to Idaho, and was held graveside at the Canyon Hill Cemetery on June 2nd.

Even though we lived much of the winter in McCall the first year, for some reason we returned to Texas in early November for a six-week stay. Because our home on Pin Oak was rented, and would be sold later, we made our Horseshoe Bay condo our Texas home. It remained our home until 1995 when we moved into a duplex in Austin we had purchased the year before. We have many pleasant memories of the time we spent living at our Horseshoe Bay condo. We had occasionally stayed there for several days, but living there day after day, week after week, was a new experience. We liked it, the kids liked it, our friends and distant family often came there to visit and enjoy the golf, tennis, swimming, or long walks into the hinterland. However, over time we realized that we often were driving back and forth to Austin, about an hour's drive, and often at night with deer and drunks to contend with. We sold the Horseshoe Bay condo in 1995 after ten years of ownership and three years of residing there from February on into May.

Near the end of March in 1992, I received a call from Jack Biddle to inquire whether I might want to do some more consulting work. We talked about it, and he suggested I contact the president at a small software company in Ann Arbor, Michigan. He had come in contact with the company, Arbortext, while doing business for his own company, and he believed they had a lot of promise but rather desperately needed help from someone with more experience. I did call the president, and she decided that there was enough mutual interest for me to fly there and visit.

That meeting was sort of hilarious. About four of them met with me in a small conference room. After about five minutes talking about their current operations, the president decided she didn't like what I had said and moved to end the meeting. One of those present, Jim Sterken, was the founder and chief technical officer. He interceded and said let's talk some more. The meeting ended with an understanding that I would be engaged to work with them. That happened, and they were important in my life for the next 13 years.

Over those years, I received a financial retainer each month and stock options to overall represent a reasonable consulting fee. I worked very closely at first with Jim Sterken, and later also with John Ford, to mentor them as they grew the company. John had been hired into Arbortext by the president but he understood when Jim came to the conclusion that she was not cutting it and had to be turned loose to do her good things elsewhere. I vividly recall the ride to the Detroit airport to return to Austin when Jim very reluctantly decided that was necessary. The growth of the company was a struggle. Several times it appeared that there was no way to fund the future, but each time their determination and hard work gave them new opportunity.

In 2005, the company was acquired by a larger company for $190 million. Jim, John, others, and I all benefited financially from their success. In April 1994, I had created a family trust to purchase some property forfeited in bankruptcy by a former partner of mine. Over the years on several occasions, I had donated property, stock, and options on stock to the trust and to our children directly. I had included options on the stock of Arbortext. When Arbortext was acquired, Pat and I, our children, and the family trust all benefited greatly from the success Jim and John had worked so hard to achieve. Both of them became multimillionaires. We have enjoyed visits together in Idaho and Austin during the years since the acquisition, and we are certainly as close as friends can be. Jim and John have been very gracious in expressing appreciation for the help I provided over the years.

In early 1993, a Sigma Chi fraternity brother from CU days, Gary Roubos, called to talk about what I was doing. He was the very successful CEO of Dover Corporation, a public company that owned 40-some companies and had annual revenue exceeding $3 billion. He explained that they were planning to spin out to shareholders one of their manufacturing groups then doing about $100 mil per year. He was trying to do all he could to make sure that the stock his shareholders were to receive would have good value and that the deal not be viewed unfavorably. There was more to the story, but in short, he asked if I would consider joining the board of the public spin out, then to be called Dovatron Corp (DOVT). The CEO to be of the company interviewed me, and I subsequently joined the board.

A somewhat humorous aspect of the process was that before I was invited to join the board, Gary had asked me what I thought about a guy who had been a junior financial officer at Storage Tech, and whether he might make a good Chief Financial Officer for Dovatron. I later was told that Gary had asked him what he thought about me when I was a board member who had often quizzed him during board meetings. Unknowingly at the time, we each recommended the other and enjoyed the additional years of working together.

I would find great pleasure in writing here about many interesting-to-me experiences over the years while on the DOVT board. [The company later changed its name to The Dii Group (DIIG).] Apart from the business aspect of it, there were side benefits, like being able to tack on a week skiing in Colorado after the February board meetings there and two delightful board meeting trips with spouses to Ireland. Some experiences were uppers, some downers, some just laughable, some quite irritating, some quite loaded with great pleasure, but all essentially valuable experience and financially rewarding for Pat and me. After all, life experience is just feedback on what we believe and how we behave, so I decided there must be something about what I was thinking and doing that was resonating reasonably well with the cosmos.

I would say that my greatest contribution during the seven years on the board was to prevent the senior management from selling the company to a buy-out firm (KKR) that would have feathered the top-management nest at the

176

expense of the shareholders. At a board meeting without prior notification, the senior management announced that they had reached agreement for KKR to acquire DIIG. The management group had lined up the outside auditing firm and legal counsel to anoint the deal terms as fair for shareholders. I quietly informed the CEO that we outside directors were now on the other side of the table and that the board needed independent counsel. Subsequently, and after I looked deeply into duties of directors, another board member and I were made co-chair of the special committee of outside directors to negotiate on behalf of shareholders. I think we did a crackerjack job.

We retained legal counsel from a very well-regarded and high-priced New York firm. They were great to work with. As part of our special committee work, I created my own estimate of what should be the valuation of the company. With help from legal counsel, we presented that to KKR, and they gracefully withdrew their interest in a deal. In winding up the affairs of the committee, I requested the law firm to present us with a final billing for services. I received a call from the partner who handled our account. He said there would be no charge and that our committee had gone perfectly by the book in discharge of our duties. He then said that the reason they would not bill us was because any amount they could in good conscious charge us would be so little that if it became known it would ruin their reputation.

The company grew and the stock price increased modestly with the growth. The industry was consolidating, and we either had to grow via multiple acquisitions or we would end up being acquired. In 1999, the board traveled to China (with spouses) to meet with regional officials and the management of our subsidiary operation there. While in the vicinity so to speak, the board as a group traveled together for a week of sightseeing in China. The experiences in

Xi'an and Beijing were the most unique for us. In Xi'an we, of course, visited the site of the unearthing of the terracotta soldiers and were given a VIP tour. We also were treated to a viewing of the wall drawings held in the vaults of the Shaanxi History Museum there. The curator told us we were privileged to view more than she showed President Clinton. I believed

Curator in Xi'an China

177

her. She even let me take pictures when the policy and numerous signs in many languages said "no cameras."

In Beijing we were housed for a few days on the grounds of a highly secured compound made available to visiting VIPs. We assumed the whole place was bugged and watched our conversations accordingly. The gate was guarded by military personnel, and we all assumed that the physically fit young people waiting on the tables for our final banquet were also military. Of course, we visited the Great Wall one day, Tiananmen Square, the Outer Palace Great Hall, and the Panda Zoo another day. We dined at very exclusive places each evening, including one evening at a dinner theatre with a beautiful performance that included Chinese traditional music and dancing.

Great Wall of China

Evening Entertainment in Xi'an, China

While in Hong Kong enroute to visit our plant at Zhuhai, we had a highly confidential board meeting on the ferry boat to the mainland to consider an offer being made by a competitor to acquire the company. We decided that they were quite strongly motivated to reach a deal and that an offer under those circumstances would likely be much greater than if we later sought to be acquired. The board voted to pursue the matter and engage in negotiations. The agreement to be acquired by the larger company (FLEX) was publically announced on December 22nd later that year. The price paid to shareholders was considerably more than twice what it would have been if the leveraged buy-out attempt by senior management had been successful.

At the banquet in 2000 to celebrate the closing of the acquisition, the CEO got down on his knee in front of Pat to tell her he was greatly indebted to me for blocking his attempted buy-out transaction. He ought to have been; the (explicative deleted) guy did his best to make my life miserable a few times during the process. He even attempted to kick me off the board on one occasion because of a trumped-up charge of conflict of interest because of my being on a board of a company he claimed was a competitor—pure BS.

178

One of the outside directors owned a large amount of DIIG stock. He had originally objected vigorously to my sense that we should resist the buy-out at the proposed price. He eventually understood how much the diligent questioning of the buy-out valuation did for his interest. After the selling out of the company was history, he invited the other four ex-outside directors and spouses to be his guests for a visit to his native Greece and a week of sailing in the Aegean Sea—a trip neither Pat nor I will ever forget. Again, that was an experience that could fill a small book, but it will only get a few paragraphs in the next chapter.

The company the DIIG CEO claimed to be a competitor was HEI, Inc. (HEII), in Minneapolis, Minnesota. It was a publically held company specializing in the design and manufacture of ultraminiature custom thick-film microelectronic devices. The CEO was Gene Courtney. As has been written above somewhere, Gene and I were considering merging MRI and his former company before Intel favored MRI for acquisition. We had remained in touch over the intervening years. Gene became CEO of HEII when it was a distressed company in 1990 and moved it from the edge of a cliff to a very comfortable operating situation. In 1994, he had asked me to join their Board. I really enjoyed working with Gene and the others, and the company made steady progress building up a nice cash reserve to fund a diligently prepared growth plan.

Unfortunately, the results of all that good work was included in the financial information filings of HEII required by the SEC. It popped up on the computer screen of a sleazy corporate raider who took aim at control of the company in order to get his hands on about ten million bucks plus a going concern. In 1998, he connived with a morally bankrupt brokerage firm in Minneapolis and a two-faced ingrate shareholder to gain control of enough shares to take over control of the company. Gene had engaged a prestigious law firm in Minneapolis to provide counsel to him and the board of directors as the situation unfolded. But the raider entered the fray with some junk-yard dog attorneys and proceeded to flout corporate law and jurisdiction by the SEC to succeed in the takeover. In my opinion, the battle was lost because attorneys of a carriage-trade law firm could not effectively deal with those of the gutter.

It was a sad day for me to see all that Gene had done so well fall from his nurturing hands. It was also a sad day for the shareholders who voted for the takeover (and all other shareholders) because they soon saw their investment in HEII become worth pennies. It was also sad for me to see the SEC be totally nonresponsive to enforcing the federal laws that applied in this case after timely and formally well-presented requests for intervention by the HEII law firm. Before moving on to another exciting chapter of my life in the 1990s, I am pleased to announce that at least a few years later, the corporate raider was convicted of some violation of laws and given a lengthy prison sentence. We reap what we sow. I wish no person harm, but it would not make me sad if they lose the key.

In 1997, Pat and I had enough of a financial cushion to want to invest some of our net worth in property of greater value than our McCall home. We looked at property around Payette Lake and decided the prices were not good value. At Pat's suggestion we brought up the idea again to build on the lot we had purchased next to our cabin on West Mountain, across Cascade Lake and 12 miles from the village of Cascade. That plan fit what we could afford and what we would want to get for our money. I created a floor plan and a description of the general appearance we desired. A high school friend's brother, who was an architectural engineer, improved and prepared the detailed construction plans required to actually build the structure. Early in July we broke ground. I loved the process of building what we later decided to name "Bru Haus."

I selected a contractor to manage sub-contractors for concrete work and framing. Working closely with him, I handled most of all other subs. Pat and I picked out what we wanted for colors, plumbing and light fixtures, windows, doors, etc. I was on the job most every day for the next four months working closely with the building crews and picking up the scrap stuff. Those doing the construction work were comfortable with my presence and on many occasions they made suggestions about how some particular detail could be improved. They contributed much more than just their hours on the job.

We were aiming to move to our new home in time for Thanksgiving that year. We even had the moving van scheduled and in front of our door in McCall. Then the snow began. They got the truck loaded and drove to our new abode, but then found that their truck was too big to get close enough to unload. The snow and ice made conditions worse. The day before Thanksgiving they drove the truck, our belongings on board, to their home base in Boise. After a day or so with time off with families, they reloaded our belongings into two smaller trucks and returned to Bru Haus. Fortunately, they picked up a strong young man from Cascade to work by the hour to help them. He turned out to be the best set of brains of the three. The unloading, more or less directed by him, went well. When it was time to drive away, one of the dingy drivers promptly got stuck down the road a mile or so. At that point they were on their own, so they had to call a wrecker from Cascade to pull them out. I am sure the moving company took a loss on that job, but they fulfilled their commitments to me.

It was nice that we had the cabin to live in while that last week of the move-in process unfolded. Within a couple of weeks of touch-up here and there, we were comfortable at home in our new home! Some weeks later, we gave a party a la "open house" for all who had contributed to building it. It was built to withstand the elements of the mountain location and to sort of "take care of itself" when we were gone for long periods of time. We had installed a propane-fired backup electric generator. It provided power for a comfortable living situation, including well pump, heating, refrigerator and microwave, and power to more electric outlets than we needed for TV, music, computers, coffee pot, etc., when the utility power went down—which it did frequently. We installed a security system and purchased a large propane storage tank. It has indeed "taken care of itself" when we have been gone over these seventeen years. We love our Bru Haus, the surrounding forest, and our view of the lake. Our neighbors are special friends.

1999 was a big travel year. In the late spring, Pat and I made a three-week trip to Europe with Mike and Pat Faherty. Starting with two days in Barcelona at the time of the European Soccer Championship Game (what a day and night that was!), we took a train to the French boarder, stayed overnight at a small border town, picked up a Citroen rental car there, and started East along the Mediterranean—at high speed. We stopped along the way to take in some food and sights but ended up that night in a place near Genoa, Italy, quite distant from the urban area. The next day included Pisa and the leaning tower, then farther on east to the sight of our first hilltop town, Voltera. I have a delightful memory there of lunch at a small family restaurant stuck in a small space along a narrow street—where every building must have been there for centuries. That is where I got another of my famous close-up pictures of a house fly in or on a glass of wine. Then that afternoon, on to Poderi Val Verde.

Poderi Val Verde in Chianti, Italy

Our week near Castellina in Chianti at Poderi Val Verde with owner Ulrike Eder was enjoyable. Each day we ventured out from our spacious unit to experience new terrain, new restaurants, and encounters with friendly people. Although we were only 45 minutes away from Florence, we all had lengthy visits there in the past, and we wanted to see smaller villages and visit special

181

restaurants. And wow—did we ever! Siena was the largest and most well-known city we visited, but we have memories just as vivid from visits to Poggibonsi, San Gimignano, Greve, Panzano, Radda, San Quirico D'orcia, Pienza, Montalcino, and Montepuliciano. (Our favorite restaurant was in Panzano.) Each day we would have our "special" food and wine lunch somewhere, and then buy some wine, bread, cheese, and maybe some pasta to take back to our villa to enjoy it out in the gazebo in the evening. Tough duty, but someone has to do it.

Our favorite restaurant-in Panzano

During the 1990s, I served on the advisory committees at ORME School in Arizona (a boarding school in a ranch environment) and continued to serve on the Advisory Council for the College of Natural Sciences at The University of Texas at Austin. For several years, I also continued as Treasurer of the Child Development Center at church and served on the board of the Foundation for Religious Studies in Texas.

The College of Natural Sciences had a special program devoted to a group called the Dean's Scholars. The program was guided by Jim Vick, PhD, who was a professor in the mathematics department and who I eventually learned was also a Sigma Chi. We decided to raise money to support research projects by undergraduates. I scheduled luncheons in the corporate dining rooms of senior executives at some companies in several Texas cities. The executives were chosen because of their UT connections, the wealth of those they were known to associate with socially, and because their company had an appropriate dining space for a group. The executives provided the meal and invited up to ten invitees to the luncheon. Jim provided from three to six Dean's Scholars for each trip. I provided transportation in our 1985 customized Ford Van.

The Dean's Scholars were generally different for each trip. Jim and I briefed them about how best to make good impressions and help seek funding commitments from the invitees. They were asked to split up for the luncheon to sit with the guests and to mingle before lunch and after the formal luncheon ended. Two or three were asked to give brief descriptions of their own undergraduate research projects and express the hope that support would come forth to provide the same opportunity to others. They were always impressive and well received by the attendees. Jim would start the presentation following the lunch and introduce the students. I would usually close the affair with a low-key pitch for generous funding from those present. As a result, we raised about $250,000 for the undergraduate research program.

I enjoyed setting up and participating in the luncheons. Even more, I enjoyed the conversation in the van driving to and returning from the luncheons. The interaction with such impressive young people always led to serious topics, not necessarily of an academic nature. One of the most interesting conversations for me was one time when Jim and I were in the front seats just driving along and listening. Behind us, three or four girls were talking about their career interests and post graduate plans generally. The most poignant part of a conversation I recall was when a girl described her conflicted desires—to be home when the kids came home from school like her mother was or an appealing career interest fueled with great passion.

Also in 1998 while at our Austin duplex, I woke up one morning when it was still dark outside and noticed the glow from the bathroom window. I opened the window and saw that about 50-70 yards away there was a fire raging at the portion of the adjacent apartment complex next to our drive way. At that time, fire engines had not arrived. Pat and I were out of our place in a flash wearing little more than pajamas. I got up on our roof with a water hose Pat handed up to me and started dousing the large embers falling on our roof. Pat ministered to our tenant girls who were in shear panic, in part due to concern for their dogs. Our driveway to the street was right in the middle of the fire zone, thus blocked. The girls knew they could climb over the back fence to escape if necessary, but what about the poor dogs? Pat told them she thought the dogs

Apartment Complex Fire Near Austin Duplex

would be up the ladder behind the first person showing the way. Picture was taken up our driveway after fire put out.

A lot of other experiences in the 1990s are great memories even if not the kind that one might call life-changing in any sense. In looking back over monthly calendar records, it looks like we skied over 20 times during the 1990s. On one in 1998, Pat was caught in some bad weather conditions and tore her ACL. It was surgically repaired, and she skied again in subsequent years.

During the decade, we had a lot of summer visitors (and a few skiers in winters) while we lived in Idaho. Many were friends from Texas who had never visited any location in the Northwest. We noticed that as friends near our age retired, they had more time to travel, and we were on the list. The preponderance of visitors, in addition to our kids, were people I had worked with and developed close friendships with over the years. Pat and I had started exploring the back country soon after we moved to McCall. We found great places to picnic, climb in the mountains or up the creek valleys, or just to drive into the wilderness area to view scenery and wildlife. We could usually show visitors some deer and elk, some viewing elk for the first time.

Our favorite place to take city folk was back into the Lucky Lad Mine and occasionally watch them begin to get increasingly nervous the farther back we went on the poor jeep road. In several places, the terrain next to the road was a very steep drop-off. There was one place where, over the years, three people were afraid to remain in the jeep and chose to walk across that stretch of road while I waited for them on the other side. Names are being withheld as a matter of kindness. The "road" went about 21 miles from the end of pavement. The trip from there to the end of the road and return was at least three hours. It took even longer if I had to stop and remove trees that had been blown over the road. Once in and out, our visitors were often quite proud of the picture of them by the tree at the mine with the tobacco cans containing the original mining claims. Many times over the years, we couldn't even get to the mine because there were trees too big to move or too many snow drifts.

In 1995, Bob Sheets made the cabin his home and office for a year while he was writing his book about the Salem Witch Trials. Bob had a distant relative, George Burroughs, who was hung as a witch. Bob never did publish the book that I believe would have been the definitive accounting for what happened in that chapter of American history. Bob loved doing the research and even the writing but in later life just grew too involved in other matters to go the final steps into publication and distribution. Bob's unfinished book reminds me of the many times I have started to write about some of my thoughts about, or implications of, quantum physics—that remain "unfinished" in the file cabinets!

There have been two times in my life when someone with whom I had a close relationship has come to me with a suicide intention. The first was an employee of MRI who asked to see me one morning. He came in, looking very much in a state of anxiety, and blurted out that his wife was threatening to commit suicide if he didn't comply with some desire of hers—a desire I have long ago forgotten. If I didn't know it before, I sure learned then that there are times when people want one to tell them what to do, rather than to help them find significance and options.

The second occasion was back when we lived in McCall. The wife of a friend said she was filing for divorce. He became very despondent and said life was a bummer. To make the story short, I sent him an airline ticket to come to Idaho for some time to visit and tour the area. He came, Pat understood, and I holed up with him at the cabin for almost a week—just hanging out together, listening to Leonard Cohen (his choice) while sitting on the deck looking out over the lake and woods. We took several jeep trips into the back country. He is now happily married again and has been for many years. We remain friends.

In the mid-1990s, a close friend from venture-investing days, Walt Rychlewski, and I devoted a lot of time and some of our money to create a plan for a start-up business for an innovative communication device to be worn as a pin or necklace. We reached the point we had a high-quality business plan and contacted some of the venture-capital people I retained contacts with since the 1980s. The only one who thought it worthy of funding would only do so if I were to run it. I went home, described the situation to Pat, and asked what she thought if we were to relocate back to the Dallas area for a couple of years. She said she would be glad to visit me on weekends. That is what prompted me to write on one page:

What Results Do We Want From Our Plans?

To be available to be of assistance to each other, our direct family, and our extended family.

To live in one or more homes that are safe and comfortable for our lifestyle with enjoyable music, reading material, and computer/communication resources.

To take care of our health to make our remaining years as enjoyable as possible, from a health and fitness standpoint, and to try to avoid being a burden upon our children or friends.

For RLB to do a good job on a few public company boards or as a consultant so that he will have some business relationships with people he likes, the medical coverage they can provide us, and income that along with properties and other modest income sources will provide us funds for our basic needs.

To enjoy the pleasure of friendships with many people, with whom we can visit frequently in pleasant surroundings at modest incremental expense, and enjoy the stimulation of their views, the pleasure of pure friendship, and occasional mutual assistance.

To have time to devote to intellectual curiosity and philosophical/spiritual contemplation as the spirit moves.

To avoid as much as possible contentious people, angry adversarial situations, and siege environments, so as to readily see the positive and experience joy from nature, people, and simple things/activities in a low- stress environment.

To be able to spend time in remote, preferably inspiring and/or exciting places that offer natural beauty and facilitate perspective.

rlb
April 1996

In the early 1990s, I discovered a small growth on my left arm changing color and growing larger. Our doctor in McCall took one look and did a biopsy. The biopsy came back a squamous cell cancer. After contemplating my early demise for a while, I learned from a doctor friend in Texas that catching a growth that early meant an almost 101% survival rate. I talked the dermatologist into removing it on my first visit. Within a year he took off a premalignant growth on the same arm—the one we let hang out the car window while driving in our youth. The dermatologist said guys my age were his most frequent clients! I have no additional such growths in the about twenty years since. I am not sure how a young person avoids all behaviors that can come back to kick him in the butt many years later, but I wish them luck like I have had. (Wear a broad-brimmed hat and apply sunscreen to exposed skin when in the sun, at least during mid-day.)

In 1998, we had an MRI employee reunion with about eighty ex-MRIers attending. I expected to hear reports of "after-MRI" experiences they were so satisfied or thrilled with that MRI would be discussed in lesser terms. Wrong. By far the more frequent report was that MRI was the experience that none had matched. I learned a lot that I didn't know for sure back then—but believed— about the things employees valued the most. We had a highly competent technical guy run off with someone else's wife and another guy caught dealing drugs, but except for those individuals in those rare situations, it was a very wholesome environment to encourage high personal performance and satisfaction. Of course, many persons wore sandals and behaved in highly creative ways, but we thought that was especially wholesome!

In the late 1990s, Pat and I started the tradition of an annual summer "cabin party" for all extended family members who had interest in using the cabin with their families or friends each year. A cabin-use privilege was available with only a few ways it could be lost. Rules and my expectations regarding acceptable use have been well communicated and even posted within the cabin. In recent years, it has also been the expectation that they would show up for the party—a long weekend to do top-to-bottom maintenance and cleaning. Those occasions have been great times to get together and have fun as well, as a way to keep the condition of the cabin the way all would like to find it when they arrive to use it.

During the 1990s, Rob lived in Sacramento, California. After the great wine-country experience in 1989 with Bob Lowe, I developed a fondness for Napa and Sonoma Counties that grew over the 1990s to be more like a love affair. Visiting Rob created an opportunity to visit those areas that we just couldn't pass up. He came to love spending time with us there also. We all learned a lot about wine together. Wine

Ski Trip Wine Committee

became a part of our list of healthy choices. The picture of Crutch Crutchfield, me, and Gerry Wrixon is from one of our skiing trips to Colorado after a Dii Group Board Meeting. It illustrates our commitment to making sure we could be depended upon to match the wine to the menu.

I had met Gerry Wrixon when we were both asked by Gary Roubos to become board members when Dovatron was spun out of Dover. Gerry was the director of a world-class microelectronics laboratory in Ireland. Both the technology and Ireland were important in the business of Dovatron. He became the other committee member when I was selected to be chairman of the audit committee. We worked well together, and Pat and I became very close friends with Gerry and his wife Marsha. Gerry later became President of University College Cork, a constituent University of the National University of Ireland.

In the mid-1980s, I had purchased the kinds of parts used by a convenience store to make their huge coolers, so I could make a small cooler of similar design for a home wine cellar. When we moved our belongings to Idaho, I sold the wine cellar unit to Crutch. He has kept it pretty full ever since. As mentioned earlier, we first became acquainted when he decided to learn more about technology venture-capital investing. We quickly hit it off, and Crutch and his wife Danna have been close friends of ours ever since. He has kept the wine cellar full of better wines than I would ever have thought of. In addition to their nice home in Austin, in recent years they purchased a beautiful mountain home in Colorado where they now spend most of the summers.

Gerry and Crutch shared my enjoyment of wine and an interest to constantly learn more about the entire process required to make it, from soil to bottle. The Crutchfield's and we have traveled together many times in the wine countries of California, Oregon, and Washington State. The pleasure and learning experience of many wine-country trips came to include restocking our wine cellars, first in Texas, then at Bru Haus. That stocking activity continues to exist to this date. Because they are closer, Oregon and Washington wine regions have replaced California as the main source of the contents of the wine cellar at Bru Haus.

Part of the pleasure of our annual months in Austin in the 1980s was to expose ourselves to more culture than is possible in Valley County, Idaho. In particular, those were the glory years of the local Austin Opera performances. Thanks to Alfred and Ellen King, founders and major contributors to both the management and funding effort, Pat and I had very good seats. I developed a love for opera that continues. I had attended opera performances at the Lincoln Center in New York City occasionally while doing business there in the 1970s and 1980s, but the bug didn't really bite hard until we enjoyed the Austin productions. I will add that both the best and worst performances I have seen of Aida were in Austin with the New York City Met somewhere in between. The worst was with staging and performance drama from the Chicago Opera organization. They turned the grand march into a vulgar show of pagan-parading prostitutes.

And finally two of my best recollections from the 1990s—time with and care of Mom, and I was able to devote a lot of time to study quantum physics and a reality beyond space-time. Regarding the latter, I believe I made a great leap forward in my insight as to how quantum physics suggested many aspects of the greater reality I wished to understand. A summary of what I learned during that effort and the years that followed will be set forth in Chapters 15 and 16, my Metaphysical Journey.

Mom was born in 1915, so her age during those years was 75-85. Before Dad's stroke, each year was bringing them greater pleasures and general joy of life. All of that changed. It all started downhill following Dad's stroke. As Dad grew less and less happy with life in general and was every day aware that all that had been so good was now but a memory, Mom's life pretty well collapsed to taking care of Dad and a household. Dad's death took quite a mental and physical load off Mom. By then she was about 81 and had moved back to the mobile home on Crestwood they had lived in earlier for several years. She was not as spry as she once was but restarted living a more active life. It included time with ladies who once were her closest friends and seemingly endless hours shopping for the most minor things.

When Mom reluctantly, but willingly, gave up driving, her pleasure in life trended downward again. Dad did not leave a large estate. Mom's code of good conduct inclined her to be so frugal she wouldn't switch to cab rides to continue her mobility. She did stretch what assets there were, plus social security and veteran's benefits. That enabled her to live without family financial assistance for the rest of her life. She moved from the mobile home to an apartment at the Valley View residence facility but later left because her rent was raised. That started a sequence of four more moves in the 2000s, which are left for the next chapter!

And then arrived the end of the 1990s—sort of. First, I had to learn how to spell "millennium." Anyone who couldn't spell millennium just couldn't engage in everyday conversation with those who could—who knew why we should care. I actually learned how to spell it, and why I should care. I was chairman of the Audit Committee at the Dii Group the year before the old would be called the past, and we would have to live with the future. We had operations with computers in seven countries and several time zones. And it was becoming clear to computer users all over the globe that something highly undesired might occur at midnight on 31 December 1999.

It is really pretty easy for humans to understand past and future. However, all computing gets done by software—as we who were in the software business used to say. And most of the computers in the world needed to refer to the current date when doing their job. If it was payroll, the software had better know how to handle dates. If it was airline-crew management, better know how to handle dates and time of day. If it was to record how much manufacturing production went into inventory this month, better know how to identify the end of months. If you were software running a computer, at the stroke of midnight on 31 December 1999, you had better be able to tell the significance between all dates ending in 99 and those ending in 00.

Because memory had been expensive for most of the history of computing at that time, programmers used as little of it as possible. So when everyone

189

knew it was in the 1900s, it was only necessary for the software to tell the difference between two numbers to tell it what year it was. As a consequence, at the stroke of midnight at the end of December in year 19xy the software would "automatically" know that the value of y would have to be increased by one to change what was happening to recognize it was happening in the new year. For instance, after midnight on 31 December 1941, the programs would know it was then 1942, and after midnight on 31 December in 1999, the software would know it was 1900. Oooops!

Thus for that historical reason, most computers in the world were programmed so as to permit that kind of problem to occur at the moment of a new millennium. The situation was well recognized. Many months, if not years before the century was to end, all software had to be analyzed to see if there would be that problem. If it existed, the computer code would either have to be fixed or replaced in advance to avoid a possible serious data-processing nightmare. That need created a lot of business for new and old firms that could be hired to analyze and change computer programs and a lot of business for companies selling new computers that did not have software with the problem to start with. The gross domestic product of many developed countries in the world was higher than expected in 1999 because of all of that new commerce.

So much for all that technical stuff. By mid-1999, we were pretty sure the Dii Group and the rest of the industrial world had taken all the actions we needed to keep things running come the new millennium, and we became even more confident by the end of the year. Knowing that, I became less concerned about the potential for chaos and disruption of life that would affect our families. Once those with responsibility knew that they had taken care of fixing the software before the new millennium, they could forget about it and join the parties to welcome in the New Year. For those people in particular, and for most people everywhere, parties that year had much greater significance than the usual New Year's Eve parties. It was not just a new year, it was a new CENTURY!

Pat and I were fortunate to be invited to a New Century Party at Fran and Larry's beautiful home. They have many friends so it was a big party, and one we will never forget. Dana and Andy were there and also Rob and his fiancé Karrie Wagner—soon in the new century to become another Mrs. Brueck.

Thus ends my story about many of my experiences and recollections during the 1990s—and the end of this chapter of that story.

A Thought or Two Looking Back from Now

Other than the beginning of a challenging and rewarding relationship with Jim Sterken and John Ford at Arbortext, there was not much in the way of new qualitatively different experiences during these years. Pat and I are very happy that we chose to build Bru Haus instead of alternatives, and also that in general we had a lot of quality time together.

In terms of what was new and important to my life experience during those years, it was clearly my time to commit to the study of quantum physics and the context of a greater reality. I think my life now would be very different if I had not had a chance to bolster my interest in the paranormal with a foundation understanding of physics.

13

Gliding into Retirement

But not retirement in the first year of this new century! Retirement was six years later, even though during those years one may not have noticed me doing much work! I will start with some very specific memories and then try to fill in between them with miscellaneous personal experience, just for the record.

At the top of the new millennium list is the marriage of Rob and Karrie in Austin, Texas, on 2 July 2000, at First Evangelical Lutheran Church (FELC), where Dana and Andy were also married, and where Pat and I and family had attended for about 36 years. In addition to our family and friends, Karrie's parents, siblings, and many of Rob and Karrie's friends who also live in the Austin area.

Several years later, Rob and his long-time "boss" left their employer on good terms to form their own urban-planning partnership. They have successfully grown the consulting work in their home stomping grounds of Northern California and around Lake Tahoe, but Rob's family moved to and remains living in Austin.

Rob and Karrie's two children, Abby and Robby, are now in 2015, respectively 13 and 11. We get to spend time with them often during our "winter" migrations to Austin, occasionally staying with them while their parents are out of town. Both have been very active in sports activities over the years, and we have been there cheering on the sidelines. It has been a delight to be so close to them as they have been growing up.

And, in general, for the first few years of the new millennium, it's easy and fun to write about travel so I will pick up the story there.

It is hard to beat the trip to China, but each of these also had very memorable qualities. The first in the new millennium was that trip to Greece with people from the Dii Group Board of Directors that was mentioned in the last chapter. Our host was Deno Macricostas. Deno was born in Greece in a low-income family. At an early age, his job to help produce family income was to go every day from village to village with his goat to sell goat milk. As Deno grew older, his father decided there were better prospects for his son in America. The problem was how to get him there. There were distant relatives there, but he would have to learn English to get a Visa, and Deno was not much of a student.

He tells this story. He went to the closest US State Department office to try to talk his way to America. They said he would at least have to demonstrate that he could read enough elementary English for him to be able to follow directions, etc. They pulled out a book, turned to a certain page, say page 74, and asked him to read the second paragraph. He failed. He waited a few weeks, tried again, and failed again. That time, he noticed that he had been asked to read the same paragraph on page 74 of the same book. He told his father. His father acquired a copy of the book and told him to work at it until he had memorized that paragraph, then return. Deno did and got a Visa. What followed was the dream of every immigrant—work hard, get rich, deserve it.

Deno eventually became the founder and CEO of a very successful company in the semiconductor industry. He became wealthy in the process. He and his wife became very generous with their wealth, in particular with large contributions in memory of his father to some university I do not recall. And of course, he funded the week-long trip to Greece in the fall of 2000. My lengthy trip report is too long to insert here, so I will just say it was one delightful day after another in a very historic part of the world and will settle for inclusion of a couple pictures and only a few paragraphs from that report.

I was sort of overcome on occasions with the historical associations, especially at the Island of Delos. When I packed for the trip, at some point I had room for just one more thing, like a thin book. I chose *The Lessons of History* by Will and Ariel Durant. I happened to be reading it while underway on the way to Delos. It really put me in the mood to "inhale" more of what I was seeing as ancient history in the Aegean and then Delos in particular.

The pictures below of our boat, the Michael R-VIII, and the statue of Aphrodite, Pan, and Eros in one of the museums were selected by lottery. ☺

Yacht Michael R VII in 2000   Aphrodite, Pan, and Eros Statue in Athens

Here is what I wrote after our trip.

****

Delos

Delos was once the political and religious center of the ancient world. There is evidence of it thriving in the Mycenaean era, 1400-1200 BC, and a fascinating history on into the first century BC. Although some of us think of it as the favorite playground of Dionysos (Bachus to you Romans), it is more widely known as the birthplace of the mythical god Apollo and his twin brother Artemis. Several of the most significant of the many temples dedicated to Apollo in Greece were on Delos.

Now as for Dionysos, Delos lays claim to the same stories you hear about Dionysos everywhere. Dionysiac Festivals were reported to have been held regularly. They included singing and the dancing of satyrs and nymphs dressed in animal skins who, when drunk into ecstasy with wine, engaged in maniacal merry-making late into the night. It is from these escapades that we have our modern word nymphomaniac, derived from nymph and maniac (ecstasy). [Research on this topic was supported in part by the Tuesday evening BS group of Austin, Texas, which was generously given and is acknowledged in kind.]

In addition to that claim to fame, Delos had/has many others. We had a guide who spoke very good English and was well educated for her trade. Many historical sites have been or are being reconstructed on Delos to provide an interesting picture of what life was like there many centuries ago. During some centuries, Delos was what we would now call a tax-free port. Goods could come in and leave the port without taxation. As a result, the citizens grew prosperous and art flourished. It is particularly galling to the Greeks that, during the time they were dominated by Byzantium, an Englishman courted favor with the powers that be in Constantinople and hauled away a lot of the nicer sculpture and other art objects. They are now in museums in London with no indication that they will be returned.

Delos may have been dry, windblown, and covered in most places with weeds when we visited it, but it also was the place that had the vibes of its great history. Once the place of power, protected from attack by its sacred status, with an oracle second only to Delphi that was consulted before all major decisions of the ruling powers, it was now mostly piles of old stone, inhabited during the day by tourists with no place to stay overnight.

****

The most thought-provoking moments of the trip for me were during those few hours on the island of Delos.

As our Greece trip ended, the four Dii Group couples and the guests of one said, "Let's do a gathering again sometime." So a year later, I gave the idea some thought and enough research to pick three or four possible venues. I sent out an email to the effect: "If we want to get together again this year, here are some possible ideas, what do you think?" I received not a single reply.

Of course while researching places I could imagine enjoying, I became sort of desirous of the idea of friends gathering there. In particular, a gathering at a particular large mansion on a hill overlooking a bay of ocean water on the outskirts of Victoria, British Columbia, Canada, seemed to me full of great possibilities. So I looked around for other couples Pat and I could enjoy a week with and engaged Crutch Crutchfield, now also one of my BS group buddies, in a discussion. He liked the idea and locale, so we quickly put together a list of three other couples we would like to invite. Two quickly accepted and the third could not consider it for personal reasons at the time. (A new wife was a recovering alcoholic, and the rest of us wanted to plan the trip around wine—sort of.)

In addition to us and the Crutchfields, Wes and Emily Marshall and Stan and Debbie Adams were ready to get into the details of a plan. It didn't take long for Pat and me to suggest a fifth couple, Kevin Wilson and his wife Jennifer Wauson.

Mike and I had invested in a start-up in the early 1980s where Kevin and Jennifer were the technical team to produce *The Personal Computer Show*, a weekly cable TV program focused on the early uses of personal computers. Kevin and Jennifer made the concept a terrific technical success, but we ran into enough business obstacles that we finally had to shut down the effort. I had enough contact with them at that time to believe many fine things about them. I had even provided some well-deserved help to get them going in their own venture. We asked if they would like to join us. We were pleased that they were flexible enough in their schedule, had enough financial wherewithals, and enough enthusiasm about the idea to quickly agree to become the fifth couple.

I had met Wes when I was invited to a gathering of the original Zinners of Austin—a group of about a dozen guys all interested in enjoying the variety and quality of Zinfandel wine. I didn't know many of them and happened to end up sitting next to Wes. He had an advanced degree in psychology and had retired from a successful entrepreneurial business owning and managing specialized medical-care centers. I found our conversation interesting and enjoyable. When Crutch suggested him and Emily as a couple for our group, I was quick to agree.

We first met Emily when we five couples gathered after arriving in Vancouver, British Columbia, for a dinner to start our trip together. As will be noted later, Pat and I made several trips with the Marshalls in subsequent years. When we were in Austin, we visited with them frequently, often at the home they designed on a beautiful setting in the hills West of Austin after Wes retired young following those successful entrepreneurial endeavors.

Wes has the largest private collection of music CDs I have ever seen. He tested and wrote evaluations of high-tech music and video equipment for several major industry companies. He is also a professional wine writer and has written two books on the subject. We always had more wine than we could taste and/or drink every time we gathered at their home. Tough duty—great friends, beautiful setting, gourmet food, and all the wine we could drink and stay reasonably sober.

All ten people of our group knew somebody, but nobody knew all. We settled on a plan to rent the mansion pictured below for the week starting the 9th of September in 2001. The mansion was built around 1900, had been upgraded periodically over the years, was located in the heart of 26 secluded acres overlooking that bay, and had six bedrooms and enough of everything else to suggest that it would be a great home base.

Wes and I worked out a plan that in part included a small jazz combo to entertain us at our digs one night, an expert on British Columbia wines another night, one day on a chartered boat motoring through the many waterways, and less expensive plans for other nights and days.

Our Group Rental Mansion in Victoria, BC

On one day, Stan took all who wanted to go along on a flight in his plane up North over Vancouver Island. He and his wife Debbie had flown the plane there from their home in Austin. They owned and managed three very popular restaurants there. When one of the restaurants was founded later, Stan's partner became a client of Dana's. Through him, Dana had met Stan who soon thereafter became a client also. He was helped a lot by Dana and decided to have her take over CPA duties for his restaurant business. In addition to her private practice, Dana is now responsible for all of his financial accounting, financial staff and systems, and tax reporting. Every time Stan sees me he manages to insert into the conversation how much Dana's help means to him.

Anyhow, we all settled in Sunday evening and enjoyed an excursion to the Butchart Gardens Monday. Tuesday started with Stan running down the stairs from the third-floor apartment yelling something about a bombing in New York. He had made an early morning business call and was talking to an employee in Texas when the news broke. We all rushed downstairs in pajamas and gathered around the small black-and-white TV in the kitchen. While we were trying to understand the nature of what had happened, we saw the real-time news reporting of the second plane striking the second World Trade Center building. We were shocked and were having great difficulty in absorbing the significance of what we were seeing and hearing.

After we broke from the TV, dressed, fixed breakfast, and shared our concerns about loved ones and others we knew who were in planes or in Manhattan, we caucused to decide what to do next. In short, we decided to continue with the plan for the week—keeping track of the news but not fixated on it. Each day a different couple was responsible for buying, preparing, and serving whatever they decided for our evening dinner that day. The jazz piano player and female vocalist were the big hit for evening entertainment after dinner. Early each evening we enjoyed a glass of wine and conversation on the patio overlooking the gardens and the bay. One evening at Stan's suggestion, we had a long discussion along the lines of what I would call metaphysics.

We also enjoyed other planned experiences, took care of quite a few matters relating to how we would all return to our homes, and departed Canada after passing border security measures. Pat and I had our car and drove Kevin and Jennifer to the Seattle airport for their flight. Stan was not permitted to fly his plane over the border for a couple of days and, when given departure approval, had to make their refueling stops in small airports enroute back to Texas. Life went on, but the implications and subsequent events initiated that week continue for all of us.

In 2002 along with three other couples we have known going back to high school days, we joined together for three weeks of traveling in recreational vehicles in the Northwest and part of Canada—in part so my golf-nut buddies could play famous courses along our route. Pat and I did not own a recreational vehicle!

RV Tour in Northwest and Canada

The others did. After looking into the cost of renting a motorhome and the fuel costs of driving it, we chose to buy a camper trailer that would serve our needs adequately, not luxuriously, and cost less. We would also have the pleasure of using the trailer occasionally for years thereafter. On several occasions, we have just gone into the boondocks to camp out, hike, fish, and just see some part of the great out of doors.

Other significant trips during those early years of the new century included a week with Kevin, Jennifer, and the Marshalls in the northern California wine country and a week in 2006 in northern Spain followed by a week in Ireland with the Marshalls.

Two of our memorable trips in the early 2000s were to gather our clan—we and our kids and their spouses—in nice places for most or all of a week. In July of 2001, we rented a large home on the ocean boardwalk at Seaside, Oregon, with a smaller apartment up the street for Rob and Karrie to sleep in. We had a great time. We were there over the 4th of July, so it was a festive time, including an Independence Day Parade.   That night during a spectacular fireworks extravaganza, we were hunkered down on the beach in front of our place. It seemed like a major war zone. None of us will ever forget it.

We also gathered the clan for a week before Christmas in Sedona, Arizona, in 2004. We rented a home once owned by a movie star, Jane Russell. The town was all decked out for the holidays, and both it and the surrounding countryside were beautiful. Of course, we have many pictures, but the pleasure was highlighted by just being together.

Family Hike in Sedona, Arizona

The gift exchange of presents was a hoot. The town's celebration of the holidays included elaborate seasonal decorations by many of the downtown businesses called the Night Lights. One evening we bundled up, including the then six-month-old Robby and nearly three-year-old Abby, and followed the directions for touring the many displays. The tour was complete with all one could imagine related to the holiday stories and music. Rob and Karrie enjoyed a romantic dinner together at a fancy restaurant while we toured.

One experience during the early 2000s was particularly challenging. That was when I started to notice that I lived in the middle of a potential forest fire! In getting acquainted with neighbors, I learned of three times when unusual circumstances started fires on private property within the subdivision that could have easily spread to the forest within which we all lived. To try to make this story also short, I went to the office of the Idaho of Lands in McCall and asked if there was anyone to give counsel on protecting against such a possibility. In other words, in addition to protecting ourselves, how do we limit setting a major chunk of the Idaho National Forest on fire—a fire that might be started in our subdivision, not by an act of nature such as lightning?

In 2001, they offered to send an expert out to walk through our subdivision and give us an idea of how to reduce the danger of fire. He suggested thinning the trees he marked as overly "mature" trees that were accidents waiting to happen if a fire started nearby. We tied ribbons to the trees, and I sent a letter to all property owners suggesting we work together to have a logger remove the trees. Most property owners viewed each way something could be accomplished as giving "the other guy" some kind of bigger advantage financially. The idea got nowhere.

However, the next year I received a call from that official to let me know there was a new government program to fund projects that would reduce the fire hazard at places where a developed area bordered a National Forest. There were grants to pay for projects. We applied for funding for a project to log and reduce other hazardous material within our subdivision area, approximately 200 acres. We received the grant and, over a two-year period, removed 39 truckloads of marketable logs and created over 100 burn piles composed of logged tree slash and many trees that were too mature (read—rotten) to be merchantable. In the process of logging, all low growth on the trees, called "ladder fuel," was removed up to about 12-15 feet. That alone reduced the threat of a serious fire by limiting the extent a brushfire could start big trees on fire and create a serious forest fire that would consume all of our homes and cabins. I managed that project and, in a certain way, enjoyed what we accomplished—but I would never do it again, even though we were selected as the best-run project of that kind in Idaho.

The actual business life experience that I retired from was pretty limited between 2000 and 2006, the year I am willing to say I retired from business obligations. As mentioned earlier, the "last supper" of the Dii Group was in the spring of 2000. We gathered for dinner at one of the most expensive restaurants in New York City, paid for by the company that acquired us. (Wasn't my decision to do that—but just another example of how our CEO liked to live high on the hog with shareholder money!) So early in the new century, I no longer had obligations to the shareholders, employees, customers, and suppliers for that large publicly traded company.

Then, my last board of directors' responsibility and mentoring experience was when Arbortext was acquired by a larger company in a transaction completed in 2006—as was mentioned in my recounting of business experience with Arbortext during the 1990s. Before attempting to describe what that meant as far as any change in lifestyle for Pat and me, I will touch on some of our personal experiences of the early 2000s and then continue on into retirement in the next chapter. A few other "early 2000's" things that come to mind follow.

I will say that my generally good health is near the top of the list. In spite of a couple of attention-getting issues, I continued to be very healthy for a guy my age. (Ditto Pat for her age.) I feel blessed compared to so many of those my age who are dealing with health issues that totally change their way of life.

As I mentioned in passing earlier, I had a history of infrequent minor seizures in my 30s and 40s and frequent nighttime panic-like experiences when respiratory rate/oxygen level was too low. In 2003, I experienced a couple of "knock-down" seizures. I was referred to a neurologist, Dr. James D. Redshaw, in Boise. An EEG scan showed an electrical anomaly somewhere in my brain (I forget where), and the doctor prescribed small daily dosage of Lamictal, 50mg 2x/day. (In two steps over the next ten years, dosage increased to 100mg 2x/day.) Dr. Redshaw had me get an MRI just to check to see if there was a tumor causing the anomaly. He informed me that various kinds of body stress could bring on seizure symptoms and that has proved correct in years since— most noticeably when I am too hot, dehydrated, or experiencing strong pain. Minor lifestyle adjustments have kept the problem from being more than a minor discomfort once in a while.

For many years, we alternated family gatherings at Christmas between the cold and snow in Idaho (Pat and I), and the moderate weather climates of Austin (Dana and Andy), Sacramento (Rob and Karrie), and Gilbert (Dave and Autumn). All were enjoyable and in some way special, but the gatherings at Bru Haus were the most unique. We often had three or four snowmobiles rowed up at night out front. Sometimes we loaded up three cars and headed for one of the ski areas north of us—occasionally pulling cars out of snow banks going or coming. And of course, many snow forts and snowball "fights."

During the 2000s, my mother moved five times in her beloved Boise before her death in October 2009. All were one form or another of independent living. Thanks to the assistance from Harley's family in Boise, and in particular JoAnne and Johnnie Davis, Mom was able to get out and about right up to the last couple months of her life. The moves in the early 2000s were the most stressful for her because she was in each instance moving because there was something about her current place that was no longer acceptable to her.

Also in the early 2000s, Mom started to have serious health issues. When she suffered a bout of pancreatitis, we thought she might not survive. Later, she fell and broke her hip. It took her a long time to recover from the surgery to replace the hip. The family believed that the fall was primarily the result of a lack of fluids and therefore a problem with her electrolytes. The assisted-living place where she lived decided that she was a risk they no longer wished to incur—read—they weren't confident their staff could provide the care they were supposed to provide! Although her next assisted living in a small home-like environment didn't work out, her next after that provided great care and comfort for her remaining years.

Which brings me to mention the death of Alfred A. King on 25 March 2006, at age 90. Other than my immediate family, up until that time I had spent more richly filled hours and days with Alfred than any other person in my adult life. I had admired many, but Alfred was at the top of my list. I miss him dearly.

During the early 1980s, I sort of got "being a member of organizations" out of my system, so there were few in my life in the new millennium. I did enjoy the time I participated as a board member in the Texas Foundation for Religious Studies and the Charles Babbage Institute and Foundation. After over 40 year's membership, I finally resigned from the Town and Gown Club in Austin because I was seldom available to attend meetings. On special occasions, I am still invited to be the guest of a member.

Although it was not a "member" thing, Pat and I enjoyed trying to help a choral music group that started in Austin during the early 2000s—then known as the New Texas Music Works. Pat and I have actively and financially supported the growth of the choral ensemble ever since. Our dear friend Fran Collmann became president of the organization early on and Larry on the board of directors. In the following years, the ensemble changed its name to Conspirare: Craig Hella Johnson & Company of Voices. Fran and Larry nurtured the group through the pains of growth, and with their guiding and financial help, Conspirare has become a world-renowned choral group.

In October of 2006, Pat and I traveled to Northern Spain and a little of Portugal for a week, then joined Wes and Emily Marshall for a very full week in Ireland. In Spain, Pat and I traveled leisurely along the Northern Coast west of Santander. Our favorite overnight was in the quaint historical fishing village of San Vicente de la Barquera located in Cantabria, where we have some of our favorite pictures and very special memories of Spain. We then spent a

Romantic Overnight at Bossaco Palace, Portugal

couple days in Santiago and three very nice places south of there—the Spanish Parador at Baiona, the historical and picturesque Bossaco Palace in Portugal, (pictured here), and the city of Oporto. I think Oporto has special charm as well as the finest port wines I have had the opportunity to sample and enjoy.

Our visits to the Baiona Parador and the Bossaco Palace were just plain leisurely and very romantic. Oporto was just as Oporto is! We loved it! Of course, it is the place where one can take a tour boat up and down the Douro River and view the tasting rooms of most of the most famous port wines in the world. But it is also historical, picturesque, both old and modern, and full of many fine tourist accommodations and culinary pleasures. We relived some great memories from that week as we flew from Lisbon to Dublin and on to Cork.

The following week in Ireland started with Wes, Emily, and us as guests two days at Gene and Barbara Courtney's Ireland estate near Kinsale, not far from Cork. From there, we traveled to Dingle for a couple of days of touring the Ring of Kerry and then on North to Galway, passing through Limerick and a visit to the Burren Perfumery along the way. The historical ruins along the Ring of Kerry were fascinating to me. Why would any humans want to choose to dwell on the Dingle Peninsula five thousand years ago? As we left the Ring, we stopped at a small village where I enjoyed the best lamb stew of my life. I have ordered lamb stew many times since hoping to experience the pleasure again—to no avail.

In Galway, we hired a guide and inhaled the long history of that part of the Ireland coast, followed by drinking and visiting with the locals long into the night. Galway just radiated happy friendly people. It's a good thing we have the memories of that day and night in Galway. The next day we moved on to our final destination in Ireland, Dublin. There we experienced the pits! One unpleasant experience after another. Wes had made reservations at a small inn in an area of Dublin where he and Emily had visited early in their marriage—a visit with many fine memories. We noticed the immediate vicinity looked a little seedy, but we checked in. We soon realized that not only were the quarters shabby but also that the lock on the front door was not operational. We also noticed that drunken young men were climbing up onto the inn from an adjacent parking garage and had taken over the unit next to ours. We didn't even unpack.

The clerk was unfriendly to the point of being ugly and would not return our money. We finally left anyway. As Emily, Pat, and I stood on the street below with our baggage, Wes ran up and down the streets in three directions trying to find alternate lodging. While we awaited Wes, Pat and Emily posed "thumbing it" for the picture at the left— while watching two passed-out druggies across the street.

Recovery from Dump Lodging in Dublin

Wes returned, sweaty and breathing hard, to tell us that our only option at that time of night was a very upscale five-star hotel a block and a half away. He had generously tipped a nicely uniformed hotel doorman to bring a cart all the way to where we were. While enduring the smiles and wisecracks of many we passed along the way, we wheeled the loaded cart to the hotel. After paying about six times what we had planned for lodging there, we flew out of Ireland after touring Dublin the next day. After going round and round with his credit card company, Wes was finally able to get a refund of all that had been paid to reserve the run-down inn.

These last few preretirement years were full of great experiences and the related memories of times with our family, frequent travel, social occasions with dear old and new friends, personal contributions of time and money to organizations providing opportunity and pleasure to many, and the opportunity to share our life together with nice homes in two very special places—in Idaho where we have our roots and lived during our formative years and in Austin where our kids have their roots and formative years—and where we have dear friends and special relationships that grew out of our almost thirty years there as full-time residents.

Some of the much more pleasant and/or particularly satisfying things about my/our personal life during these years included:

- We continued to actively ski with several trips each year to many ski areas.
- Our neighbors in Idaho are terrific friends and helpful on many occasions.
- We traveled quite a bit in wine country and restocked the cellar each time.
- Even though we lived in Idaho about nine months each year, in several years during those months, we made one- to four-week-long trips to Austin.

- One summer I took grandson's Nick and Ross camping for several days in our trailer camper at a beautiful spot on the Selway River in Central Idaho. They fished and floated the river in a raft, while I sat in a comfy lawn chair on the bank just thinking and doing a little writing.
- Pat and I started working out at the Dell Fitness Center, which is a part of the Jewish Community Center of Austin, and continue to this day.
- I continued to enjoy the monthly gathering of my BS group buddies but also endured the sadness I experienced with the deaths of two of them who had been closer to me than blood-brothers in this life.

To many, it looked as if I had already retired—and the evidence supports that view. And my strongest memory of all is yet to be mentioned. In Chapters 15 and 16, my Metaphysical Journey, I will summarize the contribution during these years toward my understanding of the nature of a greater reality.

A Thought or Two Looking Back from Now

I think the chapter was aptly titled.

There was a lot of "going" during those years, but it was "easy going". We did a lot of traveling when traveling was easier to do than in subsequent years. I truly "eased" into retirement, so the process of not being so focused on time, effort, and responsibility was spread out over the years.

Looking back, few business experiences have been as pleasing to me to see as the success of Jim and John at Arbortext. I know them both well enough to know that they will help many people and groups with their time and resources over the years. That's a big "pass it on" opportunity they will both find personally rewarding in many ways.

Looking back at all the time and effort devoted to quantum physics—I think it was worthwhile both psychologically and as a necessary step in my quest to find a personally acceptable way to view the reality I knew by then to be greater than our physical world. But lest I forget, it was and is a humbling experience. There is so much more that I do not understand than what I think I do understand. I like to think it might be more important to make the most of what I think I do understand than to be insensitive to possibly profound implications if I knew more.

It is clearer now how understanding Pat was when I devoted so much time and passion to physics instead of engaging in more activities we both could have enjoyed together. On the other hand, we have had opportunities for special kinds of pleasure far beyond what we could ever have expected earlier in life.

➤ 14 ⥽

Loafing into Old Age

The beginning of feeling on the verge of old age was the first time I had evidenced a moment of minor confusion in the presence of our kids. I immediately thereafter observed I was being given consideration ordinarily reserved for those recognized by offspring as starting on a downhill slide with a limited number of years ahead of them. Ouch! It seemed sort of like—"We better enjoy them as much as we can while they are still here!" Well, that was quite a few (by my reckoning) years ago. We seem to be holding together pretty well, but I do enjoy the increased attention from the kids and their families.

Loafing may not be the most accurate description of how we have spent our time during the last six-plus years, but it sort of suggests that I haven't been working for others for retirement income during those years. I have been most fortunate to be in good health and to have great amounts of time to pursue my interest in the nature of reality and the spiritual journey accompanying it. More on that later. I will start this chapter with what will seem to be describing more activity than there were years in which to experience it. First, there has been a lot more time with our family.

Mom found enough pleasure to make her life meaningful in her last years, right up until two weeks before her death on 9 October 2009. In August of 2010, we had about 30 family members at Bru Haus to celebrate her life.

Preceding the get-together, several family members helped Courtney prepare a slide show of pictures of Mom's life. A printed copy remains at the cabin.

Edythe Bernice (Pearce) Brueck   8/31/1915 – 10/9/2009

On three occasions in recent years, we have been able to again enjoy lengthy get-togethers with our kids and their spouses—twice with Robby and Abby included. When our 50th anniversary rolled around on 1 June 2007, neither Pat nor I wanted the kids to arrange a big affair with family, friends, and whoever happened to be walking on the streets nearby to help us celebrate our long marriage. So, we preempted. We rented a large home in Breckenridge, Colorado, for a week at the end of May and invited them all. We also invited Bob Sheets and Don Kromer to join us a couple of days. We hiked, golfed, played at the local kid park, and generally did a lot of walking and driving sightseeing in the area. And of course, a lot of just hanging out together along with some good food and wine. One highlight of the week was when Andy sang to Dana to recognize their 24th wedding anniversary on the 28th while presenting her with a card with a highly sentimental message.

The next get-together was a little different. After preparing for over a month, I invited our kids and spouses to join Pat and me in April 2009 for a long weekend at a home I rented on the shore of Lake LBJ near Austin. It was sort of a command-performance thing! The purpose was to talk about things going on in the world around us that might bring about a lot of change within the next ten to twenty years. I had prepared an agenda with five major topics and written material, Internet sites, and video material relevant to each topic. The session topics were:

The World Around Us
Technology Sampling
Longevity and Health
Societal Misc.
The US Economy

It was not a lecture. It was "let's look at this stuff and share thoughts"—which we did. A lot of the technology-related topics, including health-related science, have come about much sooner than the experts had forecast. The major changes within the fields of education have come about slower than was forecast. That is a major disappointment for me, which has caused me to look further into the situation. The forecast of relevant technology and its potential implications for changing the classroom situation in all levels of education has been in the ballpark. The implications for distant learning are unfolding big time in higher education.

In elementary and secondary education, however, in particular secondary, events in the society surrounding the educational experience are far outpacing what is happening in the classrooms. The forecast was for students to be learning much more via communication technology and social applications that would connect them to resources outside the classroom. It appears that budgetary constraints and the resistance of teacher unions have inhibited the use of the technology for the classroom educational experience. In secondary grades, students are learning a lot from the world outside the classroom but a lot of it is counter-productive to the desired educational subject-matter goals.

In my opinion, that is just one more reason I see our educational institutions graduating students ill-prepared for informed decision making in both their personal life and participation in sound governance processes within our society. The unprecedented acceleration of the rate of change in the world around us seems to me to be presenting challenges our society is having trouble dealing with.

The implications described in the material we reviewed relating to global affairs have generally unfolded in different directions than most of the potential scenarios described. The worldwide influence of demographics-related implications is unfolding about like expected. We discovered that there wasn't much we could infer from the material we reviewed relating to the unfolding of the US economy—which is no surprise. Better informed people than we daily experience the same problem.

The general assessment of our experience together was that it was worthwhile for the time and effort it required and a different kind of sharing of views than we usually experience in our gatherings together. Some of what we found most interesting was quite personal and only very indirectly related to the session topics.

In 2011, we gathered at a luxurious rental in La Jolla, California, near San Diego for a week of mostly relaxation by the pool and play of one form or another. Rob, Karrie, Robby, and Abby made day trips to the many attractions in the area appealing to family excursions. On a couple occasions, including the visit to Lego Land, Rob's cousin Jeff (Pat's nephew), his wife Lisa, and their daughter Allie joined them. It was neat for me to see the kids getting acquainted for the first time with those relatives.

One very chilly day, we visited a beach in the area. On another day, we invited Pat's niece, Amy (Benedict) Thomas, and her family to visit. At the end of the week, Pat and I drove away toward Idaho and visited Al and Helen Kosmata and places in the northern California wine country on our return. I will be very happy if I never, ever, need to drive in the heavily populated areas of Southern California again. Otherwise, great couple weeks, with many pleasant memories.

And of course, in the last half-dozen years in addition to our annual week on the Oregon Coast at Yachats each fall, we have made some special trips elsewhere, including travel to Alaska, Costa Rica, and a driving trip from Austin to the East Coast. The week on the ocean at our Yachats rental is my favorite place away from home to just relax, take walks, and catch up on reading. We always spend a few days to stock up on Oregon wines on our return to Bru Haus. Dana and Andy visited us there one year and Crutch and Danna Crutchfield another year. Since the owners added a guest room, we are enjoying the opportunity to invite family or friends to join us there for a couple days.

The way we chose to do the trip to Alaska required the travel budget for two years. In July 2008, we flew from Boise to Seattle to Vancouver, British Columbia, and on to Prince Rupert, British Columbia, where we rendezvoused with friends from Austin. There we boarded a small 100-plus foot-long boat (see picture) with only six couples as guests and a crew of five. We were fortunate that the other four couples were enjoyable shipmates. We cruised up the Inland Passage for nine days, with many anchorages in interesting places, ending in Juneau. We saw several kinds of wildlife both on land and in the water. The crew said we had more time up close with whales than any other cruise they had made in those waters. We took many pictures and videos, including calving glaciers. Just writing about it now brings back thrilling memories. (Note bibs, for the crab dinner to come.)

Whale Watching   The Safari Escape Yacht   Great Staff and Food

After we disembarked from the Safari Escape, we flew to Anchorage and, after an overnight there, took a bus to Denali National Park. At the park we stayed overnight at a lodge at the end of the road in the park. It was nice, but we would not recommend it to friends. For short visits, the main park experience is achieved on the bus ride to the end of the road and back to the park entrance—where the lodging is less expensive. Many tour companies offer that single-day experience.

We took the fabled train ride back to Anchorage, rented a car, and drove to a B&B in Seward. We really enjoyed everything about that part of our trip. We especially liked the aquarium that let us see up close a lot of what we had seen in the wild. From there, back to Anchorage and flights back to Boise, and up the hill to Bru Haus.

Our trip to Costa Rica in November 2009 was interesting, but we would not return or recommend it as much as friends had recommended it to us. We stayed at a beautiful gated resort on the West Coast and daily hired drivers to take us away to show us the best of what they had to offer. Nothing was a total disappointment, but nothing ranked high either. Have pictures, have travel receipts, have some nice memories—but would rather have gone to New York City, which was the original plan for use of the American Airlines' frequent-traveler miles.

The two-week-long driving trip East in April 2008 was much more taxing than either of the above, but we had no serious difficulties and many fine memories. We saw up close and personal a part of the USA we had not seen before. The highlight of the trip was to visit with Kevin and Jennifer in the Atlanta area, then the night in their condo at the Isha Ashram in Tennessee.

They were granted their special request that we be permitted to stay on the grounds even though we were not meditators. We were not requested to follow certain customs for those who are. The large property is beautiful and, at that time, was very early in development. We were welcomed there by everyone we visited or dined with. It is a very special place, well suited for their spiritual gatherings and programs.

We visited several tourist attractions during the trip, including the Biltmore Castle in Asheville, North Carolina. However, in addition to the visit with Kevin and Jennifer, the main focal points of the trip were to visit long-time friends Dan and Chris Appleton at their Virginia home near Washington, DC, to attend a Novak-Biddle venture-capital firm partner's meeting, and to visit Sue and Howard Cardwell at their home in Kentucky on our return trip. All three of those stops were special and memorable. It was especially nice to see Jack Biddle and a lot of my old friends from venture-capital investing days. Many, like us, are limited partners in Jack's own successful partnership.

On our migration travel from Austin to Idaho in 2013, we again went through Arizona to spend time with Dave and Autumn on the "A Gate Called Beautiful" (AGCB) property they have chosen for their retirement ministry to those in crisis within the many callings of the broader ministry. We met them on the property, and while we were there we were joined for an overnight and day by Fran and Larry Collmann. They were in Phoenix to help Fran's mom make a move to assisted living at age 99.

A lot has been accomplished at AGCB in the last couple years since Dave and I first met with the planning and zoning staff of the Coconino National Forest to learn what had to be done to get their approval for the ministry's planned use of the property. Last year the plan for development neared completion. We were all on pins and needles waiting for the presentation to the P&Z staff and hopeful approval by the Board of Supervisors. It was an emotional swing. The P&Z staff voted to decline the Conditional Use Permit application. However, Dave and his consultant prepared material to put the situation in a better light in relation to the requirements, and the Board approved the development plan.

There were many more experiences in recent years that have been special for me, or for both Pat and me, but not really special enough to get much treatment in my life story. I may want to read this again in my old age, and if so, I imagine I will enjoy seeing mention of the following:

We quit skiing in 2009 so now migrate to Austin earlier than in the past.
We both have enjoyed reunions with high school friends.
We enjoyed reconnecting with Rick Terry and his new winery venture.
A 2012 visit to the Oregon wine region with John and Laura Ford was neat.
We really enjoy having the guest suite added to our Austin duplex in 2011.
In the spring of 2013, we attended a Sadhguru program in Houston.
In June 2014, we were considered family when Rick and Leslie married.
In July 2014, our immediate family visited us here at Bru Haus.

And in the "not-so-enjoyable category," we remember:

The auto accident I caused in Phoenix on our migration to Texas in 2011.
Another of my dear BS group friends died in 2008 after a very full life.
In 2011, I suffered the first ever hard-drive crash on one of my computers.
And in June 2012, a large tree blew down and damaged Bru Haus.

Storm Damage to Bru Haus 4 June 2012

Following my formal retirement in 2006, I have again, even more so, had time to pursue matters related to my quest to understand a greater reality. These have been the years that have built upon the insights of earlier years to culminate in what I now believe. Along with the focus of prior years, I have summarized this latter part of my metaphysical journey in Chapters 15 and 16. In Chapter 17, I describe my current metaphysical perspective and how it is related to my satisfaction with my current life. But I have a more general life perspective also, so before heading into the metaphysical journey, I would like to summarize how I view the life journey I have been describing in all these many pages so far.

This part of my perspective is very important to me. It is the attitudinal starting point that I try to take with me into every new day. Oversimplified, it is just my outlook on life as I know it. In more detail, it is something I can say if I answer the first of two questions:

(1) How I feel whenever I ask myself how do I feel?

(2) What do I believe to be a metaphysically dependable guide for viewing any and all situations I encounter as a living experience?

I will take the first question first and leave the second to the next three chapters. If I ask "how do I feel," the answer is strongly influenced by how I feel about my past.

I chose to view my own life experience to date in terms of my positive experiences and memories and not how things could have been easier or better in some way. My life experience so far can be summed up in one sentence. I think I am one of the most fortunate persons on Earth. The rest is just detail.

- I was born healthy with the genetic opportunity to be intelligent. I did not earn either. Those gifts have been mine to use or abuse.
- My childhood years were without fear, abuse, or hunger.
- In my youth there was always a loving adult close by expressing that love for me and others.
- I was guided early in life by family and role models to learn right from wrong, basic decency, and other worthy values.
- Before I became a teenager, I was permitted or took initiative to engage in a lot of self-guided experience that served to build a sense of independence and self-confidence early in life. That is more difficult for a youth in this day and age.
- In my teens, I was athletic enough to experience teamwork, have leadership opportunities, and play sports under the eye of character-building coaches. I can't dance, sing, or paint pretty pictures like many people, but I was taught to run fast and how to project my voice by leading calisthenics instead of singing opera.
- My teen years were in a very forgiving time. I did not have to look forward to going to war right out of high school.
- I was able to avoid accidents or errors that would have handicapped me or someone else physically or psychologically for the rest of our lives.
- I grew up in an area where a young person could be educated and trusted to use firearms to hunt and to wander in mountains to hike and fish. These experiences helped me develop a sense of personal responsibility and independence.
- My life, all the way from birth leading up to early adulthood, included an abundance of positive confidence-building experiences with studies, work, play, friends, family, and authority figures.
- I was fortunate that the nurturing experiences in my youth helped me to develop attitudes and inclinations like fortitude, perseverance, dependability, and a general willingness to assume

responsibility that helped greatly in future years when dealing with the stress and challenges of an active and creative life.

- I learned that, with a good attitude to bring to any situation and a willingness to work as best I knew how, things would generally go well.
- I think that can be said of all humans, but I was blessed to be taught that way.
- Somewhere along the line over the years, what I experienced helped me to develop an inclination toward adaptability for dealing with a historically unprecedented and accelerating rate of change in the world around me.
- Although I later reneged on a commitment to honor its terms, the NROTC scholarship enabled me to afford to go to a major university and resulted in encounters with both opportunity and disciplines of new kinds. It was either continue to mature or hang my head and blame the world for my woes.

Being so well "equipped" for later life with good genetic fortune, healthy experiences, and a positively influenced value system—it was just up to me not to squander it. What more could a young person wish for?

And it even got better. The years that followed early adulthood were filled with opportunity and challenges not too great but to yield with reasonable effort:

- In my adult years, I was fortunate to be mentored and in critical times tangibly helped by many older and wiser.
- My employment offered me many opportunities to be successful in my work. I did not encounter any serious obstacle to keep me from accomplishing what I was asked or strongly desired to do.
- I may have been oblivious of potentially negative circumstances, but for whatever reasons, disappointment or discouraging experience did not deter me from trying to make something positive happen—within our family, at work, or at play.
- I was blessed with a marriage relationship of love, value, compatibility, and mutual recognition of responsibilities.
- Pat and I were blessed to have healthy children who learned to be responsible for their own actions at an early age and, each in their own way, to pursue education and work providing opportunity for their accomplishment and pleasure.

- My optimistic nature enabled me to see stimuli from day—to-day experience providing opportunity for constant learning and other meaningful-to-me aspects of growth.
- By working as best I could with some luck along the way, we are well enough off financially to support a good but not extravagant retirement.
- And of great personal importance (as must have been noticed if one has read this far), I have had the opportunity to pursue a metaphysical quest that has resulted in a satisfying personal perspective with which to wake up and live each new day.

So of course, I think I would be as dumb as a fence post if I didn't realize that I am one of the most fortunate persons on Earth! I choose not to dwell on any lesser view of my life experiences. I choose not to be unhappy or disappointed because of anything lacking in my present circumstances nor apprehensive about my future, even about death (most of the time!)—although I am enjoying life and hope to enjoy more of it. It comes natural for me to expect a positive future. My life perspective is simply not much burdened with negative recollections or expectations—some regrets, yes, but now a perspective within which to view them that is not upsetting. Call it selective memory or whatever; it is what I choose to think about such a neat life. I am eternally thankful.

I realize that not everyone can be so blessed. I think I understand that. However, I have seen many people create a future outlook more satisfying than might be expected from a difficult past. They read books, maybe seek counseling within a church or other relationship, maybe learn to meditate, or maybe are fortunate to have a close personal relationship with someone to guide them to a different perspective about what is possible. I hope that those young people less blessed than I can get beyond any difficult circumstance of their past and find a route to a more blessed future. I like to try help when opportunities arise.

A Thought or Two Looking Back from Now

Looking back in the rear view mirror, there were several very special people and a relatively small number of life choices that guided me into the most important paths and away from others. I am especially grateful for that. The most special of all were those that brought Pat and me together—as I am convinced was "meant to be." I am a little overwhelmed when I think of how much of our joy together has been possible because of all she has brought to our marriage as lover, wife, and mother of our children. I hold the belief that our life

217

experience is working out to be "according to a metaphysical plan" for each of us.

And reading back through recent chapters, I am reminded of what we have chosen to write about in our annual letters at Christmas time each year. We always look back on the year and realize how much pleasure we have experienced during visits and activities with many friends and family. I see that same pattern as I review what I have written about lo these many years. And in the most recent years, it has been a pleasure to see the next generation, our great grandchildren, get their start in life. In a sense, this story is for them.

Time with family and friends, in many sometimes distant places, continues to be the blessing of living longer. For that I am grateful.

I have very much enjoyed this life. I hope that shows from what I have documented. It comes natural for an older person to want to offer advice. I have decided to not go there ... -except for ... the advice I received from that high school football coach. His advice would be that for the rest of our lives we just look ourselves in the mirror at the end of every day and ask if we have done our best.

The next three chapters are for the few who want to work hard to try to follow me down a rather difficult path—both difficult for me to describe, and if I at least somewhat succeed, then a path that I believe is difficult for a reader to assimilate unless they bring with them some kind of head start. All I can say is, you don't have to go there. If you do, I suggest you keep in mind the part that describes how difficult it has been for me. Maybe it will help a reader to sort out their own beliefs about reality if they consider what I am providing as at least a few questions that won't go away unless one works pretty hard to find answers.

During this life story, my family has made an appearance in one form or another many times. To sort of bring things up to date, the current Rogues Gallery of our adult family follows.

Chapter 15 begins after my family's pictures. Join me in my metaphysical journey!

Best wishes. rlb

Bob, Pat, Dana, and Andy

Dave's Family: Nick, Autumn, Courtney, Dave, and Ross

Dana's Family at Thanksgiving 2013

Rob's Family Ski Trip 2014: Rob, Robby, Karrie, and Abby

➤ 15 ◄

My Metaphysical Journey

Part 1—From Physics to Metaphysics

Before I start down the path of these next two chapters in greater detail, I would like to mention a few things about the path and what will be encountered.

First, this is just my metaphysical journey. These two chapters are a somewhat tedious description of my journey of many decades which started with an interest to find connections between physics and paranormal phenomena. Along the path, the importance of other connections has been added to the quest; including a major contribution from channeled material to show what reality would look like if it works like described therein. I hope that what I have concluded as meaningful to me during this journey is based on solid premises, but I know others who have covered some of this same ground have arrived at a different destination. So be it. After all, "reality" is only a symbol for what one believes to be the big stage upon which all viewpoints are only a part.

Most certainly that group with alternative viewpoints includes many with an understanding of quantum physics. If some encounter what I have to say, it is possible they will not readily agree with my conclusions derived from the physics that I have found worthy of mentioning in support of my view of reality. So be that also.

I am aware that a lot of the metaphysical traditions with similarities to what I will describe utilize a different terminology to characterize them. In particular, the terminology often includes terms familiar to one with a physics background such as vibrations, fields, and probably not explicitly stated, also terms suggesting superposition of field metaphors. The conceptual mapping between terminologies should be thought-provoking, even a pleasant diversion—except possibly for the concept of "probability fields" like assumed in quantum physics.

I eventually discovered that I would have to venture well beyond physics. That included the need to investigate the evidence for something very weird to me—reincarnation. And even more difficult, I ran into the long-running war amongst the learned concerning issues of duality between body and mind. I even touched the historical third rail of physics—the nature of consciousness and how to relate it to what we describe within physics. I believe no understanding of reality can omit inclusion of each of the above in a definitive way. And, as if that wasn't enough, I finally was forced to decide if I could believe the enlightenment of a soul dictating books from life after death touching upon all of those highly contentious topics. What a great trip. I will start with the search for input from quantum physics.

Input was a little difficult to come by. I quickly realized that there remain many serious issues to be dealt with in quantum physics where disagreement was evident. I discovered that many physicists are aware of problems within current, often conflicting, theories within physics, but I didn't find much to help me identify and discuss those issues then.

According to physicist David Pratt in his article titled "The Farce of Modern Physics," there are a lot of very bright physicists who hold views contrary to others—"Fundamental differences between scientists with equally excellent credentials." In his new book *Supernormal*, Dean Radin lists eight assumptions or doctrines within generally accepted physics that are currently taught in colleges and universities as established fact rather than assumptions. In each case, I now believe there is evidence to simply classify many such assumptions as essentially false or very incomplete in some way! For instance, Professor Richard Conn Henry of Johns Hopkins University has unquestioned credentials but has put forth and defended several conclusions contrary to generally accepted physics. Inferring such an example, he has been quoted to have said, "How grotesquely badly we teach how special relativity encapsulates the practical problem of teaching physics to the freshman physics major." Right on, Professor.

Although one can take issue with some of what Pratt takes issue with, his articulation of serious inconsistences and flat-out contradictions in generally accepted physics is a tour d' force of a maze of assumptions and questionable interpretations. If one takes a little time to search the current Internet, they will find that there are now many others with excellent credentials who have also concluded that there are major contentious issues within generally accepted physics today. As many are finding out now, it is difficult to extend physics if one is hide-bound to a base model that is starting to creak and groan. There is a lot being represented by theories within physics today that does not even describe something about the same reality. Some say we are ready for a paradigm shift. I agree.

I do not describe any new physics in this chapter. However, by replacing two assumptions of mainline physics with one assumption of my own, I think I have been able to milk a lot more meaning from the physics we have to work with at this time.

Physicist Bohm treated the topic of meaning several years ago, and I don't think it is any different today. His work offered interpretations of quantum physics that raised major questions about what was being accepted as "mainstream." Bohm was asked why some of the work of his and others was rejected even though there were conclusions to show that the mainstream was obviously incomplete or based on questionable assumptions. His answer was: "Because nowadays no physicist understands this at all except by very complicated mathematical arguments which are so distant from his intuition that he regards it largely as something that is significant when he talks about his work, but not as something connected with anything else at all." He went on to summarize further that "they just present quantum physics as a set of formulae you've got to learn how to 'use', but need not 'understand' in terms of what it means."

One problem when thinking in a context of meaning is that the primary development of physics has evolved to explicitly avoid that which is not supported by experiment—even though violating that dictum often. As a consequence, there is a definite, ground up, vocabulary of terms and the relationships they combine that makes it difficult to describe concepts involved in any attempt to understand the meaning behind the model without creating incompatibility. I think sometimes physicists sort of fall in love with the terminology and inadvertently lose a grasp of the concepts, and in the process potential meaning is unnecessarily limited. I recently came across two quotes that put in words part of the difficulty that I experienced trying to come up the curve to understand quantum physics. In their 2012 book, *Quirks of the Quantum Mind*, Robert G. Jahn and Brenda J. Dunne pointed out that:

... common concepts of physical theories, such as mass, momentum and energy, electric charge and magnetic field, the quantum and the wave function, and even distance and time, are not more than useful organizing strategies consciousness has developed for organizing its world.

In their book they also quoted James Jeans from his book, "Physics and Philosophy",

...the physical theory of relativity has now shown that electric and magnetic forces are not real at all; they are merely mental constructs of our own, resulting from our rather misguided efforts to understand the motions of the particles. It is the same with the Newtonian force of gravitation, and with energy, momentum and other concepts which were introduced to help us understand the activities of the world—all prove to be mere mental constructs, and do not even pass the test of objectivity."

In particular, the "concept" of energy that was given to some relationships back in the antiquity of our physics models was the one word that caused me the most difficulty in my own journey to characterize an extended reality. Energy is at the core of cause and effect within current physics. Energy has the fundamental role in how those many "concepts" hang together as "physics". Issues relating to "time" and the treatment of the physical Universe as a closed system with conservation of energy are right up there in my list also. More on a relationship between energy and consciousness later, but the point is that the terminology is just symbolic language of physical theories and models, and the historical connotation of the terms may inhibit the search for the meaning underlying the model.

There is a "catch 22" (as one might say in the vocabulary of this era) that physics has left the meaning to be the work of others, but then the others are expected to incorporate an inadequate and sometimes misleading terminology of physics to explain the meaning.

Many pages back, I included a formal definition of that word "metaphysics," as follows: [Metaphysics = attempts to clarify the fundamental notions by which people understand the world, e.g., existence, objects and their properties, space and time, cause and effect, and possibility. A central branch of metaphysics is ontology, the investigation into the basic categories of being and how they relate to each other.] That is good enough for me. If we could indeed "clarify" all of that, we would totally identify all that there is to ultimate reality. But I will just emphasize the words "attempts to clarify," and settle for that.

Alternatively, a physicist I respect defines "metaphysics" this way: "If it is not acceptably described by physics, then it is metaphysics!" Again, I think that would be great if there were agreement on what should be accepted as physics. But, there is no such condition as agreement as to what is accepted physics. He is highly regarded within the physics community of today, but I think that statement is hollow. I think that view demonstrates he doesn't understand either physics or information that might suggest that what he understands is incomplete. So, I choose to just set forth as metaphysics—that for which there is credible evidence concerning aspects of reality that has not as yet been incorporated into an extended view of what is currently "mainstream" physics.

The physics of our everyday reality works. It may work based on questionable assumptions and thus differently from the generally described reasons, but it works. Such macro physics rests upon a basis that does not require any assumptions about the ontology of quantum physics. The quantum physics that works to make semiconductor technology is actually macro physics. The correlation statistics used to build across the gap of the indeterminacy of quantum change are based on macro measurements. We go forward creating our directly experienced world based upon a probabilistic underpinning. I don't think that is always kept in mind.

I hope that what seems to me to be growing highly credible evidence of anomalous phenomena and of the now widely recognized significance of unanswered questions will encourage some of our best and brightest within physics to become open to consider what physics as practiced today cannot alone explain about that greater reality. In the meantime, I have explored this territory as best I can. If it turns out that my insights regarding a new assumption on which to interpret important aspects of quantum physics will pass muster, then the implications are profound.

As I have gone back over the physics part of what I have written about this journey, I keep finding others who have traveled their own path to reach many of the same conclusions. The ground that I covered tediously in my journey is now being articulated from an increasing, though still small, number of sources.

There appears to be a growing number of physicists or other physics-savvy bright people who are writing and lecturing about the same issues and questions, some in books written as far back as 2002 that I wish I had seen then. I am willing to bet that, by the time anyone reads this material, there will be even more. Those I am currently aware of include physicist Bernard Haisch's book *The God Theory*; physicist Peter Russell's many books and an excellent lecture now on U-Tube titled "From Science to God: A Physicist's Journey into the Mystery of Consciousness;" the distinguished Ervin Laszlo's many books devoted to integrating material to describe an extended reality; Dean Radin's two books *Entangled Minds* and *Supernormal*.; and again, Robert G. Jahn and Brenda J. Dunne in their book *Quirks of the Quantum Mind*. Other physicists, such as Templeton Prize winner Paul Davis, have written extensively to popularize some of the more thought-provoking research results within quantum physics and raise questions with no current answers.

It is actually thrilling to me to see such outstanding scholars focus on these topics—those I have also found important. Several have arrived via different routes to some of the same physics conclusions I have reached without their extensive physics knowledge to think with. However, I am not aware of any other published work that has tied as much together as I have in one place—in particular to include the detail I have in Chapter 16—to extend the physics framework.

Anyway, the point here is that this is *my* journey. It is not a physics lecture just because it does include focus on several fundamental aspects of quantum physics. This chapter describes my sometimes torturous journey to answer questions meaningful to me. What I do know for sure is that because of this journey and what I have learned from it, I have now, to my satisfaction, answered many of those questions. And the resulting view of reality helps me to live a more enjoyable and morally responsible life.

So, moving on. I would like to expand upon some of the hints earlier in my story that this day would come. In particular, I mentioned in Chapter 10 when reporting on my experiences in the 1970s that I rubbed shoulders with a little of the paranormal for essentially the first time in my life. Those were the years when I was about 35-45 years old, and indeed I had no, or only an indirect, awareness of the paranormal prior to that time.

However as you may have noticed in Chapter 10, I actually engaged in a little more than casual shoulder rubbing. It was enough to plant a seed that I have nurtured ever since. It is rather ironic that at what might have been the busiest and most stressful period of my life, I devoted many precious hours to reading about what to me at that time was weird but fascinating stuff. In part, I would guess that some of my interest was just because there seemed to be so much weird and fascinating stuff all around me.

Those were the years when the New Age movement sprang into life in American culture. [The term New Age refers to the coming astrological Age of Aquarius.] The Wikipedia website (in this era) describes the movement in this way:

The New Age movement is a Western spiritual movement that developed in the second half of the 20th century. Its central precepts have been described as "drawing on both Eastern and Western spiritual and metaphysical traditions and infusing them with influences from self-help and motivational psychology, holistic health, parapsychology, consciousness research, and quantum physics."

I would certainly not describe myself now or then as afflicted with some of the reputation of the New Agers of the time. The usual connotation associated with that label referred to people engaged in some pretty flaky beliefs and practices.

In my case, I would just say that I was highly curious about some of the off-shoots of the intersection of several currents: the drug culture, the growing focus on the paranormal (that may have been spawned by that drug culture), the spill-over from the 1960's interest in Transactional Analysis Theory to improve one's life, the popularizing of connections between paranormal topics and the new theoretical work within quantum physics that brought forth ideas about "connectedness," the publication of the work said to be channeled by Jesus titled *A Course in Miracles* , and in general, the many books on all these topics—many combining more than one of the topics together in a single book.

The book, *The Dancing Wu Li Masters: An Overview of the New Physics* by Gary Zukav, was published in 1979—and as noted on the back cover—to provide an understanding of physics "for those people who have heard of the mind-expanding, psychedelic aspects of advanced physics, but who have no mathematical or technical background." Even without equations, it is a daunting task to understand the depth of what is presented in the book. The author combined a good bit of metaphysical perspective with the physics to make it fit with the times. If one didn't already know it, the book is enough to convince them that one does not spring from the womb understanding quantum physics.

Those were the days of Carlos Castaneda and his books such as *The Teachings of Don Juan* describing the drug-induced altered consciousness way to experience a Yaqui way of knowledge of a greater reality; Robert Monroe and his book *Journeys Out of the Body;* J. Allen Hynek and *The UFO Experience* following the closing of the USAF Project Blue Book; the book by Andrija Puharich about Uri Geller, the psychic spoon-bender, mysteriously enough called *URI Geller;* Kelsey and Grant's book *Many Lifetimes* reporting on what they heard from clients about prior lives during regression hypnosis; a #1 best seller for a while by Thomas A. Harris titled *I'm OK-You're OK;* many new or new editions of books on religions of the East and Theosophy, etc., such as the Eckankar movement created by Paul Twitchell in 1965; and a whole lot of other books on topics of the then fads and hot buttons.

And I forgot Transcendental Meditation (TM) as popularized in the 1950s and 1960s—and on into the early 21st century—by Maharishi Mahesh Yogi. Maharishi is reported to have trained over 40,000 teachers of TM, and to have taught more than five million people, including the Beatles singing group and other celebrities. His worldwide following and good works brought fame to him and several others still recognized as famous—a lasting popularity not achieved by many in the New Age of the era.

Not so lasting was Chandra Mohan Jain, a.k.a. Acharya Rajneesh, but known notoriously as Bhagwan Shree Rajneesh—a self-proclaimed guru from India. Rajneesh ended up giving the word "guru" an undeserved negative connotation. He established a commune in Oregon where he and his associates ended up acquiring 74 Rolls-Royce automobiles before their teachings and manipulation ran out of steam, and it was shut down. Zukav's book and others with themes related to metaphysical possibilities also turned out to be exploitive opportunities for others. Many books of highly speculative content were published to springboard off the growing number of issues unanswered within physics, paranormal phenomena, or the seemingly profound teachings of the gurus.

It was also the time when the direct off-shoots of the 1960's drug culture brought into being workshops, personal transformation-focused programs such as the Erhard Seminars (EST), residential communities and retreat centers like the Esalen Institute in Big Sur, California, and a boom in the lecture circuits for anyone who could say much of anything about this new ocean of stuff to talk about. All of that must have caught my attention a bit because I just refreshed my memory by looking through my book shelves! Gad, I read a lot of that and more. Some was absolute trash. Thinking about it, leads me to recall again the sage advice of Fritjof Capra in his thought-provoking book, *The Tao of Physics* :

Mystics understand the roots of the Tao, but not its branches;
Scientists understand its branches but not its roots.
Science does not need mysticism and mysticism does not need science;
But man needs both.

Yes, some anomalous phenomena seemed mysterious to me then and is even likely to seem weird now. But a lot of what we can learn from physics and other sources is also weird. I believe that we have to get over this idea of labeling as "weird" anything that is quite foreign to our personal experience. Well then, what might be some really weird things about personal experience? To refresh your memory, one current dictionary definition of weird is "noticeably different from what is generally found or experienced." That is sort of putting it mildly when thinking of the paranormal stuff I was reading about. The definition of "unbelievable" describes what many people think about the paranormal in more grabbing terms, "too extraordinary or improbable to be believed."

However, after years of reading the results of carefully conducted research related to several kinds of anomalous phenomena, I became strongly convinced that when the conclusions being published from credible research became more widely known there would be a great leap forward in physics and life sciences in general to incorporate a greater reality. It took about 50 years after the articulation of quantum physics before there was widespread understanding and acceptance in technology, culture, and commerce. At the rate of change we are seeing in the world around us at the time I write this, and in particular with the kinds of change being spawned by the Internet and social media, it should take less time to assimilate the implications starting to become understood and accepted regarding the paranormal—that which is now referred to as "the anomalous phenomena" of physics.

I intend to describe why I think physics is quite ready to give greater consideration to such phenomena. But first, I think it is about time I write a little more about that "anomalous phenomena" I mentioned back in Chapter 10. It puts many questions on the table to be answered—in particular with some help from physics. In the following and many other areas of the paranormal, the formerly unbelievable has been shown, using analytical measures appropriate for the tests, to only be weird. No longer unbelievable—just weird. And weird is good. That means there is a lot to think about. It is basic within information theory—if there is no uncertainty, there is no information, and where there is great uncertainty, there is also potentially a great amount of information to be discovered. Thus, if serious research is devoted to the study of some of so-called weird phenomena, we should learn something.

As mentioned above, in Chapter 10 I commented in passing that I personally experienced mild forms of paranormal phenomena such as Telepathy, a little Remote Viewing, and moments of intense "knowing." I have never experienced much more than that kind of thing. However, I have extensively studied the evidence for a much broader range of phenomena. Here is a small sample of anomalous phenomena that our reality includes—and some of the questions it suggests—that inclined me to look to physics for explanations.

Remote Viewing: There is a lot of credible research data to indicate that some people can report accurately, without benefit of any local stimulus, what is happening somewhere else in the space-time we live in. It is called Remote Viewing. Joe McMoneagle (from his book *Remote Viewing Secrets*) describes the phenomena this way: "The ability to produce information that is correct about a place, event, person, or object located somewhere in time/space, which is completely blind to the remote viewer." (McMoneagle was one of the most consistently successful persons to be trained in a US government program called Stargate.)

Many people have been trained to perform like that in government-funded programs like Stargate. Others, having a natural personal knack for it, demonstrate the capability without training. Just think a minute: The neurons of their brain are getting some kind of nonphysical stimuli that produce their awareness of something for which we have no theory to describe how that is possible. Data of this kind clearly demonstrates something occurring that is "anomalous." It also strongly suggests that our view of the fundamental incorporation of space and time in current physics must be extended. Information is being received without limitations imposed by distance or time. How can that be? Is that weird or, if not weird, what is? If that is happening without consideration of time or space, how much awareness of other stuff is also possible but not explained within the space-time dimension of reality?

Presentiment: There is also evidence from experiments replicated in many places in the world that our body responds to some things before our brain has even been able to notice that they happen. These are "Presentiment" experiments, sometimes referred to as evidence of precognition. Data of this kind is again clearly "anomalous." There is no known explanation for what is not yet perceived but is being measured by the sensors attached to the body.

These experiments show that human beings in controlled experiments, when confronted with pictures of highly emotional content, exhibit measures of body awareness on average about 2-3 seconds before they see the pictures their body is already somehow aware of. The phenomenon was even detected in one set of experiments when earthworms responded about one second before the earth around them was disturbed with a mechanical vibration. In both cases, the organism is responding to something before their brain neurons are aware that it has occurred. There is not only an issue with "time" there but also with a question something like, "What is it about a body that detects a visual source before it becomes a visual stimuli to brain neurons?" That is evidence of a sensing other than the five we are all familiar with. "What kind of 'sense' is that?"

Psychokinesis: There has been credible evidence for many decades that human intention or desire can cause certain random processes to become nonrandom in the manner expected by the intent and can even influence a particular face of dice to show up more often than chance when the dice are rolled. There are also more dramatic examples of Psychokinesis than those, but they have in common that human "thought" can cause change to occur in a physical process. "Is that scientific support for prayer?" "How does an effect like those occur without a known physical explanation in terms now understood as physical?" "Is it possible that just a small quantum effect can have a large physical effect such as intention to influence the function of a person just by tweaking a few atoms within body water or brain neurons?" "Does that mean that every intention may have a physical consequence?"

The Global Consciousness Project: And the plot thickens so to speak, when something initially random becomes nonrandom without a directed research attempt to create the effect. Based on earlier experiments at Princeton University, there is now a Global Consciousness Project to study Psychokinesis when large numbers of people around the world are focused intently on an event of worldwide significance. In these instances, devices in many places in the world that have been, day after day, minute after minute, always producing random data suddenly and simultaneously deviate from randomness to a degree statistically well above chance.

Between August 1998 and April 2005, 185 such events were documented, representing anomalous phenomena estimated to be 36,400-to-one greater than chance. Two such events, with exceptionally high deviations, were the funeral for Princess Dianna on 6 September 1997 (London time) and the terrorist attack on the World Trade Centers in New York City on 11 September 2001. One can quibble with use of the word "consciousness," but there is strong statistical evidence that the emotions of large numbers of people can produce physical effects on objects in locations around the world unknown to them but objects that are sensitive in some way to an influence originating with the event. It is certainly evidence of some process clearly nonphysical (by today's physics) that is creating a change in the atomic structure of many recording devices that are physical. Is there any way physics can be extended to characterize the information exchange that describes how our knowledge of an event causes an effect on the functioning of the purely physical devices as if such large numbers of people directly intended to do so?

Reincarnation: As mentioned earlier, I believe there is evidence of several kinds to support the belief that something akin to reincarnation exists. The channeled material from Edgar Cayce and the early research of Ian Stevenson eventually convinced me that something akin to reincarnation needed to be considered seriously in any effort to learn what constitutes a greater reality. The early work of Stevenson focused on credible instances (after study of many more) of apparent recollections of previous lives by very small children. Many years later, he researched the evidence suggesting that some bodily injuries associated with a death in a prior life resulted in bodily markings at birth in a current life. He published all his evidence to that effect on the Internet so it could be reviewed and challenged if necessary by others, but it was essentially ignored. (Apparently so weird as to be generally viewed as unbelievable.)

There is also other evidence for reincarnation but little that can be evaluated via a formal research/scientific method conducted in laboratory experiments.   There are many accounts of reincarnation-type experience reported in incidences of hypnotic regression. Many of the oldest established religions of the world include reincarnation as a certainty, often with matter-of-fact reporting of details about prior lives of mystics. The channeled Seth material actually provides some detail on how reincarnation fits in with a greater scheme of things. I now believe that there is plenty of evidence that, when the various sources of data and insight are taken together, they will suggest an overwhelming case for some form of reincarnation. I think the issue for all of us is: Should we take this seriously enough to see what it might say about how we live our lives? Once the idea is put on our plate, we all decide that for ourselves.

As some would say, if you believe in reincarnation, you open up a real can of worms. In that sense, I agree. If one wishes to try to understand the implications, things become incredibly difficult to characterize what the situation is outside of space-time, when we only have space-time language we are familiar with. Our thoughts and language are sometimes insidiously loaded with space-time underpinnings. For instance, we think of evidence of reincarnation as a relationship between a person alive now and something the person recalls about being alive physically in a prior time. Where has that information been stored? How are they gaining awareness of it? Should we imagine that any relationship that ever existed must also exist throughout "all time"—a.k.a. "eternity?" Questions like those make the challenge of understanding how reincarnation might fit in a real up-hill journey, but one with a destination that I have found undeniable and very meaningful within the workings of a greater reality.

Though noted as certainly curious, the many unanswered questions were not enough for me to make a study of either physics or such phenomena a primary focus of my interest at that time. However, the questions raised by paranormal evidence and discussed in some of the books mentioned above did cause me to think a little more about my then naive thoughts relating to the physics of reality. I knew just enough from trying to read those new-age books to know that I was never taught the physics that was supposed to tell us about how our world might work in those ways. The books were presenting a whole new vocabulary for me to try to understand.

It seemed reasonable to look to physics for answers to the questions raised by the paranormal, but I discovered that I really couldn't "think" physics anymore and that my advanced math that was needed to learn anew was way down my memory stack. I could recall basic material from a lot of courses relating to the physics of electricity and magnetism, optics, thermodynamics, and classical mechanics—but not about hearing a single bit worth mentioning about anything called quantum mechanics or the theories of relativity.

I recall feeling very depressed (figure of speech) that I couldn't think physics when I really, really wanted to. During the 1980s, I just recall that I sort of muddled along, banging from pillar to post, trying to integrate what I was reading and hearing but essentially avoiding the challenge presented to me to study physics. I totally missed the newest major topic within quantum physics at that time, the discovery of what became known as nonlocality.

However, with the passage of a lot of time, by the early 1990s my interest to find a relationship between physics and the paranormal did finally shift seriously toward physics. A growing awareness of the paranormal was occurring with little effort on my part—wonderment yes, but effort no. I finally developed a serious desire to try to understand quantum physics.

Quantum physics had originated in the early 20th century based on the physics subjects I had learned something about. It was just the natural evolution of the physics that had come before. Measurements and subsequent theories based on what could be seen and touched produced some improved equations to describe how physically evident things fit together. However, it finally became clear to me that the new quantum physics was more like a revolution. Even the brilliant mathematicians, who derived the theory, had a tough time accepting what the math was telling them. And there were a bunch of different assumptions used by different physicists to describe the variety of implications depending on what was assumed. It was even hard for those steeped in the subject to see where it was all headed. In a letter to D. Liplein as late as 1952, Einstein wrote: "This theory reminds me of the system of delusions of an exceedingly intelligent paranoiac, concocted of incoherent elements of thought. ... If correct, it signifies the end of physics as a science."

I had no idea about how difficult it would be to learn about quantum physics. I kept hanging up on some stuff of the kind a student can ask the professor about—but I had neither the professor nor the Internet or even a readily accessible-to-me library. I vividly recall that the things that bothered me most were related to action at a distance (field theory), several puzzles relating to the nature of time, and that I couldn't see how to relate any physics to the credible evidence of paranormal phenomena.

So in those years, I was staring at the basic level of some highly interesting physics stuff that was new to my vernacular:

What was the new way of viewing the nature of "matter?"
How did the form of "matter" change in quantum (discrete) steps?
What really was this thing called a "photon?"
"How" was the Schrödinger Wave Equation (SWE) so basically important?
On what was the Heisenberg Uncertainty Principle based?
What the heck was the Special Theory of Relativity?
And I had no clue regarding the negative energy solution of Dirac.
And I am sure there was more!

And also, I was encountering nagging questions like these:

How could a photon be called "a particle" but have no rest mass?
Was the photon energy or did it just "carry energy?" Just a force?
How to view "energy" other than as a name of something within physics?
How could an electron-photon absorption/emission take place in no time?
How could the SWE be defined in the macro but describe the micro?
What caused quantum indeterminacy?

Antimatter? Zero-Point Energy Field? (Everywhere, but nowhere?)
What makes the Special Theory of Relativity and speed of light special?
And, of course most importantly, if space-time is not fundamental, what is?

It became clear to me that the gut of the new physics was the focus on how "change" in the form of matter from one moment to another takes place in our physical world at the subatomic level. Based on the work of Max Planck that triggered the revolution in physics around the turn of the 20th century, the words "quanta" and "quantum" had come into the physics vocabulary with a special meaning. The words came to refer to the small discrete units of anything that is involved in any physical action. The common example is a quantum of light energy called a photon. I learned that a photon is defined to be a particle but has no mass. The amount of energy it represents depends on its "frequency" when alternatively considered to be an electromagnetic wave. Each photon is defined to be a unit of "action" regardless of frequency. But the term "action" occurs rarely in a physics context. For me, things started to get very complicated when I attempted to learn all there is to know (or is assumed) about a photon. However, I soon realized that one cannot even talk about and understand how change takes place without including the role of photons.

In our physics models, the "change" from one atomic-level configuration of microscopic matter to another (simple "change" as we all think of something changing) requires a change in the energy distribution among the atoms in the area that is changing. The electrons in the atoms of matter have infinitesimal levels of energy, and all change in energy at that level is modeled by quantum physics and chemical processes. Within physics, examples occur when an atom is said to absorb or emit energy in the form of a photon or when atoms collide. All change taking place in the atoms and molecules of our physical world is in one way or another based on that simple energy-exchange phenomena. Energy is defined that way. That is how the word attains inferred meaning in a physics context. As I will write about later, the same word, "energy," is used to infer somewhat different implications in a broader context of "creative" processes. What really bothered me was when I read that the change in the energy level of the electron was assumed to happen "simultaneously" with the emission or absorption of a photon.

There was much about what was said to be quantum physics that was confusing when I was trying to better understand how it fit with how the passage of time is experienced in our day-to-day world. Eventually, I think I have found a way to extend physics to make moot some of the problems imbedded within mainstream physics arising from assumptions about the nature

235

of time. But to get there, I had to deal head-on with Einstein's Special Theory of Relativity (STR) and the idea of his space-time interval. I recall wondering what might be the significance of something moving at the speed of light. I didn't have the slightest idea then as to what that might mean.

According to the theory, for anything traveling at the speed of light, time has slowed to a stand-still, and space has contracted to a point. Well then, what about a particle of light moving at the speed of light? Does that mean that a photon experiences no time and doesn't go anywhere—all the "time?" Yes, I guess. As Peter Russell writes in his 2002 book, "From Science to God," "This points toward something very strange indeed about light. Whatever light is, it seems to exist in a realm where there is no before and no after. There is only now." As will be described later, experimental evidence has confirmed that observation.

At least that is what the STR indicates. Well then, "light just is", and one way to think about a photon being absorbed by an atom is to view the atom as having received some energy—period—and has sort of been "kicked" to change its situation in the physical world at each "now".

At the time I was first trying to understand the implications of the STR that was just a puzzle with no explanation. More recently, I like to think of that as, "Light does not move, we do," but that is not relevant to my journey so I will leave that there.

And then there was the main equation within quantum physics. The Schrödinger Wave Equation (SWE) represents how change "might" occur, but it does not completely represent the "why" the change occurred or the "exact" outcome. It is not even clear "what" the wave function says about the underlying reality to which it is associated that specifically determines the outcome of the change. That latter issue is where things are left for various "interpretations." The manner in which it was derived may be useful to provide probabilities for the likelihood of various possible outcomes but nothing more specific than that.

That equation begged for an interpretation of why these infinitesimal levels of change take place in that manner, and there have been several ideas about that, but none resolved the question sufficiently for me. I read what others had to say to help me hypothesize a little about the reality underlying the phenomena. However, the SWE did not provide me with much in the way of "built-in" suggestions about what that reality might be. It simply does not describe the nature of nature—but we know it works! The SWE is basically just a mathematical equation, but it took me a long time to realize that is so because it has been described in several different ways to arrive at the "interpretations" of what quantum phenomena is believed to represent about reality. More on that later when I write about my own "interpretation."

At the time, there was no obvious reason to me why deep down every minute change in the makeup of matter at the microscopic level could only be characterized via probabilities, thus giving all change an aspect of unpredictability. That was a totally new phenomena for me to try to understand. Quantum physics described the world beneath what we see and touch in a new way—a statistical way. It is interesting to me to note in retrospect that the realization that reality is statistical to the core actually led to the evolution of the semiconductor technology that is ubiquitous within current developed societies today.

My loss of faith in the validity of assumptions associated with the various ideas about the reality underlying the quantum equations (the "interpretations") thus became a growing issue for me. Until the early 1990s, I had never had enough time to come to grips with sorting out the four or five most widely accepted of those ontological interpretations. However, like many others, I kept asking myself that question: "What does the weirdness of quantum physics say about the nature of existence—an underlying reality?" The answer was and is—not much when the best physicists in the world can't agree!

Prominent physicists such as Richard Feynman claimed that nobody, including himself, understands quantum mechanics—they just know how to compute things in order to get predictions that fit the facts observed after looking many times at how things change. He is reported to having also said, "If you think you understand quantum mechanics, then you don't." That point was later proved by a poll among 33 leading thinkers at a conference in Austria in 2011. That group of physicists, mathematicians, and philosophers were given 16 multiple-choice questions about the meaning of the theory, and their answers displayed little consensus.

Even though the formulation of quantum physics was a revolutionary "paradigm shift" in understanding how change takes place at the level of microscopic particles like electrons, protons, and neutrons—the stuff of atoms said to comprise every physical object—for me it sort of created more questions than it answered. It was just another incomplete picture in what science could determine about the working of our physical world. What was new was that,

that picture had some new and pregnant gut issues built in, including one that was basic to all others. I think the sense of "incompleteness" was more obvious than had been the case with the equations and models before quantum physics. In the vernacular of quantum physics at the time, a particle could be somewhere without being in any particular place—someplace but other than within some bounds—we don't know exactly where within space-time focused physics. There was obviously more to be learned about that. (And there has been.)

Grossly overly summarized, it was like everywhere you looked there were houses full of furniture without knowing how the house came into being or how or why there were different kinds of furniture. Further, when one looked in a house, even houses with the same furniture, the way the furniture would be arranged in the house could not even be known for sure before you looked. If one started down a path looking at lots of houses, it was possible to determine how much of the time any certain arrangement might be observed, but what would be seen when looking into any one house was indeterminate in advance. All you would have to work with were some probabilities for one kind of arrangement or another.

I learned that in the context of quantum physics, it was like there is a microscopic level in our entire physical world where something unknown to us, except in a statistical sense, selects one outcome instead of another from possibly several others at each small step when anything changes physical form or makeup. We don't directly "see" that level of indeterminacy when we look around and go about our daily life, but it is there. I learned that the change steps happen so fast, so to speak, that we only know details of the outcome when many change steps have occurred or when the quantum-level phenomena are closely studied and technology developed to identify and measure (macro) the results of subatomic change statistically.

In fact, according to our physics models that provide the language we use to talk about the subject, the subatomic change steps may occur many millions of times per second (maybe even greater than ten to the 44th power). We have no technology to directly measure something happening that quickly—so even to call them microscopic is a technology issue. Our best current technology can only directly record a subatomic changed state after about a million times a million times a million times a million change steps may have already occurred. (That's only ten to the 24th power.)

Even at that rate, what we see or measure as change is actually the result of a sequence of interim change steps. No particular material object exists long enough, as an indivisible or identical or rigid thing, to change or age. The energy behind it weakens. The physical pattern therefore blurs. Each recreation at each blink therefore blurs. Each re-creation after a certain point becomes less perfect. After many such complete re-creations, that could not have been perceived physically by a person, one will notice the difference and assume that a change in some object has occurred.

Neither our eyes nor our technology can even come close—but what might be happening that fast is at the heart of any attempt to understand a greater reality than presented by the models and equations of current physics. I learned that through study that was not a part of my education nor from sources I am familiar with outside of quantum physics.

The implications of that statistical nature of nature were and are wide reaching. I learned that physics research related to that seemingly small window of quantum level indeterminacy has led to many questions relating to reality that physics cannot answer. What is the source of that indeterminacy? What causes it? What is the relationship of the indeterminacy at one change step with the next change step? Is it just some randomness in nature that can never be identified? As will be covered in many pages to follow, I managed to sort out those issues and arrive at answers meaningful to me.

When I first learned enough to grasp the significance of this quantum indeterminacy, it seemed to me that I should have seen more evidence of work to extend physics to relate the obviously related unknowns in physics to the unanswered questions prompted by the study of paranormal phenomena. In both areas, it seemed obvious to me that there were *conditions outside of space-time* that would have to be discovered before many substantive questions could be answered. That thought guided me to subsequently question the support for key *assumptions* buried in the physics models to limit cause and effect to space-time representations. In my view at the time, there was little evidence to indicate that many physicists had focused on that issue, even though I learned later that many have done so.

I began to devote more time to those issues in the late 1990s. If I had to pick a turning point in when I started to sort out and try to improve upon some of the fundamentals of quantum physics I knew about, I would pick 1998. Since first reading the Seth material as far back as the 1970s, I had also been prompted to think at least a little bit about where the nature of a consciousness outside of space-time might fit in. I had begun to realize that what I was looking for was something akin to answers to that question described above—how

239

physics might be extended to allow or explain what it was that I had read about in Seth or was reading and thinking about in parapsychology. However, I certainly had not tried to better understand the nature and forms of consciousness, and that is almost all of what Seth was talking about. (I have included background information related to Seth and channeling in the next chapter of this long story.)

Consciousness was controversial. I had/have over ten books about the nature of consciousness, but they don't even give a degree of certainty that they are talking about the same thing. As George Miller noted in 1987, "'consciousness' is a word worn smooth by a million tongues." More importantly to me at the time, it seemed like everything significant that I was reading and/or thinking about created more issues about the nature of time or even space-time. I left the topic of consciousness for later but did put more effort into thinking about how our models within quantum physics could be extended to incorporate the data describing newly studied paranormal phenomena. For a long time, the Seth material continued to be just a neglected source of insight that didn't make it to my frontal lobes. I was fixated on my need to better understand quantum physics. (Looking back, I think that was a good thing to do at the time.)

Soon after it was published in 1996, my longtime friend Gene Courtney read the book by John Gribbin, *Schrodinger's Kittens and the Search for Reality*. He was so sure I would want to read it that he sent me a copy. It was interesting, but it wasn't until toward the end of the book that it became a "wow." That was the first time I heard about the work of Bell (1964) and Aspect (1981) that introduced the theory and experimental evidence of something called "nonlocality"—but at that time the then-current physics provided few leads about where that fit in! Then, as is the course of physics, bright people had begun engaging in work to find answers.

I also discovered that a Nobel Prize winner, Brian Josephson, was exploring the border between physics and certain areas of the paranormal. His stature and the substantive nature of his work enabled him to challenge many in physics who had a knee-jerk reaction against the paranormal data. Josephson said that some scientists feel uncomfortable about ideas such as Telepathy and that their emotions sometimes get in the way. He was repeatedly rebuffed within the physics community for his open-mindedness regarding the paranormal, but later in the mid 2000s, he was given an opportunity and took advantage of it to blast his critics in a scholarly manner. There were others who shared his interest, but it was his stature that caught my attention.

The work of Bell, Aspect, and others established nonlocality as fact within our equations of quantum physics, basically that any change anyplace in the universe could in theory be influenced by what was happening in any other part of the universe! This evidence of a certain level of "interconnectedness" within the greater reality did not and does not (as some believed) provide a theoretical basis adequate to explain all that might be occurring in paranormal phenomena, but it did add a major piece to the puzzle. Said another way, *they proved that the belief in a purely objective reality requires cause and effect and was demonstratively false*, and the nonlocality theory arising from quantum physics could be experimentally verified. (But the lack of an objective universe does not take away the beauty of a sunset. More on that in the next chapter.) <u>They established that there must be more than a physical, objective world</u>—*that there must be "an outside of space-time."*

Nonlocality also did make it clear that there was a kind of "wholeness" within physical reality. The message seemed clear: One could not look at the world and try to understand it as just a collection of independent and separate particles—or separate anything. I just kept wondering about matters related to nonlocality. The time had come for me to get a lot more committed to try to learn enough to actually develop ideas about what might be *that reality beyond space-time*.

However, easier said than done. In the process, I discovered that there was a lot more depth to quantum physics than I had imagined or can even imagine to this day. I had a hard time sorting out what I should be learning from the broader areas of quantum physics and what was really relevant for the project at hand. I was banging from pillar to post reading a vast spectrum of research papers with little of significance for me. They were mostly just mathematics devoid of meaning directly related to my interest at the time. The good news was that I discovered that more and more was being published about a growing amount of evidence of the paranormal phenomena. It was beginning to be referred to within physics as "anomalous phenomena." (I regarded that as progress.) I gave up trying to know more than I needed to know about physics in general and settled for what seemed directly relevant to me as a contribution that basic quantum physics could provide for understanding paranormal phenomenal and a bigger picture of reality.

When trying to find quantum theorists with work that might be highly thought-provoking in seeking a way to bring together physics with the evidence of paranormal phenomena, I studied the interpretation of quantum physics characterized by the work of David Bohm. Sometime during the 1990s, I had encountered and read the 1993 book, *Bridging Science and Spirit* by Norman Friedman. He wrote about the common elements between the physics of Bohm and reality according to Seth. In that book, he also loosely compared those interpretations of reality with the interpretations of others. The model and the descriptive terminology of Bohm sort of required "going to language school" to understand his particular interpretation, but I am glad I eventually worked my way through it with Friedman's help.

Bohm's interpretation of how to view quantum phenomena includes the possibility of "hidden variables," and as a consequence, it can be extended in *possible meaning* to be more than just the mathematics. Bohm also had more to say about the quantum vacuum than I had encountered before. It was of interest because I had earlier encountered the derivation for representing the quantum vacuum when studying the work of Nobel Prize recipient Paul Dirac. His work included a representation for "negative energy" and speculation about "antimatter." Both topics intrigued me, but it was years later before they became (highly) meaningful in my view of things—in particular as to how to relate quantum field theory to conclusions based on more elementary physics.

Bohm's deep dissection of what was assumed and accepted in Einstein's Special Theory of Relativity went far beyond any such assessment I had encountered before or have since. His articulation of the Special Theory of Relativity indicated to me that, even though there is generally accepted experimental verification, the Special Theory of Relativity raises some interesting questions. Bohm went so far as to say: "Einstein's relativity theory is a central plank of 20th-century science and is commonly said to have passed every experimental test with flying colors. However, there are plausible alternative explanations for all the experimental data and astronomical observations cited in support of the special and general theories of relativity, and the internal inconsistencies and unwarranted assumptions of standard relativity theory have been pointed out by dozens of scientists." In my later study of the topic, I discovered there were a lot more than a dozen with issues related to the Special Theory of Relativity.

Month by month in the latter part of the 1990s I learned and remembered more and more. I began to understand how and why there was much more to the meaning of the word "reality" than I had ever considered before, but I was also beginning to pull together a way to view it. It took another few years of rather intense study for me to start to make a personal breakthrough in the quest to greatly expand my view—but I was past the point of no return.

In 1998, I coined the word "binks" to describe my baby steps in the direction I was headed. Eventually, binks brought quite a few thoughts together into sort of a combined physics/consciousness framework. The word "binks" was a play on words because my view included what I thought at that time might be the way to consider the "collapse of the wave function" in the Copenhagen Interpretation of quantum physics that was developed by Heisenberg, Bohr, and Einstein in Copenhagen, Denmark, in 1927.

I decided to assume that the quantum steps of change all took place simultaneously within the entire universe, and I decided to call this assumption "binks."

I realized I could assume that to happen at the boundary of the current physics model of the universe where the Heisenberg Uncertainty Principle applies—at the Planck dimensions where the measurable universe is too ill-defined (fuzzy) to be precisely described by quantum physics. Within our models, that is where the limit of simultaneously representing space, time, energy, and motion occur. As a consequence, my assumption did not violate any existing quantum physics I was aware of. That assumption in binks also did away with the physics and philosophical issues associated with the "Measurement Problem" related to the (so-called) collapse of the wave function.

In essence, the "binks blink" replaced the collapse of the wave function to create a new version of the (entire) physical world independent of how it might be observed or measured. The Schrodinger Wave Equation thus became a way to compute statistical data and not to otherwise be an indicator of the nature of the reality from whence the statistical uncertainty. It provided no other basis for direct physical interpretation. The binks assumption placed all the "indeterminacy" within quantum physics to come and go faster than the blink of an eye, so to speak. ☺

Furthermore, the binks assumption provided a way to understand the speed of light as just a consequence of the rate of that blinking. (That turned out to have widespread ramifications—see Note in Passing below.) That helped me to better understand the Special Theory of Relativity and made moot the need for Einstein's "assumption" that the speed of light was constant for nonaccelerating frames of reference. In a sense, the binks assumption replaced it.

I recently traced back in the evolution of our physics models and equations to see why Einstein had to "assume" that the speed of light was the same in nonaccelerating frames of reference rather than state it as fact—if he knew it was fact. It appears to me that he did so because he incorporated the Lorentz transformation that in turn had evolved from the work of Maxwell that had "assumed" the existence of an aether that led to the incorporation of constants within the E and M equations that later were shown to establish the value for the speed of light (without the aether assumption) and the conclusion that light is an electromagnetic phenomena. Some physicists claim to have reason to believe that Einstein just made the assumption so as to make the invariant space-time math work.

However, in the worldview of the binks assumption, there is no need for the idea of a speed of light with the usual connotation of "speed," or even the concept of a tachyon within certain explanations. The measurable changes in the physical world just occur at the blinking rate or slower. All "speeding" is just a word connecting the concept of time to blinks occurring so fast we cannot see or measure anything but what appears to be or has been the result of change— perceived or measure and sometimes called motion—in essence, the rate of changing manifestation of the universe. (The role of the photon of generally accepted physics must thus be understood quite differently.) The "speed" of light is just the fastest rate of change of space per unit of "time" (the Planck reference rate) as the variable "time" is embedded within the model of physics.

The binks assumption provided me an opportunity to extend the meaning to be derived from quantum physics in a major way. In essence, it has nothing to do with speed but a lot to say about "change" within our physical world. It provided a way to take the "outside of space-time" aspect of nonlocality into a much more enlightening perspective of no space and no time.

Note in Passing: [Although I didn't understand the full implications at the time, starting with the binks assumption as a way to view the "speed" of light ("c") as a fundamental attribute of *all* change taking place in the physical world helped me to later understand much more physics. In particular, it changed how I view the significance of the Maxwell Equations, the evolution of relativistic quantum-field theory, the fundamental relationship between light and all energy as energy is characterized within physics, the way to characterize negative time, the nature of antimatter, the significance within physics that the photon is its own antiparticle, the connection with what is attributed to the zero-point field, and an entirely new way to extract *meaning* from quantum physics that I think would have delighted David Bohm. The two centuries of study regarding the nature of light culminating with Maxwell's equations created a basis on which much of modern physics is built. Accepting the binks assumption does not require changing those relationships depicted within the models and equations of experimentally verified physics, but it does make apparent the need to examine certain assumptions that are associated with those relationships and a much different and greater meaning to be associated with them.]

The binks assumption did not create incompatibility, and I thought it would open the door for extending physics to help explain paranormal phenomena if it had anything to say about "time." It turns out that it did. It shed a whole new light on the topic, pun intended.

To summarize, those aspects of binks were not incompatible with basic quantum physics but described a universe that blinked in and out at the tremendous rate provided by the Planck interval to bring about all steps of change at the quantum level. (There is a transition issue between blink states—sort of a fading out and a fading in. That is immaterial here. I will come back to the question of what might be going on between blinks in the next chapter.) The outcome for each blink remains indeterminate throughout the universe, but the issue of when a change could be assumed to have occurred—just the "ordering" is specified—leaving cause and effect as an open issue. That was a very important insight because as my views developed *it served as a "synching" of where the inside and outside of space-time intersected*.

The great mathematician Gottfried Wilhelm Leibniz (1646-1716) obviously had that idea in mind when he said, "Space and time are merely bookkeeping devices for conveniently summarizing 'relationships' between objects and events within the Universe." That seemed interesting when I first read it, but at that time I didn't realize it must actually be one of the most profound insights of the 17th century.

Most importantly, from these very basic insights it became clear to me that "time" and "light" were just attributes of a blinking in-and-out universe! Time is not a dimension, it is just a measure we use to record and observe changing conditions in the physical part of reality, and a name we have associated with the psychological experience within the changing world around us. Time is just an attribute of change per se. The ordering of the change steps may involve much more than what we typically refer to as past and future—the change steps just "are"—they are just a "now."

The possibility of negative time, so to speak, became something to keep in the back of my mind because within the binks model, the use of the variable "time" as used in physics models can have meaning *independent* of the order of the change. Although I didn't realize it then, that fact became important later when negative time had meaning in a very special way that made sense for explaining retro-causative paranormal phenomena and to even provide meaning that helped to connect physics and consciousness.

With the binks assumptions at the quantum level, more doors were opened to consider and put the focus on how change occurs. The idea of the *passage* of time becomes secondary. With each new pattern for the universe, *there is only the "now."* And without "need for" the passage of time to describe/model how the change occurred, there will just be a subsequent "now" to follow—and with it that *indeterminacy* regarding where the influences causing the change come from and the details of the form it will take.

That idea of the immaterial direction of time is not inconsistent with the Heisenberg Uncertainty Principal or with quantum physics in general. The application of the math of quantum physics is not a cause-and-effect model. The predictive statistics characterizing the possibilities of what might be occurring at the macro level of each "now" do not fully address what might be "causing" the change in energy states that takes place with each blink. There is just incompleteness within the current framework of quantum physics. That is why I hoped that physics could be extended by incorporating the growing amount of credible evidence of anomalous phenomena.

I was pretty excited about binks.

Binks provided me a framework for incorporating how not generally recognized influences might be involved in the evolution of the entire pattern of the universe as changes happen in quantum steps.

It changes the way of thinking from "past" and "future" to a framework of "prior" and "subsequent" "nows," where the insidious incorporation of "time" into our terminology disappeared. That was my start to put meat on the bones of an interpretation of my own. Binks was a starting point to extend what I thought physics could contribute to a much greater understanding (and related meaning) of what was behind that word-symbol "reality." Binks thinking eventually just got folded into my more extensive view of reality, but it gave me my first big step.

Although I had begun to spend more time studying physics in the late 1990s, it was during the first few years of the new century that I started to bring together additional sources and thoughts that supported the initial binks framework as a path by which to extend physics to help understand the paranormal as normal. It helped that I could include a friend with related interests in the evolution of my thoughts.

Following our unforgettable 9/11 experience shared with Kevin and Jennifer that I mentioned in Chapter 13, our times together became more frequent, and our friendship with them grew to be much deeper over time than with all but a few friends in my adult life. By the late 1990s, Kevin and I had started sharing questions of a metaphysical nature. We continued those discussions into the early 2000s—mostly trying to find some connections between physics and the evidence of anomalous phenomena that was being reported with increasing frequency during those years.

In one of those discussions, Kevin added a new dimension. He happened to mention that his dad had several experiences of awareness of ghosts in his adult life and, finally, that he had had his personal experience. Kevin said that he had been contacted psychically by his uncle who had died during WWII on a bombing mission. This was a report of a paranormal experience of a different kind than I had ever personally experienced or ever heard about from a person I viewed as highly believable. I became much more interested in that kind of altered consciousness (psychic experience) but still primarily focused on trying to learn more of an ontological nature of reality via my own interpretation of what could be gleaned from quantum physics. The significant contributions from Kevin to help me understand the connection between physical reality and the role of consciousness as a part of psychic experience came later.

During those years, my growing passion to understand quantum physics turned into a borderline obsession. Every day I arose and scanned all the announcements of new research papers that were listed on the website http://arXiv.org in the field of quantum mechanics. I had also studied daily the email dialogue between top-flight physicists on the discussion list moderated by Paul Davies as part of the Science & Ultimate Reality Symposium in honor of John Archibald Wheeler on his 90th birthday in 2002.

That is where I encountered the work of Ulrich Mohrhoff and his "Pondicherry Interpretation of Quantum Mechanics." The key within his work was to recognize that the starting point of interpretation, the Schrodinger Wave Equation, was simply a probability calculus. That was a confirming, but also a more in-depth view of what I had decided about it when worrying about the SWE while arriving at binks. He put a lot more flesh on those bones. His work was a major stepping stone to my advancing beyond the creaking gigantic edifices within the literature that were built on the assumptions of other "interpretations" relating to quantum physics.

Mohrhoff's interpretation rejects the time-varying treatment of the wave equation and also deals with all the issues of "the measurement problem." It better articulates what I had considered the speculative assumptions and questionable conclusions associated with the Copenhagen Interpretation. It also departs from classical physics in rejecting the usual assumption that physical reality could be limited to the way atoms and constituent particles or, the objective universe in general, were characterized in the models and equations of modern quantum physics (consistent with nonlocality). It made clear that the statistics of indeterminacy were determined by what change occurred at each discrete macro change step rather than what "caused" the change. It was the first strong support known to me of key aspects of my binks interpretation in work by a first-class physicist. I would not mention it here if it was not a big deal in my view—helpful both psychologically as well as a source of new insights.

I knew I had to change my ways when I began to realize that my blood pressure went up every time I became highly intent for a prolonged period of time on something difficult for me to understand. For a couple of years, I often laid awake an hour or two many nights—focused on the same issue night after night, week after week, and even month after month. At some point I realized that obsession was unhealthy—in several respects. I backed off—a little—enough. I think it helped that I had a growing confidence in what I understood.

In late June 2006, I attended a three-day symposium in San Diego on the nature of "time," which was organized as part of a week-long meeting of the Pacific Division of the American Association for the Advancement of Science. The formal title of the symposium was "Frontiers of Time: Reverse Causation—Experiment and Theory."

Before attending the San Diego symposium and probably in part what helped develop my interest to attend, I discovered research papers describing very thought-provoking research tests relating to time. I briefly exchanged emails with both researchers to ask questions. The one who in turn asked me a question that at the time I could not answer was Antione Suarez, but that question has been in my memory bank all this time—and with my current belief about how reality works, I think I can finally answer it. Running into his paper, I had learned that in 1997 he and Valerio Scarani had proposed a certain experiment to test an aspect of nonlocality that indirectly was also a profound probe into the fundamental nature of "time." In 2001 Suarez and Nicolas Gisin had performed the experiment.

Based on his work, Gisin had reported experimental evidence that *no story in space-time can explain the evidence for nonlocality; the evidence seems to emerge somehow from outside space-time.* That confirmed by experiment the implication that there is no objective reality, as was a conclusion based on the theoretical nonlocality research earlier. In early 2006, Suarez subsequently performed another experiment, one that really got my attention. In the conclusion of his paper describing that experiment he wrote:

The entanglement bringing about nonlocal correlations is insensible to space and time, and cannot be described in terms of "before" and "after" by means of any set of real clocks. ... *In the nonlocal quantum realm there is dependence without time, things are going on but the time doesn't seem to pass here.* (My emphasis.)

It was this last sentence that sort of blew me away. Here were physicists that reported they had experimental evidence for some of what I had concluded when deciding on the blinking assumption when arriving at my binks interpretation. Their wording in that sentence cut to the core of the matter. Wow. That just made me all the more determined to understand more about how that could be, and more importantly, what were the implications related to expanding upon binks and providing support for paranormal phenomena.

In summary, by the mid-2000s theoretical and experimental research results in the prior few decades had clearly established that the models and equations described by current physics must be extended to eliminate wrong or misleading assumptions, to account for nonlocality, to recognize the fact of change occurring without the passage of "time" cannot be explained solely by current physics models, and to deal with the uncertain direction of cause and effect.

After attending the San Diego symposium, I wrote a report summarizing my "take away" thoughts. It is in my files as "San Diego Symposium Report—A Perspective and Summary" and describes the list of session topics and the presenters who were about half physicists and half researchers within some area in parapsychology. The non-physicist researchers also had a solid background in physics. I think the San Diego symposium was a watershed event in establishing a basis for accepting the research evidence of retro-causation but that the tough issues relating to time per se were not addressed deep enough for me.

I had heard about retrocausality and read one or two papers, enough to get the idea based purely on statistical data. But the San Diego symposium helped me to understand the wide implications when some condition in what we call the future can "cause" certain conditions (as "effects" created by the cause from the future) so as to bias the earlier change steps toward that specific future. That is, *an effect preceding the cause, as we conventionally measure/order time!* So with the Suarez conclusion and this, there clearly can be an influence from outside of time (time doesn't know about it—it is independent of time) related to observable change in our physical world—but it is not clear if it is to change the past or the future as we think of "time."

That work drove a nail in the coffin of the cause-and-effect direction built into our current physics models if they are understood without these considerations. That possibility was anticipated by what I described earlier—that at each "now" the direction in time of the cause and effect may not be known. That indeed has wide-spread implications because our widely accepted basic physics and life experience always assume that cause precedes effect. I now count on unpredictable events to create an open parking space where I want it before I get there! ☺

In a more technical sense, there were enough research results discussed during the San Diego symposium to record retro-causation in my feeble brain as a fundamental aspect of reality, and one that seriously challenges how erroneously committed we are to a sense of time just flowing along. The conventional belief is that retro-causation is impossible. I knew quantum physics allows for the possibility of negative time, but the San Diego symposium gave it a little flesh and blood, so to speak. It also drove home—again—to repeat—that the cause and effect that depends on the arrow of time that is firmly built into parts of our current-day physics is a weak reed to build on. Binks did not have a problem with the ordering issue—as was pointed out earlier. Once thinking with a context outside of space-time, increments of time per se are just not what determines the evolution of influences that create changing relationships.

I did find one technical paper in particular to be highly thought provoking. Richard Shoup of the Boundary Institute presented a paper in which two points were made clear to me. One, with analysis strictly supported by existing physics, he demolished the often-made assumption that the indeterminacy within quantum physics was the result of simple randomness within nature. I later encountered a paper written by David Pratt back in 1997 that, in a different way, supported the same conclusion. Following his study of Bohm, Pratt concluded "Quantum indeterminism is clearly open to interpretation: it either means hidden

250

(to us) causes or a complete absence of causes. The position that some events *just happen* for no reason at all is impossible to prove, for our inability to identify a cause does not necessarily mean that there is no cause." One could just say that is the logical conclusion that one "can't prove a negative." However, he continued:

The notion of absolute chance implies that quantum systems can act absolutely spontaneously, totally isolated from, and uninfluenced by, anything else in the universe. The opposing standpoint is that all systems are continuously participating in an intricate network of causal interactions and interconnections at many different levels. Individual quantum systems certainly behave unpredictably, but if they were not subject to any causal factors whatsoever, it would be difficult to understand why their collective behavior displays statistical regularities.

Of course, it is those statistical regularities (correlations) that underlie our semiconductor technology and the ubiquitous incorporation of electronics in society at this time.

Shoup also rigorously established that, because of the possibility that retrocausality might be operative in any situation, all quantum steps of change within the physical world (as modeled within physics) should just be viewed as the difference between measurements of one set of relationships and another set of relationships without any built-in incorporation of time because, with the interconnectedness, there is no way to determine the time ordering of cause and effect. In discussion with him then, and in email exchanges since, he is strongly committed to be working totally within the current models of physics and seems particularly averse to considering possible influence of any kind from "outside of space-time." I hope he will come to consider "outside of space-time" broadly.

Shoup and Mohrhoff did agree on two points: (1) Nothing physically is the result of a purely random event or condition. (2) Because the direction of cause and effect could not be known *for sure*, we really should not think in terms that our physical reality can only just change from one form to another because something called time marches on with the future solely determined by the past. If one wants to talk about the result of any change from a "now" to a "subsequent now," all that can be said is to describe the form of the relationship between things in the vicinity before the step and again after. It takes some kind of information to know why and how it happened. *That can be extended to another vote for interconnectedness on a grand scale.* They also brought the

251

words "relationship" and "information" into my vocabulary as technical terms in the context of how reality works in the view of two highly competent physicists.

The realization that it takes some kind of information to characterize why and how the relationships change was especially cogent. The importance of incorporating relationships into my thinking and the new-to-me way to think about information was further driven home when I ran across another research paper by Shoup. In it he again focused on this fact that there is "information" associated with every describable relationship. He used a different example to make that clear, but my paraphrase goes like this.

Imagine some large number of tinker toys, say about 836 just to pick a number, that a person forms into a small model race car or a house, whatever. Now think deep about the Gestalt of the situation. The whole (say race car) is greater than its parts. It equals the sum of its parts (the 836 tinker-toy pieces) plus the relationships among them (the structure). I will add, note that the parts are physical but the relationship (say, that which describes the particular whole race car) is a nonphysical subjective belief, idea, or opinion (information) of the car builder. *The relationship is crucial information that is not contained in the parts and is not material but which must be available and manifest materially in the arrangement.*

Generalizing, one can think of all relationships as just information about............whatever the relationships are about! And also that *information is nonphysical but critical.* The nonphysical design information and the physical action of how to assemble it are both required to build a tinker-toy race car. The brain is certainly involved in the process, but information becomes subjective before it becomes *manifest in our objective world.* Perception makes the information manifest, but in essence, information itself is nonphysical. Perception of information from a source other than the basic five senses is an example. Much more on that topic later when I note the nature of some kinds of information I realized that we generate each day to create our own reality.

The focus on relationships provided an important key to a door I had tried to open for several years. The fact that the significance of "relationship" could become so important to me was in part because it tied so much "non-physics" together that could be supported by physics. My path starting with the binks twisted and turned a lot, but it yielded a framework for extending physics to help explain the greater reality originating with my interest in the paranormal.

252

I think the path described in the many pages above provided enough insight from quantum physics for me to venture forth into the more speculative and controversial terrain involving <u>human perception</u> associated with paranormal phenomena. Before describing that part of my journey, however, I summarize what may be obvious to the more learned but which is what I believe my study of physics yielded as:

- The entire physical pattern of the universe blinks in and out simultaneously (assumption) with quantum steps of change.
- The Schrödinger Wave Equation is not a basis for inferring physical cause and effect; it is just a probability calculus.
- What we think of as "time" is just an attribute of the blinking, not a dimension nor a cause to make anything happen.
- If any change within space-time is influenced from outside of space-time that influence must occur at a quantum blink step.
- At each blink, there is indeterminacy associated with the nature of the change in the physical that will occur at the next blink.
- The indeterminacy between change steps in the physical is not a result of a random process but rather indicative of a not-yet understood process of change of the connecting relationships.
- The new "now" we experience at each blink does not create a "time-ordering" of how actual cause and effect took place.
- Nonlocality is a fundamental characteristic of the physical universe.
- Nonlocality precludes the existence of an objective universe, demonstrates that there is at least a potential degree of interconnectedness of all within the universe, and that there exist physical relationships and observations that cannot be explained within the current physics describing the nature of space-time. (Nonlocality *requires* the existence of explanations from outside of the generally accepted four dimensions of space-time.)
- Nonlocality demonstrates that space is also not a fundamental dimension within a greater reality existing outside of space-time.
- Change in the physical can come about as a consequence of retro-causation, where a condition in what we call the future may have caused a preceding effect, and if and when thinking in terms of "time," it is reasonable to include the possibility of "negative time."
- All change in the physical just represents the changing relationships between a prior and a subsequent "now"—both the "cause" and the direction of physically manifest cause and effect may be uncertain.
- The form of a relationship exists solely as "information" describing what is being referred to as the relationship and such information is

253

not physical—not existing in space-time to require either space or time. (Note, the pattern of neurons of a brain may represent the perceiving or perception of a physical manifestation of information, but the nonphysical information must exist a priori to create the forming of the pattern.)

- The pattern of the universe at each blink is a gestalt of all the information related to all objective relationships within the universe. Because there is conceptually a relationship between any one and all other relationships (i.e. the thought of such a connection as an example), there is information demonstrating the potential interconnectedness of all. Nonlocality is no surprise.

- And because there is no distinction between outside of time and all time (as we think of "time"), what is to physically happen to form the next "now" may theoretically be influenced by complex information intensive processes utilizing any physical event or human thought that has ever occurred—processes and influences originating from outside of the space-time described by current physics—and processes occurring between each blink without requiring the sense of duration existing within the physical world.

- Because of these considerations, it is not at all clear that the definition and connotation of "energy" as incorporated within the model and equations of current physics is appropriate to use to describe or be a factor in some causes of change.

- The manner in which nonphysical information influences the objective form of a change within physical reality at each quantum change step is not determinable using the model and equations of current physics.

I do not think what I have represented is contrary to experimental results, proven formulas, etc. As mentioned at the beginning of this chapter, there are many assumptions incorporated in what is now considered current quantum physics. I do not believe that offering an alternative assumption, or declining to accept an existing questionably supported assumption, automatically creates unsupportable incompatibility with the mainstream model. It might take considerable effort and the careful examination of what I have set forth to insure that it is indeed "contrary" rather than plausible but not certain. An example issue is the generally accepted pillar of current physics, the conservation of energy. I believe that there is a good argument to be made that the physical system in question is NOT closed, and that assumption may not be correct—which is what I now believe. The issue of that conservation theorem is now at the heart of developments in recent years relating to zero point energy, the nature of "light" and energy-related processes such as electron tunneling.

The blinking at the Planck edge of what is described by current quantum physics was the only "just plain assumption" leading to this extended picture of reality! However, that blinking rate is just because it is the edge of our models. If "time" within our models was measured differently, the blinking rate would still remain the edge of our models represented by the uncertainty principal. It is the theoretical and experimental research within physics in recent decades that has established the framework characterized above, so any person with an open mind may explore its implications. Quantum physics does not answer the "why do things work this way?" questions, but as just summarized based on the blinking assumption, it provides a lot for one to consider if they are interested in digging into what might exist outside of space-time that produces this physical world picture we observe and measure.

By the time I managed to grasp that much of what we can learn about an extended reality by digging a little into quantum physics, I had also been reading the Seth material more thoroughly. No other source I was familiar with came as close to credibly describing a view of reality in such detail—detail that seemed to be supported by physics. During those years I also continued to read an increasing amount of material relating to research in paranormal phenomena. I then thought I was ready to seriously focus on trying to see how I could answer the questions with their origin in my experience derived from such phenomena. The Seth material was also a gold mine with which to work to do that.

So, my journey headed on in that Seth direction—sort of reluctantly—in the absence of any more promising path.

Once I came to understand the basics of quantum physics described above, it became clear to me that the slavish focus limited to objective space-time information considered to "cause" change in the physical world is the major disjoint between current mainstream physics and what must be considered if we are to learn how to incorporate the data representing paranormal phenomena. The Seth material supported and augmented that view.

Looking back, and with the advantage of hindsight achieved at a high cost of time and frustration, I decided that the importance of looking at both space-time and outside of space-time aspects of reality in terms of relationships cannot be overstated. Every change occurring within the physical world may be viewed as a change in relationships. It seemed to me that anything we want to think of

255

as existing outside of space-time must be thought of as having meaning in terms of a gestalt of relationships and how they evolve independent of time. And as was previously noted, all our desires, emotions, expectations, intentions (actual or just maybe), and all thoughts in general do exist as nonphysical relationship information—possibly forever throughout eternity available to be used to influence the continued unfolding of the physical world—if there is a process by which that can happen. (According to Woody Allen, "Eternity is a very long time, especially towards the end.")

The general acceptance of nonlocality, and to a lesser extent retrocausality, have at least made increasing numbers within physics open to take a look at anomalous phenomena looking for a possible connection. However, unless many others join them, current physics, chemistry, biology, and methods of doing science in general will continue to be incapable of digging very deep for new insight incorporating the role of nonphysical information to influence the nature of any change occurring in the physical universe at any "time". In my opinion, an open mind to at least take a look at the Seth material would help that process along, but I do not expect that to happen with but a few exceptions, even though quantum physics seems to have brought many to where that should be a natural step.

As described in this chapter, physicists now know that processes and relationships existing outside of space-time can *in theory* connect anything and everything, in or outside of space-time, to cause the evolving patterns we perceive as a physical universe. The framework of quantum physics represents an undifferentiated whole! The big picture includes the fact that the physical cannot be completely represented without the nonphysical, and the influence of the nonphysical cannot be probed and determined without some extension of current physics. Physics alone cannot provide the detail of how nonphysical information works to affect the indeterminacy that is fundamental to all change occurring in our physical world at the quantum level. But I think it is also quite clear that it does provide a framework to work within if we wish to learn more about the what, why, when, or how questions that arose earlier when surveying some examples of paranormal phenomena.

In the first part of my post-retirement years, I wrote a 27-page document to put in one place my thoughts at that time about what must be reconciled for quantum physics to be extended to allow room for that growing evidence of anomalous phenomena. I decided to summarize what I believed at that time about both. I titled it "RLB Thoughts Relating to Consciously Influenced Change." It is in my files and begins with two quotes:

Consciousness fits uneasily into our conception of the natural world. On the most common conception of nature, the natural world is the physical world. But on the most common conception of consciousness, it is not easy to see how it could be part of the physical world. So it seems that to find a place for consciousness within the natural order, we must either revise our conception of consciousness, or revise our conception of nature. (David Chalmers)

It seems pretty clear to me that we need to revise our conception of *both*—significantly expanding a consensus view of what we think we know about nature but also with a willingness to explore totally new ideas about consciousness, and in both spheres to accept and incorporate the evidence of anomalous phenomena and the nonphysical aspect of human existence. (rlb)

I learned a lot by reading David Chalmers. I think he is one of the more insightful and forthright academics I am aware of in the field of psychology/philosophy, and his use of "psychophysical. He is the one who has written extensively on the subject of how does subjective experience spring from plain old matter, even if the matter is a brain? An easy answer is embedded in beliefs I had encountered in some of the very old religions of the world or in the expositions of philosophers like Kant, Berkley, Whitehead, and Bergson—but I wanted to leave the so-called supernatural and highly abstract ideas out of the picture, at least until I thought I might be able to paint a more detailed picture such that supernatural had a different connotation.

In that document, I summarized my then understanding of the basics of quantum physics—a small part of what has been embedded in this life story. I also described various forms of anomalous phenomena, which I only summarized earlier in this chapter. I touched briefly on reincarnation and NDE's. I even included a description of how I imagined that the human experience of perceiving paranormal phenomena might occur. I used the terms "self" and "consciousness" but didn't have as much to characterize what I meant as I do now. I summarized eight conclusions—but that was before my interest turned to the Seth material, thus none mentioning any insight from it.

Somewhere along the way, it occurred to me that there were two questions that had to be answered in some way to characterize the nature of the self and consciousness that are part and parcel of a considerable amount of the paranormal evidence: (1) What was the scope of the potential sources of the non-normal stimuli that was being perceived by a person's brain? (The stuff perceived for which we had no physical explanation.) (2) How could the person even perceive stimuli that did not originate from our normal five senses?

The common objective of the research in paranormal phenomena was to gather evidence concerning the first question—to identify the nature of the non-normal perception and to determine if it was a real effect or just some kind of unusual, but chance, perception. Example: Could person A really perceive what person B was thinking about? Example: Could person A really describe a condition remote in space and/or time? Example: Could the body of person A be reacting to a stimuli not yet perceived by the brain neurons of person A?

It seemed impossible to gather data from formal research methodologies to suggest answers to the second question. In particular, as mentioned regarding Presentiment, how could the person's physical body be responding to something the brain neurons didn't know about? Persons doing research in neuroscience have claimed "it's all in the brain," but they haven't convinced me. All the work I have seen published just ignores the possibility that there could be something more than the cause and effect they are studying. There are correlates, but *correlations do not prove cause.* The existence of correlations between some part of the brain functioning and the measured or reported perception of some kind has not even satisfied highly qualified people in the field—David Chalmers in particular. The Seth material seemed to offer me little additional insight.

Fortunately, as I read many of the increasing numbers of reports relating to parapsychology, I had also encountered the interesting papers within psychology and philosophy, as well as a few within physics, that caught my interest regarding the subjective nature of the observer/perceiver. At the same time, as I returned to reading more of the Seth material, I encountered even more material and insight of similar kind that seemed to be important. All these sources shouted things about "consciousness." I decided I had to try to sort out and improve my understanding of the many differing views and the differing language associated with the words "self" and "consciousness." In considering somewhat the same issues, philosopher Thomas Nagel put it this way:

... such an understanding would be to explain the appearance of life, consciousness, reason, and knowledge ... as an unsurprising if not inevitable consequence of the order that governs the natural world from within. That order ... will not be explainable by physics and chemistry alone. An expanded, but still unified, form of explanation will be needed, and I expect it will have to include teleological elements. (*Mind and Cosmos: Why the Neo-Darwinian Conception of Nature is Almost Certainly False,* p. 32.)

258

I will touch on my view of the "teleological elements" in Chapter 17. In the meantime, on to Part 2 of my metaphysical journey, Chapter 16, and what I have become comfortable with when thinking in terms involving "self" and "consciousness" at the heart of a much greater reality than I ever could have imagined when I started this journey.

Science cannot solve the ultimate mystery of nature.
And that is because, in the last analysis,
We ourselves are a part of the mystery
That we are trying to solve.

(Max Planck)

⤜ 16 ⤛

My Metaphysical Journey

Part 2 — A Metaphysics of Personal Reality

Whether we know it or not, our views that amount to a personal reality are subtle, complex, and often not given much thought other than a possible religious faith. Our reality is pretty much evidenced by what we see and do each day. It is tempting to just say, reality is something like the total ocean that we swim in and let it go at that—but I couldn't.

I think that for most people, a reason to think more deeply about such things is just not necessary for living the way they choose to live every day. I know many people who care deeply about their conduct and thoughts as a reflection of their personal values without feeling a need to explore the depth of reality more deeply. I think that is an accurate description of some of my closest family and best friends. Only a few know how deeply I care about extending my view of reality. Of course, Pat is the exception. She knows my nature intimately (thank goodness) and accepts me as I am.

As covered in the prior chapter, my journey to try to find connections between paranormal phenomena and physics—for the most part—failed. Each seemed to make major contributions to the subject, but my tour through each had led me up against a figurative wall representing the need for a working definition of consciousness. There was an experiencing, observing, self on both sides of the wall without a connecting consciousness of the other. The physics framework made it clear that what needed to be added to the picture was not physical, and thus would need to start outside of space-time. My bookshelf loaded with books describing various views of how human consciousness should be understood provided me no connecting link.

I then accepted the idea that my greatest potential source of insight relating to the nature of consciousness had indeed been under my nose for years, but I had not been ready to totally accept it. After reviewing parts of the Seth material with growing interest, and without seeing a better way to go, it seemed to make much more sense to me than all the other stuff I had looked into. I ended up studying and understanding it in great depth—and breadth!

When I had encountered the Seth material in the 1970's I noticed a few bits of content that I believed to be supportive of physics I had earlier studied in college. I definitely recall that gave me a sense of credibility concerning the Seth material I was reading—but only a touch, not a hit in the face. But, after working my way through the journey described in Chapter 15 as summarized on pages 259 and 260, I was absolutely convinced that major representations within the Seth material were clearly supported by my conclusions from physics.

Seth became much more than credible. I thought the Seth material might provide the connecting link between the paranormal and physics, so my journey continued as I describe in this chapter—a journey to try to bring consciousness into the picture via the Seth material—and as it turned out, via a lot more also.

The "self" was at the core of the Seth material description of reality. I had never really sorted out the duality issue, so I proceeded to learn more about it so I could tell if what I learned and the Seth material seemed to be talking about the same thing. I discovered that there exists a vast amount of published material relating to the differing views about the existence of a self or the many views regarding the source and definition of both a "self" and "consciousness" together. (The philpapers.org website of this era provides over 1,000 papers devoted to related metaphysics.)

I recently discovered that the founders of quantum physics also thought there exists an unyielding mystery as to how their quantum theory related to consciousness and reality in general. (All were classically educated in philosophy.) The 2012 book "Quirks of the Quantum Mind" by Robert G. Jahn and Brenda J. Dunne includes many pages devoted to that topic in Appendix A, "Observations from the Patriarchs." For instance, in the preface to his book, *Matter and Light*, Louis de Broglie wrote, "...it is fair to observe that the advance made by quantum physics has opened entirely novel perspectives on a great number of questions, and that the future orientation of metaphysical doctrines will almost inevitably be deeply influenced sooner or later."

Soon thereafter the physicist and philosopher Arthur Eddington summarized his thesis in his book, *The Nature of the Physical World*, as follows, "Recognizing that the physical world is entirely abstract and without 'actuality' apart from its linkage to consciousness, we restore consciousness to the fundamental position instead of representing it as an inessential complication occasionally found in the midst of inorganic nature at a late stage of evolutionary history." It would be difficult to be much clearer than that, but it took me a long time to clearly see the need for the connection and to subsequently arrive at the supportive physics framework I described in Chapter 15.

In Appendix A, with permission from the authors, I have included a number of additional quotes from the Patriarchs to characterize their common intellectual search for the "reality of nature." I think it is clear that these key players among those who laid the foundation of what became quantum physics saw the implication connecting physics and a person (self) within an aspect of nature akin to consciousness.

Also probing into that connection in depth, collaborating with the Patriarchs in the process, Yale physics and philosophy Professor Henry Margenau wrote the book *The Miracle of Existence* to extend that intellectual search. Much of his work also helps connect quantum physics and paranormal phenomena. It seems to me to be amazing, if not appalling, that physicists and the physicalists within science in general, have seemed to ignore those (and others) who so clearly in much of their writing pointed to the nature of those connections.

I think Nikola Tesla was "right on" when early in the 20th century he said, "The day science begins to study non-physical phenomena, it will make more progress in one decade than in all the previous centuries of its existence." I now think that day is dawning. I have learned a lot from those giving it birth.

John Wheeler, a recent and renowned quantum physicist, was instrumental in drawing attention to those issues brought up by the Patriarchs. He put forward many implications of quantum physics that seem to me to be totally compatible with what I have concluded without his extensive knowledge to work with. In particular his delayed choice hypothesis, later confirmed by experiment, supports much of what I have tried to explain and will extend. Dirk K. F. Meijer, in his March 2015 paper in J. of NeuroQuantology, "The Universe as a Cyclic Organized Information System: John Wheeler's World Revisited," has described many implications of Wheeler's work in extensive detail.

My conclusions from quantum physics described in the summary in Chapter 15 were a giant step for me toward the plausibility of non-local influences in how change takes place in our physical world. However, the quantum- physics framework offered no directly connective role for the person exhibiting a paranormal event. Yes, it appeared that some form of consciousness was involved, but consciousness was not a well-defined phenomenon at that time, and one might argue, not even now, in my view.

Telepathy and remote viewing are examples of the intimate role of human awareness without support within the physics framework, even with nonlocality as part of it. In neither phenomenon was it clear how nonlocal cause and effect might explain how the nonlocal "information" became available to the persons perceiving it. It had become obvious that I had to get beyond just the quantum framework to help explain the human perception aspect of paranormal phenomena.

From many sources over the years I had already accepted a view that our self was more than just the working parts of our body. Even before I understood much about quantum phenomena, it had become clear to me that what was missing was how the "outside of space-time" information being perceived "paranormally" by neurons in a brain got there! There had to be some kind of sixth sense. Somewhat similarly, there was the question of how human cognitive processes, information thought to be originating within the brain, could experimentally influence physical material well separated in space-time from the brain. There was a growing body of research evidence that human thought could indeed affect matter. Those were issues intimately related to the depth and breadth of what our self is like.

I initially thought that the binks interpretation of how change occurs removed the role of a human observer to "collapse the wave function," which was the quantum event assumed by many to describe a particular kind of human connection within an experimental situation.

However, one can't prove a negative—in this case, that the influence of humans has no role even in the binks interpretation. Binks *did not* solve that problem. In fact, the nature of indeterminism that was described in the extended framework of the last chapter theoretically cannot preclude *any* source of influence. And in the paranormal situations, the human was clearly a source or receiver of information in unknown ways. The question for me at that time was where to start looking for a path to understand how that works.

That sent me back to the thinking lamp and raised a lot of very old questions regarding the duality of body and mind, or as I prefer, body and self. I prefer "self" because I have come to believe that the self is a broader consciousness structure than the mind and that there is a need for "self" and

263

"mind" to be carefully defined to show a distinction as two separate aspects of consciousness.

Historically, the discussion of this body-self distinction is as old as humanity, particularly in the forefront within early Greek philosophy. More recently, the "mind-body" dualism became a major issue within epistemology via the work of Rene Descartes in the early 17th century. Descartes identified the nonphysical mind with consciousness and self-awareness and distinguished this from the brain/body. Before I gave serious thought to the topics of this chapter, but after reading many books and papers, I came to ascribe to that view in a somewhat qualified sense. The details of how I characterize a personal reality start with how I came to view a self as much more than a body in a metaphysical sense.

Even though I knew nothing about what the Patriarchs had written, I had read views of several highly competent physicists that easily make the case that the nonphysical self is not in conflict with anything the quantum-physics framework of the last chapter has to say.

Piero Scaruffi, a somewhat obscure modern-era physicist whose thinking I found very thought-provoking, has written extensively on the nonphysical mind-body distinction. Based on his study of quantum physics, his conclusion is that the nature the consciousness of a self begins with, "Any paradigm that tries to manufacture consciousness out of something else is doomed to failure. Things don't just happen. Ex nihilo nihil fit." Scarfuffi goes into the topic in great detail to the edge of, but not encompassing, the view that all matter might be/include consciousness in some as yet unknown manner.

In an entry dealing with the use of the term "qualia" in philosophy, the Stanford Encyclopedia of Philosophy provides an analogy much like I did with the tinker-toy race car to make much the same case. That is, information is nonphysical, and the stuff of our mind is information. It took me awhile to distinguish between the thought and the arrangement of neurons that physically confirm the thought, but as noted, I found a few clues to think about.

In a paper published in the "Journal of Consciousness Studies" in 1996, University of California professor Arthur J. Deikman wrote extensively from an approach that distinguishes the process of awareness—of being aware—from the content of the awareness—of what the awareness is about. He views awareness as "something apart from, and different from, all that of which we are aware: thoughts, emotions, images, sensations, desires, and memory." And thus "the word 'awareness' to mean this ground of all experience." In other terminology, that is the distinction between the observer and what is observed.

The distinguished neuroscientist, V.S. Ramachandran, has written: "One of the last remaining problems in science is the riddle of consciousness. ... '*Who am I' is arguably the most fundamental of all questions.*" After reading a lot about what people like those just quoted had to say, I decided that for me the answer is clearly that humans have more than a brain at work and that the non-brain part is nonphysical. As a shortcut way of viewing that, I came to the conclusion that I just "am." *My self is not my physical body parts,* rather it is a nonphysical something or other that is capable of being aware. That is, a self that is distinguished from the vernacular of "yourself," "myself," and/or a reference to some attribute such as self-esteem or my dressed-up-to-go-to-the dance self—all of which are really just talking about a physical being.   My nonphysical workaday self is "the one who observes and decides how I feel about it," the one "who answers questions," and the one "who has thoughts about things of an entirely subjective nature." That self is nonphysical, a consciousness entity of some kind outside of space-time—and *just is*.

Those are characteristics associated with the self Descartes distinguished from a body. That is the self that cannot be constructed from electrons and protons. That is the self that cannot be objectified in a universe we know from nonlocality and other evidence to, in essence, have similarities with an illusion. (It is only an illusion when we confuse the reality we experience with the physical reality. More on that later.)

I decided that for me there *is* an answer to that "hard problem" posed by David Chalmers.   His actual question is "Why does awareness of sensory information exist at all?" My answer is, it is because it is the awareness that "just is"—the awareness that is part and parcel of my nonphysical self.   In essence, I think the "hard problem" should be expressed the other way around. How does consciousness give rise to "change" in our bodies and the physical world in general? That is sort of like, "How does the physical world exist and change in relation to our subjective view of it and how it works?" That is essentially the question the Patriarchs were asking.

I have decided that for me my conscious awareness is not emergent or just somehow acquired—it just is!   Individual awareness is not just a limited consciousness that may simply be an aspect of a brain in any live person. It is not possible to demonstrate that a self *cannot* have characteristics a brain does not have! I think it is easily possible to demonstrate that a brain cannot have all

265

characteristics of a "self." At some point this distinguishing aspect of "being" must be given a label. I decided to call it a "self." Others often use the terms "soul" or "spirit" to, in essence, refer to a view with an overlapping nature. As will become clear, I eventually came to believe a lot more, a very lot more, about the nature of our selves.

Sometime along the path, I quit wondering when or how did humans, and thus "selves" come into being. In the context of the reality I came to accept, the question becomes moot or just speculation. It doesn't matter! As we saw in the physics framework, *time is not a unit of measure having meaning within the greater reality!* Outside of time is all time—eternity. We came to exist. We do exist. Eventually the subject of the nature of the self led me to deeper thinking about a much more fundamental kind of consciousness than just the self-consciousness of a person.

With an "acceptable to me" working idea relating to the existence of a nonphysical "self," together with the relevant quantum-physics framework of the previous chapter, I started to think more deeply about where and how the *role* of consciousness of some kind might fit in.

I read several books about nature of consciousness, but my primary conclusion was that the distinguished authors were each describing something different and quite limited compared to what was needed to answer many obvious questions. Eventually, the Seth material and the experiences Kevin shared with me became the two major inputs to my sorting out of ideas so as to arrive at a belief about how to understand the word "consciousness." I had first encountered the Seth input, so I will cover the background there first.

It took me awhile to be willing to seriously accept what Seth had to say about the fundamental role of consciousness because of the channeling phenomena. Channeling seemed weird. (And even a total show-stopper for most people) However, I took into consideration the widespread acceptance of channeling by others and devoted a lot more time reading the detail of what the nonphysical personality Seth had to say.

The Seth material has been the best source for me to develop an understanding of the channeling process. It has also been important to me that the Seth material is totally compatible with, and supporting of, quantum physics. They overlap in significant areas—much more than will be included in what follows. The Seth material is even a source of teaching new aspects of physics. It is sort of fascinating to me that this fount of knowledge is sourced by a dead man. (Seth referred to himself as "An energy personality essence no longer focused in physical reality.")

Reading Seth again, I discovered that Seth had mentioned a blinking aspect of the physical universe in those books. I had failed to remember that from my reading of the Seth material in the 1970s, but it was obvious that idea must have helped direct my attention within physics to the Heisenberg Uncertainty Principle and the Planck dimensions. That was clearly a focus that helped me formulate the most important aspect of binks that I described earlier—the blinking nature of the physical world at the edge of the time-dependent physical world that our physics equations describe.

The Seth material goes into great detail—one might say the core theme of all that is covered in the material—to describe how we individually and collectively create our personal reality. Since changes in our physical reality occur in the quantum steps, understanding the detail of the blinking phenomena is where we must discover how the unfolding of those changes in our experience are influenced, and by what. However, both our personal awareness and our science knowledge are well short of providing us experimental details of all that happens between each blink, in part because of the high rate (as pointed out in Chapter 15) at which the blinks occur.

Fortunately, as mentioned with emphasis in chapter 15, as I came to a better grasp of quantum physics I learned how to rephrase many questions so that they could be posed in terms of "changing relationships," in our objective universe and the void outside of space-time rather than in terms of space and/or time. With the changing relationships framework to start with, the blinking importance within the Seth material became of greater interest.

My belief back then, and now, is that there is no question concerning the nature of our greater reality that is more challenging, important, and possibly unanswerable than, *"What is the detailed nature of the process that determines what all happens during a series of blinks that influences the personal reality we individually experience during life?"* I also came to believe that to understand as much as possible about that process was important to me. It has been a fascinating part of my journey, so on with the story of it.

As previously mentioned, the Seth material was channeled by Jane Roberts. Because I am going to share how meaningful this material has been within my journey, and how difficult it was for me to accept, I am first going to provide a little background on channeled material in general before getting into the specifics of why I view the Seth material to be a reliable source of information.

I would not be surprised if anyone reading what I am writing would wonder about how this or any other channeled material could be taken seriously like I am saying that I do. Even though 75% of persons in America in a Gallup News Service survey in 2005 believed in at least some form of paranormal phenomena, only 21 percent believed that a dead person could communicate with a live person. Thus, at this point in history, I would not expect most people to know what the word channeling referred to, and if they do know, I would guess that most would likely associate it with mediumship or possibly as some kind of new-age phenomena of questionable credibility. Apparently Yale University knows the difference.

Yale University is now the depository for the archive of all of the Seth material—not just books but including personal channeling sessions for the Roberts and transcripts of Seth participation in the frequent sessions held for gatherings of people to learn about and discuss related topics determined by Jane Roberts. There are currently 498 boxes archived in the "biographies" classification within the Sterling Memorial Library at Yale, Manuscript Group Number 1090.

Although the mediumship process is recorded as far back as Greek and Roman times and has occasionally become a big deal in some part of human societies, it is not well studied, and there have been charlatans galore to taint the general perception. The historical characterization is that of a mediating communication of some kind between spirits of the dead and living human beings. However, when it comes to channeled material, there is much more than that to think about—and more examples than just the Seth material.

The most advanced form of channeling is known as trance mediumship, which is the nature of the Jane Roberts channeling of the Seth material. There are other well-known examples of trance-channeled material in modern times. One of the most well-known and widely published has been *A Course in Miracles* (ACIM) dictated to Helen Schueman by the Jesus personality starting in 1965. The material was first published for wide distribution in 1975 by The Foundation for Inner Peace. I have not studied all of the material but have read a small book describing the history and a summary of the message, plus a 111-page study-guide publication of the foundation titled *The Fifty Miracle Principles of a Course in Miracles*. It is clear that a major focus of the material is related to the fundamental importance of forgiveness.

Although expressed in different terms within a deeply spiritual paradigm, the material describes a reality with *extensive* overlap of the Seth material description of how our personal reality works. It is often characterized as echoing the teachings of Jesus recorded in the historical Bible—but as a contemporary revealed scripture—a modern-day message from God to mankind. There is a lot of information related to ACIM on the current Internet, including a foundation site with a great breadth of material. The site currently reports the existence of over 2000 study groups in 65 countries.

As mentioned in the chapter covering my life in the 1970s, the first trance channeled material I encountered was that channeled by the faith healer and psychic Edgar Cayce. Cayce (1877-1945) is reported to have had psychic experiences as a child. Over a 40-year period later in life, he gave over 14,000 "psychic readings," each generally to relate to a specific request. Cayce believed that his source of information provided during the readings was from what he called the Akashic Record of life experiences of all people who have ever lived on Earth. The information generally included information related to the history of the physical world and the reincarnation history of those requesting the reading. Cayce was religious and a biblical scholar, but became accepting of the reincarnation framework of the Akashic Record.

When I first encountered the words "Akashic Record," I had no perspective with which to imagine how the information could be available, let alone how he could retrieve it. With my background in computing, I wondered how such an "addressing scheme" might work, but it took a few decades before I could answer that and other related questions to my satisfaction. (More on that topic later in this chapter.)

To me, the vocabulary used in his readings was very much like that of the King James Version of the Bible. In 1931, he founded the Association for Research and Enlightenment (A.R.E.) to be a depository of his life readings and to make those readings available to anyone who wished to study them. Many books on specific topics have been written to summarize content of Cayce readings. I own and have read seven of those books.

A.R.E. international headquarters are in a modern building complex in Virginia Beach, Virginia. The A.R.E. has several regional and urban centers in North America. These organizations serve as communication links to the Virginia Beach headquarters with the primary goal to foster spiritual community throughout each geographic locale.

The A.R.E. centers worldwide offer workshops, study groups, lectures, and related programs in over 37 countries with members in over 70 countries participating. The organization also has a publication-press division to offer for sale books and other media based on the archived Cayce readings covering a vast array of subjects. The material is compiled within the following five categories: (1) Health-Related Information; (2) Philosophy and Reincarnation; (3) Dreams and Dream Interpretation; (4) ESP and Psychic Phenomena; and (5) Spiritual Growth, Meditation, and Prayer. There is also a vast amount of information relating to Edgar Cayce on the Internet of this era.

I am less personally familiar with another work said to be the result of trance channeling, *The Urantia Book*. From what I have read, the name of the person who channeled the material was known only to five people, all now deceased. The word "Urantia" is the name in the writings to identify Earth. The source of the work is said to have been revelation from celestial beings. (Note how different that is from how Seth labeled "himself.")

The book was transcribed as 186 papers, covering 2,097 pages of text in the book between 1925 and 1935. The Urantia Foundation was created as custodian of the transcripts in 1950 and headquartered in Chicago, USA. The English version was published in 1955. The book has been translated into over 15 languages. After litigation of issues related to the copyrights, the work became in the public domain and is now readily available on the Internet as well as the published book form.

As excerpted from the Urantia Foundation website: "The writings in *The Urantia Book* instruct us on the genesis, history, and destiny of humanity and on our relationship with God the Father. They present a unique and compelling portrayal of the life and teachings of Jesus. They open new vistas of time and eternity to the human spirit, and offer new details of our ascending adventure in a friendly and carefully administered universe." I have the book but ceased trying to read all of it when I encountered the need to learn an entirely unique vocabulary to understand it. However, I learned enough to read and find highly interesting quite a bit written about the life of Jesus.

Another trance channeled work I am familiar with is the many readings of a spiritual nature channeled by Ray Stanford. Much of the material was published in the journals of the Association for the Understanding of Man (AUM) between 1972 and 1977. Selected readings were also published as the book *Speak Shining Stranger*. The organization was headquartered in Austin, Texas, where I lived at the time. I was a member of AUM and have read and reread the journal articles and three books published by AUM over the years. I have no idea as to the membership of the AUM, but the number was small compared to the thousands or millions of readers of the material mentioned above.

The stated purpose of the AUM organization was "through its research program to elucidate the physical, mental, and spiritual natures of man." The readings were initiated by requesting the nonphysical "Source" to provide information concerning specific questions. The resultant material was either from the Source or from those who called themselves "Brothers." Like the Cayce and ACIM language, I view the material as in the language of the King James Version of the Bible but at least in a vocabulary I was familiar with. I found the primary focus of the Stanford readings to be on meditation, prayer, and "how to" think and behave spiritually—usually with references to teachings of Jesus.

The only otherwise-focused readings known to me in the Stanford material were two readings in 1975 titled *The Universe: A New View,* specifically requested to answer questions posed by a group of physicists led by James Wray, PhD, from Moorhead State College in Minnesota. Whereas the Seth material is expressed using more or less an everyday familiar vocabulary to attempt to describe phenomena that is difficult to describe in everyday terms, the material provided by the Source of these two Stanford readings was presented (with obvious difficulty) to explain metaphorically within a physics perspective the reality behind physical phenomena. The metaphorical readings are thus difficult to absorb but present a clear elucidation of some of what is going on behind the scenes represented by modern physics models and equations and extensions thereof. Overall, I think the Source did a good job of communicating difficult physics to competent physicists.

Although the Stanford physics material covers less ground than Seth, the material is also entirely compatible with the Seth material and, in several areas, much more detailed to connect space-time with outside of space-time phenomena. The Stanford material provides more detail than Seth regarding certain details of how nonphysical information becomes physically manifest during blinks. I believe that only a few copies of the AUM journals with these readings are likely to exist today. I have created a public folder on the Microsoft OneDrive (in "The Cloud" of current computing fashion) with scanned copies of those two readings and have sent copies to two physicists and two others who I believed might find the material of interest. I only know for sure that one found the material clearly meaningful.

271

I have selectively read channeled material from two other sources: Elias (channeled by Mary Ennis) and Charles (channeled by Kurt Leland). I am told that not much of the Charles material has been transcribed, but I have obtained paper copies of five sessions covering material additive and consistent with Seth and with interesting perspective regarding its significance. The main topic of one session was the importance of living with a core belief of compassion for all—consistent with the Seth material relating to the importance of "to *be* love," rather than to think in terms of "to love" as when describing a directed thought or intent related to an object/person. That seems credible to me when I put it in the context of religious philosophy I am a little familiar with.

There is a vast amount of material from the trance channeling of Elias by Mary Ennis. Thousands of pages from sessions have been placed in digital form on the Internet, as well as an index to topics touched upon in the sessions. The names of people present at the sessions are included. I have read very little of it, but a close friend was at many of the sessions and views the material as credible and very consistent with the reality characterized in the Seth material he has studied.

There are, however, several "popular" channeled sources in recent years that from what I have seen do not pass muster. It seems that many who accept what is to me ludicrous material have either had no way to check the validity of the channeled material or don't wish to. On the other hand, there are research institutions, such as the SOPHIA Research Program directed by Dr. Gary Schwartz at the University of Arizona, testing reported mediums/channelers and the content of the channeled information. There are other similar programs testing some form or another of channeling in private institutions devoted to that subject. There is a vast amount of reported research results on the Internet.

Now on to Seth and, finally, to a meaningful understanding of what I think should be understood as "consciousness" and how important that understanding is in how I view reality and try to conduct my life consistent with my beliefs.

I have 14 books that were dictated by Seth and channeled by Jane Roberts, and I know of five more that I don't have. I have read and reread most of this material. At first in the 1970s, it just seemed sort of surreal to me. But later, with a significant amount of quantum physics insight under my belt, certain key aspects of the Seth material seemed credible and maybe even more "in tune" with a view of reality that might actually be directly supported by physics.

272

I had already accepted the idea of reincarnation of some form, and for me, thinking in terms outside of space-time was not a show-stopper even though at the time I didn't have physics support for that idea. As mentioned earlier, the core message of the Seth material I encountered seemed to be that *we create our own reality.* That seemed a little challenging in a way that resonated with me.

In a few pages, I can only touch on the voluminous extent of the Seth coverage of what constitutes a reality that is much greater and more complex than our physical universe. I certainly cannot provide the "tutoring" manner of coverage that was so well provided by Seth—so I won't try. Similarly, I cannot describe here the step-by-step insights that resulted as Kevin and I worked together to connect details of his altered states of consciousness to the views arising from physics and Seth.

Rather, I will just try to summarize what Seth added to my beliefs relating to the nature of our greater reality—and in particular, material providing a tour d' force defining "consciousness" and how it is so fundamental if we are to understand how the world around us works. And in less detail, I only wish to characterize the contribution of the Seth material to the general terrain, without every rock, tree, and gully, but with enough to tell my story of what I have come to believe about that greater reality.

I intend that this chapter will sort of "top off" the list of all the sources that have helped me conceptualize the view of reality that has enabled me to live more fully and with less "friction" within the world around me in these later years of my life. In the next chapter I will attempt to describe some of how that reality is taken into consideration day by day to help me create the reality I experience.

I have decided to describe and then summarize the Seth contribution via these four topics: (Glossary guide to terminology is provided in Appendix B)

Regarding Fundamental Consciousness
Regarding the Nature of a Self
Regarding How We Create Our Own Reality
Regarding Uncommon Ways of Experiencing Reality

The Seth view of the greater reality is grounded in the belief that Consciousness is the source of energy and creative urge that pervades the unlimited extent of both the space-time universe and the "Oneness" of the nonphysical eternity outside of space-time—including the energy that created the universe and all that can ever exist or happen within it. Seth actually refers to that Consciousness as "All That Is," but for me, I just decided to refer to All That Is as "True Consciousness", often using just Consciousness with the capital "C." (The important reason to use the capital "C" is to distinguish True Consciousness from the common use of consciousness that is used in so many different ways to refer to some body/brain function, unrelated to it being a fundamental basis for All That Is.)

This assumption of there being a Fundamental Consciousness and the binks blinking assumption are the two assumptions with the most ramifications underlying my belief about the nature of reality—those on which all else is based. It seems to me that an increasing number of others are beginning to see a reason to also assume a Fundamental Consciousness as a necessary direction in their effort to extend physics to provide meaning concerning our reality. I have a list of 16 Ph.D.'s, most physicists, who have written on the topic of how the objective world has deep roots out of space-time and that quantum physics essentially requires consciousness and that Consciousness is fundamental.

True Consciousness is the source that creates everything that can be defined—given a name—information describing relationships—including every atom of the universe—including every self and every thought of every self. All the parts are a limited part (expression) of the one True Consciousness. They are all connected—there is no separation except by the labels we give them to represent some particular creation within True Consciousness. Each part is just an Organization of Consciousness (OC) representing some aspect of reality for which we give identity and attributes—whether physical or nonphysical.

Starting there, it follows that all such Organizations of Consciousness (OCs) have meaning within reality and that each such OC has an energetic creative propensity to evolve to fulfil its role to change the pattern of the universe as the on-going Creation within True Consciousness. The Seth material views relationships as within the physics framework, but the context is usually as an Organization of Consciousness, so as to sort of keep the focus on Consciousness as the context and starting point. In both frameworks, information is nonphysical and defines relationships, whether they are as objects, or thoughts such as desires, intentions, expectations, etc. Also in both frameworks, the nonphysical information exists prior to any manifest objective form within the universe.

Organizations of Consciousness are just globs (expressions) of always evolving True Consciousness that represent the information about the

274

relationship they define. That is, every OC, an atom for example, has an awareness of what it is (Consciousness), what it is for (propensity), and in a sense has a role to be involved (energetic) in relevant-to-it "change" processes to become a part of something greater. To do that, each OC relationship may combine with any other OC relationship to form the gestalt of a subsequent more complex relationship—and that is happening and never stops as the evolution of Creation.

Thus, I had to understand what "to become a part of something greater" means. I had to learn to think in terms of the gestalt nature of everything—that everything is an evolution of something or some condition that existed in a lesser form along the way to becoming something of greater complexity. A terrific example is that of a human body. It is composed of trillions of parts (cells) that evolve working together to represent something greater than just the sum of its parts—they form a constantly evolving physical body—something much more dynamic and of greater complexity than a large bucket of cells of various kinds.

The entire Universe may be viewed as such a gestalt of relationships.

The Seth description of all that in great detail emphasizes, importantly, that "total awareness of all" is an attribute of True Consciousness, and therefore, because all else is an expression of that True Consciousness, all that is formed via the evolution of Consciousness is intrinsically enabled to be aware of all other expressions. Thus, there exists connectedness such that everything may be consciously aware of all information about everything else should the relevance of information related to some other expression need to come into play as part of the continual creative evolving propensity of all OC's. That is another and more profound characteristic of the interconnectedness demonstrated within quantum physics. It is sort of a generalized "if you need to know, you may know" attribute of all evolving expressions of Consciousness—that is, including all change occurring in the physical world. In essence, if important, one may be aware of every sparrow that falls!

Seth explained it this way—"Information does not exist by itself. Connected with it is the Consciousness of all those who originate it, understand it, or perceive it. So, we do not have to think in terms of objective, forever-available banks of information into which you tune as if via some addressing scheme. Instead, the Consciousness that held, or holds, or will hold the information, may attract it like a magnet. ... Your 'self' Consciousness attracts the Consciousness that is already connected with the material." (Of course, that explains how people experiencing some form of paranormal perception access the information available from another person or place.)

This means, that everything physical within our objective universe and the complete detail of every kind of historical or ongoing act or thought occurring within nature, exists first as nonphysical information evolving to new forms. If we even observe or measure anything in the physical universe, we have also "created" new information—to thus create a new more information-intensive OC. All information related to all OC's (relationships), once created, is never erased— it is nonphysical—it just exists--it remains for all eternity. (Note, here comes that Akashic Record concept again! And it won't be the last time.) So, in this manner, Seth connects the Oneness of all gestalts of Consciousness within eternity with the existence of the eternity outside of space-time that was also shown to exist as a consequence of the basics of quantum physics.

The changes we observe or measure in the physical world are thus created by evolving gestalts (relationships) of Consciousness. That evolution is continuous and unstoppable, thus "energetic" in some form, possibly in some manner related to the use of the term "energy" with our physical models and equations. (Seth describes that relationship, but the considerable detail of the process is beyond what I have chosen to include as a part of my journey.)

A more comprehensive coverage of these main points of this general summary of what Seth has to say about Consciousness is:

Regarding Fundamental Consciousness

- All of reality exists as the Consciousness of All That Is.
- All That Is is unbounded and indescribably great creative energy and presence. (Creator of all characteristics and substance within reality.)
- Religions of mankind refer to All That Is by many names. (God, Brahman, Allah, Yahweh, I Am, and many others. I will choose to refer to All That Is as True Consciousness [Consciousness for short] with the understanding that no name places any limit or attempts to objectify the full nature of All That Is.)
- All That Is = Energy = Consciousness = Creator — these meanings are synonymous. (Consciousness is both the source and the sum of all energy and awareness, and the whole is more than the sum of its parts—i.e., a gestalt.)

- All that can be said to exist within the Oneness outside of our physical space-time universe or physically within it is an expression of Consciousness but not separate from Consciousness. (As True Consciousness but with limited expression potential—like us!)
- There is even a degree of Consciousness in every atom of matter.
- There is no relationship representing an object, process, or experience within the perceived physical universe that did not first exist as an Organization of Consciousness (OC) within the nonphysical Oneness.
- It is within the nature of every such Organization of Consciousness (OC) to be aware of and capable of connecting and exchanging information with ALL other OCs.
- The unceasing Creative energy of True Consciousness endows every such OC to seek fulfillment of its own propensity toward its purpose by unceasingly increasing the complexity of relationships within which it is a part.
- Mankind views the change in our physical world from a sequence of "nows" as passage of "time," a measure given by mankind to the change in what can be physically observed or measured from one blink to the next. (With both Seth and quantum physics, "time" as viewed by humanity is an illusion [only an attribute] caused by the change occurring in the physical world. There is no sense of "time" in the Oneness, where there is no time that is also all time—eternity.
- The evolving Oneness brings forth the constantly changing pattern of the physical universe as a sequence of new "nows," blinking from one to the next. (Which is an enrichment of what was characterized within quantum physics in Chapter 15.)
- Every OC that exists in the Oneness of eternity is available to influence the pattern of the universe at the next "now," subject to a sufficient level of significance.
- Within the Oneness, all OCs that have ever existed or will exist remain and according to their nature *may continue to evolve* throughout eternity. (To really understand reincarnation, we must understand the *may continue to evolve* part. More later on that.)
- That continual evolution of OCs in the Oneness is represented by changing (evolving) *relationships* not by a process related to the sense of time and/or space within the physical world. (Recall that thinking in terms of *relationships* was necessary within quantum physics to understand how all change in the physical world is characterized to occur independent of "time.")

277

- Consciousness with the form of our initial physical universe existed prior to the universe actually becoming physically manifest. (An OC to creatively evolve to become the physical universe and all within existed first in the Oneness, undoubtably with aspects different from what can now be accepted on the basis of our physical evolutionary history. Some assume and believe a particular reason that the universe was created, but I see no need to speculate about that—it clearly was created!)
- There can be an infinitely complex change in relationships within the Oneness without passage of time in the physical world, such as between blinks and as occurs within the OCs of our dreams. (Seemingly, near- instant cures of medical conditions may be a good example, where trillions of cells in a body may essentially in an instant change from unhealthy to healthy.)

Thus, according to Seth, reality is "top down," starting with Fundamental Consciousness! These views relating to the significance of Consciousness as fundamental within the greater reality became an additional "framework" for me to work with. But many questions remained unanswered and many more were subsequently raised.

The question where Seth eventually became my only "fount of knowledge" was "How do information-intensive processes that take place in the Oneness manifest one 'now' after another within what we observe and experience as the changes taking place within the physical world?" And another deep one: "How should we even understand various kinds of 'processes' within the Oneness that relate to our changing physical world when there is no time within the Oneness— where new Organizations of Consciousness evolve but do not require "time" to do so?" And another biggie for me: "How do people who have paranormal experience, particularly when they can do so at will, become aware of (perceive) content existing within the Oneness?"

It is clear now that the framework of True Consciousness figuratively built on my framework of physics as regards several topics, including interconnectedness/nonlocality, the focus on matters outside of space-time, information as nonphysical, and the significance of relationships in preparation for understanding in Seth terms the nature of a "self". The Chapter 15 framework was deep down, related one way or another to how energy is characterized within the cause-and-effect model of physics. This current chapter is essentially Seth talking about the creative nature of some kind of energy to evolve relationships as expressions of True Consciousness within the greater

278

reality, and in particular the nature of a self as a special Organization of Consciousness.

To grasp what Seth had to say about ourselves, it is imperative to understand how our selves are so totally immersed within the framework of True Consciousness. WE ARE, from the point of view of "our" greater reality, an expression of that Consciousness—the same stuff—just limited by comparison! WE ARE Organizations of Consciousness (OCs). WE ARE the most complex, energetic, and creative OC within this reality. (There may be other realities inaccessible to us.) WE ARE a part of the Oneness—that realm of the no time—no space zone—to exist throughout eternity—impossible to be erased. WE ARE interconnected with all other selves and all other nonphysical relationships within the Oneness—as both the physics and Consciousness frameworks represent. WE ARE co-creators of the physical universe—every second, every minute, and year by year—and we have been in times gone by. Recognizing that we are one of those structures of Consciousness characterized above must be the starting place if we are to learn more about what Seth has to say about our self. All that is sort of easy for me to write "in retrospect" but to put it together in depth with many implications took me years!

When I revisited some of the Seth material relating to what I just described, I realized that Seth had been in a sense describing the nature of our self with that depth and breadth all along—I had just not gotten enough of the big picture to understand what was being taught. In retrospect, I realize that part of the problem I was having was that it was all presented in our familiar language that is full of words containing an insidious embedded context of time and space — like the word "process," for example. That was the problem that Seth had to deal with over and over again! It really helped when I found that I could think of ANYTHING in or out of space-time in terms of "relationships" because relationships just exist, no space or time required! In essence, they are just information about whatever they are about! Everything is an example. There exists nothing in the Oneness or physical world that is not so representable and represented as a Consciousness structure—no matter how small or large in some sense of size or significance.

It is easy to think of examples—anything one thinks about is an example—physical objects such as a chair, city, ocean, firecracker, animals, and atoms—and also nonphysical relationships like those associated with the thought of going to the store or the desire to bowl a strike or the intent to kiss a girl or the expectation of a nice present at Christmas. All involve complex information relationships made up of simpler relationships to form a greater gestalt—just like the thought of going to the store includes relationships like store, car, streets, doors, etc.

Of course, the gestalt of the each of those is the collective result of "building-block" relationships that are in turn gestalts of many more relationships, etc., ad infinitum. These kinds of collections of building-block relationships include an infinity of infinities of potentially related consciousness structures that is a concept easy for a physicist or biologist to relate to but may be quite difficult for most people, even a musician. However, if my understanding is even in the ballpark, a willingness to accept the complexity and unfathomable extent of infinities of infinities is a necessary headspace for even the most basic thoughts about the greater reality. The bottom line is to accept that there are a lot of relationships and a lot of potential interconnectedness comprising the evolutionary history of essentially every OC in both the Oneness and the physical world.

And of course, to get into the nature of our self, Seth revisited the subject of reincarnation to make clear that we must think in terms of our many "Selves" as well as our "Self." As mentioned earlier, prior to really getting into what Seth had to say, I had come to accept the evidence for some form of reincarnation even though I could not answer a certain question that begged repeatedly for attention: How is it possible for there to be a "process" of evolution of many physical world lives evolving within the Oneness (simultaneously) where there is no "time" for change to take place?

From physics I had moved to accept out of space-time as fundamental—thus, our objective world as "derived" from the processes taking place in that unchartered domain I later came to call the Oneness. The basis for a lot of paranormal phenomena began to look possible long before it was possible for me to know exactly why—so that was encouraging—but reincarnation presented a special problem for me.

Multiple lives on Earth occur where we think in processes that take "time," so we think of such lives as sequential. How can there be "sequential" in the Oneness—without "time?" At first it seemed like it couldn't be. But I finally realized how to relate that "process" of changing relationships within the Oneness to multiple physical lives in space-time. In the Oneness where there is no time, the OCs of physical life relationships "just evolve" and remain with no separation. They just are!. They cannot do otherwise. They are just different but interconnected Organizations of Consciousness that evolved with our "self" as the common OC connector.

For instance, one prior worldly experience might include a life learning to shoot an arrow to acquire food. In another life, we may learn what a car is and how to use it to get from one place to another. In another life, we may be a cheating scoundrel, etc.—thus maybe to "have been" any life experience we have ever read about or heard about. And that is the same as realizing we "are" in some way all of those "life experiences"—NOW. Within the frameworks I found believable to me, each of us "is" in each physically manifest life potentially continuing to benefit from multiple life experiences of our "self" that are documented for eternity within the Oneness, but generally details of them are not knowingly a part of our day-by-day awareness.

We think of each life in terms of certain "experiences," but as was described within the True Consciousness framework, those life experiences are actually evolving relationships within the Oneness before they become manifest as that experience we are consciously aware of in each life. (More detail on that as this all unfolds.) I think that is now easy for me to say, and it is the answer to the question regarding reincarnation that bothered me for so long, but it was a real challenge to see why it is so. Our expression of Consciousness as a self is really a gestalt of experience from many lives. Our self is not just our physical bodies. Our bodies don't experience many lives, but our selves do.

Later I ran across some Seth material that added to my understanding of this "process" that does not require time nor space but with the sequencing aspect. The relationships change in the same way we experience time and space within a dream. We have a sense of changing time and space in a dream, but it is not the same as the time and space experience of our waking state. A dream is, however, an evolving OC of relationships within the Oneness. In a sense, we can think of our multiple physical lives as like dreams. ☺

Summarizing, as was pointed out in the True Consciousness framework, all expressions (OCs) of Consciousness have energy and are unceasingly evolving to increase to gestalt nature of their relationships within Creation—the cause and effect between the nonphysical and its manifestation within our physical world. Being just different expressions WITHIN True Consciousness, each OC is potentially part and parcel relationally aware and connected with the entire details of EVERY other OC. Information relating to one expression is always available to any other expression of our self via what we might think of as a kind of telepathy connection. There is plenty to "connect" with (all of eternity, including the progenitors of our "future") for every OC to be constantly evolving with new relationships. Some just happen to be OCs representing different lifetime experiences. A new life is sort of like a new car or any other OC connected via a relationship to our eternal self.

When all of what I think I have learned is put together, it becomes clear enough to me that every Consciousness structure that has ever existed remains within the Oneness to theoretically be "in play" as a possible relationship to be included in the evolution of any other relationship—such as those of our next "sequence of nows." At each quantum step in any change process of any kind in any part of the physical universe, the Consciousness structure building blocks (OCs) for a new pattern of a "now" are selected by some not predictably known (and maybe unknowable) process to create the always changing physical reality we know and love. That "in play" process is probably unknowable in detail, but factors that play a role, and how the selection process occurs, is what the Seth material is all about—how we create our own reality. It just takes many books and a lot of setting of the stage—creation of head-space—to explain how we can influence the process. It requires a view of reality as a context. The Seth material is a view of reality. The physics framework seems compatible.

Seth's message is that we can learn how to strongly influence the process to create our own reality experience without knowing all there is to know about that selection process occurring at each "now." In a sense, what Seth conveys in all of his books in our common English vocabulary is the background that helps give personal meaning to the terms "a now" and "in play," so the process of how we create the reality of our experience can be influenced by us as we live our lives. That helps us become aware of our role and responsibility within the process of creating our experience via thoughts and actions that, in conjunction with the thoughts and actions of others, become "in play" as that experience evolves "now" after "now".

To do that, to help build our understanding regarding the nature of our self and how our worldly experience unfolds, Seth uses terminology like our "Inner Self," our "Outer Self," and our "True Self" (sometimes a.k.a. our Whole Self) to try to help tie everything about the enormously extensive nature of a self together. I think I understand a good bit of what Seth was describing, but I am certain I have also missed a lot. Seth makes clear that there are no such actual inner/outer boundaries within the Consciousness extents of our self but introduces the terminology as an aid to help us understand the nature of how our body self can improve the way we interact with the greater reality. I will use that Seth terminology in what follows.

I realize that Seth was using True Self to represent the gestalt level of Consciousness that includes as constituent relationships the aggregate collection from all of our self experiences within many physical lives. The True Self Consciousness gestalt is too great (infinities of relationships) to be obtainable through one life experience. Our experience in any one life becomes a part of our True Self experience, but also there are ways in which each life benefits by being a part of the complexity of that True Self. Our body-related self that manifests as "us" at each blink in each incarnation remains in contact with our nonphysical True Self within the Oneness. It is up to us to learn how to benefit from the other life experiences that are available to us via such contact. Reminder! Seth's focus within his teaching material is, over and over again, to describe how we create our own reality. Given that, it is not surprising that so much Seth material is devoted to the nature of our "self."

The Inner Self is described as that inherent capacity of the self of any life experience to connect us, sort of like a channel, with the depth of awareness within the Oneness that is inseparable from us in both our nonphysical and physical expressions, but is not a channel we are generally aware of day by day. The Inner Self has a virtually infinite reservoir from which to draw knowledge, experience, and guidance. We would go insane if we accepted it all at once!

Seth teaches that the important essence of the Outer Self (often also referred to as our Ego Self) is to help us to act based on our decisions and intentions when we are embodied in the physical. I think Seth refers to the Outer Self as our Ego to sort of tie-in with the references to ego behavior and language within psychology, as an identifiable aspect of our existence but not as the common connotation of egotistical or just the waking awareness.

Seth's characterization of the relationship between our Inner Self and our Ego during each lifetime is sometimes entertaining but always insightful in some way. The Ego is described as providing our direct, brain conscious experience with the world that has the option of sort of listening to our Inner Self—or of sort of pushing such guidance into the background—sometimes with immediate or more eternal unpleasant results. That listening—the conceptual boundary between the Inner and Outer selves—is referred to as the commonly talked about subconscious. It filters/selects perception by our brain of the information available from our inner Self. Among other things, it is what provides us the sense of identity. The Ego is nothing more than the top portion of the subconscious. Through reincarnational experience, the Inner and Outer Selves come closer and closer, and the intermediary subconscious function disappears.

In that Inner/Outer relationship, the Ego is spoon-fed, being given only data related to those feelings and emotions that it can handle. It frequently forgets its "whole" nature. When it becomes swept up in a strong emotion, it seems to lose itself. When the Ego most vigorously maintains its sense of separateness and individuality, it is no longer aware of unity with the Inner Self. It is sort of off in a world of its own. Those are times when meditation or some form of disassociation is particularly helpful to get back in balance.

Our Ego is the aspect of our self that experiences time as continuity between before and after. (Dummy, it doesn't realize that there is really only "now." A dog knows better!) However, its focus on helping us to manipulate in the physical world is facilitated by its experiencing the world as a series of stimulus and response; thus we experience worldly causes and effects. Seth says more about the Ego, but that is essentially what I needed to know to understand the helpfulness of talking about the self in terms of the Inner Self looking out at the depth and breadth of the Oneness and the Outer Self (Ego) looking constantly forward to the physical world where we need to work with our body and brain. Again, doing that leads to our sense of identity.

The mission of the Ego aspect of our self is to help us manipulate within a physical existence, from getting up each day to retiring each night. One mission of the Inner Self is to enable us to benefit from any information in the Oneness that might be helpful to us if we are aware of it—including contributions from our True Self to share with our current life what we have learned in prior lives. The kicker is that we have to learn how to open up to our Inner Self and listen.

I think a lot human behavior and experience can be characterized with what has just been written about in the last few paragraphs. Much of what follows is intended to provide what I believe to be the benefits of an understanding of the importance of the interplay between the Inner and Outer Selves. If we are Ego bound, we cannot reap the vast resources of our Inner Self.

Seth says what we decide (control selection) via the working of our Ego is determined by the everyday decision making of our "mind." In my experience, the word "mind" is often used as some abstract "something" sort of synonymous with an also abstract ill-defined waving at something called "consciousness." Seth would have none of that. Seth carefully defines and then proceeds to often use "mind" as the working together of our nonphysical self and our brain, which then functions to help us physically perceive, think, and know stuff that is offered to our Ego for consideration and action.

Our mind assesses whatever is relevant for the moment within the physical world and has behind it all the energy, power, and connectedness of the Inner Self to the Oneness at its disposal. Subconsciously, it is always trying to give our brain a clear picture for our decision making and other physical functioning. Just like the Inner and Outer aspects of our self, the mind is always with us, takes up no space, and needs no time to function. All three are the nonphysical aspect of our self that co-exists in and out of space-time. Our brain is the purely physical, working connector that perceives physical or nonphysical stimuli to translate the focus of our mind into our living experiences.

I refer to the relationship between our Inner Self and the full expression of our mind as a figurative "Gateway." I think my life experience has greatly improved since I learned how to open that gateway. To experience and function exuberantly within the greater reality, I believe it helps to learn how to develop our awareness to pull good guidance from our gateway and to learn how to use our mind to create useful information from that source. It is our access via the Inner Self to the awareness and unlimited knowledge available to us from the collective experience of our True Self and all other OCs of the Oneness.

This is the gateway that is opened by intent or without apparent conscious brain control, by those who acquire awareness of nonphysical information in the form of impressions, knowings, revelations, intuition, unusual insight, etc.—a lot of everyday awareness that adds depth to life experience. The gateway is also in an open state when experiencing some unusual form of non-normal phenomenon or altered personal awareness. Our gateway through the Inner Self has the potential to provide information with value we can depend on. (There are those who believe there is a physiological opening [gateway] for nonphysical stimuli to reach perception in the neurons of the brain via the synapses and/or microtubules, but I have no reason to go into that here.)

When I eventually realized the role of the gateway to our Inner Self, and therefore to the Oneness, it helped explain the connection between paranormal phenomena and our physical functioning. For example, Telepathy and Remote Viewing are readily understood as accessing and perceiving information via the gateway to the self of another human. It requires a little more explanation for perceiving "the future" situation, as we think of our "time" experience, but that became clearer when I learned more of what Seth presents on how we create our own reality by thinking about what we put "in play" to influence what becomes manifest as our future.

I have come to believe that when we are inclined spiritually, we use the gateway to hear and witness the guidance via the Inner Self to help us evolve a self that is closer to the nature of the True Consciousness of which we are a part. (Again, some would use "soul" instead of "self.") The reported spiritual bliss of religious figures in history is an exceptional example. Experiencing a state of spiritual bliss is also reported often by experienced meditators.

Seth says we can learn to open the gateway if we practice. Practice suggestions are provided in the material along with the general benefit to be derived from each. I now understand what was going on back in the 1970s when I learned to "go to alpha" as a brain state for experiencing psychic impressions. I think that is a practice easy for most of us to learn if we desire to do so. It can become life experience enhancing when our wandering thoughts or moments of habitual routines (housework, dressing and body care, arising from sleep, etc.) are sort of trained to be moments of unplanned insight. Seth provides suggestions on how to open our gateway in that manner.

There are a few obvious questions arising from these Seth teachings. For one: "Is our experience in another incarnation in any way a factor in a current one whether we seek to be aware of it or not? If so, why aren't we more aware of those multiple incarnational experiences?" Well, occasionally some humans are. That is where Ian Stevenson and others have discovered the research evidence they have concluded is akin to reincarnation of some kind.

I found that subject to be quite complex, but in essence, I decided the answer to that question is definitely yes. Not only is there bleed-through of other life experiences but, as mentioned a few paragraphs back, there are benefits if we learn how to be aware of them. Seth describes many subtle ways that our current life insights and inclinations are often connected to those learning experiences of our True Self in other incarnations. Many attribute the exceptional capabilities of some artists, musicians, leaders, child prodigies, etc., to some prior life experience, and Seth acknowledges that can be true.

In a less obvious connection between this life and a prior life, Seth's summary comment is that we draw to ourselves in this existence and in all others those qualities upon which we concentrate our physical or nonphysical attention. A lot of times, we are probably being aided or hindered in what we do by a prior life experience, but we are not aware of it. The somewhat related and widely viewed importance of personal "karma" is intimately connected to multi-life experience. (More later in this chapter regarding karma.) Hopefully, multiple

286

life experiences help us reduce the limitations of our True Self compared to the True Consciousness nature of All That Is.

It was tempting to say, "Ah ha, I have confirmation on what the purpose in life is supposed to be." Well, yes and no. I found the Seth answer to the question very thought provoking. Seth would say, "The purpose of life is being—as opposed to not being." "The purpose is to live it"—period—the way reality works will guide us during multiple lifetimes (teleologically) toward an increasingly full participation within True Consciousness. In all experience in all lifetimes, there operates a teleological focusing within reality to guide us to an always-improving expression of a spiritual nature.

Our purpose in life is just to get the experience we encounter and deal with it. Experience, and learning from that experience, is the name of the game of life. We evolve in a way to learn from counter-productive or dissatisfying experience just as well as experience that provides feedback that is more joyful, fulfilling, and spiritually insightful. Seth says, "Just go do it," but you will find something possibly more meaningful if you pay attention to what you choose as your value system and beliefs while you do it. Essentially, Seth says, "You have a mind, use it."

At a more detailed level, Seth teaches that the way reincarnation works leads our True Self to equip our personality self to enter each life with a "plan for this life" that we have prepared each time we are born for a new life experience. In each life, our purpose is to have the experiences and make the most of them. That will help us evolve spiritually. There is a special meaning in all of our lifetime relationships, attitudes, and experiences. If in one life, for example, a man incessantly hated women, he might be a woman in the next so as to face what he had dished out to women in a past life. If one had no empathy or sympathy for sick people in one life, sickness may be chosen for a next life as a way to encounter and endure such attitudes. If one gained great enlightenment in one life, one would likely plan a life to experience enlightenment of a completely different kind—even if a stressful life to achieve it. No life plan is prepared so as to focus on one such lesson only but is prepared by a self as a developmental opportunity via physical experience—not to be wasted.

If we make predominately good choices at key life junctions—plan fulfilled. If we don't—well, there will be more opportunities in this life and a subsequent life to work on it. That is about all I want to take space for right now on views about the generally understood meaning of karma. More later. For me, the True Consciousness of our self is all that is needed to guide us—*we just need to learn how to open up our gateway to the resources available via our Inner Self.* In our terminology, Seth also teaches that the more we open that inner gateway and are open to "listen," the more we will also perceive the spiritual nature of the greater reality and thus "learn love."

It finally also dawned on me that when once a person accepts that the real self is nonphysical and not just a part of our physical body, then many doors open that are of a deeply spiritual nature, and that has been true for me. Accepting that my True Self is nonphysical brought back some questions from my youth: "Where do we go when we die?" "Are there reasons other than basic faith to believe in God?" "Are heaven and God out there someplace or something different?" "Do we need to be saved?" And so on and on and on ... Those questions had been on my mind for a long time because there are issues arising from questions like those that lead to a variety of religions staking out claims based on a variety of answers. I have chosen to work on answers for myself—but with help wherever I could find it within a more "fleshed-out" and believable-to-me reality.

Of course, "God is Love" is core Christianity, which was my upbringing, remember. Seth agrees, making clear that Love is without an object—that love is a nature "of love" rather than a nature "to love" (a person or object). Seth closely relates the nature "of compassion" to that "of love." Other than to mention that learning to be love is the lesson we learn as we evolve through as many lifetimes as it takes to believe that is important, Seth doesn't provide a value system guaranteed to speed that process along. He does mention that the combination of the evolution of our True Self and the feedback we receive from our life experiences will result in a trend toward a spiritual awareness of the nature of our Fundamental True Consciousness. I think that is good to hear. ☺

The focus of all such generalized guidance, and there is a lot in the Seth material, is to recognize first and foremost that all that we see in our world is a result of the ongoing Creation originating within True Consciousness—even persons engaging in behavior we are inclined to label in a negative way. The guidance then is like the advice of Jean Piaget for parenting, "the behavior may not be ok, but the person is ok." I personally think that connotation regarding "love" is also the true starting place of sincere, unquestioned, "forgiveness." Pat and I have recently seen such forgiveness "without qualification"—from a young woman neighbor whose husband and father of their child was gunned down and killed by Islamist jihadists while teaching children in the Middle East. Her witness was an amazing example of forgiveness as pure love in action.

288

Regarding the Nature of a Self

- There is a portion of each of us, our truly deep identity that decided that we would be a physical being in this place and time. This self is the psychic seed from which we became an expression of True Consciousness.
- Before we are born, our self creates a desired plan for various experience situations during a new lifetime, and we are born into the appropriate family, gender, genetic makeup, world location, and future, with the potential challenges and opportunities to enable us to fulfill our desired plan. (If we don't, we learn by our unrewarding choices and await a new incarnation with a new plan.)
- It is more correct to think of the self not as something we have, rather, what we are—a highly complex expression of True Consciousness.
- The True Consciousness awareness of every self cannot be severed.
- When conditions suggest significance, every self may by the working of desire and our self propensity within Consciousness to attract as relevant to its experience any and all other Consciousness within the Oneness to create a more complex expression of itself. (That is a very strong and important statement. To grow via experience, we have access to all OCs that our self would like to be aware of within the Oneness—a total connectedness that includes potential awareness of every thought, intention, or emotion we or others have ever experienced in any lifetime—to be available if we listen via our gateway to our Inner Self as we create our own reality within the current lifetime.)
- Every self is a (tremendous) gestalt of component OCs that seek each other out (attract each other) in accord with the fundamental nature of Consciousness to evolve via the feedback from experience within both the physical world and the Oneness to fulfill its nature.
- Every self is a boundary of Consciousness but of potentially unlimited awareness and energetic Consciousness within its personality boundary. (A self is not invisible, rigid, and limited in potential from being a special evolving personality gestalt.)
- Part of the self knows and <u>knows</u> it knows. Part of the self knows and <u>does not know</u> it knows.
- Selves have a unique personality that experiences many lifetimes with the gestalt of its personality attributes evolving within each lifetime.

- Within the personality self that we call our own, there is access to our greater True Self (a.k.a. Whole Self) that has experienced many lives as many personalities.

Seth dictated books and provided much additional material to describe the depth and breadth of a greater reality within which our beliefs create the reality we experience in each lifetime. I came to believe that the more we understand how that occurs, the more we can assess and over time change our thoughts and behavior so as to create for ourselves a satisfying life experience. That's the general statement. Once we accept the implied responsibility for the results of our choices, the details start by recognizing that the primary consideration is the importance of using our mind to listen to our Inner Self.

The detail provided in the Seth material is to help us learn to do that. Our Inner Self will help us guide our life of choices so as to create the best we can do to implement the plan we created for this life. The places, people, world conditions, opportunities, and challenges we need to execute the plan will "just happen" to be there at the appropriate times. I have come to look at my own lifetime that way. Reviewing my own life to write this life story seems to suggest and confirm that there has been a plan. Note: The plan was never clear to me until in retrospect—in the rear view mirror. ☺

Seth does not set forth a basket full of "should of's," "ought to's," or in general tell us how to make good choices at that level of behavior. Rather, the Seth material provides another framework regarding the nature of reality—how within that reality our thoughts, desires, intentions, emotions, expectations, etc., have their origin in our beliefs. The intent of providing us with this framework of understanding regarding beliefs is to help us identify how the choices we make as a result of such thinking and feeling create the physical life we experience. This framework adds another to those of physics, the nature of Fundamental Consciousness and the complex nature of our self.

Given that we are an energetic and creative OC, Seth teaches that the feedback resulting from action based on our beliefs is what we learn from. As has been and will be repeated over and over, physical lives are to experience feedback. The associated implication, and a fact according to Seth, is that between lives we ponder what we have learned and make the plan for our next life accordingly. We have no choice. That is the way reality works. We are expressions of True Consciousness, and thus co-creators as we evolve to become selves with fewer limitations and to experience a greater depth and breadth of reality. Seth directly touched upon the fact that it can be difficult to connect the experience and what we are to learn from it. Two common and worrisome questions were used as examples: "How does a loving God permit evilness to exist?" and "Why do bad things happen to good people?"

Seth guides us with examples and context within the Consciousness and Self frameworks to first recognize that "the Universe is of good intent; evil and destruction does not exist except as a scenario of experience." That is, one cannot define evil and destruction except by labeling—they are not conditions inherent of a self or situation, but rather they are labels for what any consciousness created to create can create. What is, is. Then in one passage, Seth speaks to the first of these questions as follows: "Evidence of evil in the world *appears as such to our senses* in order to let us know the consequences of the beliefs we hold, but mankind may awaken from that sadness as from a bad dream." That is, there is no "The devil made me or they do anything."

I have often heard others claim something like: There can be no God because, if there is a God who let evil be a part of Creation, that would be a malevolent God. And if there is a God who cannot prevent evil, that is a God without power and presence. Either way, they cannot believe in such a God. I believe their life could be a lot more satisfying if they realized there is the Seth way to view evil as a label we give to behavior, but that there is a teleology of love in process in all experience. With the help of the Seth material, I have been able to answer those questions in a meaningful context of reality for myself. I have decided that for me the idea of bad things happening to good people is more complex to think about because even "good" must be thought of in a similar way.

The basic starting point for trying to answer both questions was that there is purpose in life experiences that we and others, as an expression of our True Selves, have decided to encounter in this life to learn from. If we do, we will no longer think in terms such as good and evil, pretty and ugly, or as a mistake or as a stroke of brilliance. That leads to another question for each of us to answer on our own: "What is it that I am to learn from the experiences within my current life and, maybe even more importantly, to learn within the context of others involved in my experience?" Our experience is often intimately related to the experience of someone else also. I now believe that is a set of relationships we should learn to subconsciously keep in mind if we believe that our beliefs create the reality we experience.

As mentioned before, the Seth's answer to what is the purpose in all this is don't worry about "a right answer," just keep plugging away with the idea to learn from experience, and the more we learn to discern the rules of the game from the feedback from that experience, the better we will perform and feel about it. And in my opinion, by acknowledging and whenever possible following our impulses, we can discover a meaning for our lives and learn how to act in such a way as to benefit both ourselves and the world. If we do not like some aspect of our world, then maybe we should examine our expectations from a new perspective. If we feel guilty about some aspect of our behavior, that is a good place to start.

One of the rules of the game of life is that, although there is a game we all play together (called life within the physical), the main game is personal—we are ultimately in it alone. The reality we encounter is uniquely our own. I learned from physics, then Seth, and some help from Kevin, that no two humans are experiencing the same reality. If we look at something in the middle of the room from opposite sides of the room, we see a different object (set of relationships). If we see a child cry, the pattern of neurons within our brains and our subjective perception may have a lot in common, but they are not identical. We can think quite different thoughts while seeing the same flag, etc. We only "know" our physical world by the many, many thoughts in our head—to us the world is a mental construct—and what we see is uniquely our own idea of what it looks like. Objects within the physical world are often most meaningful because of the thoughts they give birth to. The Patriarchs quoted in Appendix A realized that.

We, of course, agree on many things when we see pretty much the same thing close enough to give it a name—like a tree, a car, a cloud, etc., and to share concepts about the nature of our world that arise from shared experience, like that of weather, ocean waves, popping balloons, etc.—even when we see different storm details, different waves, a different view of the balloon, etc. The general form and changing patterns of our world are the result of humanity jointly participating in a shared Creation—"a consensual reality." Through our collective desire and expectation to share a world of objects we essentially "create" all the matter that it takes to do so.

Once Organization of Consciousness's are created, exist, and evolve, those expressions of the True Consciousness are just there for eternity and available to be in play for any and all where there is a strong enough significance connection. Mankind collectively produces the pattern of all matter subconsciously at each blink. Many connections that support consensual reality came into being long ago. Others exist when we develop a cultural experience together such as the invention of a horseless buggy, airplane, etc. I find it sort of entertaining to look around for something to watch that is not currently consensual reality to many, and watch it become consensual reality to many, and maybe even many more.

At the nonphysical level, this sharing of a view of the nature of our physical universe is accomplished via that Inner Self telepathy operating constantly between the infinities of OCs of humans when we subconsciously agree on the existence and properties of objects. Until I understood why we could all agree on some things, I kept wondering how come the airplane I was flying on was working if all passengers were supposed to be experiencing a uniquely personal reality. ☺

To repeat, however, in every moment there is a perception of objective form within the universe that is seen and experienced differently by each of us. That is, at each "now" there is essentially a separate pattern of the universe and state of mind uniquely our own—soon to be replaced by the next sequence of "nows." As made clear within the prior frameworks, objective *relationships* may change with each "now"—and the most important are the relationships unique to each of us. The uniqueness of our individual reality is generally not taught or recognized. Accepting the belief that it is can be an important beneficial factor in all decisions we make.

As Professor Conn Henry has noted: "Galileo was able to educate the world to understand that the Earth goes around the Sun, yet physicists today have utterly failed to inform the public to understanding the purely mental nature of the universe—with all that that implies for the meaning of human existence. That is a tragedy, and it should be rectified."

Because we are all born with a unique-for-us purpose and predisposition for certain situations and desired choice patterns, it should be no surprise that we perceive and create a reality uniquely our own. And the most personal aspect of all is our beliefs. As I think is important enough to mention over and over, our beliefs are thoughts and positions formed by imagination and emotion concerning the nature of the world as we see and experience it. A lot of the Seth material is one way or another related to how our beliefs are what help us separate some possibilities within the Oneness from alternate possibilities. Through our thoughts, etc., our beliefs attract and actualize other Organizations of Consciousness to be considered by our self for inclusion in our own creative processes. Collectively, the result is to create our choices—uniquely our choices, even if great significance is given by us to the choices of others. *Our beliefs are our screening, sorting, discerning, and directing agents.*

Many beliefs influence the way we perceive possible, or even what we think are probable, conditions in what we think of as our future. An example would be the expressions of a desire for some future event or condition. Another might be a prayer for someone. Another might simply be following a plan created by and important to someone else, like an employer. A common denominator of many situations is when there is desire or expectation about events in the "future."

Seth reminds us that such expectations or general thoughts touching on possible future situations become Organizations of Consciousness in the now, and therefore information immediately and firmly established as existing within the Oneness even though about the "future." That is, every thought that we have continues to exist, and depending on how strong we are attached to it, may be in play in what we will subsequently experience. The information is available to be taken into account consciously or unconsciously along with all other OCs in subsequent choices to be made by us or others.

I will refer to such OCs of thought, desire, expectation, etc., that represent a personal view about some "<u>possible</u>" future situation as a *probable reality* that we might experience—without regard to the degree of the probability. We are figuratively surrounded by possible but not yet manifest thoughts and conditions that might influence our experienced future. Our Ego essentially guides us to choose single events or actions from all of what could be alternative probable ones.

To repeat what has been mentioned in several different ways: The nature of our self to expand experience is unceasing, as is the nature of all expressions of True Consciousness—each according to its own propensity. That is the ongoing nature of Creation. Creating is what all OCs have in common, from the smallest particles of matter to the complex gestalts like our True Selves or the entire universe. So for me the questions were: "How does that work for us, our self?" and "Do we care how it works?"

The Seth material describes the ongoing Creation of the physical universe in terms of how nonphysical relationships, both OCs and potential realities, <u>materialize</u> to create a changed state of matter within the physical world at each "now." Again, our physical world is created by the Consciousness structures within the Oneness at each blink. Each blink is advancing the creative evolution of every OC. What we create as nonphysical Consciousness structures become the stuff that determines our unfolding *physical* world experience. I decided that I personally cared and do care enough about how it works to read, study, and ponder information that seems credible that relates to the process. We all decide for ourselves about such things, so I certainly don't think that one size fits all.

We know that all change in our and everyone's physical reality occurs during sequences of those blinking steps characterized in the physics framework and also as mentioned often by Seth. We know there is indeterminacy at each change step, but with such small change steps, it is hard to say much about them at that level. As a more comfortable way to think of it, we can talk about the changes unfolding as continuous sequences of nows to characterize events and situations. As we also know from quantum physics, that the statistical process involves selection of some outcomes and not others at each of the "nows." That is where we look when we ask, how does the nonphysical stuff ready to be in play as probable realities formed by our thoughts, etc., actually influence the form of changes taking place hour by hour, and so on, in our experience?

Seth offers the conceptual basics of how that works, some in the language and processes of physics, to describe how one "now" fades out and a new one fades in to create the blink of a new "now." In essence, it is a process describing how the energy and information representing the nonphysical Organizations of Consciousness selected to be "in play" is transformed from creative Consciousness energy into electromagnetic relationships within the physical world of our observations and measurements based upon the same information. The total level of detail in a physics sense of how each such change step is determined is just a part of the creative nature of True Consciousness and is and always will be to some degree a mystery to us.

The Ray Stanford channeled material does provide highly insightful detail relating to aspects of that general process from a physics context, but not of a complete transition step. I think of the nonphysical to physical transition as "bridging" the "nows" from one to the next. As was mentioned in the prior chapter, physics as we know it does not focus on how consciousness might have a role in the steps of indeterminacy that create observable/measurable change. I think there is a growing number of highly educated and insightful physicists such as Tiller, Haisch, Puthoff, Mohrhoff, Meijer (and I am willing to presume many others) that are starting the long haul that will lead in the direction of seeking a role of meaning behind physical processes. Similarly, there are also others in neuroscience, psychology, and philosophy that are seeking a better understanding of consciousness in their work. I think they will find a growing common ground.

295

In this chapter I am trying to share what Seth does have to tell us about the kinds of things that occur during the transition process and how they work to create our reality in the context of our beliefs. As I have already mentioned, for me, how we create the reality we experience is a big deal. Learning more about what that means has been very important in how I have chosen to live the remaining years of my life. That is why I wish to share the essence of what I believe about the manner in which we have some influence as to how our physical experience unfolds.

It is important to keep in mind the fact that all physical and nonphysical Organizations of Consciousness within Creation are expressions that seek fulfillment of their continually active creative nature according to their degree of allotted True Consciousness. Sort of like atoms evolve to be molecules, molecules evolve to become cells, cells evolve to grow and maintain bodies, bulbs evolve to become flowers, kittens evolve to be cats, etc., and if we think in geological terms, a river became the Grand Canyon, etc.

And as mentioned earlier, Seth informs us that all of our thoughts, desires, intentions, emotions, expectations, etc., are such nonphysical expressions of Consciousness and that once formed are part of the record we create as our reality that will remain unique to us throughout eternity. According to Seth, the strength of the emotion involved in any thought creating those nonphysical expressions of Consciousness is very important in how we create our own reality. Strong emotion is often sort of "attached" to desire as well—which makes desire also of special significance in how we create our own reality.

As mentioned pages ago, a thought once created (An OC) cannot be erased; however, Seth teaches that the significance of any OC is clearly changed if and when we create a new OC with a clearly desired alteration of the prior one.

An example might be that at one time we have a thought like "I hate that guy," but later based on a new insight, we regret thinking such a negative thought and honestly recognize how clearly that is not really the way I want to be—or something like that. The net experience can be positive—sort of like "with the help of my Inner Self at work, I want to replace such views with a new belief that we are all made of the same stuff, and we also behave poorly sometimes, but I should just view his bad behavior as what I don't like and not him that I don't like." Or, an even more significant net positive might be: "I have come to the belief that I should view all people with compassion and look beyond a judgment about sometimes poor behavior or their personal limitations.

That is a high priority. I am trying daily to change my thoughts and behavior." This replacing of old beliefs with new beliefs is important to understand and is absolutely necessary when I get to the Seth version of the nature of karma.

To summarize again how this fits together: Seth teaches that all Organizations of Consciousness (OCs) in the Oneness may be "in play" at each "now" to influence the change taking place *if* there is a context for significance. That is, the unfolding of events in our life and the world around us is the result of a process of selection from infinities of possible OCs to form the gestalt of the next "now." Seth characterizes that selection process in terms of the intensity with which OCs came into being—in particular as related to the significance of imagination and emotions. Little significance—little contribution to our subsequent experience! In short form, that is how our beliefs are in play to create our physical reality.

I believe that our beliefs thus step-by-step create our worldly experience. Depending on how we use our mind, we have guidance available to us via the gateway of our Inner Self and our free will to change our beliefs and create a more satisfying reality for ourselves based on the feedback from that experience—if we choose to assume responsibility for the reality we create for ourselves.

Regarding How We Create Our Own Reality

- We create our own reality—we have no choice—we cannot do otherwise. Our only choice is to decide what we think about all that.
- We evolve to understand a greater reality as the result of our experience, both as our True Self within the Oneness and via our many lifetimes within the physical world.
- The life plan we create before birth places us in the general situations, including genetics, that create the challenges and experience we will encounter in that lifetime.
- We create our reality as we make day-by-day free-will choices in each lifetime resulting in one particular future experience rather than available possible alternatives each time we make a choice.
- The reality we seek and that is experienced personally in each life is determined by our beliefs and is uniquely our own. Though some or many beliefs may be similar to beliefs of others, there will be nuances that are consciously or unconsciously unique to us. No two people see or experience the exactly same reality.

297

- Our beliefs are the basis for our choices in thoughts and deeds.
- Our beliefs determine how we screen, sort, discern, and direct choices.
- We confuse beliefs *about* our worldly experience as *actual* characteristics of the world itself.
- Our thoughts, emotions, desires, intentions, expectations, etc., are all influenced by our beliefs, and create Consciousness structures that are then available to effect subsequent life experiences.
- The likelihood that such Consciousness structures will be selected to affect our future experience depends both on the emotional intensity of what created them and the significance they represent to us in terms of the unfolding experience.
- The probability of an event in the future of our experience may "cause" our interim choices (quite possibly not otherwise related) to result in an experience ("effects") that will lead to that future "cause," even though free will is always available to us in all choices. (This is the retro- causation scenario.)

To sort of sum up this framework, I would like to close it with this quote from Seth: "You make your own reality or you do not. And if you do not, then you are everywhere a victim, and the universe must be an accidental mechanism appearing with no reason. That is a belief that the miraculous picture you have seen of your body came accidentally into Creation, and out of some cosmic accident attained its miraculous complexity. And that body was formed so beautifully for no reason except to be a victim. That is the only other alternative to forming your own reality. You cannot have a universe in between. You have a universe formed WITH a reason or a universe formed WITHOUT a reason. And in a universe of reason, there are no victims. Everything has a reason or nothing has a reason. So, choose your side!" Of course, it would be easy to incorporate "free will" into that exposition, but I will refrain. Our free will is a fact that is part and parcel of the nature of our self.

And I will summarize Seth's contribution to my personal insights and beliefs about the nature of True Consciousness, our self, and how we create our reality this way. As compared with religious philosophy and speculation from many sources that proclaim to say something about the nature of the connection between the nonphysical and physical world, the Seth material has been the single most complete source that has passed muster for me. It was, and is, a comprehensive body of material that appears to me to be compatible with every other source I am aware of and deem importantly related to a greater reality— and it is delivered in the English language. Seth used language we are familiar with in our common experience in the physical world to try to describe aspects of the Oneness, where using our space-time based language makes doing that very difficult.

Before moving on and as sort of a refresher for some of the main topics above, this chart below is something to ponder relating physics and consciousness frameworks. It is interesting to me that although I first started thinking about the "physics of reality" those many years ago; it now appears to me that my journey has taken me much farther. Early in the next chapter, I will put closure to my thoughts about where the most commonly discussed evidence of paranormal phenomena fits in a context with these frameworks.

Physics Framework	Consciousness Framework
Outside Time and Space	The Oneness
Relationships/Information	Organizations of Consciousness (OC)
Blinking Nature of Physical Change	"Nows"
Energy As Defined within Physics	Energy of Creative Consciousness
Connectedness as in Quantum Physics	Connectedness of All Consciousness
Personal Mental Uniqueness of Reality	Personal Fact of Uniqueness of Reality
Nonlocality View of Outside Space-time	Gateway to All Within the Oneness
Retro-causation	An Influence on Current OC Creation
Unknown Cause of the Big Bang	All That Is—True Consciousness Just Is

Regarding Uncommon Ways of Experiencing Reality

The fourth area of growing insight in recent years has come from some reading and discussions with Kevin. The scope and depth of those discussions of metaphysics with him increased greatly after 2004 when he and Jennifer attended a lecture by the East Indian mystic, Jaggi Vasudev Sadhguru. The presentation generally described how the formal practice of meditation helped people experience better health and more joy in life. Jennifer was immediately attracted to what Sadhguru had to say. She wrote me an email in April that year telling me about the experience and suggesting that I read a couple of books about Sadhguru and what he had to say.

I did, and became curious but not much more. It seemed to me that what he had to say was directed solely to people unhappy with their life experience, and I didn't feel that way. I really didn't want to spend time wondering what "bliss" might be. Kevin seemed interested but not as much as Jennifer. Then in July that year I received an email from Kevin where he wrote:

"I just finished the yoga training that was taught by Sadhguru. It was absolutely amazing. It changed my life, and I was very skeptical going in. He talked about something very close to the bink theory. He called it "Creation" and explained that it happens billions of times each second. Space and the void of nothingness that seems to have potential for binking in and out of existence is where God lives. And of course, within each of us that same god lives in between the clutter of our thoughts, emotions and ego. The practice that was taught helps you clear your mind of the clutter. So far, usually the result is only one or two seconds of thought-free space but sometimes as much as ten seconds. Once you give this nothingness an opportunity to be, amazing things happen to your point of view. You realize what the 'I am' really is. You realize where YOU really are, and you feel that everything is a part of you."

"But there are some side effects ... good health, well-being, and happiness. I'm already feeling them all in just a short time. I'm looking forward to telling you more."

Kevin and Jennifer have learned and personally experienced much of what Sadhguru teaches and demonstrates. They have engaged in many yoga courses, workshops, and other programs to help them make Isha Yoga a more comprehensive perspective of reality and life experience for them. [Isha Yoga's flagship program is "Inner Engineering," where individuals are initiated into meditation in part based on breathing practices and a powerful Kriya or internal energy process, distilled from the yogic sciences to effect a profound self-transformation. It is a method of bringing one's entire system into alignment, so that mind, body, emotions and energy function in complete harmony.]

After Kevin attended his first introductory meditation program, I was surprised at the increasing number of reports from him involving what I thought were complex states of his altered personal consciousness while meditating. Within my thought processes, much of what he had to share from them seemed to relate to subjects we had discussed while talking about Seth, physics, and the growing amount of material in the general area of the paranormal. Kevin also quoted Sadhguru a lot and suggested I read another book about him, which I also did.

In 2005, while attending a Sadhguru Program in Michigan, Kevin had an altered consciousness experience during a meditation focused on death he will never forget. (His book describing the experience in great detail, *Beyond Heaven*, will be published in 2015.) We have discussed that experience many different times and from many different viewpoints over the years. Immediately following the meditation, he returned to his sleeping quarters at the Boy Scout camp rented for the program to draw a picture containing the many symbols he recalled from the experience. I think the diagram is interesting, and I intend to mention some reasons why some of the symbols are of particular interest. I have inserted the diagram below.

As will not be a surprise if one looks at the diagram, it is the source of the special meaning we now assign to the technical term (ho ho) "Basketballs." We believe that those symbols within his dream were to guide him (and subsequently me) to a very important aspect of physics and personal reality. The frameworks I have attempted to characterize earlier in this chapter provides the information necessary for me to describe why I believe basketballs are important in how we experience reality.

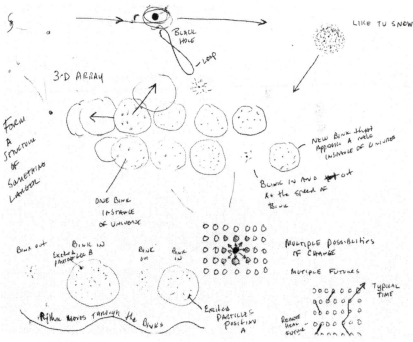

THE DIAGRAM OF SYMBOLS CONTAINED IN KEVIN'S 2005 MEDITATION

But first, I would like to again mention what I wrote earlier: Our True Self is the essence of our human existence as an expression of God Consciousness. It gains the experience of each of our lives within the physical world and shares some of that experience with us in each life if we open our gateway to let that happen—and it does happen often without our knowing about it. When we think of "I" or "me," it is important to keep in mind that we are consciously connected with our True Self in the Oneness in each experience of many lifetimes—and "the experience of many lifetimes" means we are the collection of every act, thought, desire, etc., and the nonphysical True Self OC has been a part of our many lifetimes. (We are getting closer to a karma conversation. ☺)

In June 2010, while Jennifer was in India for a special Sadhguru program, Kevin visited us in Idaho, and he and I adjourned to the cabin for most of each day to talk about physics, metaphysics, and our attempt to connect symbols from his diagram with aspects of our unfolding view of reality. Prior to that visit, Kevin had meditation experience where he gained insight on the connection between our individual True Selves and the basketballs. Those discussions raised more questions than we answered—for which we are forever grateful.

The starting point for discussing basketballs was Kevin's perception during the meditation that the basketballs represented the changing pattern of the physical universe at the rate of what we then called binks—the rate of change in the make-up of anything manifest as physical. (Remember that every personal "now" brings its own unique past with it.) He also reported that there were many basketballs (the more he noticed, the more he perceived) and that he witnessed something like an electrical spark zigzagging its way through the unending array before him. As you can see, there are many notes and symbols on his diagram, but to him, one of the strong memories when he awoke from the meditation was that the spark had something to do with the life force of a person experiencing the pattern of the universe from one blink to the next—like a life.

The more we discussed things, the more I was sure there was strong overlap between his altered-consciousness insights and some of my evolving thoughts. I switched from a disconnected observer to looking for compatible beliefs. Kevin and I have subsequently spent a lot of time clarifying, carefully articulating, and documenting our mutually held understanding and beliefs. With the possible exceptions of a few fuzzy areas, I haven't found clearly conflicting issues yet between what I brought to the conversations and what Kevin contributed based on his experiences and the teachings of Sadhguru.

We began to see connections and in particular with the Seth view regarding the role of the self at the core of human experience within the greater reality. I decided to add Kevin's reports and some beliefs from the Hindu/Sadhguru religious/mystic philosophy to the material I was constantly comparing for compatibility, or lack thereof, relating to the nature of a greater reality. Although the Hindu metaphysics are expressed in terms of fields and vibrations, it was easy for me to interpret that material in the framework I have used. I talked in considerable detail to many people about their meditation practices, but I did not encounter any reports of the metaphysical depth as those experiences of Kevin. Thinking back on our history of discussions, I am quite aware of how those discussions leading to my understanding of several things have been so important to me.

Early in the discussions, I kept trying to understand how what I have been referring to as an OC could select or contact or even know about any other OC. Yes, there is interconnectedness, but connectedness in general does not describe "how connected." As mentioned previously, I considered that question, "the addressing problem," obviously because of my database computing experience. Part of my problem was that I was fixated on the belief that all human perception was via brain neurons. That did not help at all to answer a question relating to OCs within the Oneness.

It was Kevin reporting on his death meditation who represented that he was able to "address" (connect with) other OCs within the Oneness just via the idea of wanting to be connected, or even as more of a tour without intent; he could "perceive" what was there, and even communicate with it, in his altered consciousness state without any thought process within the physical to tell him how to do that or even what he was going to be connected to. Seems to me now that such totally nonphysical connectedness should have occurred to me before, but it hadn't. Later, I read Seth where it was described the way I described it back within the framework of True Consciousness—every OC just is aware of all else in the Oneness, and in its normal creative evolution it will utilize any contact relevant to such value fulfillment. That can be and is an addressing perception!

Now back to basketballs. I haven't gotten to the punch line there. Another part of Kevin's death meditation was the grid with the darkened sphere at the center with the arrows going off in different directions. His interpretation of that was: When put in the context of the basketballs as described above, the dark sphere was one of the basketballs, and it represented a human self at a "now" before physical manifesting of the next "now." In the context of the physics

303

framework, we took the arrows to convey the idea of indeterminacy between "nows" (In quantum steps) as the immediate changing physical reality of that self as it evolves in accord with the significance of the most relevant OCs within a sequence of "nows."

I forget exactly when we decided to conversationally test the idea that the basketballs represented the reality as it existed for a given self at a "now." That was a more challenging conclusion than it might look on the surface. So much seems easy when looking back from our current understanding, but it was challenging along the way to arrive at current beliefs. Because a new pattern of the universe exists first in a probable sense of potentially a very large number of OC's within the Oneness before some become "in play" to manifest at a "now," each basketball would contain information about all OCs with any association with that human self, as well as all information related to its perception of physical reality at that "now".

Working together with both the physics and Consciousness-related frameworks pretty well already established, we thus arrived at the conclusion that each basketball represented a uniquely single self-reality at every "now." And therefore that, taken together with the sequence of prior basketballs, represented a lifetime of "nows" for each self in each reincarnation. In one of Kevin's death meditation experiences, he reported the specific awareness of revisiting and reliving events that were a part of basketballs representing the life experiences of his own and others.

Eventually, we extended that to be another way to think of the True Self gestalt—as the basketball history of all selves that contributed to the collective experience of that True Self. Another way of saying it is that the True Self OC is a record within the Oneness containing all it's experiencing of reality via many lifetimes—and it exists for eternity.

Summarizing again, we decided that at each "now" (blink) of the physical, all information relating to a self and all relationships it has with the state of the universe are represented using the metaphor of a basketball. For each and every self, there exists a sequence of basketballs for every "now" of every physical lifetime—the information representing the total mental and physical lifetime experience in a context of all relationships in the gestalt of the universe related to that experience. Each such basketball for that self exists as energetic Consciousness outside of time and, therefore, throughout eternity. The aggregate of basketballs from each lifetime of a self represents the

304

Consciousness gestalt of all relationships of information ever experienced as its True Self.

In Kevin's meditation experience, the lightning bolts represented the way the free will of the life consciousness of a self-created life sequence of experience from one basketball to the next via the selection process converts all probable OCs potentially in play to an actually experienced "now."

I should also mention that, in addition to working with our beliefs arising from the physics and Consciousness-related frameworks, Kevin and I were also at the time wondering about the nature of the "Akashic Record" that Edgar Cayce and others said was where they got some of the information for their channeled readings. The record of Cayce's readings contains a great variety of information related to the person requesting the reading. That information included detailed personal experiences during several lifetimes, description of world events during those eras, relationships with other persons (selves), physical body health information, etc., and even prophesies regarding the future. The idea of the Akashic Record is also an integral aspect of Eastern religious philosophy. Such a record (data source) is also viewed as the possible source of information available to persons participating as subjects in some research related to paranormal phenomena. The way Kevin and I have chosen to think of the Akashic Record, it handles all these requirements quite nicely—just basketballs, up, down, and all around! ☺

Kevin's experience provides evidence of a record of human history from which all of the information from every evolving relationship ever physically manifest would be available—which is totally consistent with the Seth material. There are many humans given special recognition within (primarily religious) history who are said to have demonstrated the mystical ability to perceive all of that, and by joining their consciousness with others, to even relive the thoughts and intentions that never became represented as part of the manifest physical record.

To me, our current belief regarding the origin and significance of basketballs fits within the context of my beliefs about related topics I arrived at in different ways. I see the compatibility as supportive, as well as an extension, of my prior beliefs. My beliefs are the result of personally very challenging mental activity. Kevin shares such beliefs but more because his conviction is based on his experientially (rather than mentally) perceived "knowing" during meditation and other similarly challenging yoga exercises.

305

Just in passing, I will note that I believe that basketballs are a finer degree of detail about reality that connects with the negative time and antimatter topics of (more or less) commonly accepted physics at this time. Both topics were commented on extensively by the Source of the Stanford readings mentioned earlier and are entirely compatible with the physics framework of Chapter 15. The energy that is thought to be associated with the zero-point energy of the quantum vacuum is something I have thought a lot about—as also the issues associated with the photon and light in general.

In particular, it took me years and many hours of sleepless nights to think through to my satisfaction that "light just is." (Several well-recognized physicists have found support for that view, though arriving at that conclusion differently.) In particular, it is an interesting and, for me, an entertaining exercise to mentally view all I know about cosmology in the context that "Light Does Not Travel, We Do." "We do"—meaning changes in the blinking physical reality, the "kick" of newly manifested energy at each quantum step that shows up as a change of some kind in our physical world. Anyhow, on with the metaphysics instead of just controversial physics.

From the git-go of Kevin and Jennifer's meeting with Sadhguru, Kevin's reports of what he has learned from Sadhguru often mention the word "karma." Of course, for almost 40 years I had seen references to karma many times and even definitions of karma and religious teachings that included a belief in karma. But I had never really accepted the word itself as understood or meaningful to me. It was generally used to mean something along the lines of a record of good and bad life choices in a context of reincarnation, where possible punishment and/or un-doing bad karma was important if one wished to evolve to an exalted spiritual state.

Kevin has shared quite a bit of Sadhguru's references to, and characterization of, karma. I have also read and listened to some of what Sadhguru has said about it. The significance of karma was on my mind and many times in discussions with Kevin.

I think Kevin and I have now decided that Seth describes a personal reality in much the same manner in which Kevin understands karma in the light of Sadhguru's teaching. As mentioned earlier, Seth describes the topic within a different background context than Sadhguru. However, in both representations, the karma-type characterization of thought and behavioral choices during one's life creates an important reality for representation of human experience. A karma-like process within both is clearly associated with how we create our reality—not just in one lifetime but throughout our experience of many lifetimes.

I think there is at least one difference between Seth and Sadhguru in the description of the importance of Karma, however. The teachings of Sadhguru devote a lot of attention to the nature of the purpose for changing one's beliefs and related conduct by describing (in part by teaching proper meditation) where it is supposed to lead—the goal to be fulfilled. Seth teaches that purpose is just to have life experience and learn to listen to one's Inner Self (open the gateway) and that one's beliefs and conduct will then be guided *teleologically* toward fulfillment of the spiritual goal of physical experience. I do not recall where Seth has provided as much detail about that teleological embedded spiritual goal as do the teachings of Sadhguru.

Sadhguru informs us that "karma means action—physical, mental, emotions and energy action—and that karma is accumulated past action, thought, and emotions." Seth informs us much the same—that "existence is action," (Organizations of Consciousness are incapable of non-action) and that the energy and creative nature of our self creates a nonphysical record derived from the action of our thoughts, intentions, desires, and emotions, etc. Of course, that history of our experience is, in both representations, our basketballs.

Because all lives are evolving in the Oneness simultaneously, there is agreement in both views that basketballs represent "the memory of life"— the total record that is an attribute of each True Self—the Akashic Record. I think that is also saying, in Sadhguru's words, "Karma is what you bring with you into each life." Significantly, both sources also ascribe importance to the manner in which individuals may "change" the current state of their evolution at any time to accomplish growth in a desired direction.

As previously mentioned, Seth teaches that, because there is only the "now" (or the "Moment Point" in Sethian terminology) we may change the belief that created a prior action and then continue our on-going evolution in accord with the revised belief. We don't change the basketball history; we just add new ones demonstrating by our current choices that whatever created the no-longer-desired choices in the past is no longer relevant. Once we fully act in accord with the new belief about that part of reality—it is our reality! Deeply held belief is the new real, and we behave and experience accordingly—with more enlightened choices if the revised beliefs support them.

Sadhguru also teaches that the karmic history of any self may also be altered. In particular Sadhguru teaches that, through the action generated by a Kriya meditative practice to manage a person's life energy, it is possible to dismantle the prior action, thus dissolving the related karma. It appears to me that "life energy" in Sadhguru terms is the same as the energy we have available to us as an Organization of Consciousness in Sethian terms. According to the Sethian terminology, the energy for existence of anything, including life energy, is a share of the unlimited energy of True Consciousness; the life energy for a physical body Consciousness structure runs out when our self has decided to call it quits for any lifetime.

Sadhguru's teaching is that the endgame is to experience via meditation a perception of reality beyond what can be discerned mentally, and that once perceived, one will live in an enlightened way think and behave to dissolve karma so as to reach that desired state that has been perceived. I understand dissolving karma to essentially be losing attachment to the fruits of our actions.

In the terminology of both, as I understand it as just written, they are basically similar, and potentially the same as to the result—that there is a process that is available to enlighten one to make choices that are in harmony with evolution toward an end condition. The difference seems to me to be that, in the teaching of Sadhguru and other Eastern religious beliefs, it is possible to *perceive* during one's life an experience-based belief about the nature of that end-condition goal during advanced states of meditation.

Beyond those two paragraphs, however, the comparison of belief systems gets very different and a little fuzzier—possibly even to the point of some incompatibility. I do not intend to go into the subject that deep because I don't even understand enough about it to do so. In this short story, I haven't but touched a small portion of the depth of detail included in the Seth material, and I am not at all informed enough to understand much at all of the great depth of what is explained by Sadhguru. However, it does appear to me that the goal within both teachings is the same, to one way or another in different ways, to find the teleological purpose of our part of Creation within the greater reality and where it leads us. The detailed description of the teleological process of the two is just different.

That is, in both viewpoints it seems to me, there exists a belief in the teleological workings of reality that as long as we live lives and don't get the message, the more lives we will live until we do; the aim is to get it right and not reincarnate further. My Sethian way of bringing the two viewpoints together is in words such as: "Karma is a name for the built-in workings of the feedback and response system that guides us toward where we are supposed to go and are guided to go if we are really listening via the great potential of our gateway." I think that direction is toward a self with less limitation compared to that of True Consciousness that Seth refers to as "All That Is" and Sadhguru refers to as "That Which is Not" (the indescribable nothingness from which Creation unfolds.)

I believe there are a variety of paths within our lives that are said to help us to eliminate our Consciousness limitation gap altogether. Those who accept the reality of reincarnation, as I do, believe that some level of spiritual awareness is eventually possible within a life that will eliminate the desire of our True Self to create a self-development plan to initiate another life experience of the kind we have in this physical world. Our True Self will no longer desire or need to benefit from the feedback of a physical life experience.

I have also come to believe that indeed meditation appears to be a way to potentially "speed up" the diminishing of the karmic attachments and counter-productive tendencies during our lives. I think I finally understand what Sadhguru was pointing out when he said something like, "One does not 'do' meditation, one experiences meditation." I obviously think there are other benefits of meditation in addition to improving health and reducing stress. It is obvious to me that Kevin has experienced levels of uncommon awareness, including occasions of nothingness—no awareness—that I believe represent a deep and fulfilling nature of spiritual development.

I don't think meditation nor Seth nor any one view of reality is necessary for one to achieve any particular spiritual nature in life, but I believe that if anyone really desires to experience a more spiritual nature they must care about it—and one way or another acquire beliefs that will permit them to create that reality as their own. Meditation, institutional religious faith and rituals, drug-induced altered consciousness, and even success in living "love" no matter how obtained, are all belief-improvement paths of seeking that come to mind.

Kevin reported experiencing "Tornadoes-Bathed-In-Light" (TBIL) during his state of altered consciousness. It has been a much more difficult topic for me to try to be sure I understand, and to explain. I will provide my few interpretations of the TBIL metaphor and will depend on Kevin to over time discuss more fully his much more important "first person singular" recollection and significance—and his corrections where I currently miss or mangle that significance. I expect his book to shed more light on the topic (pun intended) and to set the record straight where I may have missed the mark.

Basically, it appears to me that the TBIL symbol was the "connector" between the perception realized by Kevin's nonphysical self and what he was to connect with next during his experience within the Oneness, where any OC (like Kevin) may connect to any other OC instantaneously. I view it as the symbolic connector glue of the entire greater reality, and, in particular, as between a human's current self, True Self, and potentially anything/everything within the Oneness.

The symbolism seemed to be clear with metaphors of connection like a black hole, or the binding forces that connect all matter, and even the life force connecting our new "now" with the old to create the basketballs within eternity. The latter seems to me to be of special importance because it ties the new "now" with the information within the Oneness that represents possibilities that had not yet materialized at a prior "now." I understand the symbolism of what he described as the path of "nows" zigzagging through the potential futures as free will—a graphical description for Kevin's benefit of how free will is similarly described within the Seth material.

A lot of Kevin's experience seems to me was to make clear to his manifest self of this lifetime what was described above as the significance of the basketballs that form the record of the pattern of physical reality that is unique to each of us at each blink. It also seems to me that there was a special purpose in his being connected with so much "memorable experience" during his "tour de force" within the Oneness—so that he could have an experience of "interpretation" per se. I think he has made good use of it.

I think the interpretations were uniquely his own but certainly something I am glad he shared. They provided Kevin personal meaning associated with some of the depth and breadth of the Oneness—in such dramatic and personal ways as a life-changing experience rather than as a mental possibility—experiences that he will never forget and neither will I. Without our discussions and exchanging of what seems like zillions of emails, I would not now hold a view of the greater reality where so many sources of seemingly credible material all hang together for me.

Kevin and I have combined our thoughts and experience to reach a better understanding of some important things—with the clear message being that they all describe different ways to gain insight concerning a same greater reality. If I have accomplished what I tried to do in this chapter, I hope my story and my resulting beliefs contribute to a message that indeed describes something meaningful about a greater reality.

From only two assumptions, the binks assumption and the assumption of the nature of an energetic and creative Fundamental Consciousness, all relationships that describe reality can be characterized. It is a reality complex enough to answer all questions except one: What is the complete detail of how the selection process works to create each "now" pattern of our universe? The Seth material and beliefs regarding the active role of karma describe aspects of that process, but I am not aware of any way to describe the process in complete detail. I am not even sure it is meaningful to ask a question about detail for such a process. It is possible that some relationships just evolve—period.

At this point I have to make it clear that I doubt if very many people will find any reason to read this far along in my journey—it is just too weird. I admit to having had that feeling many times. Each time I sort of went back to a believable starting point and proceeded to "build the case" again—again—and again. On the other hand, multitudes within mankind believe there exists a God of indescribable omnificence that nothing I have said would be but a shallow description of what might be the reality created by that God—and don't think of that as weird. I am amazed at what all is ascribed to many such gods. As I will mention in the final chapter of this journey, I have a belief in a God. Ontological questions can only be answered on the basis of faith. Whatever we choose to believe is essentially just a matter of in what we place a faith.

Now, before I share a few beliefs in the next chapter that have helped me to personally live a more satisfying life as I have aged, I would like to add two more topics. The first is to follow up on how an understanding of the physics and consciousness frameworks does indeed provide the basis for answering questions about what is called paranormal phenomena. The second is to share a summary of what the Seth material has to say about the consciousness nature of the cells within our physical bodies.

I sort of started down this metaphysical trail with interest to see how physics might be extended to explain what was going on with paranormal phenomena. That led me to cover a lot of ground, realizing in the process that physics alone wasn't going to get me there. I hope that ground covered in this chapter has provided the rest of the story—so to speak. I will try to quickly answer the questions and summarize the explanation now available related to those phenomena I first mentioned on page 136 and had a little bit more to add on pages 230-232.

First, **Telepathy** is a snap. People are first and foremost nonphysical Consciousness, and any OC is capable of total awareness of another. However, that just says it is possible. As I have tried to describe in the above pages, there are many factors at work in setting up the connection—in this case, primarily the opening of the gateways of the individuals exchanging information. Researchers of telepathic phenomena have written extensively about the variability of participants to open the gateway, without calling it that. I have experienced telepathic communication with another person many times. I think most people have also.

Next was **Precognition**—perception involving the acquisition or effect of future information that cannot be deduced from presently available and normally acquired sense-based information. To put this in perspective, we need to remember that what we call the future is but the physical unfolding of possibly infinities of probable OCs, each with varying degrees of probability. Once they were created, such probable realities are available in the Oneness; therefore, any person OC can theoretically be aware of them and thus perceive them ("see" them).

That information about the probable realities of subsequent "nows" is most likely enough to create infinities of possible physical outcomes. A person exhibiting precognitive awareness must therefore somehow (usually without anticipating doing so) be aware of the particular set of most significant influences that will materialize. That is how it is possible. As with all people actually exhibited any psychic phenomena, the gateway must open. In research experiments it is not uncommon for the precognitive effort to describe an event that "almost" happened or quite possibly could have happened instead of connecting with that which did. It is widely believed that animal behavior may be influenced by precognitive awareness.

Psychokinesis is non-physical change in the relationships of physical matter. It may be exhibited where the nonphysical mind of a person influences the physical manifestation of some condition of matter—often referred to simply as mind over matter. All matter is just the physical objectification of a relationship of some form in the Oneness. A person's mind exists, whether or not the thinks of it as the combination of a brain and all relationships of the Oneness. All change in the physical must be an OC in the Oneness before the change can be manifest in the physical. Thus, the person's mind connects with the gestalt OC of the relationships comprising the form or placement in physical space of the object to be changed to bring about Psychokinesis. The most common credible evidence I think of is the situation when people influence the statistics of a random-number generator by their intention to do so. However, there are many other examples. Healing intentions are also a common version.

What I believe to be a rarer form of Psychokinesis is when the relationships describing two or more physical OCs are changed whether or not any manifest personality with intention to cause that is present nearby. A simple example would be a vase falling off the mantle in the middle of the night with no other possible explanation other than being displaced by the intention of a nonphysical self. I can make up all sorts of fascinating stories on what might bring that to happen, but I need to move on with this. A person can easily find such information on the Internet or in libraries—or in whatever form of societal information storage that may exist in a subsequent era.

Presentiment is just a particular type of precognition coupled with Psychokinesis. A highly probable yet-to-be-experienced OC in a future "now" of the person causes a physical effect prior to that subsequent "now." Although the experimental evidence I described earlier is based upon precognitive awareness of a condition designed to illicit a strong emotional significance and therefore a high degree of a subsequent probable reality, there is no reason to believe that high probability is a necessary condition. That kind of process is fascinating to me. Whether we are perceptually aware of it or not, it is obvious that it is occurring with some degree of probability all the time. Our physical bodies are possibly experiencing psychokinetic change before our gateway to the mind opens to let the brain know—if brain neurons ever do. As is to be mentioned below, Seth informs us that every cell OC of our body is precognitive.

Remote Viewing is also simple to explain with the frameworks of physics and Consciousness. We know from both frameworks something about the connectedness of all—the all of the Oneness. That "all" includes the information which represents the "target" for remote viewing. Add a personality OC with an open gateway to the Oneness, and that is all there is to potentially perceive anything anywhere in the physical world—whether the experience is being described to others or not. I always think it is sort of humorous when a person perceives the right place at the wrong time—as has occurred in controlled experiments. It is also possible for a person to experience altered-conscious awareness of something somewhere within the Oneness without it passing thru brain neurons as a bodily perception. For instance, that may be what happens when a person without knowing it precognitively avoids a serious danger existing at a particular time and place.

Of the many experimental confirmations of Remote Viewing (Clairvoyance), the one I like to use as an example of an open gateway is the 1973 experiment with Ingo Swann. As part of the Stargate Program in progress at that time, Swann foresaw the rings around Jupiter before they were experimentally confirmed by the Voyager spacecraft six years later.

Again as with Presentiment, remote viewing type information is always available to our Inner Self as a potential nonphysical stimulus to our brain, but I think it is uncommon in this era for many of us to experience Remote Viewing. There are, however, credible records of people being trained to do so. I have evidence that when attempting to do so I may have had the experience at least once.

We, by tradition, call these forms of perception paranormal, but if one thinks about it a little, there is no phenomenon that cannot be explained within the frameworks of Chapter 15 and this chapter.

In my journey I encountered much more Seth material than I have referred to here. There is just way too much to include it all during my attempt to characterize the essence of it. For instance: the significance of dreams, the story of the creation of Earth and humanity, the nature of sexuality within the human species, more detail regarding "sensing" that is possible via the gateway, exercises for readers to help develop their gateway, the metaphysical underpinnings of "mass events," considerable detail on the life and purpose of Jesus, the prior civilizations of Lemuria and Atlantis, health/illness/death and healing, life between lives, war, other bodies and other realities, and much more.

There does exist (with copy included in the Yale University archives of the Seth material) a 39-page Index to all Seth books that was created by the diligent work of Sue Watkins. Other individuals have created other indices and concordance documentation of the material. Many others have extracted material from the many books into summaries by topic or even entire books. One quite comprehensive book is, *A Seth Reader*, edited by Richard Roberts. Paul M. Helfrich has authored many works, including the book, *Seth: The Ultimate Guide*, which extracts from and puts in context the Seth material.

In addition to the many books, including the ones dictated by Seth, there is also a lot of attention given to the Seth material on the Internet of today. I have copies or pointers to much of it included in my own files. Other than the Seth books themselves, the most concentrated summary of the material I am aware of, much in the words of Seth, is that which can be accessed via the www.sethnet.org website in this era. In particular, the contributions of Lynda Dahl include much, much more than I am able to summarize within my story.

There is, however, one additional topic that didn't seem to fit in my story earlier but is a topic that is very meaningful to me and I think worthy of comment. (My comments are certainly not in the great detail offered by Seth.) It is the nature and importance of the cellular consciousness of our body cells. That topic is mentioned frequently and emphasized strongly in the Seth material. In particular, Seth provides a great amount of detail on the nature of how the functioning of our physical body is related to the gestalt consciousness makeup of the atoms, molecules, chromosomes, and genes within each cell. And also, how the consciousness makeup of each cell and organ knows its function within the whole body and works to fulfill that purpose.

Seth teaches that cells also have a precognitive comprehension of the subsequent pattern of our body from one "now" to the next. That enables our body to function in a sequence of "nows" independent of how we think of cause and effect. That is, our cells have information from both prior and subsequent "nows" available to use in their evolution. To the nonphysical and eternal self of our body of True Consciousness, that evolution of our changing physical body is perceivable in terms of probable realities. Cells just know more about potentially subsequent "nows" than we might realize, and Seth teaches that they use that information to help us maintain a healthy body—especially if the beliefs that are leading to those subsequent "nows" are based on a desire to maintain a healthy body!

The implications of cellular consciousness are too many to mention. That precognitive nature of cells even at times creates miraculous healing that can be thought of as retro-causation. Many of what we perceive as miracles are the result of cellular consciousness functioning in this way. The evidence for the working of prayer and imaging to improve health is another. Our health is in important ways determined by this gestalt of body cellular Consciousness. I now like to think in terms of how taking good care of my body helps determine how my body takes care of me!

Our health and life experiences, in general, are influenced genetically and in other ways too many for me to totally understand. That genetic influence is particularly apparent within our life plan for each life. How we view and treat the body we have is one way we can have a very direct and strong influence in every life. I believe that the flip side is that bad life-style habits and risk-taking also very directly affect health. Within the overall context of how our beliefs

315

create our reality, I believe that how we view body health is very important. I wish that I had come to explicitly understand that at an earlier age, but I think that in some ways I was learning it bit by bit by just observing and "listening" to the world around me. I have been fortunate to experience mostly good health, and I am grateful.

I think my journey has resulted in a way to view reality that goes far beyond my initial desire to understand how my experience and the general evidence for the paranormal could be explained at least in part by physics, and vice versa. I encountered a much greater role for consciousness than I could have imagined when I started on that journey. I would never have encountered or understood the significance of Kevin's experience without what came before. The gestalt of the views I have described may only provide me a peek into the nature of a much greater reality within which we exist, but for now, it is what I choose to believe. So I will move on to the last chapter of my book and share some reasons why I think my metaphysical perspective helps me to live a greatly satisfying life.

➤ 17 ◄

A Wrap Looking Back

We are not human beings having a spiritual experience;
We are spiritual beings having a human experience.

(Teilhard de Chardin)

Ryleigh, Cory, and Ellie (if you have come this far): This chapter is not only for me in my next life, but it is also for you and your cousins. I hope it will be of interest to you. It is not advice nor is it intended to be preaching. It is my effort to express and share how some of what I believe matters in my life. I hope that you learn a lot about what others believe and why what they believe matters to them. There is a wealth of material available to you. Pick thoughtfully. After all, this book has just been about my journey—my story—my way of recording it. You are creating your own story. You are the star of the movie about you. Best wishes in your own journey.

****

So, I guess the obvious questions for any descendent who might stumble across and be reading this years from now is: "Why was all this metaphysical stuff of interest to Bob? Why should it matter?"

Turns out, they are sort of interesting questions for me to try to answer. I look back and see how oblivious I was during much of my life. But then I see that at some points described in earlier chapters, I began to be more curious and more inquiring, at least about some things. It appears that the more involved I became in the world around me, the more I had to make choices and decisions as part of my experience. I left the figurative cocoon of near vision. I encountered new ideas as I began to meet more and more people—some of great accomplishment and learning. And out of all that and reading many books, the metaphysical kinds of questions just started to bubble up. I began to frame questions relating to things I was curious about, including the beliefs of several religions, the credible weirdness of the paranormal, and finally, questions about the possible meaning behind the equations of physics.

But then, I ran across the above quote from Teilhard de Chardin and some of his extensive thinking and writing. I didn't buy the entire enchilada, but I bought a large number of bites. I know his thinking raised a lot more questions with me than it did answers. It took me back to the questions related to "What is the nature of being spiritual?" I read highly thought-provoking questions embedded in the works of others that created related questions. At some point, it appears that I came to have a quest to get some answers—for certain kinds of questions anyway—many of which as mentioned in preceding chapters. I didn't know it was a quest then but looking back, that's what I call it.

I think the nature of the quest has been to discover what I believe to be meaningful foundational aspects of a metaphysically dependable guide *for me* for viewing any and all situations I encounter as a living experience. I believe it has helped me to "mellow" over the years of trying to put journey-inspired beliefs into practice. Some will say that is just called maturing. Maybe so, but my guess is that my "maturing" has been greatly aided by this journey. ☺

I say *for me* because I realize that a perspective for living is unique for each one of us. Others who might read what I have written will come to their own conclusion about "does it matter." If they have read it in hope of discovering something new that will enable them to find greater meaning and satisfaction in their life, I hope I have not disappointed them. The message of the material is not just that we create the reality we experience; it includes beliefs that help us create one we will be happier with.

I certainly realize that many people, probably most with a moral compass, don't need all this metaphysical stuff to go about each day with spiritual faith to live an admirable life of love, morality, and personal satisfaction. And they may have achieved greater insights than I have and maybe even earlier in their lives.

However, this view of reality that is fundamental to our worldly experience at least provides answers to many serious questions that are acceptable for me, and there exists for me a way of living that is consistent with those answers. And probably most important, I now think I live a more satisfying personal life and help make Pat's more satisfying also. I cannot imagine living without this "metaphysical stuff" covered in Chapters 15 and 16. It has changed my life in the direction of greater meaning and happiness.

So it seems to me that it might matter if someone's life journey leads them to this material hoping to also find insight for improving their pleasure with life.

Or, maybe it only matters if someone is already searching for something to answer questions of their own. Or maybe it only matters if some words or ideas they have encountered here lead someone to think, "It might matter." If any of the above, then I would suggest that the "metaphysical stuff" that really matters—that which is sort of the foundation of the world behind the scenes that is a factor in our everyday life whether we realize it and benefit from it or not—would start with:

- That there IS an "outside" of space-time, and there is a lot we can learn about it. "Reality" is not just the physical world recognized by our five senses and our brain. Cause and effect occurs outside of space-time. The cause and effect we are used to sensing and measuring is a consequence, not the real cause.
- That I and WE are not bodies and are far more than bodies. Bodies are what we have, not what we are!
- That all of Creation is an ever evolving Energy Gestalt of Fundamental Consciousness of which we are an important part. We are a unique expression within God Stuff. God is not "out there" or separate. Our awareness is a part of God's awareness.
- That reincarnation is a fact—hard to believe—but an evidence-supported fact. I have accepted the belief that life plans are formed before each physical birth to guide us toward the life experience we desire for further spiritual development. That belief is supported by hypnotic regression transcripts and confirmed by Seth. That belief alone has terrific implications if we think about it.
- That we do actually, day by day; create our own physical life experiences in a context of our life plan. No experience of ours is caused without our participation as a causative agent. Nothing happens to us, desired or undesired, without our having been involved to some significant degree in creating it.
- That there is a strong connection between what we choose to believe and the specifics of our life experiences. If we wish to improve our life experience, we should look deep into our beliefs to see what needs to be changed to create the experiences we desire.
- That understanding that we have and can learn to open an awareness "gateway" to information from the greater reality is a terrific way to enrich our life experience and our resulting sense of confidence, peace, and satisfaction. The context provided by the "metaphysical stuff" tells us how that works and guides us to experience life-enriching benefit from such "listening." In a sense, we are all psychics! We have and may develop further ways of

"knowing" that in many situations are more helpful than thinking. Information is an intrinsic aspect of the Oneness. Every relationship about anything within eternity, including every thought or experience, is information that is potentially available to us if we learn how to open our gateway to become aware of it.

It is my belief that this "metaphysical stuff" is not just an abstract idea, a philosophical concept, science fiction, or just a possibility! It is the essence of the heart and soul of how the world works—every day—whether we like it or not. A reader must decide for themselves what they think—accept or reject—and move on in life, creating their own reality whether they realize it or not. The choice is sort of like, take responsibility for it or just eat drink and be merry, as the expression goes. You read, you think, you "sense", you decide. This "metaphysical stuff" has been described to try to make clear that there is something to believe or not believe that I think matters. You get to decide.

The rest of this chapter and book is just sharing a glimpse of how accepting the view of reality provided by this "metaphysical stuff" works its way into everyday life experience—at least into mine. If one is going to "walk the walk" instead of just "talk the talk," then it might include some similarities with this sample.

Looking back, I now also believe that my long-held desire to better understand the nature of reality has actually been a "spiritual" quest—a background spiritual purpose, so to speak, for this terrific lifetime experience. I think I have arrived at a life-enriching understanding of what Teilhard de Chardin wrote.

Before seeking my personal view of what constitutes reality, I had sort of given up thinking much about church dogma! Even as I grew to think more deeply about religious beliefs, I really didn't find a spiritual comfort zone until I was well along in the journey I have described. In a sense, a form of spiritual seeking was really the driving energy of my quest, a spiritual posture upon which to build a way to view the world around me that makes some sense even though one can argue that the world doesn't appear to make much sense at all. I realize that there are many religious group teachings that don't seem to fit well with the focus of my own. I am not alone.

In recent years I have seen an increasing number of articles on the topic of growing spirituality within the world unassociated with traditional religious identity groups. In his 2010 book, "The Purpose-Guided Universe," physicist

Bernard Haisch writes, "The distinguishing feature of the new spirituality is that it needs no mediator between God and you: No church, no priest, no guru. We are learning how to connect to God directly, and the key to this is an expanding consciousness."

Long after getting pretty deep into my quest in the early 2000s, Fran Collmann gave me a copy of the book *How to Know God* by Deepak Chopra. He began his book by noting that a large percent of our population acknowledge their belief in God, but there is not a consensus on how that God fits in with a view of reality that is based on what we experience day by day, which he referred to as a "gap" needing to be filled. He then describes his view of facts to help fill that gap and his answer to the book title. He writes that the facts would be:

Everything that we experience as material reality is born in an invisible realm beyond space and time, a realm revealed by science to consist of energy and information. This invisible source of all that exists is not an empty void but the womb of Creation itself. Something created and organizes this energy. It turns the chaos of quantum soup into stars, galaxies, rain forests, human beings and our own thoughts, emotions, memories and desires.

Sound familiar?

(His views should help many in their search for a personal reality. His books, CDs and video presentations have been purchased by millions.)

Even though I was reluctant to undertake this writing venture, I now think my life story would just not seem to be complete without having had the opportunity to bring this all together for my own benefit and at least offer to share it. I am thankful I have been, and still am, fortunate to experience so much in this life. Writing my story—my journey—is now part of my journey.

I have written about this life journey for some current family and, who knows, maybe even a few friends might find it interesting. But also, there is another reason I have thought it worthwhile to record in Chapters 15 and 16 so much of what I believe to be believable. I think I have set forth a foundation that gives credibility to the thought that there is quite possibly an important message here. At the very least, it should be thought provoking if anyone really wants to dig into it with an open mind. If one person living in what we call the future ever reads this and is inspired to seek a greater understanding of their own reality, it will have been worth it for me to devote this effort to share it as I see it. In particular, I hope that I will see it early in my next life. ☺

Because it might be important to such a person, I have attempted to describe the essence of many "nonmainstream" sources of fact and insight so as to merge in one place what I have found meaningful to me regarding the nature of a greater reality than we see at each sunrise and sunset. In addition to those who have inspired and guided me to learn how to think during my life, the primary sources from which these beliefs are derived have included: the channeled material of Seth, Stanford, Elias, and Charles; my interpretation of material within quantum physics that seems to me to be the most relevant in describing how change occurs from one moment to the next within our physical world; the growing amount of credible evidence of anomalous phenomena not explainable in the context of current physics; and Kevin's interpretation of his altered-consciousness experiences and the teachings of Sadhguru that augment and/or provide support for the beliefs suggested by the other sources.

Bottom line, I think that setting forth this basis for my beliefs is an important way to try to contribute something worthwhile to anyone guided to this source by the working of the reality I have attempted to describe.

So—on with the story. What do I think worth summarizing from these beliefs about the nature of reality as important for me to live by and to be such a source of satisfaction in my daily life? Here goes the dash to the finish. I will mention a few specifics.

There are many details that sum up "to be satisfied." However, for me they can for the most part be gathered together under the broad umbrella of my understanding that *our beliefs create our reality and that the purpose of our life is worldly experience to provide feedback to help us understand that connection.* In that context, these metaphysical beliefs are very important to me. If we -- desire to know "what is perfect behavior?"—no one knows! If we then ask: "What should we do?" My answer has become: "Listen to that Inner Self that was characterized in Chapter 16 and sort of keep a close check on your beliefs." I hope my own current beliefs that help me to be satisfied with my current life will be further apparent in what follows.

First and foremost, I will start with what one might call my creed. For the first time in my life, "belief in God" has real significance for how I live each day. Of course some, possibly many, people might say that the God I am talking about is not their God. I certainly accept that. However, I believe God is the

Creator—the Almighty—the Omnificent—the All That Is—the True Consciousness—the God that is not limited by any description—the God continuing to express as our physical experience—and that we are all part of such a God, warts and all. I am only using the name "God" because the word God was what mankind decided many centuries ago to have meaning to so many people of the world in so many important ways similar to my own belief. My use of the word God is to make clear that it means many important things to me. In essence, in my opinion, the God I believe in deserves to be viewed as just as worthy of the inference from the name as any other.

Having said that, there is no doubt but that there are some differences between my idea of God and the idea of "the God" followed with varying beliefs by others for centuries. I think any differences are so clearly in the eyes of the beholder that I can leave it at that and just try to share why, for the first time in my life, belief in God has a real significance for me.

The "God as True Consciousness" that I characterize is not out there somewhere, separate from me and others, looking over our shoulders. I am not a chunk of flesh separated from God. I think all of Creation is God stuff—from the smallest of what we call an atomic particle on up the complexity hierarchy— we selves included. My physical self is just as much God stuff as my nonphysical self. I am looking over my own shoulder! I look at myself and all others in this light. I believe the unbounded awareness of God is aware of each of us and can be called upon for awareness of our need for assistance or guidance. God's love is the name for this fundamental nature of being.

I can listen to the God that exists as the Oneness at any time I desire to open my gateway and say, please come in. I even think we get a steady stream of information without even asking, but I do not view that as a God that intervenes in our lives to "cause" us to act one way or another. I believe that we have free choice—we are responsible—only we can change our personal beliefs, thoughts, and behavior.

I believe that *one* of God's most important messages to me and others was delivered to mankind via that highly evolved self we call Jesus, even if not every story about what Jesus said and did has come to us exactly as intended. I believe that the highly evolved self we call Jesus chose to manifest physically and share spiritual insight to a world in need of the message then and now. I believe that such an especially highly evolved self may choose to manifest physically again someday and express another very special message for mankind in ways and terminology well matched to that era.

323

We are told that Jesus made it clear for all to see during his physical life that it is possible for a physical person to perform what we call miracles and be psychically gifted like—like, wow! I think if we dwell on these ideas about our possible reality, we can understand more about how that all comes together and even experience a good bit for ourselves—without waiting around for pearly gates. I really love this God and am undefinably grateful that God is at work in my life experience every single moment that I live and breathe without my making that a special request. I believe that God is at work in every other life that way also, even though it doesn't always look that way. Part of what makes me so joyful about all this is because I do believe the same God is there in the same way for every living human being.

What I have just written is more important to me than every bit of what I will continue to mention but that doesn't mean that what follows isn't also important to me. Almost every word is intended to relate to something important to me.

One fundamental reason I can think of God and life in general with a big helping of joy and satisfaction is that I think I have gained a clearer understanding of a purpose for being alive in the first place. Heaven and hell may be meaningful concepts for many people but are much distorted ideas about reality as I see it.

The messages I took away from Sunday school class were stories to instill desirable thoughts about morality and behavior. I am sure they helped me develop beliefs that were supportive of many good choices as I matured. On the other hand, the take-away from sermon topics dealing with the God-man relationship rarely resonated with me. The good news for me now is that I do strongly resonate with the belief that arises from this metaphysical journey that *every single life experience is in a sense sacred. Everything is sacred. There exists nothing that is not sacred.* It is really difficult to engage in negative or profane behavior when that belief is held unconditionally!

I believe that because of the way we influence our own reality we essentially live in unceasing prayer. I express it that way because I believe that is the way reality works. In a sense, we get what we pray for. We know from religious practice, paranormal research, and what has been covered in the prior two chapters, that our thoughts do affect physical change. It doesn't matter if what we experience must be prayed for or not. I think we are all well served to be grateful for our many blessings, but I don't think they were delivered to us by

324

a God that intervenes directly in our lives. God guides us to author our own lives!

As I will repeat over and over in varying contexts, I believe that our beliefs create the constant unfolding of our personal experience within reality—that is what I think of as unceasing prayer! Because we can never be totally without doubts, our beliefs depend a lot on where we place our faith (both in minor and major areas) and how strong we feel about it. Whether we think about it this way or not, a faith of some kind is at work in all we do and think. I believe what Jesus taught to be true, that the power of faith can move mountains—even though I have had to settle for much less. ☺

I have used the word "teleology" a lot because it is a terrific reminder for me to pay attention to the reality I create via my beliefs. Teleology is when something is "built-in," the very nature of a process—not added as a step in a process—but inherently a part of it so basic that it cannot even be separated out of the process if one wanted to. A teleological process guides something forward toward an end condition.

In the working of our reality situation, teleology refers to the process experienced by every personality self and True Self to evolve over many lifetimes toward a nature of True Consciousness—with diminishing distinguishable separation from all Consciousness within the Oneness. All of us have such moments of "at one with all" at least once in a while. I view my moments of undefinable joy as a glimpse into such a state, and at other times, it just seems like there is nothing separating me from everything around me. I just smile. I always hope there will be many more such times—but that is up to me.

I believe that feedback from our experience is what can provide insight about what it means to be an expression of God that is increasingly in harmony with God Consciousness. If we are listening to our Inner Self, we will be guided to behavior that is in general satisfying rather than disappointing. That is that teleology—where the ultimate "purpose of living" is inherently built into "the process of living!"

As mentioned earlier several times, I believe that the purpose of living is for a self to gain experience that guides the path to beliefs that in turn nurture the path to the reality we desire to experience. And more lifetimes means more experience with which to evolve spiritually. In the book *The Afterlife of Billy Fingers* by Annie Kagan, her deceased brother Billy communicates with her from the afterlife. He tells Annie, "The world is your oyster; you are the pearl and you are the oyster."

A message of this chapter of my story is in part the same. Our worldly life experience provides the sand that eventually creates a fully formed pearl. Thus to say it again, I believe that experience is a sacred process—why waste it! I choose to have faith in the evidence that teleological guidance exists within reality. *For one to accept that there is a teleological purpose being served by all worldly experience it is necessary to understand and accept the significance of a view that a greater reality requires.* And our reality is unique for every one of us. I am only trying to share a little of what mine is like for me. Everyone creates their own. Organized religion provides a variety of beliefs in support of teleological processes.

There is another inference from teleology. The Seth material leads me to believe that as we evolve over lifetimes of making choices to sort out experience our True Self will eventually outgrow the need for physical world experience. Further physical life experience will become of marginal significance. We will move on as a higher level of personified consciousness—which Seth, Jesus, and others report is more loving, especially if we think in terms of "to be love" rather than just "to love" people, things, and situations.

To be love, it now means to me that we, without judgment, must live lives in this world with growing tolerance and compassion for others. Forgiveness is recommended also—until we realize that there is nothing really needing forgiveness. Just as love is without an object, I like to think of forgiving as not necessary except for the psychological nature of interpersonal relationships. I believe the reality I have attempted to characterize helps me do that. I guess these really gutty things sum up a lot. They are also good indicators for how many people define and find satisfaction via some path and thus a satisfying life experience for themselves. I think I am fortunate to have joined them.

I believe that life experience and the resulting feedback is how we *learn to learn* and practice love. Also, I believe that paying attention to feedback from my decisions and actions will help me to discover what characterizes the full nature of being a human. I think it helps to become aware of all the information the nonphysical greater reality offers us. For me, that means to try to understand and be guided by what I can obtain through the gateway to the Inner Self as much as I am able to do before this life experience ends. And I believe that seeking to become aware of "all the information" means to gain as much insight as possible with which to try to create a personal reality experience evolving toward a behavior consistent with love. I hope I am in this life helping my True Self to experience a step along the path of that kind of evolution.

I am confident that in the long run I will sort things out to improve the expression of my True Self of God Consciousness. In the short run, it is meaningful to me that I have a view of reality that suggests that I can speed up the process by taking some responsibility for my choices in a context that beliefs seem to be the key to lining things up for the long run. It is again the message that we create beliefs based on feedback from how we manage our experience and that our beliefs create our reality.

Looking at it another way, I am convinced that when we change our beliefs so does our experience. When I came to accept that my beliefs create my own reality, it meant accepting that I am the one most responsible for what kind of reality I experience. That sort of takes away the options to blame stuff I don't find satisfying on someone or something else. Tough, Bob! Buck up soldier! That's just the way it works!

When viewed in yet another way, that just means I want to be generally attentive as much as I can about the thoughts, desires, opinions, etc., that I choose to use to label people and events in the world around me. For a long time, I didn't find that very easy to do and at least to some extent still don't. There seem to be a lot of subtleties in how all this works. Even when I have been sure I wanted to change a belief and the thoughts that emanate from it, I have had to learn patience. I think it is more difficult than just changing a bad habit. However, it seems to me that we have the opportunity to grow toward greater and greater satisfaction with our reality whether we experience resistance and some failure or through the feedback of joy and celebration. Given the opportunity to choose, I prefer the joy and celebration. ☺

As noted in Chapter 16, it seems that how much emotion or intensity we associate with thoughts, etc., determines how much they are likely to manifest in some way to influence a subsequent sequence of "nows," a.k.a. the reality we will experience. But the Seth message makes an important distinction between the intensity of emotion and the *significance* of the thought in the first place. For example, if I were to think the negative thought "I think that guy is a nutcase" with strong emotion, I will probably see some influence of that belief in my life not long after as confirmation that I indeed hold that belief—and a reminder to think about whether I would like to change it. However, if I were to think "I think that guy is a nut" as a passing thought, one not dwelled upon or emotionalized, then it is highly unlikely to create undesired circumstances. We all have such kinds of passing thoughts. Passing thoughts without great attachment or emotion to their content are not major contributors to creating our own reality! Thank goodness!

I sincerely believe that one of the greatest contributors to my current general state of satisfaction with life is to be able to attach so little emotion to most of my thoughts—not just passing thoughts. Before Seth, I ran into something similar in the concept of nonattachment within the Hindu religious philosophy. I even put signs on my wall as a reminder to watch out for counter-productive attachment. Seth just put much the same message into a context I could better interpret and practice. I try to keep it in my mind.

According to Seth, we change our beliefs via the significance we associate with our thoughts, emotions, desires, intentions, expectations, etc. When existing beliefs have some sense to become actionable, or a desire that they become actionable, then there is significance. As we change our beliefs, we create the opportunity to become more discerning about thoughts with a high degree of actionable intent. In general, as we pay more attention to the desired significance of our beliefs we may choose more often to make observations rather than judgements with actionable desires. That's the theory.

With some attention to the topic, I think I came to understand how the significance of a thought can be recognized in practice. I am glad I tried. As I understand it, even though all of our thoughts create the Organizations of Consciousness that are in the form of probable future real events, there must be some degree of this significance for such thoughts to be "in play" for the actualization to take place. Thus, it is not just the intensity of emotion but the significance we *attach* to the thought. All thoughts are potentially in play, but attaching significance to them increases the probability they will actually influence subsequent experience.

I still think that the "significance" is sort of a fuzzy aspect but is of fundamental importance. I am guided to pause and think about it every once in a while. It was easy to accept that passing thoughts (per above) need not be either emotional or significant. But that was not enough to help make a connection between what I think and whether it is likely to be significant enough to matter to me or to anyone else.

So the issue became "what makes some thoughts significant or insignificant in creating my reality, and others just to be more like passing thoughts that will not be in play as my experience unfolds?" For lack of a better understanding, I have taken significance to be determined by how strongly we invest attachment of some kind with a thought, rather than just emotion or a half-hearted prayer of desire or wishful thinking. I think there is attachment when _we in a sense believe it has merit_. Or stated another way, how strongly are we willing to commit to make, or wish to make, some imagined event become a real event because we think it deserves to become a real event. I think it is different than just an intensity, such as to desire some situation strongly. For instance, wishful thinking may not necessarily anoint a thought with enough significance! Eventually, I came to think that _significance is more associated with something like an investment we are willing to make by using our creative capacity in that manner._

It has helped me increase my satisfaction with my current life by thinking of significance more than I used to do. Little significance, little influence in life experience. That's ok, a half-hearted expression of desire with no skin in the game wasn't meant to happen in the first place. I don't think much about significant imprinting from what is said during a bull session with the neighborhood guys. Also, it seems like a "rant" on some topic need not be significant if we don't invest too strongly in our belief that it has so much merit that we should expect some result. It is sort of: it's ok to be right but not ok to expect that the world should do something about our opinion. If we want action, we need to do something, such as contribute money or join a cause with others of like mind.

At the other extreme, we take seriously and fulfill our plan for each lifetime by the measure of our stewardship of significance as it is related to creating the general nature of the life experience we desire. Our sense of significance determines how we create the building blocks along the path. I like to think that being a steward of significance is a positive way to think of being sort of constructively self-centered—without behaving self-centered as we normally think of the words.

If we think deeply about it, the universe we experience attains its reality through ordered sequences of significance we have invested to guide the evolution of the cause and effects that manifest that experience. I hope I have shared something about the significance issue worthy of a little thought—it was for me. I will leave it at that. (Seth has also included references to the hormonal effects related to the significance we attach to certain kinds of thoughts, but like a lot of other things, I don't think they need be mentioned in detail here.)

So we have beliefs, we have thoughts, and we take actions based on those beliefs. And depending on some subtle factors, they become in play to influence our subsequent reality—or they don't. I think I have learned to have more worthy thoughts when it is important for me to do so. However, if I have a second thought and think I may have put a tint of significance into a negative thought, I try to back it out—replace it—counter with a modifying thought with significance. I try to take all emotion and intensity out of the negative thought—and be sure I claim it unworthy of any possibility of significance.

Bottom line, I think it is good for me to pay attention to the basics of what I have learned about all that, but there is just no reason for me to get up-tight about it or obsessed with examining every moment. I think I have the general message that is meaningful to me, so I just try to keep an eye on what beliefs I am putting to work. Gradually, over recent years I have experienced enough satisfaction with that level of effort that I don't want to lose it by trying to be an overachiever!

Trying to pin-point favorable and/or unfavorable *beliefs* can be more difficult than I had imagined. A person with a very comprehensive familiarity with the Seth material, Lynda Dahl, expresses the difficulty this way:

- Since everything we experience is a reflection of our thoughts and beliefs, they're behind which emotions we feel, what actions we take, the condition of our bodies, the possessions we own, our thoughts of the future, and the guilt's we harbor. Our lives unfold based on our beliefs about ourselves, our upbringing, our supposed past, the condition of the world, our prejudices, our views of religion, health, illness, safety, vulnerability, love, and money. They can be seen in living color in the kind of friends we choose, our fears, our home and work environments, our reactions, our selection of career, the associations we join, our political positions. *What we believe, we experience.*

I think it is hard to argue with anything she said.

One way I have found to start tracing thoughts and behavior back to an underlying belief is to watch for "trigger words" of an attitudinal nature. Those, for example, are words that just reek of opinion or position—what we might think of as representing "good or bad"—or as "observations vs. judgmental." There are a lot of "trigger words" in our everyday lives that really point back to our beliefs. Any word that creates a tendency to "react" is a trigger word.

Here are some example common trigger words to experiment with: Hate. Would like. Terrible. Deserves. Behaves. Concerns me. Truth. Angry. And so forth. With a little practice, I think it is possible to very quickly make a good guess about whether the underlying belief helps to create an improving reality for me (and others) or is it a belief that limits opportunities or invites feedback that makes life less satisfying.

Accepting responsibility for our beliefs can be rather daunting until one gets the hang of it. But after a while, I have actually found it quite satisfying to explore the possible relationship between my thoughts and actions, seeking to discover the underlying belief so that, in a low key way, I can decide whether I like it or wish to replace the belief with ... with what? And there we go, more to think about.

I think the cause and effect of one particular kind of belief is important enough to single out for special mention. I think that what one chooses to believe as truth, no matter how accepted, promoted, or honored by others, is really just a belief. Truths are just beliefs rarely supportable as a permanent belief. Like any other belief, truth is sort of in the eye of the beholder. The changes that take place in our experience as we create our own personal reality can often change the belief that was earlier deemed to be truth. I think that is sort of neat.

Even though I realize that we have individual pre-birth plans for what we desire or expect to experience in each life, I still have a sense of sadness when I see or hear about someone's misfortune or outrageously anti-social behavior. I used to feel overcome with a kind of deep sadness when there was someone or many suffering in some situation. Now there is still that feeling of sorrow but without deep emotional attachment because I believe there is purpose in everything, and the purpose of situations is totally personal for all directly or indirectly involved. (It took me a long time to articulate that as my belief related to abortion.) In some sense, a personally disastrous situation may be a part of a plan that an individual has for their experience in this life.

That has led me to think differently about natural disasters, war, crime, serious human illness, and deeply personal decisions such as abortion, suicide, and death. It helps me to remember that the main game in town is taking place with purpose within the Oneness—out of sight of our limited awareness of all the possible influences associated with whatever is happening. I find it helpful to just realize and accept that there is much more "in play" than I can know about or understand. Nothing happens in our physical world without first being determined outside of space-time within the Oneness. However, that's sort of intellectual—it still hurts when I see suffering or aggressive conflict.

Another take-away thought I have on the topic of life plans is to assume that we don't have to reinvent the wheel (so to speak) in each life. As was mentioned earlier, I believe we have the opportunity via our gateway (practice helps) too intuitively, or based on a meditative request, benefit from the experience resulting from our other lives that are evolving within the Oneness as a part of our True Self. We have the opportunity to learn in this life from those other life experiences to keep us from holding tight to counterproductive beliefs and choices. We most likely are not aware when we are receiving insight or inclinations through our gateway from other of our lives within the Oneness. However, those prior life experiences help provide us the opportunity to "move on" with new experience from which to consider new beliefs. That is another reason to develop a way to live with an open gateway. I think I do much of the time.

If we truly believe that in a prior life we have quite possibly experienced what those we observe are presently experiencing, it offers a different perspective to bring into our own current life experience. No question about it, we have suffered also and maybe that is what makes us sensitive to the suffering of others now. Life experience is very personal. Believing that, I am less inclined to think in terms of assertively inserting my life into the experience of others than I used to be. (I continue to believe that empathy, if not too emotional, passes the Seth muster.)

On the other hand, I get satisfaction when I can do something others appreciate, and I can deeply from my soul say, "It was not a burden, it was an opportunity." I really mean that when I say it, and I am finding more opportunities all the time. I have been told by many people that the idea of viewing many situations as an opportunity rather than a burden was very meaningful to them. But primarily, I just plain find helping others to be a source of satisfaction within my current life situation. Many situations present an opportunity, not a burden.

Once I accepted that our beliefs create our personal reality, it became easier to go about my life sort of happily humming as I go along trying to improve beliefs. In general, I am consciously aware that I am contributing to a possible future if I put emotion or intensity of feeling/opinion into some thought or act. It has become automatic—no thought about it is necessary. Similarly, it feels ok to have opinions, and even a critical thought or anger, without any emotional attachment—being more discerning than judging. That really, really helps when I observe politics in America these days.

Of course, I don't have to think about these things so much that spontaneous behavior becomes impossible. "That is a good thing," as one of our grandsons used to say about what, from his perspective, were good things. The message from Seth is that spontaneity is a desired behavior—sort of like letting the Inner Self handle the situation. I think I often fail on that score. It is still difficult for me to be totally spontaneous when for most of my adult life it has been almost a duty to look ahead and try to make something happen or avoid something happening. However, I do catch myself being spontaneous more often these days, which is mostly for the good. Every once in a while though, my spontaneous expression is something I wish I had expressed differently—so be it, do better next time. I love the feeling that comes with being spontaneous. I guess that is a kind of satisfaction.

That reminds me of how my current view of how reality works has helped me with my problem of living with regrets. I am sure there have been hundreds of times in my life when I said or did something I later regretted, and sometimes the memory comes back. At other times, I regret that I failed to see and benefit from opportunities—sometimes failing to capitalize on an opportunity that prevented benefit to others also. Living later with both forms of regret sort of took the edge off my satisfaction with my accomplishments at other times and under different circumstances. Late in life I still occasionally regret something, but I can also see the purpose in the experiences and try to learn from them. Experience is sacred, whether I liked it or regretted it. Think about it—then move along.

Both what I learned from the Seth material and my own observations have led me to believe that fear attracts fear. That is, if we put emotion with intensity into the fear of something, we may be inviting the experience we fear or something similar. In a sense, we give life to it as an Organization of Consciousness to be a part of our potential (or probable) future. I often see that in the lives of others around me. In a couple of ways, I even see it in my own life. I am sort of fearful of fear. ☺

I still remember when as a child losing a dollar was a big deal. A dollar was a significant portion of what I had to work with then. I feared losing a dollar. Today, I don't fear losing a dollar, but I am very annoyed by my constant thinking of "what is the worst that could happen" in situations. I have "imagination thoughts" that confuse what "could" go wrong with what "actually might" go wrong. I must have a deep-seated generalized fear of unpleasant things happening. I don't have reason to feel that way. I don't want to feel that way. I immediately feel foolish, a failure, and maybe even a hypocrite, because I can't seem to once and for all change that belief and create a reality where there is *absolutely no expectation* associated with thoughts of what might happen that I wouldn't like. I now try to think of such potentially unpleasant thoughts as just another form of day dreaming—of no significance.

When I sense a negative expectation, I immediately have to stop whatever is in progress to regale myself and try to "erase" the knee-jerk thought by thinking how what I implicitly feared is unsupportable. I try to quickly find a thought to help view the situation differently. I try to think of a way to create a new thought in the positive light that whatever comes about a situation will be a meaningful experience—to be viewed as a sacred life experience and not to be criticized or feared. Dealing with this problem does not take much satisfaction away from my life, but it sure is annoying. ☺ I now believe that *expecting* something negative is a failure, and I guess that I have a belief that failure itself is negative. ☺

One of the related topics I think about in those situations is how much the Seth material dwells on the message that we live in a safe universe. That message is, in part, that we have no valid reason to expect something fearful or negative in any way. When I first encountered that message, I was somewhat in disbelief. At first blush, with all of the crime, war, and suffering in general in our world that we see so much of during the nightly TV news—that message seems absurd. However, after I stepped back and carefully examined my beliefs, I think I see the point.

It is not that "the universe is safe," it is instead that "we live in a safe universe." Enjoy a glass of good fruit juice or wine while swirling that around a while. If we have accepted a view of reality like I have accepted and attempted to describe, we have in theory left behind the assumed knowledge that the universe is not safe and the forms of fear that such a belief engenders. That universe that is not safe really exists as an aspect of creation, but it need not be the aspect of reality we experience. Whatever we experience is a life opportunity to evolve our self. For some, that means the experience of evil behavior or misfortune. It is all experience with meaning for them and those also involved in their experience.

Of course, *the point is that we are the creators of the universe reality that we do uniquely experience.* If we don't screw it up too bad, we probably live in a universe safe for us. With that thought in mind, pun intended, I try to hold down the emotion and any wisp of significance when I trip up and think of what might go wrong with some expected near-term probable future. An excellent resource for a much greater perspective on this topic is provided in Linda Dahl's book *Living a Safe Universe* (currently published as three volumes).

A special kind of fear—at my age—is the common one, a fear of death. I succumb to that fear occasionally, particularly when there is a minor but new kind of hiccup in my normally good health. Because I think fear of death is inconsistent with my beliefs, it bothers me. I have decided that it is not just a lurking fear of death as much as also somehow related to concerns about the manner of death. The negative concern seems to be the uncertainty about whether a hiccup is the start of what will eventually be a dying process or well—just a hiccup. (I have experienced a few hiccups, so I know wherein I speak!)

There are times when I wish I weren't inherently curious. Alfred King expressed that same view when I visited him shortly before he died. I could do without being so interested in the personal view of dying. Anyhow, I am attempting to heed the advice of Seth, prepare for death as if preparing to go on vacation. In the meantime, I try to keep the idea of a safe universe in mind and try to make good choices about taking care of my body and mind. In moments of concern about my health, I have found the best remedy is not to think about my view of reality—but to get busy doing something like mowing the lawn or cutting firewood. I really cherish old age, but sometimes I have to remind myself of that.

And finally (for the moment), one of my favorite sources of satisfaction—my imagination! Even before I studied Seth, I got satisfaction from the creative aspects of my imagination—for personal pleasure, business-related matters, or simply planning related to family matters. Then I ran into Seth, and the topic took on a whole new dimension—literally!

Now, the good news, bad news. The good news is that the use of our imagination is one of the most direct ways we can create aspects of a personal reality strongly influenced by our desire. The bad news is that the use of our imagination is one of the most direct ways we can create a personal reality strongly influenced by counter-productive desires. According to Seth, our imagination and emotions are the most concentrated forms of creative energy that we possess as humans.

335

A super-charged imagination is therefore an engine of creation. Our imagination is what opens up our future for new journeys of experience. But again, it matters how it is engaged. In my case, I must have been born with a genetic inclination matched to my life plan to gain experience by learning to use my mind for imagination. It seems to me like another of those gifts bestowed on me at birth, rather than something I had to earn on my own. I sincerely believe it has been a major positive factor when I have been some form of leader, especially in innovative situations. We all have or can develop some positive kinds of imagination. I think we can all benefit from our imagination if we give a little thought to where it might lead us.

My imagination has probably also got me in trouble, but I don't recall those troublesome outcomes! I do recall writing about imagination in a short epistle I sent to our closest family members in November 2012 titled, "Thoughts on Thanksgiving." It says so much about how strongly I view our capability for imagination that I want to include it here. The satisfaction I experience from the use of my imagination may not have originated with my metaphysical journey, but I now view my imagination as one of the most important factors in how I create important aspects of my personal reality. My journey has given my imagination significance, responsibility, and an increased source of satisfaction within my life experience. Here is what I wrote.

Thoughts on Thanksgiving

Thanksgiving legends are typically soulful accounts of groups thankful for sustenance and some degree of opportunity after hardships in traveling to a new land or after release from some form of bondage or restricted freedom. It is not unusual for such accounts to be of an almost spiritual nature—of something that is more felt than tangibly described. And often, the message comes to us with overtones of new beginnings, recognition of new horizons, and even an eagerness to explore what used to be the unknown.

The historical words in which human journeys are wrapped are typically about the actual physical experiences of encountering the new state of affairs, but the literature involving journeys is also full of allegorical stories symbolic of the greatest potential for life-changing destinations of insight. Such stories, books, and movies leave a lot to our imagination—they are available to provoke a nonphysical journey—a form of travel to anywhere our thoughts take us—made possible by our imagination. Generally, they also provide a guide for the trip.

That capacity for imagination is a human attribute most of us don't think about when making the list of what we are most thankful for. Yet, it is our imagination and subtle meditation that provides the richest possibilities for human experience. It is our imagination that distinguishes us from other animals. It is our imagination which frees us from the limitations of the five senses—providing the journeys of our dreams, our desires, thoughts of our future, our intuition, our spiritual sense of meaning, and sometimes even our sense of "just knowing" instead of "thinking." No scholar, poet, or mystic has ever defined the limits of imagination.

Our inner journeys provide opportunity to transcend the limits imposed on physical journeys. An unlimited variety of inner journeys are available to us all. Journeys in the calm environs of our imagination enable us to find new insight, new choices, new horizons to reach, new expressions of our love, and gateways through which to experience new joys of being alive. Our imagination defines the form and substance of our unique individual future. For that gift, we should be thankful indeed!

I am thankful for my imagination.

rlb
2012

It is probably all too clear that creating our own reality is a pretty complicated process—but so be it! I hope that in the last three chapters I have made some of that complexity a little less complex. I like to think of it as offering a few hand holds. I don't think this stuff gets sorted out overnight. However, for me personally, just by caring about it over the last few years, it has become a second nature. My viewing and interacting with the world this way doesn't take away the pleasure of life nor bother others around me—very much. It adds pleasure, thus satisfaction!

To make it as easy as possible to think I am doing a reasonably good job of creating a satisfying experience for myself and possibly others, I have simplified the process down to pretty much one word, "choices." My brain alone doesn't choose. My mind does. The message is, *that I am that nonphysical self that gets to choose*. I tell my brain what to think—it doesn't tell me what to think or do! And my mind is in touch with the riches of the Oneness if I just learn to open up the gateway. A starting point is to believe there is indeed a gateway.

Living with a little extra consideration for "choices" related to thoughts and behavior has sort of become much more natural, effortless, than it was only a few years ago (which is not to imply always and only good choices). I sort of "listen" through my gateway to get a sense about how I feel about what I did or am doing. I know that my intent is to develop beliefs that prompt behavior that

337

produces a satisfying experience. I don't even have to think about that all the time.

To repeat, I just have to "listen" to how I feel about how I am thinking and acting. It has eventually become a natural part of my being and not as if it is work or something difficult. I smile a lot. (I like the feeling) I think I listen more, speak less. I know that I generally accept (maybe with a smile), rather than react. What is, is! If my gateway doesn't seem to be functioning up to my standard, I take time to engage in periodic meditation, exercises suggested by Seth, or more general alpha-dynamics exercises to get back to being able to "un-focus" and listen.

If some of what I have written about my view of the greater reality appears to be of further interest, I hope some of the references I have provided will be helpful. If it even looks appealing to learn more about how you may create a more satisfying reality, I suggest you do a little research with sources available to you and find one with the "create your own reality" content. For starters, I would suggest a reread of Chapter 16 and then direct to the Seth material books or some of the excellent books written by those intimately familiar with that material. Others might suggest a tour through the many books about the Eastern mystic traditions. I also know that over the last few decades there have been a growing number of books each year devoted to guidance in creating a satisfying spiritual and generally helpful life experience. Look at the reviews and see if something moves your meter—so to speak—in your era.

The thing to remember is that we *are* all creating our reality; it is only a matter of how much we want to take that into account as we guide ourselves through our life experience. For me, reality TV, as it is labeled in this era, is not very helpful in that regard. ☺

In the recent era, there are only two physicists I know of that publically share much of what I have concluded to be the contribution of quantum physics to a greater reality—Peter Russell and Bernard Haisch. Haisch has been particularly attention-getting for me because of his major research contributions in areas of physics I believe are ground breaking—the physics related to the quantum vacuum in particular. Several years after I extended physics (in my view) with the binks assumption and the reasons for doing so, Haisch published a book in 2006 called *The God Theory*. In it, he builds upon his extensive knowledge of physics to support his belief. There is an amazing degree of overlap in our conclusions, even though the route to getting there is quite different. However, he attributes a lot of what I considered the rationale for binks to result from the same questions. In his case, the questions arose from his extensive knowledge related to his zero-point field theories. It is a fascinating and informative book, which I think should be a "must read" for anyone interested in what I have described as my journey through related territory. I think he makes the physics have meaning. One does not have to have an extensive knowledge of physics like he does to discern that meaning. He delivers it as his journey and invites his readers to come along.

Without reference to the Seth material, a great deal of what Haisch presents are totally compatible with what I have come to view as the greater reality based on the frameworks of both physics and Seth. His route to his conclusions includes many inferences that one could draw solely from Seth. In his introduction to the book, Haisch writes:

> My wager is this: As science integrates the in-depth knowledge of the physical world accumulated over the past three centuries, it will be channeled into a new and exciting line of inquiry that acknowledges the expanded reality of consciousness as a creative force in the universe and the spiritual creative power embodied in our own minds.

How about that sports fans! And he goes on and on during the book with related views. In comparing his view versus the view expressed by Stephen Hawking's, Haisch writes:

> How is the physical universe manifested? How are the characteristics of space and time defined? How are the properties of matter created and sustained? My theory, in short, proposes that we regard the laws of physics as the manifestation of God's ideas, not the limits of God's creative potential.

WOW!

Haisch also, via a different path, ended up with a view I share though neither one of us nor others can "prove" it. In my words, the view is that "light just is," "light does not move, we do." I think it cannot be disproved within current physics, but it cannot be proven either. That view is 100% compatible with the Seth material regarding how the "now" fades from one to the next, transitioning from outside of space-time to a new "now" within space-time. I really like the way Haisch got there and what he says about the ramifications of believing that to be true. With his conclusions about the nature of consciousness, it appears to me that Haisch concludes, as I do, that the fundamental significance of Consciousness *equals* Energy *equals* God is to realize that is the fundamental reality from which all else is created.

So as I come to a close of this entire story telling, the first thing that comes to mind is to think again of those who have been so helpful in guiding me along to fulfill my life plan. I occasionally hear their echoes. In particular, after Pat, they are:

The most heartfelt man in my life, Grandpa John
The most heartfelt woman in my early life, Grandma Edna
My high school coach who first spoke to me man to man, Wes Johnson
My employer and Dutch uncle who spoke to me as man to be, Chuck Banks
My most influential professors, Paul Hultquist, Jack Britton, & James Broxon
My mentor in situational awareness and crisis management, Glen Powers
My wise business mentor, life mentor, and intellectual comrade, Alfred King

My parents had to deal with many challenges in the lives I was a part of. I think they did their part also to love me and attempt to nourish me in loving and positive ways as I grew up. My love for them has grown as my view of much of reality has evolved in recent years. If it is important to them now, they know how I feel.

So, I have told my story in the most honest way I can contrive. ☺ Au contraire, not contrived, I really do believe what I have shared, and I try to live that belief daily. I have found many sources and reasons to guide me to believe that the nonphysical subjective self and the brain indeed work together as our mind so as to offer all of mankind the *opportunity* for a greater life experience. As I hope I have mentioned, there appear to me to be many ways—paths of thinking, meditating, or religious ecstasy, for instance—for a person's mind to help them create a sense of enlightenment about the greater reality. I think a desire to do that starts with the belief turned to conviction that there is a greater reality.

A couple of years ago, a small group discussion resulted in the following definition of enlightenment, "Enlightenment is a human mental and psychological condition that permits that person to 'move on' to participate more fully in the context of a greater reality than is currently experienced by that person." A reader will be much more enlightened by reading some of the many books and articles on the topic of the Perennial Philosophy. ☺

However, I don't think there will be a rush to study up on the perennial philosophy within mankind until science and culture come up with something to free humanity from the bondage of thinking about life experience solely in space-time terms. To paraphrase Deepak Chopra, I think the time has come for science to attempt to prove that a Fundamental Consciousness is not fundamental as the framework from which all else may be described—rather than the other way around as is the current paradigm. I think it will also be necessary for religious faith to become reconciled with an extended understanding of a greater reality and for a lot of dogma and fanaticism to disappear from within the major religions. Wish humanity luck on that one!

I hope that those conditions will come about gradually during the decades ahead when more becomes generally known about the greater nature of reality and incorporated into the cultures of the world. I expect the collective disciplines of science to contribute to, but not guide, that evolution. Barring any worldwide calamity that brings about greater compassion and acceptance between the peoples of the world, I think that the greater life experience for all of humanity is a long time down the road—as we think of and experience "time."

But on the other hand, coming from my usually optimistic self, there is light at the end of the tunnel for those who are looking for it. I am convinced that once one defines for themselves, accepts, and seriously adopts *any* expanded view of reality as a guide meaningful to them, life experience just takes on new dimensions in accord with that view and that the built-in teleological nature of reality will eventually guide them to harmony with True Consciousness. I hope there are or will be many other views that hold promise similar to what I hope are provided by what I have described.

In my life journey, it has been increasingly easy for me to live each day with a personally satisfying life perspective because I accepted reality to be, at least in essence, as described in Chapters 15 and 16. It is good fortune beyond putting into words that I have been blessed with a fulfilling marriage and children I love and admire for whom they are. Our many friends are a rewarding bonus. I am grateful. I sincerely wish that such great good fortune will be the overall life experience of many other people. I look forward to—and expect more—experience and opportunities to practice my beliefs for the rest of this life.

The end. ☺

Appendix A

Quotes from those who formalized the equations to represent Quantum Phenomena *

From Max Planck, in *The Universe in the Light of Modern Physics*:

... We have seen that the study of Physics, which a generation ago was one of the oldest and most mature of natural sciences, has today entered upon a period of storm and stress which promises to be the most interesting of all. There can be little doubt that in passing through this period we shall be led, not only to the discovery of new natural phenomena, but also to new insight into the secrets of the theory of knowledge. ... scientists have learned that the starting-point of their investigations does not lie solely in the perceptions of the senses, and that science cannot exist without some small portion of metaphysics.

From Werner Heisenberg, in his book *Physics and Philosophy:*

... we have to remember that what we observe is not nature in itself but nature exposed to our method of questioning. Out scientific work in physics consists in asking questions about nature in the language that we possess and trying to get an answer looking back from experiment by the means that are at our disposal.

... modern physics has perhaps opened the door to a wider outlook on the relation between the human mind and reality

From Niels Bohr, as quoted as follows by Werner Heisenberg in his book, *Physics and Beyond*:

... I consider those developments in physics during the last decades which have shown how problematical such concepts as "objective" and "subjective" are, a great liberation of thought. ... (And also to have said)

... The real problem is: How can that part of reality which begins with consciousness be combined with those parts that are treated in physics and chemistry?

From Wolfgang Pauli, from his book, *Essays and Lectures on Physics and Epistemology*:

... in recent times there is an empirical parapsychology which claims to employ the approach of exact science and which works with modern experimental methods on the one hand, and modern mathematical statistics on the other. Should the positive results in the still controversial realm of "extrasensory perception" (ESP) finally turn out to be true, this could lead to developments which cannot be envisioned today.

From Erwin Schrodinger, in his book *Mind and Matter*:

... the "real world around us" and "we ourselves", i.e. our minds, are made up of the same building material, the two consist of the same bricks, as it were, only arranged in a different order—sense perceptions, memory images, imagination, thought. It needs, of course, some reflexion, but one easily falls in with the fact that matter is composed of these elements and nothing else. Moreover, imagination and thought take an increasingly important part (as against crude sense-perception), as science, knowledge of nature, progresses.

From Carl Von Weizsacker (Student of Heisenberg) when introducing an essay in his book, *The Unity of Nature*:

... The essay shows systematically in what sense a theory of the unity of matter and consciousness is compatible with quantum theory, even if such a theory is not deducible from quantum theory.

From Arthur Eddington, in his book *Space, Time and Gravitation*:

... the proud place in human knowledge which physical science holds today (is)...only an empty shell—a form of symbols. It is knowledge of structural form, and not knowledge of content. All through the physical world runs that unknown content, which must surely be the stuff of our consciousness.

From Louis de Broglie, from "Reflections of an Elder Scientist" in his book *New Perspectives in Physics*:

... human thought of the future may well be able to look beyond the confines of space and time to behold the veritable meaning of the work which man, extending and crowning the efforts of life, has striven ceaselessly to accomplish.

*Excerpted with permission from *Quirks of the Quantum Mind*, 2012, Robert G. Jahn and Brenda J. Dunne

Appendix B

Word or Term	Page First Used	General Description
Ontology	89	The study of the nature of being
conscious	274	Common expression for personal awareness
Consciousness	274	To distinguish Metaphysical vs. Common use
Seth	137/266	Personality channeled by Jane Roberts
ATI—All That Is	274	Seth name for what others refer to as God
Fundamental Consciousness	274	When referring to the creative energetic Consciousness of All That Is
True Consciousness	274	Same as Fundamental Consciousness
OC—Organization of Consciousness	274	Aggregation of Consciousness within Reality Involving any gestalt of relationships
Oneness	274	Nonphysical eternity outside of space-time
Creation	274	Evolution of Universe of True Consciousness
Self	265/278	The nonphysical essence of the True Consciousness aspect of a person
Inner Self	282	The aspect of a self that may be aware of the full extent of the Oneness
Outer Self (aka Ego)	282	The aspect of a self-focused on physical experience
True (Whole) Self	282	Total Consciousness of a self resulting from all lives
Gateway	285	For our mind to access Oneness information
Akashic Record	269/305	True Self physical and nonphysical history
Basketball	301	The pattern of the Universe at each "now"
Telepathy	136/312	The transmission of information between persons without using any of our known sensory channels or physical interaction
Precognition	136/312	Perception with access to future information not deduced from presently available and normally acquired sense-based information
Psychokinesis	136/312	The ability to influence changes in matter or energy through mental processes—sometimes referred to as "mind over matter"
Presentiment	136/313	A form of precognition creating an emotional response before the stimuli is perceived
Clairvoyance	136/314	Seeing objects or actions removed in space or time from natural viewing—in this era most often referred to as Remote Viewing or variations thereof.
Remote Viewing	136/313	See Clairvoyance

Robert (Bob) L. Brueck graduated from the University of Colorado in 1962 with a MS degree in Applied Mathematics and a minor in physics and was a full-time instructor 1959-62. While a student, he was elected to membership in the physics honorary Sigma Pi Sigma, the engineering honorary Tau Beta Pi, and received two grants from the National Science Foundation for study and research programs. After working in applied science at Texas Instruments and the Southwest Center for Advanced Studies in Dallas for several years, he founded MRI Systems Corporation, which was acquired by Intel Corporation in 1979. After leaving Intel, Bob engaged in venture-capital investing and technology company management mentoring until his retirement in 2006. He served on the Board of Directors of four public companies, as an active board member of over a dozen other companies, and in various capacities with a number of nonprofit organizations.

Bob was born in Boise, Idaho, in 1935. He and his wife of 58 years lived in Austin, Texas, for 30 years before now splitting residence between Austin and Valley County, Idaho, each year. They have three children, seven grandchildren, and three great-grandchildren.